PSYCHOPATHOLOGY OF
PERCEPTION

Officers of the

AMERICAN PSYCHOPATHOLOGICAL ASSOCIATION

for 1963

D. Ewen Cameron, M.D., *President* .... Montreal, Canada

Jerome D. Frank, M.D., *President-Elect* .... Baltimore, Maryland

Franz J. Kallmann, M.D., *Vice-President* .... New York, New York

Fritz A. Freyhan, M.D., *Secretary* .... Washington, D. C.

Bernard C. Glueck, Jr., M.D., *Treasurer* .... Hartford, Connecticut

Lauretta Bender, M.D., *Councillor* .... Long Beach, New York

Reginald S. Lourie, M.D., *Councillor* .... Washington, D. C.

Committee on Program

Paul H. Hoch, M.D., *Chairman* .... New York, New York

Joseph Zubin, Ph.D. .... New York, New York

PSYCHOPATHOLOGY
OF
PERCEPTION

Edited by **PAUL H. HOCH, M. D.**

Department of Mental Hygiene, State of New York; College of Physicians and Surgeons, Columbia University, New York City.

and **JOSEPH ZUBIN, Ph. D.**

Department of Mental Hygiene, State of New York; Department of Psychology, Columbia University, New York City.

THE PROCEEDINGS OF THE FIFTY-THIRD ANNUAL MEETING OF THE AMERICAN PSYCHOPATHOLOGI-CAL ASSOCIATION, HELD IN NEW YORK CITY, FEBRUARY 1963.

G R U N E   &   S T R A T T O N

NEW YORK   •   LONDON   •   1965

SAMUEL W. HAMILTON AWARDS

NAME		SYMPOSIUM
Clarence P. Oberndorf, M.D.	1952	*Depression*
John C. Whitehorn, M.D.	1953	*Psychiatry and the Law*
David M. Levy, M.D.	1954	*Psychopathology of Childhood*
Stanley Cobb, M.D.	1955	*Experimental Psychopathology*
Sandor Rado, M.D.	1956	*Psychopathology of Communication*
Karl M. Bowman, M.D.	1957	*Problems of Addiction and Habituation*
Bernard Glueck, Sr., M.D.	1958	*Trends in Psychoanalysis*
Sir Aubrey Lewis, M.D.	1959	*Comparative Epidemiology in the Mental Disorders*
Franz J. Kallmann, M.D.	1960	*Psychopathology of Aging*
Nolan D. C. Lewis, M.D.	1961	*Future of Psychiatry*
Franz Alexander, M.D.	1962	*Evaluation of Therapy*
Heinrich Klüver, Ph.D.	1963	*Psychopathology of Perception*

LILLIAN AND HENRY STRATTON AWARDS

Name		*Symposium*
James Birren, Ph.D.	1960	*Psychopathology of Aging*
Benjamin Pasamanick, M.D.	1961	*Future of Psychiatry*
Heinz E. Lehmann, M.D.	1962	*Evaluation of Therapy*
Charles W. Eriksen, Ph.D.	1963 }	*Psychopathology of Perception*
Ronald Melzack, Ph.D.	1963 }	

Library of Congress Card Number 65-19219

Copyright © 1965
Grune & Stratton, Inc.
381 Park Avenue South, New York, N. Y.

Printed in the United States of America (K-A)

CONTENTS

PREFACE

PERCEPTUAL ANOMALIES in the mentally disordered have been known ever since the beginnings of history. The importance, however, of normal stressful experience as opposed to disease processes in the production of perceptual anomalies such as hallucinations has remained undetermined. In order to cast some light on the sources of perceptual distortion that occur in the mentally ill and the mentally well this symposium attempted to cover the full range of phenomenological, clinical, and experimental approaches.

As might be expected, only samplings from these areas could be included and these consisted of excursions into the phenomenology of hallucinations and depersonalization, neurophysiological and psychomotor aspects of response, experimental approaches to perception of time, pain and taste, and the influence on perception of such special states as sensory deprivation, early experience and sleep.

The results of this symposium indicate that though the questions we have raised are far from answered it is possible to be more specific about the sources of some of the deviations, and this may lead to further research in exploring these fields. Perhaps we will never know the full answer, but the search itself will reveal much new knowledge.

The three elements that are involved in any perceptual task are: sensory afferents, reticular activating systems, and cortical association activity; or, if you wish, sensory input, alertness or arousal, and memory storage. The attempt to discover the relevance of impairment at any one of these levels to perceptual deviation is one of the foci of interest of this symposium. It is quite possible that each of these three levels may in itself remain intact in psychopathological conditions, but that the interaction between them may be faulty in schizophrenia or other mental disorders. The various papers in this symposium direct their attention to each of these levels and to their interaction.

In answering these questions it becomes apparent once more that in order to understand the abnormal we must study the normal.

THE EDITORS

HEINRICH KLÜVER

HEINRICH KLÜVER

Samuel W. Hamilton Memorial Lecturer, 1963

To BE WORTHY OF having received the Samuel W. Hamilton Award from the American Psychopathological Association, obviously one must have certain outstanding attributes. Judging from the recipients of previous awards it would appear that one must be either an outstanding psychiatrist or have made some unusual contribution in the field of psychopathology. In fact almost all of the previous recipients have been psychiatrists, and all have been Doctors of Medicine. Why, on this occasion, has the association deviated from its previous course and chosen Heinrich Klüver who holds the degree of Doctor of Philosophy (Stanford University) and is Professor of Biological Psychology (Emeritus; Sewel L. Avery, Distinguished Service Professor, University of Chicago)? The reasons are not obscure. The choice of this remarkable man does credit to the judgment of the Association. There are few if any men in this century who have so influenced the world's thinking as to the relationship of the brain to behavior and to psychological activities, including pathological ones, as has Heinrich Klüver.

He was born in the north of Germany, in Schleswig-Holstein, in 1897. He was 17 years old when World War I erupted. He was soon in the German Army on the Western Front where he miraculously survived years of fighting, being wounded only once. The rest of his company of 120 men were not all so fortunate. In a year and a half those killed were replaced by approximately 1,500 others. Shortly after the end of the War he enrolled first in the University of Hamburg and then the University of Berlin (1920-23). In Germany his psychological interests were stimulated by such men as William Stern in Hamburg and Max Wertheimer, Wolfgang Köhler (later of Swarthmore College in Pennsylvania) and Kurt Lewin in Berlin.

In the summer of 1923 he boarded a freighter—the lone passenger —and headed westward, via the Panama Canal, to California. After only a year (1923-24) Stanford University awarded him his Ph.D. in physiological psychology. While at Stanford he, in his lectures, brought Gestalt Psychology to American shores for the first time. Although he enjoyed California, and he still has a great affection for Stanford, he left immediately after his graduation to become an instructor in psychology at the University of Minnesota. In spite of the contentions of certain "educators," great books are not everything in one's intellectual development. For most of us, great men have far more influence. This was true for Heinrich Klüver. At Minnesota he became associated with the man who for him was the "most brilliant neuropsychologist the world has seen," Karl Spencer Lashley. In 1928 Klüver followed Lashley to Chicago—first at the Behavior Research Fund (1928-33) and then at the University of Chicago. That Lashley exerted a great influence upon Klüver is not to be denied, but in a very real sense Klüver has hewn out his own destinies.

Probably the one thing which has influenced the career of Klüver more than any other has been the peculiar drug, Mescaline, with its unusual hallucinatory properties. His interest in this drug led to the publication of his monograph in 1928 entitled, "Mescal, the 'Divine' Plant and Its Psychological Effects." It was his interest in this drug and his endeavors to elucidate its psychological and physiological effects that led indirectly to his study of the functions of the temporal lobes and the effects of bilateral temporal lobectomy. But this came somewhat later. In the meantime Klüver was becoming an expert in the handling, understanding and studying of the monkey and its behavior. He developed his famous "method of equivalent stimuli" which has been so important in the experimental psychological analyses of the complexities of normal and pathological behavior in animals and in man. In 1933 he published another monograph—"Behavior Mechanisms in Monkeys"—and shortly thereafter studied the functions of the occipital lobes and the effects of occipital lobectomy. With these years of experience in studying the behavior of monkeys it is not surprising that he so promptly recognized the profound effects of temporal lobectomy. "Aurora" was a mature female rhesus monkey. She had been an experimental subject of Professor George W. Bartelmes. In her maturity she had become vicious. Because of the widely recognized ability of Klüver to handle any monkey, Aurora was offered to him and he accepted her. Klüver and I were already engaged in attempting to localize the effect of mescaline in the brain of the monkey, and it was decided to study the effects of this drug after temporal lobectomy with Aurora as the first subject—a fortunate choice. On December 7, 1936 her left temporal lobe was removed. Early the next morning my telephone rang. Klüver's excited voice came over the wires. "What did you do to my monkey"? "Why," I asked. "She's tame," exclaimed Klüver. I hastened to his laboratory. It was unbelievable. This formerly vicious, unmanageable beast was indeed tame.

As soon as her condition stabilized we removed the right temporal lobe (on January 25, 1937). The amazing clinical picture which Klüver later studied so meticulously was immediately apparent. The behavioral state resulting from bilateral temporal lobectomy which is characterized by tameness, psychic blindness, strong "oral" tendencies and an excessive tendency to attend and react to every visual stimulus were soon apparent. The alterations in sexual behavior and the changes in dietary habits characteristic of these animals were detected later. The next few years were spent in studying this state in many other animals.

These and other researches of Klüver's have led to literally hundreds of investigations on the temporal lobes of man and of animals, and to an extensive revision of the conception of the organization of the so-called "association areas" of the brain. He has stimulated research on the anatomy and physiology of the temporal lobes, on the relation of this part of the brain to endocrinological activities, and most important of all on the relation of the temporal lobes to the behavior of man and animals. Probably no one in our generation has done so much to concentrate the world's attention on the subject of the relationship of the brain to behavior and psychological activity as has Heinrich Klüver.

To those of us who know Heinrich Klüver well, all of this is not surprising. These are the expected accomplishments of the world's most distinguished experimental biological psychologist. What never ceases to excite our amazement is the broad scope of his interests, knowledge and understanding. Heinrich Klüver is not just an experimental psychologist. He is an authority on the porphyrins, and particularly on their presence in the nervous system. He, together with Miss Elizabeth Barrera, is the inventor of one of neuropathology's best staining technics—the Klüver-Barrera method for the simultaneous staining of neurons, glia and myelin sheaths. He is a most knowledgeable person on the care and handling of monkeys.

As was noted earlier, Dr. Klüver is not a physician, yet over the years he has always been at home in or near medical schools. His closest friends and associates—Karl S. Lashley excepted—have been clinicians and medical investigators. With the untimely death of his good friend, Stephen Polyak, Klüver assumed the very heavy responsibility of finishing Polyak's encyclopedic treatise, "The Vertebrate Visual System," and seeing it through the press. This was a two-year labor-of-love for his close friend and colleague. Klüver has been interested in studying the development of diabetes mellitus and other diseases in his monkey colony. In his laboratory he has found more cases of simian carcinoma than has ever been found in any other collection of non-human primates in the world. He has found and studied pituitary tumors, endometriosis and many other conditions in his animals. Although Klüver is undoubtedly one of the world's greatest specialists (in biological psychology) he is also one of its greatest generalists.

This has been a great privilege to bear witness to the great contributions and to the outstanding interests, knowledge and ability of a dear friend.

PAUL C. BUCY, M.D.

Part I: Neurophysiology of Perception

1

NEUROBIOLOGY OF NORMAL AND ABNORMAL PERCEPTION

Samuel W. Hamilton Award Lecture

by HEINRICH KLÜVER, PH.D.

FIRST OF ALL, I should like to express my deep appreciation to the American Psychopathological Association for selecting me as this year's Samuel W. Hamilton Award Lecturer. No doubt, there are "psychopathological" reasons why this honor should come to me on February 23, 1963. The American Psychopathological Association is about as old as Karl Jaspers' *General Psychopathology*—a book first published in 1913, that is, 50 years ago. But as it happens, its author was born on February 23, 1883, and is, therefore, celebrating his 80th birthday today. I greatly appreciate that the American Psychopathological Association (whether by chance or forethought) picked the 23rd of February for this year's Memorial Lecture, so much the more since I have recently joined others in trying to convince the University of Chicago Press—successfully, as it turns out—to market an English translation of the magnum opus of Jaspers.[56]

When I saw a list of the previous Samuel W. Hamilton Memorial lecturers I became slightly depressed since I noticed that all of them have been eminent clinicians and it is somewhat depressing to find that I cannot qualify as a clinician in such an illustrious company. In my defense it may be said that I did acquire some clinical experience and that it took me 40 years to acquire it—in dealing, however, chiefly with subhuman primates. I even learned, many years ago, about mother love in monkeys or rather about the "psychopathology of perception" involved in the absence of such love. There are brain operations which completely eliminate mother love—that is, maternal behavior. But what happens to the baby left lying on the floor of the cage? You may take

1

a hand in bringing it up—supplying food for its mouth and a pad of soft white cotton for bedding. You may then ultimately discover in case the baby happens to be a Java monkey baby (a species with a rather long tail) that two things are sufficient for providing psychological and social "security" for such a baby, namely, a piece of white material, even if it be only a square inch of white paper, and grasping and holding on to its own tail at the same time.[88]

I sincerely regret that I have not known Dr. Hamilton personally but when recently looking through some index and abstract journals I came across two entries, "Hallucinations, visual" and "Hamlet, psychoanalytically interpreted," and between these two items the entry "Hamilton, Samuel, biographical note on." Unfortunately I shall never know whether Dr. Hamilton would have felt at home between visual hallucinations and a psychoanalytical interpretation of Hamlet but there is little doubt that the man who wrote the biographical note, namely, Dr. A. A. Brill, would have felt very much at home there. In this connection, it was another prominent psychoanalyst who was responsible, some 30 years ago, for my talking here in New York City on problems closely related to those I am going to discuss today. It was Dr. S. E. Jelliffe who had a hand in putting me on the program of the December 1932 meeting of the Association for Research in Nervous and Mental Disease. My paper at that meeting[75] was chiefly concerned with psychological aspects, particularly with the behavior of certain types of pseudohallucinations—pseudohallucinations in the sense of Kandinsky—that is, with phenomena generally referred to in the literature as eidetic phenomena or eidetic images.

In retrospect, some of the results obtained in my eidetic researches started in 1923 and pursued for many years[65,66,68,70,72,73,75] still appear to be of special interest to me. I should like to call attention to only three points.

1) The first concerns a *technique* which I used in studying negative after-images, eidetic images as well as hallucinations.[81] The technique consists in applying an insensible alternating current which, within a certain frequency range, will produce flicker phenomena that can be observed with open or closed eyes. Only a beginning has been made in studying eidetic and hallucinatory phenomena in the presence of electrically produced flicker but there is little doubt that further use of this method will yield significant results when used in the experimental analysis of a wide range of subjective visual phenomena, including dreams. For a start, one might profitably investigate the be-

havior of very stable eidetic images, that is, images formerly referred to—in the name of a wrong theory, I believe—as eidetic images of the tetanoid or T-type.

2) The second point which I wish to stress for only a moment is the role of *motor factors*. More than a century ago the French psychiatrist Morel insisted that hallucinations are "psychosomatic" phenomena. Since then many sensory-tonic and sensory-motor theories of normal and abnormal perception have seen the light of day. One of the eidetic cases (a medical student) I studied at Stanford University 40 years ago had such strong and stable imagery that Dr. W. R. Miles was able to photograph his eye movements during the reading of an eidetic text. This subject had no difficulties in producing, with sensory vividness, the eidetic image of a printed text on an objectively empty screen in front of him (empty except for a fixation point). This suggests the possibility of "photographing" hallucinations or at least pseudohallucinations by way of photographing the eye-movements involved in seeing them. The role of motor factors in relation to phenomena, such as eidetic images, appears to be of particular interest since it is highly probable that eidetic phenomena, physiologically considered, generally involve central regulations and the operation of cortico- and centrifugal systems. This raises a number of questions which cannot be considered at this point but which have a bearing on recent and, it seems, successful attempts to eliminate all eye-movements, by means of stabilized retinal images, when studying visual phenomena. In fact, it is not even necessary to use a special optical device for doing so when the phenomena under observation are represented by Haidinger's polarization brushes (which are stationary with respect to the retina). Perhaps one of the most interesting results reported by investigators working with stabilized retinal images is the fact that visual phenomena may disappear and reappear or disappear and regenerate in characteristic fragments.

3) This brings me to the next point which concerns the *problem of fragmentation* in normal and abnormal perception, particularly in visual perception. It was this problem which I discussed with Paul Schilder when I met him for the first time (it was on the West Side of Chicago and it must have been in the late 20's). What was most interesting to me in Dr. Schilder's published account[148] of his own eidetic images was the tendency towards fragmentation in his images. Recently there have been reports in the literature insisting that the fragmentation or regeneration of stabilized retinal "images" of faces,

shapes, and other configurations is chiefly determined by the "meaning" of what the subject sees and/or by visual Gestalt principles. However, the extreme instances of spatio-temporal fragmentation I encountered when studying eidetic images many years ago led me to consider a more radical possibility—namely, the existence of fragments devoid of all connections, organization, and meaning, that is, a level on which even the most primitive Gestalten are no longer possible.[70,72] I raised the question whether, instead of seeking the correlate of Gestalt *qualities*, we should not entertain the idea of an emission of quanta to cope with a functional level on which all organization is lost and only fragments reign supreme. To be sure, the question I raised has not yet been answered. It remains to be seen whether molecular biology in trying to cope with brain mechanisms will more readily cope with "fragments" than with organized wholes or Gestalt factors. In a book posthumously published,[149] Schilder returned to these problems and pointed out that he, Klüver, Freud, and Pötzl had demonstrated that "a whole" may be produced by a "piecemeal gathering of single pieces."

I shall now leave the more psychological aspects of eidetic phenomena and turn to more neurobiologically oriented approaches although, again, with reference to the problem of hallucinations. It is true that even 30 years ago there was a man who had not only the courage to talk about a "neurobiology" of hallucinations but to write a book of more than 400 pages about it. This was Raoul Mourgue whose book,[122] *Neurobiologie de l'hallucination*, appeared in 1932. His *Introduction biologique à l'étude de la neurologie et de la psychopathologie* written in collaboration with C.v. Monakow had been published in 1928. After reading and analyzing some 7,000 publications on the subject of hallucinations, Mourgue concluded that the facts then available were not sufficient to formulate a *theory* of hallucinations.

When turning now to neurobiological approaches I should like, first of all, to emphasize two points, one in connection with experimental studies of the effects of mescaline and one in connection with the hallucinations encountered in patients with acute intermittent porphyria.

1) In 1935 I visited Professor Brouwer's clinic in Amsterdam. It was during this visit that Brouwer and H. de Jong gave me a demonstration of *"experimental catatonia,"* that is, of a cat immobilized by bulbocapnine, with mice running over her and one or two sitting on

her head. We observed after a while that the cat's eyes suddenly moved: she looked or seemed to look at one of the mice. I shall never forget Prof. Brouwer's comment: "I wish to God I knew whether the cat really *sees* the mouse and can recognize it." Whereupon I hurried back to Chicago eager to answer this question or at least related questions. At that time I was engaged in studying the behavioral effects of mescaline and other phenethylamines in normal and lobectomized (frontal, parietal, and occipital) monkeys and even in monkeys in which the sensory roots of the trigeminal nerves had been cut by Dr. Bucy previous to removing the somesthetic areas. In these experiments I used animals which, in the course of several years, I had trained to respond differentially to a variety of stimuli, such as visual, auditory, and weight stimuli. Today I shall refer only to the results obtained in tachistoscopic tests. These tests—I had invented a special technique for them[76]—provided information whether a given animal was able to perform an appropriate motor response to one of several visual stimuli appearing simultaneously, in different positions, for only a short time, such as 0.1 sec. or 0.01 sec. The stimuli I used differed, e.g., in brightness, color, size and/or shape. It turned out that the correct performance in tachistoscopic tests was not impaired even if the mescaline doses were so large that the monkeys appeared stuporous and exhibited some of the symptoms of de Jong's "experimental catatonia."[26] In other words, they were—in the short time at their disposal—objectively capable of recognizing and differentiating visual stimuli although they appeared stuporous or at least semistuporous and their general behavior indicated a very low degree of alertness and wakefulness. This leads me to a point which, I believe, needs special emphasis in the present stage of psychochemical and psychopharmacological researches. In general, I am somewhat disturbed when it is rashly claimed that a given region of the brain is an "attention" center or that stimulation of another region provides evidence for an increase or decrease in "alertness." Furthermore, I am unfortunately aware that the literature nowadays is full of "hallucinated" cats and monkeys. But a monkey grabbing into the air under the influence of a supposedly "hallucinogenic" substance does not necessarily grab for hallucinated objects; a monkey who scratches himself does not necessarily itch, and when sticking out his tongue rhythmically does not necessarily have paresthesias. It requires evidence of a sort not easily obtainable to justify such inferences from motor movements or other objectively observable changes. Yet it happens again and again that an investigator hastily insists that a given animal reacts with reference to some sensory information or misinformation or that sensory concomitants can be inferred from motor phenomena. It cannot be too strongly emphasized that some of the behavior data currently obtained in many investigations are of a sort that cannot, or at least should not, be utilized for correlations with anatomical, electrophysiological, or biochemical data since they can serve only as a basis for unwarranted interpretations and misleading conclusions.

2) The second point which in my opinion needs emphasis was brought home to me when I attempted to understand the genesis of hallucinations and related phenomena in cases of *acute intermittent porphyria* (one of the hepatic forms of human porphyria). This is a truly protean disease which often appears in the guise of neurological and psychiatric disorders.[82] In fact, porphyria patients have at one time or another been diagnosed and treated as cases of acute encephalitis, encephalitis lethargica, myelitis, poliomyelitis, polyneuritis, periarteritis nodosa, progressive muscular atrophy, arsenical poisoning, nicotine poisoning, diphtheria, brain tumor, psychoneurosis, hysteria, neurasthenia, acute psychosis, or manic-depressive insanity. Such patients have even been sent to mental hospitals and have died there before a correct diagnosis was made. It is perhaps not surprising that neurological and psychiatric diagnoses of this kind have at times been made in view of the fact that the symptoms characteristic of this disease may range from motor disturbances and transitory amaurosis to hallucinations, apathy, delirium, personality changes, and attempts at suicide. The fact that hallucinatory phenomena happen to be among the symptoms produced by a metabolic disorder, such as acute intermittent porphyria, should bring home to us how futile it may be, not only therapeutically but also scientifically, to consider the hallucination an isolated symptom that can be detached from other symptoms to be studied and analyzed without analyzing the conditions and factors associated with it. No doubt, the large variety of nervous and mental symptoms in this disease points to an involvement of the central nervous system. Although there are cases of acute porphyria in which the neuropathological changes in the brain and spinal cord may be responsible at least for the neurological symptoms, we are, despite great strides in elucidating the biosynthesis of porphyrins, as far as ever from understanding how a disorder of porphyrin metabolism can produce psychic alterations and psychiatric manifestations. At the present time it is generally agreed that it is not the porphyrins which are responsible

for producing such manifestations. I still remember the night of the 2nd of January 1945 when I carried the brain and spinal cord of the first acute porphyria patient I studied from the autopsy table to the dark room of my laboratory. Incidentally, this was to my knowledge also the first brain of a porphyria patient (of the acute intermittent type) that was used for spectrochemical and chemical studies. If I ever had visions of discovering a brain glowing in the beautiful red fluorescence of porphyrin compounds under near-ultraviolet light, they vanished during the first minutes of my examination. As it turned out, extractions of this brain furnished only the small amounts of normally occurring porphyrins that I had previously discovered in "normal" brains.[83,87,91] However, in examining the peripheral nerves of this case I found a pronounced red fluorescence and a porphyrin fluorescence spectrum in some spinal nerves or merely in some segments of a given spinal nerve. In some spinal nerves, however, red fluorescence and a porphyrin fluorescence spectrum could not be detected at all. The spectroscopic findings when subsequently correlated with chemical and histological findings suggested that metal-free porphyrins may invade the peripheral nervous system in an irregular and patchy fashion. The fact that the psychic disturbances could not be associated with an abnormal "porphyrinization" of the brain or a "cerebral porphyria" is perhaps not too surprising since at an early stage I discovered that the blood-brain barrier is impermeable to circulating porphyrins or at best, in certain regions, only slightly permeable. In the light of present-day knowledge the possibility must, therefore, be considered that in this disease the genesis of hallucinations and other clinical manifestations referable to the brain must be sought in the extracerebral environment. It has been suggested, for instance, that the liver is the site of metabolic disturbances capable of affecting the brain. Recently a chemical pathologist, such as Rimington, one of the outstanding investigators in the field of porphyrins, has expressed the opinion that the various symptoms of the acute porphyria attack can best be explained by assuming some biochemical disturbance in the metabolism of the nervous system. He has become more and more convinced "that everything points to a disturbance of acetyl-choline metabolism. . . ."[142] Unfortunately, current theories do not seem to provide an adequate understanding of the pathogenesis of the symptoms generally encountered in acute porphyria. If our information on the location and nature of the metabolic defects involved in this "inborn error of metabolism," to use Garrod's expression, were more complete, a more adequate treatment of this disease would no doubt become available, with the result that psychiatric manifestations, including hallucinations, not to mention other symptoms, would vanish. As it is, therapies ranging from electric shock therapy to psychoanalysis, from the use of vitamins, hormones, and tranquilizers to that of chelating agents and a host of other compounds, have been and are being employed.

It seems then that for the time being the nature and genesis of psychic disturbances in acute porphyria cannot be entirely understood in terms of biochemical and physiological relations. At least, my own efforts in this regard have failed, but all has not been in vain. As so often happens, while you are on the road, you discover things you did not mean to discover but which are nevertheless of great interest and possibly even of some importance. I shall give two examples.

1) When I looked for a system in which the relations between heme compounds and free porphyrins might be less complex than in the mammalian organism, I became interested in the root nodules of leguminous plants and discovered that their cells contained not only hemoglobin (as reported by previous investigators) but also a free porphyrin which, in the nodules of *Phaseolus vulgaris* (var. Red Kidney bean) appeared to be characteristically different from all previously described naturally occurring porphyrins.[84,85,86,87] I even succeeded, finally, in crystallizing the methyl ester of the legcoproporphyrin, a uro-type porphyrin, occurring in the nitrogen-fixing cells of *Phaseolus vulgaris* nodules.[95]

2) When I pondered the extremely small quantities of porphyrins occurring in regions of myelinated fiber masses in mammalian and avian brains and the great difficulties resulting therefrom in determining their relations, if any, to structural elements in the nervous system, I became interested in the question whether porphyrins and related compounds might have an affinity for particular fibers or cells. In pursuit of such questions I found that azaporphin derivatives (phthalocyanines) gave excellent results in staining myelin sheaths. As a result, it became possible to stain myelin sheaths, neurons, and glial cells in the same section by using copper phthalocyanine in conjunction with suitable counterstains. This stain—because of its simplicity, stability, and unique tinctorial features—is being widely used, here and abroad, by neuroanatomists, neuropathologists, and other histologists engaged in the study of neural (and even of extraneural) tissues.[94,95]

In analyzing the history of various attempts to relate hallucinations and kindred phenomena to brain mechanisms, it becomes apparent that theories in this field, at an early stage, were largely dominated by anatomical considerations. It was assumed, for instance, that the production of hallucinations is primarily due to pathological changes in the so-called "association centers" lying between and surrounding the sensory projection areas of the neocortex. There seem to have been few, if any, attempts to go beyond the neocortex and consider the role of the archi- and paleocortex, that is, of the rhinencephalon, in the genesis of hallucinations. The distinction between a neocortex on the one hand and an archi- and paleocortex on the other—a distinction made by comparative anatomists—is often considered essentially the same as the distinction advocated by the Vogts, namely, between an isocortex and an allocortex. In the opinion of von Economo, onto-genetic and phylogenetic considerations as well as the methods of cyto- and myeloarchitectonics led essentially to the same result in separating the new parts of the brain, the neopallium with a gray cortex, that is, the homogenetic six-layered cortex or isocortex, from the rest of the brain. However, difficulties soon arose in dealing terminologically with the older parts of the brain since the term "rhinencephalon" (applied to the olfactory bulb and tract by R. Owen about a century ago[47]) has functional implications and, when it was subsequently applied to a region with ever wider boundaries, anatomists and neurologists began to develop misgivings about the size of the territory included under the term "rhinencephalon."[5,47,140,176] It is obvious that Schwalbe's "falciform lobe" and Broca's "great limbic lobe" have structural rather than functional connotations. At the present time, MacLean's[114,115,116] suggestion to replace the misleading term "rhinence-phalon" by "limbic system" (consisting of Broca's great limbic lobe and its subcortical cell stations) has been widely accepted although "rhinencephalon" appears justified if, in the words of J. D. Green,[42] it is applied only to that "part of the brain associated with the nose." *At any rate, the question must be raised whether or to what extent the "old" parts of the brain play a role in the mechanisms underlying normal or pathologically altered perception.*

To begin with, we may first inquire into the psychological and behavioral consequences of eliminating, by surgical or other methods, some of the "old" structures of the brain. I spent many years, in collaboration with Dr. Paul C. Bucy, studying the effects produced in monkeys by removing both temporal lobes, including most of the rhinencephalon.[18,19,87,90,92,97,98,99,100] There is little doubt that the behavior changes thus produced represent the most striking behavior changes ever produced by a brain operation in animals. "The temporal lobe syndrome" as described about 25 years ago is, I believe, by now so widely known that I shall limit myself to merely mentioning the outstanding symptoms. This syndrome (now frequently referred to in the literature as the Klüver-Bucy syndrome[3,22,43,57,112,132,163]) comprises the following symptoms:

1. Visual "agnosia."—The animal appears to have lost the ability to detect the meaning and significance of animate and inanimate objects on the basis of visual criteria alone. "Elementary" visual functions are not impaired since the ability to discriminate visually can be readily demonstrated. However, in the case of such an animal, visual criteria alone are not sufficient for detecting, for instance, that an object is "dangerous" or "edible." Since there is an apparent non-recognition even of simian faces the "agnosia" may be said to include a prosopagnosia.[14,24] Furthermore, the visual "agnosia" may be correlated with agnosic symptoms in other (auditory, tactile) sense fields.

2. Oral tendencies.—There are exceedingly strong tendencies to examine animate as well as inanimate objects in various ways by mouth. This hyperorality also manifests itself in contacting objects or parts of objects directly by mouth instead of first using the hands for picking them up.

3. "Hypermetamorphosis" (in the sense of Wernicke).—The animal appears strongly stimulus-bound not only in exhibiting an excessive tendency to take notice of and attend to visual stimuli, events, and changes in its environment but also in constantly trying, as if acting under some compulsion, to contact and touch every object in sight.

4. Changes in emotional behavior.—There is a complete absence or at least a diminution of emotional reactions and of such facial "expressions of emotions" as are characteristically associated with emotional behavior in monkeys. Even live snakes and other objects which normally produce extreme excitement or avoidance reactions generally do not produce the motor, vocal, and other forms of behavior that are typical of simian anger and fear reactions.

5. Changes in sexual behavior.—There is a truly remarkable increase in sexual activities and a striking intensification of sexual responses manifesting itself in diverse forms of hetero-, homo-, and autosexual behavior. Such hypersexuality may become apparent even in the absence of other animals or human observers. Changes in sexual behavior may also appear in castrates and pseudohermaphrodites.

6. Changes in dietary habits.—Normally frugivorous monkeys will accept and consume large quantities of various kinds of meat. There may also be an increase in appetite and food consumption.

At this point it is unfortunately not possible to consider the various changes in, and the fractionation of, the temporal lobe syndrome brought about by the passage of time after the brain operations, let us say, during postoperative periods of 15 to 20 years. It should be noted though that this syndrome, in the opinion of K. Akert[3] and his coauthors, "has undoubtedly been the stimulus for an unprecedented interest in the neurological basis of behaviour." Others have pointed to an "almost frenetic experimental activity" in this area of research. In reviewing some of the studies in this field several years ago, Teuber[161] found that "the major concern of those who experiment on the neurology of emotion seems to be how to take the Klüver-Bucy syndrome apart." After considering various attempts to do so he raised the question whether the "parts" found, taken together, actually add up to the complex Klüver-Bucy syndrome and concluded that "they probably do not." At any rate, an analysis of the literature readily shows that since 1937 the rhinencephalon whether "associated with the nose" or not has become increasingly a focus of interest for investigators in the fields of neuroanatomy,[4,8,36,41,64,139,166] histology,[23, 111,113,125,126,177] electron microscopy,[42] neuro- and electrophysiology,[4,33, 58,129,131,141,153,155] histo- and biochemistry,[42,117,118] endocrinology,[48,53,123, 136,137] neurology,[9-13,30,31,130,151,162,167,168] and neurosurgery.[32,108,124,152,158, 170] It is not surprising that biological psychologists,[17,39,54,62,63,127] psychiatrists,[46,50,106,133-135,145] and even psychoanalysts[128] have joined those whose experimental or theoretical efforts are increasingly directed towards this region. Furthermore, this region has not escaped the attention of workers wrestling with problems of cerebral dominance and interhemispheric relations since Downer[27] reported a reversible Klüver-Bucy syndrome in a split-brain monkey subjected to a unilateral amygdalectomy.

In considering the outcome of the "almost frenetic" activities during the last 25 years some investigators are beginning to experience great difficulties in trying to cope with the oversupply of facts and theories now available. For instance, Green[43] and his coworkers looked into the literature before actually placing lesions in the amygdala-pyriform cortex and in other rhinencephalic areas in cats to undertake "an analysis of the Klüver-Bucy syndrome with particular reference to normal and abnormal sexual behavior." They reported in 1957 that at least 29 different physiological and behavioral effects following lesions and stimulation of the amygdala and neighboring structures had been described. There is little doubt that at the present time the list of such effects would be still longer; in fact, it appears likely that the number of different effects in such a list could be doubled by including available data on every part of the limbic system. It is not surprising, therefore, that some researchers in this area are beginning to sound a pessimistic note. In 1957, the same year in which the Green *et al.* analysis was published, Cragg and Hamlyn[23] reported a combined histological and electrical study of some commissural and septal connections of the hippocampus in the rabbit and concluded that "the functions of the limbic system can as yet be defined in only the vaguest terms, and the addition of the connexions described in this paper to the already complex circuit diagram of the hippocampal-fornix system provides little further illumination." It deserves special mention that as long as 60 years ago Zuckerkandl[178] (working in the Neurological Institute at the University of Vienna) related the septum to eight fiber tracts; in the meantime researches centered on limbic structures and connections have turned every region into a "center" of increasingly complex circuits, no matter whether we are dealing with the septum, the amygdala, the mammillary bodies, or any other structure. Apparently Cragg and Hamlyn believe that further advances do not so much depend on learning more about ever more complex circuitry as on undertaking "many more physiological and behavioural studies."

Under the circumstances we should perhaps have the courage to ignore the plethora of facts and theories—at least the hundreds of *petit faits* that have accumulated during the last 25 years—in order to take a look at the phenomena from a great distance to see whether something like the outlines of a general structure of limbic functions may become visible. Paul MacLean[114,115,116] has occasionally taken such a look and I shall do the same today in the name of "psycho-pathology."

First, in looking back as far as the days of the early vertebrates we discover that with the development of distance receptors, such as vision, there started "a morphological battle that has raged for the past three hundred million years for the functional control of the frontal end of the cerebral axis"—to use the striking formulations of Stanley-Jones. If we consider the evidence from comparative sensory physiology as presented, for instance, by v. Buddenbrock[20] we find that there are microsmatic as well as macrosmatic animals among the fishes, amphibians, and reptiles—in fact, even among the birds as Stanley Cobb[21] has pointed out. It is only when we come to the mammals that the sense of smell becomes dominant: it becomes, as Henning[51] puts it, *the* sense. All available studies and observations appear to justify the conclusion that mammals are macrosmatic animals with the exception of cetaceans, such as whales, porpoises, and dolphins, and that the sense of smell is poorly developed in the higher primates, including man. However, in studying the brains of man and other microsmatic mammals the somewhat disconcerting discovery was made that large parts of the "olfactory brain" or so-called rhinencephalon are not directly, if at all, concerned with mediating olfaction. For instance, various lines of evidence indicated that the chief function of the hippocampus which once upon a time was considered to be the olfactory center in man and other mammals must be sought in other spheres and that its relation to smell, if any, can only be an indirect one. The fact that the hippocampus is relatively and absolutely such a huge structure, particularly in man, raises the question as to its non-olfactory functions. It has been suggested that the olfactory centers in microsmatic animals have in some way become "modified" by a tremendous development of non-olfactory functions although such suggestions have unfortunately not specified the nature of such functions. The general question is, just what are the non-olfactory functions mediated by the "rhinence-phalon"? We are faced here, as Stanley-Jones[156] has so picturesquely put it, with the problem of the "untenanted rhinencephalon." If "smell" is no longer the only tenant, who, then, are the other tenants? The experimental data accumulated during recent decades, especially since 1937 when the "Papez circuit" caught the attention of the neurological world, indicate—no matter what the final picture may turn out to be —that at least two other tenants may be identified, namely, "sex" and "emotions." Let us assume then that the rhinencephalon as a whole (that is, when including an "olfactory" as well as an "non-olfactory" brain) is involved in 1) olfactory phenomena, 2) emotional phenomena, and 3) sexual phenomena. The question to be answered is whether these three "tenants" have a family resemblance.

It is generally known that in macrosmatic animals the sense of smell plays a very important role in locating, choosing, accepting, or rejecting food, sexual partners as well as friend and foe. However, we are not inquiring here into the role olfaction may play in the emotional and sexual behaviors of macrosmatic and microsmatic animals. It is true that even Freud[35] was concerned with such questions. He was of the opinion that the decisive step in phylogenetic development, in fact, the step that led to the "threshold of human civilization," was made when the *Urmensch* got his nose above the ground or rather above the level of the female genitalia and assumed an upright position and a bipedal gait, with the result that olfaction became secondary and vision the supreme sense. Freud called this a "theoretical speculation" which, he suggested, should be checked by studying animals closely related to man. In passing it should be mentioned, therefore, that in recent years Schloeth[150] studied encounters among animals of 244 different species and found, for instance, that in lemurs the first contact was naso-nasal; in monkeys and apes, after the first visual contact, the contacts were naso-genital and naso-anal.

To repeat, we are not concerned here with the problem of determining the role of olfactory, emotional, and sexual factors in ongoing behavior but with the question whether an examination of phenomena in the olfactory, emotional, and sexual spheres will lead us to recognizing common features—something like a general structure typical of limbic functions in general. Approaching this question historically, we may ask, first of all, whether the *Thymopsyche* Stransky talked about when he considered affects, drives, and instincts (in contrast to a *Noopsyche*) has by now found its home in Turner's[164,165] *thymencephalon* ("the affective or temperamental part of the brain") and, furthermore, whether the thymencephalon is, for purposes of localization, the *"non-olfactory rhinencephalon"* Vigouroux[169] talked about. The boundaries of the non-olfactory rhinencephalon are likely to shift with further experimental advances and a more thorough understanding of its connections with the brain stem reticular formation and other parts of the brain. However, in the light of present-day knowledge it appears justifiable to relate this region to emotional and sexual phenomena even though its boundaries may be expected to shrink and expand as the result of future researches. It may be argued that in asking the question—*what do thymencephalon and rhinencephalon have in common?*—the precise location of a thymencephalon does not matter as long as we are interested in a functional analysis only. For the time being though, it appears more profitable to start from structures and connections of the "olfactory" and "non-olfactory rhinencephalon" as presently identified (although unfortunately not with any finality) by anatomical and physiological researches. I shall not be able to go into questions of localization nor can I hope to do more than offer a few suggestions as to the common "features in the architecture of limbic functions" (to modify Joseph Barcroft's famous phrase only slightly). Although it is true, as Buddenbrock has pointed out, that the olfactory experiences of a microsmatic animal, such as man, cannot give him any concrete idea and understanding of the experiences mediated by the nose of a dog, I shall make an attempt to approach the problem of common "architectural features," first of all, from the standpoint of a "phenomenological psychopathology"[110] and ask, *just what are the common features, if any, of olfactory, emotional, and sexual phenomena?*

1) Let us first turn to olfactory phenomena.[1,16,51] It has been said that such phenomena come and go as the wind blows or the waves roll by. The olfactory world does not provide us with "objects" casting shadows. There are no "olfactory rays." "Object odors" do not emanate from olfactory "objects" but are merely associated with events and objects localized in a visual, acoustic, or tactile space. Whatever olfactory localization there may be it is continuously or suddenly changing. Instead of well-defined objects we encounter a "rubbery flexibility," that is, diffusion fields surrounding diffusion centers. For Helen Keller,[60] who was dependent on tactile and olfactory impressions, touch seemed to "reside in the object touched . . ." whereas odor seemed to "reside not in the object smelt, but in the organ." She found touch impressions to be "permanent and definite" in contrast to odors which she pronounced "fugitive, changing in their shades, degrees, and location . . . ." "By themselves, odors suggest nothing." No wonder that she considered smell "the fallen angel." It seems then that olfactory phenomena provide essentially a non-spatial world. While odors may constitute a "space-filling something" they do not constitute "things in space." The external world as unlocked by olfaction does not contain well-defined "things" coexisting in the presence of other "things" in an articulated space.

In brief, the world of olfactory experiences, at least for man, may be said to be essentially a world of fluctuations, oscillations, and inconstancies. And so is, we may add, the world opened up by emotional and sexual experiences. There is little doubt that a phenomenological account would disclose inconstancies, changes, fluctuations, and oscillations as characteristics of the olfactory as well as of the emotional and sexual spheres.

2) The world of olfactory phenomena is a world which seems to

be devoid of "constancy" phenomena, that is, of those forms of invariance which are so abundant in the visual world. In contrast to olfaction which does not provide "objects," vision provides an external world structured in terms of objects with properties which stay put, such properties as brightness, color, size, shape, and position. In microsmatic as well as macrosmatic animals we find, therefore, an approximate constancy of brightness, color, size, and shape in the presence of enormous fluctuations in radiant energy affecting the retina. For instance, in the normal monkey, responses to "size" are within wide limits not disturbed by changes in distance, brightness, color, shape, and position.

Furthermore, the olfactory world seems to be devoid of such forms of "transposition" as are found, for instance, in the transposition of melodies in the auditory world. The visual world likewise provides transpositions. For instance, visual stimuli belonging to a "size" series may be transposed in terms of the "larger than"- or the "smaller than"-relation. They may be transposed in terms of such relations even though the stimuli belong to a multi-dimensional series, that is, differ in shape, brightness, color, and other characteristics as well as in size. "Transposition," as I have previously pointed out,[80] is merely a special case of "equivalence." There do not seem to be forms of equivalence based on common factors operative in heterogeneous and widely different odor stimuli. To transpose heterogeneous visual, auditory, or olfactory stimuli in terms of Gestalt principles or factors is possible only if such factors can be identified and recognized at all. Obviously, there can be no olfactory melodies and a transposition of such melodies if all of us, as has been maintained, are Gestalt blind in the world of smells.

Even Henning,[51] who was never one to underrate the sense of smell, had to admit that no olfactory "abstractions" are possible since no human being is capable of ignoring the differentiating properties in various odor stimuli for the sake of "abstracting" one common olfactory property. The "isolation" or "abstraction" of one common olfactory property presupposes the ineffectiveness of numerous other olfactory properties. To be able to "abstract" the property of "white" from albino rats, lilies, sugar in a black cup, and a laboratory coat implies the ability to ignore heterogeneous visual aspects in the stimulus situations. Even a monkey, in such situations, will do so although he will not designate the abstracted property by saying "white."

In brief, since the world of olfactory phenomena does not provide "objects" with properties which stay put, it is devoid or practically devoid of "constancy" phenomena. And so, it seems, is the world of emotional and sexual phenomena. Whatever its differentiation and richness, it is not a richness in forms of invariance.

3) The world to which we have access through olfaction has often been contrasted with the world to which we have access through distance receptors. Although some physiologists have spoken of a "distance" reception for odors, it is not olfaction that provides immediate and direct information on objects located at a definite distance. It is chiefly vision which opens up the world of distances. Odors are in and around us. Olfactory phenomena, like emotional and sexual phenomena, are characteristically phenomena of nearness. MacLean[115] has insisted that "emotion is the only form of psychological information which, short of physical exercise, is associated with extensive behavioral changes inside the body."

4) When comparing visual phenomena and pain it becomes apparent that there are differences and degrees in what von Kries[105] has called the "objectification of sensations." According to him, we consider any information provided by the sense of sight immediately as definite information on external objects and their properties and not as some information about our subjective states. Pain, however, is chiefly subjective and only in some instances of localized pain does it attain a low degree of objectification. In our relations to the sensory world there are, therefore, tendencies towards "objectification" as well as tendencies towards "subjectification." Olfactory phenomena exhibit at best a low degree of objectification (in the sense of v. Kries). Similarly weak tendencies towards "objectification" seem to be characteristic of emotional and sexual experiences. The information made available through them is not primarily concerned with properties and interrelations of objects and events in the external environment. The world unlocked by them is chiefly a world of subjective (instead of objective) reality.

In this connection it is of special interest that it was C. J. Herrick who called attention to Starbuck's[157] distinction between "defining" and "intimate" senses. Starbuck held that there are senses—chiefly the higher senses, such as sight and hearing—that are very proficient in defining objects and their properties and setting them off in relationships to each other. There are other senses that report qualities without relating them spatially, temporally, or in other ways—reporting immediately and directly, for instance, that something is desirable or undesirable, attractive or repulsive, agreeable or indifferent. The olfactory sense, in Starbuck's view, is chiefly an intimate, not a defining sense. The character of intimacy inherent in olfactory experiences is no doubt also present in emotional and sexual experiences.

To conclude, our analysis, although very preliminary in character, has brought to light some family resemblance among the "tenants" of the rhinencephalon. By way of summary it may be said that olfactory, emotional, and sexual phenomena may be considered as

1) phenomena involving fluctuations and oscillations;
2) phenomena devoid or practically devoid of "constancies";
3) phenomena of nearness;
4) phenomena associated with a low degree of "objectification" (in the sense of von Kries) and a high degree of "intimacy" (in the sense of Starbuck).

Our approach has thus made it possible to discern at least some of the common features in the architecture of limbic functions. In trying to specify functional correlates of limbic structures we have been led to a consideration of characteristically unstable and fluctuating phenomena, and the question now arises whether such a result will throw light on the psychology and psychopathology of perception.

In returning to the subject of hallucinations it is of great interest to find that Mourgue, in his fundamental treatise on the neurobiology of hallucinations,[122] reached the conclusion that variability and inconstancy represent the most constant features of hallucinatory and related phenomena. For him the hallucination is not a static phenomenon but essentially a dynamic process, the instability of which reflects the very instability of the factors and conditions associated with its origin. *In other words, his analysis has led essentially to the same result as our preliminary survey of limbic functions: the instability, fluctuations, and oscillations characteristic of olfactory, emotional, and sexual phenomena are also characteristic of hallucinatory phenomena.* It follows that, even if nothing were known about the cerebral localization of hallucinations, it would seem reasonable to consider their association with the temporal rhinencephalon and the temporal lobe in general. It would seem reasonable and profitable to do so even if no clinical neurologists had ever worried (as they have done) just why complex hallucinations are generally associated with the temporal instead of the occipital lobe and even if no neurologist or neurosurgeon had ever learned about subjective phenomena in temporal lobe epilepsy and no Penfield[175] had ever stimulated the temporal region (to obtain, as he expressed it, "psychical illusions" and "psychical hallucinations"). In fact, the literature—even that published before 1900—abundantly demonstrates the association of diverse subjective phenomena with the temporal neocortex and temporal rhinencephalon, for instance, such phenomena as complex hallucinations, déjà vu phenomena, visualizations, illusions, dreamy states, depersonalization, and derealization phenomena (to employ such terms as used in the literature[2,56,64a,75,119, 120,122,144]). But leaving aside questions of cerebral localization, let us consider for a moment only *visual* hallucinations and related phenomena. It turns out that in dealing with subjective visual phenomena investigators at one time or another have found it necessary to speak not only of hallucinations but also of positive and negative hallucinations, not to mention many other kinds of hallucinations, and, furthermore, of pseudohallucinations, eidetic images, eidetic images with reality character, hypnagogic images, dreams, illusions, memory-images, projected memory-images, memory-after-images, pseudo-memory-images, *Sinnengedächtnis*, re-perceptions, and "phantastic visual phenomena," to mention only a few of the technical terms used in this area of research.[68,69,73,75,81,107,122,149,154,159,160,172] The history of investigations in this field shows that never-ceasing efforts have been made to evolve suitable criteria for describing and classifying the varieties of subjective visual phenomena. It became also necessary to cope with such facts as that a hallucination, an eidetic image, a hypnagogic image, or a dream may have the *same* content, let us say, a particular object or person. Not only may a given object, scene, or event be subjectively experienced in many different ways, there may be, in ongoing behavior, a transition from one kind of subjective experience to another so that, for instance, a negative after-image may be followed by, or "transform" itself into, a pseudohallucination; a pseudohallucination into a hallucination; and a memory-image into an eidetic image.

It seems that classificatory attempts have never caught up with the richness and varieties of subjective visual and non-visual experiences. It is not surprising, therefore, that many investigators have felt that they could not do justice to the enormous wealth of normal and pathological phenomena in the field of perception. In investigating such an apparently simple problem as the characteristics of hemianopic hallucinations in his patients, Klein[61] found that all current definitions were of no use in adequately describing and classifying them and concluded that they might be best considered as simply "special forms of pathological experience." It may be argued that there is no sense in continuing to draw more and ever finer distinctions since such distinctions are merely an expression of the fact that the range from transient subjective phenomena to normal "objective" perception is tremendously wide comprising many different levels of "reality" and many different states of consciousness. Great difficulties have consequently been encountered in coping with the distinctions within this range since on the perceptual, hallucinatory, imaginal, and other levels, different kinds of "reality" are continuously judged and experienced. Under pathological as well as normal conditions we operate on, or relate ourselves to, many different levels of "reality," and are able to shift, or are forced to shift, from one level to another.

It has been our contention that there are parts of the brain which are primarily involved in tendencies towards shifts, fluctuations, oscillations, and inconstancies. It has been our further contention that for the time being we must assume that such tendencies and the tendency to operate on many different levels of reality are chiefly tied up with the temporal cortex and temporal rhinencephalon and that they can be most easily and effectively influenced by processes and conditions in, or related to, that part of the brain. In brief, the temporal lobes and their rhinencephalic components, in coping with a world of shifting and fluctuating phenomena, are primarily concerned with *poikilofunctions*. Since shifts and fluctuations associated with olfactory and affective phenomena as well as shifts and transitions from one level of (subjective or objective) reality to another are *normal* phenomena, we may expect certain parts of the brain (such as temporal and limbic structures) to be normally involved in mediating such shifts and fluctuations.

At the same time there is an ever-growing body of evidence for a *pathology of poikilofunctions*. Such a pathology of poikilofunctions may manifest itself in a pronounced *increase* in variability and an intensification of fluctuating aspects for beyond "normal" limits. It has been said that temporal seizures and various forms of temporal lobe epilepsy may be associated with a gamut of emotions from A to Z (with "the sensation of life, of conscious existence" multiplied tenfold) and with an alternation of "opposite feelings." It has also been stressed that the gamut of aura phenomena ranges from a visual, auditory, or vestibular aura to a "psychic" aura involving alterations in states of consciousness.[171] The close association of the temporal region with hallucinations and a large variety of other subjective phenomena needs no further comment. It has not escaped the attention of surgeons who have tried various procedures ranging from small cortical extirpations (even in the 19th century) to amygdaloidectomy to banish or suppress, for instance, auditory hallucinations.[34,174]

A pathology of poikilofunctions, however, may also manifest itself in a *decrease* of "normal" variability and at times even a radical reduction, if not an almost complete elimination, of fluctuations and oscillations. While normally there is a differentiation of various levels of subjective and objective reality, under pathological conditions, for instance, under the impact of an anterior cingulectomy,[173] there may be a "confusion" of levels in the sense that the individual is temporarily reduced to a level of vivid daydreaming on which he cannot, or only with great difficulty, distinguish his thoughts and imaginings from objective events in the external world. That the most striking behavior alterations ever produced by experimentally eliminating a part of the brain—namely, the "temporal lobe syndrome"—should at the same time be the most striking manifestation of a pathology of poikilofunctions is perhaps not surprising. It may seem surprising though—at any rate it could not have been easily predicted—that this pathology takes the form of an almost complete elimination of "normal" tendencies to cope with shifts, fluctuations, and inconstancies. It is true that the Klüver-Bucy syndrome has never been analyzed in the light of such considerations. I believe it would be a matter of great theoretical importance to do so but while it cannot be done here I shall make at least a start and perhaps point in the right direction. Although possibly a somewhat misleading procedure, I shall first reduce the complex symptomatology of this syndrome to a few terms and expressions, such as 1) "agnosia" and other types of amnesia, 2) hyperorality, 3) "hypermetamorphosis" (stimulus-bound behavior), 4) loss or diminution of emotions, 5) hypersexuality, and 6) a change from frugivorous to omnivorous habits. It is apparent from such an enumeration that this syndrome involves striking changes in perceptual, cognitive, mnestic, emotional, sexual, and other functions. No matter which one of the symptoms is studied the functional changes always point in the same direction, namely, towards a dedifferentiation of functions. On every functional level there is a diminution, or even a complete loss, of the differentiating and fluctuating aspects characteristic of normal emotional, sexual, perceptual, and other forms of behavior. The temporal lobe monkey appears to be dominated by one tendency only, namely, the tendency to react indiscriminately.

Within wide limits the nature and characteristics of objects reacted to do not seem to matter: there are only general determinants of behavior, such as "something to be approached," "something to be examined by mouth," "something to react to sexually," etc. *It may be said, therefore, that the Klüver-Bucy syndrome is essentially nothing but a striking manifestation of a dedifferentiation of functions, perhaps the most striking one ever discovered. All its symptoms point to a radical disturbance, if not loss, of normal poikilofunctions.*

Let us now turn to a part of the brain which, instead of being involved in fluctuations and inconstancies, is involved in "constancies." Let us turn to the occipital lobes[67] or rather the geniculo-striate system. My studies of this system[77,79,79a,80,87] have led to the conclusion that its chief function lies in guaranteeing an approximate constancy of the external environment. In the absence of this system the "objects" of the external world are destroyed, as it were, since the "approximate constancies" of brightness, color, size, shape, and position characteristic of such objects have disappeared. In studying the behavioral responses to "color" after bilateral removal of the occipital lobes in monkeys I found, for instance, that relative effectiveness curves similar to the scotopic luminosity curve of the human eye can still be obtained although color vision is no longer present: the approximate constancy of "hue" in the presence of intensity changes and of numerous other changes has vanished. The stability and spatial structure of the external visual world are gone and the only visually induced responses left seem to be those to fluctuations in the density of luminous flux at the eye. In fact, the eye or rather the pathologically altered visual system may now be said to behave like a photocell that merely registers and responds to intensity fluctuations. After destruction of the striate cortex the functions mediated by the retina and various subcortical structures of the "visual sector" of the central nervous system are no longer sufficient to guarantee an approximate constancy of the external visual environment. The intactness of the striate cortex (or only portions of it) is a prerequisite for the operation of *isofunctions* establishing constancies and stability, in brief, a homeostasis in the *milieu externe.*

Our attempt to clarify the role of brain mechanisms in normal and abnormal perception has, therefore, led to the suggestion that *the temporal lobes, and especially the temporal rhinencephalon, are primarily concerned with poikilofunctions (that is, functions involved in fluctuations and inconstancies) and that the occipital lobes, and especially the geniculo-striate system, are primarily concerned with isofunctions (that is, functions involved in constancies).* One might be tempted to express the same thought by simply saying that *the isocortex has isofunctions and the allocortex allofunctions* were it not for the fact that this represents an oversimplification and attributes too much importance to the cortex itself.

The great success in accumulating new facts in diverse areas of research during recent decades has apparently not made it easier to make equally great strides in developing original theories dealing with the functional significance of the rhinencephalon and, more particularly, the non-olfactory rhinencephalon (or only parts of it). In considering the hippocampal formation Turner McLardy,[113] for instance, advanced the theory that the mossy fiber system has properties contributing to two "detector-coder mechanisms," the one for intensity-gradients and the other for complex temporal patterns. It is true though that most theories have dealt with larger structures, such as the hippocampus and amygdala, or with the significance of complex circuits. In Grünthal's[44,45] opinion, the hippocampus represents a "catalytic activator" which is basic for the proper functioning of affective and even neocortical activities although not participating in specialized functions itself. For C. J. Herrick[52] the non-spatial character of olfactory phenomena was a fact of prime importance since it became for him an important point of departure in formulating his theoretical views on the functions of the "olfactory parts" of the cortex. The olfactory sense having no localizing functions of its own—which is, indeed, a "curious thing" about exteroceptive olfactory functions, as Herrick insists—may consequently cooperate with many other systems sensitizing and activating the nervous system as a whole or "certain appropriately attuned sensorimotor systems in particular." Other lines of evidence have suggested the idea of a "modulator" to a number of investigators. On the basis of extensive electrophysiological studies of the amygdaloid projection system, Gloor,[37,38] for instance, arrived at the idea that the amygdala acts as a differentiated and flexible "modulator" on somatic, autonomic, and behavior mechanisms that are dependent upon and integrated in subcortical structures. Morsier[121] seems to hold a similar view since he maintains that the rhinencephalon functions as a "modulator" for autonomic, somatic, and behavioral mechanisms. In line with this, Bornstein[15] considers the rhinencephalon a sort of damping device for the neopallium, blunting, subduing, and regulating exogenous and endogenous stimuli before they can become fully effective.

In terms of such theories the pathology of poikilofunctions involves essentially a loss of the modulatory, dampening, and regulatory role of the limbic system; the result is that fluctuations and oscillations no longer remain within normal limits. For a better understanding of such modulatory and feedback mechanisms it has become increasingly important to consider *the role of the endocrines*. As Lissák and Endröczi[109] emphasized only a few years ago, the most important factor in the regulation of all endocrine processes is the central nervous system. The limbic forebrain structures assume special significance since they have a wealth of connections with the hypothalamus. I once pointed out[92] that the poikilofunctions of the limbic system are poised between the isofunctions of the cortex (involved in achieving an approximate constancy of the *external* environment) and the isofunctions of the diencephalon (involved in achieving an approximate constancy of the *internal* environment). Nauta considers it "a reasonable assumption" that the functional state of the hypothalamus is continuously determined by neural events occurring in the limbic system. To separate the limbic poikilofunctions from the isofunctions involved in an external or internal homeostasis is justified, I believe, for the sake of an analysis aiming at a better understanding of these intricate interrelations. In reality, however, not even the homeostasis in the *milieu interne* is quite perfect since "the body is not always wise and the environment often unfit," to quote Drabkin's[28,29] view on the "imperfection of homeostasis."

Even 25 years ago I doubted that all the behavior alterations characteristic of the Klüver-Bucy syndrome could be understood by merely considering the destruction of nuclear structures and fiber tracts in the brain, but only at the 1948 Hixon symposium[87] did I have the courage to suggest that symptoms, such as the changes in sexual behavior and the eating of meat, should be studied with reference to alterations in hypothalamico-hypophyseal interrelations and the occurrence of possible disturbances in endocrine functions. The possibility that a bilateral temporal lobectomy may affect the endocrines was brought forcibly home to me at an early stage when one of the monkeys in my first series exhibited what I took to be a fugitive acromegaly (in addition to exhibiting all other symptoms of the temporal lobe syndrome). Except for the last days of its life this animal appeared to be in good health for more than 20 years after the operations. However, the autopsy revealed a pituitary adenoma extending as far as the corpus callosum. I should also mention that Dr. Bartelmez and I[96] once suggested that the development of an extensive pelvic endometriosis in one of my monkeys, which had to be sacrificed 7 years after the brain operations, was due to an endocrine imbalance resulting from a disturbance of hypothalamico-hypophyseal mechanisms initiated by the lobectomies. In the meantime endocrinologists,[48,53] biochemists,[117,118] physiologists,[6,7] anatomists[49,136,137] as well as numerous investigators in other fields,[123,146] including clinicians, have become more and more interested in the endocrine aspects of limbic functions. Koikegami,[101, 102,103] who has carried out such fundamental studies on the anatomy and functions of the amygdala during the last decade, was also one of the first to pay particular attention to the endocrines. For the time being most neuroendocrinologists have not gone beyond the hypothalamus in analyzing the role of nervous structures in the central nervous system regulation of hormones.[123,147] However, the complex role of neural and even "psychic" factors in hormonal regulations has received thorough attention in a 1960 monograph by Lissák and Endröczi.[109]

It is easy to understand why in general, when trying to account for a disturbance of poikilofunctions, attempts are made, first of all, to locate the responsible factors within the organism. The subject of an "environmental endocrinology" may seem full of promise as long as it concerns itself with such relatively definite problems as the photo-neuro-endocrine effects in circadian systems, with particular reference to the eye. However, merely assuming that there are environmental stimuli or stimulus constellations that are equivalent, for instance, to an electrical stimulation or an ablation of certain limbic structures in producing a change in plasma 17-hydroxycorticosteroid levels cannot greatly advance our understanding of relevant mechanisms as long as the environmental stimuli are not specified. Once specified one may hope to determine the factors involved in such an equivalence.

The problems are becoming even more complex when we turn from a pathology of poikilofunctions to pathology. For instance, if it is reasonable to assume that an endocrine dysfunction initiated by damage to limbic structures can lead to an endometriosis,[96] is it equally reasonable to assume that the operation of environmental factors can produce the same or a similar dysfunction and ultimately lead to the same disease? Or are both assumptions ill-founded? We were confronted with such questions when (in studies with Dr. Paul E. Steiner) we found that seven of the last eight female macaque monkeys that came to autopsy in our laboratory had developed an endometriosis. However, only four of the seven cases had previously undergone a brain operation and in only three cases did the operation involve limbic structures. To complicate matters, some of the endometriosis cases had also developed "spontaneous" diabetes mellitus.

There will be general agreement that *the fluctuations, oscillations, and inconstancies characteristic of the functions associated with limbic structures should be more thoroughly studied in the light of neuroendocrinological relations.* While a Klüver-Bucy syndrome, or at least a fractionated Klüver-Bucy syndrome, may be produced in both microsmatic and macrosmatic animals, the problem of differences in symptomatology in these groups has apparently never received systematic attention. From the point of view of comparative neuroendocrinology[40] it may also be of interest to study poikilo- and isofunctions not only in homeotherms but also in poikilotherms. Even 30 years ago Mourgue[122] was keenly aware that, in man, disturbances in poikilo-functions as exemplified, for instance, by hallucinations may be closely related to hormonal factors; he called special attention to the fact that the appearance of hallucinations is often correlated with the hyperfunction of certain endocrines. Endocrinological considerations have also loomed large in theoretical views on eidetic phenomena. It was claimed, e.g., that eidetic images of the B-type (referring to Basedow's disease) are "optical stigmata" associated with a complex of basedoid symptoms.[75] Furthermore, it was maintained that the eidetic phase is a phase in the normal development of children which, however, is generally terminated by changes occurring during puberty.[72] The striking differences in the incidence of eidetic imagery in different geographic districts as reported from various countries, including the United States, have often led to interesting geopsychological speculations.

There is no doubt that at least some of the functions we have thought to be associated chiefly with the limbic system have in the meantime, in the thoughts of other investigators, become associated with the reticular system[55] or, since this did not always prove a satisfactory solution, with a combination of the two systems. Perhaps the best that can be done, in the present unsettled stage, is to develop a few theoretical approaches in the hope that they may become fruitful for further experimentation. I am reminded that, in a symposium on brain mechanisms and consciousness,[25] Adrian raised the question whether we should consider the reticular system as simply something "to wake us up in the morning and to send us to sleep at night" while Lashley inquired whether it is this system which provides the "vigilance" of the brain. Morison speculated on the problem whether the reticular system as a non-specific primitive sensory system cooperates with the classical sensory system and Penfield's centrencephalic system to cope effectively with "external reality." At this point I should like to recall some experiments on children who were unable to produce negative after-images since peripheral stimulation merely led to eidetic images in natural colors; such children also could not produce memory-images since they, too, immediately turned into eidetic images.[104] The investigator suggested, therefore, that in childhood, instead of a differentiation into various levels, only a primitive "undifferentiated unity" may exist. It is undoubtedly the somewhat poverty-stricken psychological repertory of the reticular system and the scarcity of more complex psychological phenomena associated with it that has kept investigators in this field from considering the psychological implications of possible changes in the functioning of the reticular system in the course of ontogenetic development or engaging in speculations along "geopsychological" or "geophysiological" lines.

All speculations on genuine psychological matters, if meant to establish definite relations between psychological functions and particular parts or systems in the brain, are doomed, of course, if Jaspers' views enunciated half a century ago still hold, namely, that even the simplest psychological phenomena are neurologically so complex and heterogeneous that they cannot come into existence without the activity of the whole brain. Perhaps Jaspers is still right . . . . Furthermore, if Hughlings Jackson's "duplex theory" of positive and negative elements is still pertinent we cannot avoid the conclusion that a bilateral temporal monkey, for instance, not knowing (visually) that a snake is a snake and a grape is a grape and not knowing many other things merely exhibits Hughlings Jackson's "not-knowings" and that the more difficult problem consists in determining the psychological structure of the "wrong-knowings," to use Jackson's term, and relating it to what is left of the brain. Nevertheless, we may hopefully entertain the idea that an analysis of Jackson's "wrong-knowings" and "not-knowings" and their interrelations in man and animal will yield concepts or even procedures that will, despite Jaspers' pronouncement, ultimately prove helpful in elucidating brain mechanisms.

In closing I should like to comment on only one of the tools that may prove useful in such an analysis. To start with a simple example, let us suppose a monkey is required to attend to one constant feature of its environment, that is, to respond positively to a circle instead of a square. On completion of the training, the animal when tested with hundreds of other stimulus pairs may, without requiring further training, respond immediately to only one of the two stimuli in a given pair. It may, for instance, at once respond consistently to the configuration FOOD instead of the configuration FAKE or to the picture of a duck instead of a silhouette representing the skyline of Chicago (with its rectangular elements). Since experimentally numerous stimulus pairs are thus found to be "equivalent" to the stimulus pair originally used in training (in the sense of immediately eliciting a differential response) the experimenter may readily conclude that there must be a property or set of properties in terms of which the stimulus configurations are similar for the animal. On inspecting the stimuli he may find that all stimuli positively responded to are roundish or "curvilinear" in contrast to "angular" stimuli negatively responded to. We are then confronted with one of the most challenging problems in the field of psychology, namely, *the problem of an equivalence and non-equivalence of stimuli and responses*. This problem appears in the analysis of perceptual as well as of cognitive, mnestic affective, and other psychological functions.[71,74,78,93] For instance, in the tool-using behavior of a Cebus monkey, the following objects may be found "equivalent" in obtaining food (a piece of banana) beyond reach: a stick, a sack, a towel, a newspaper, branches or strips of bark (removed from a tree), a piece of meshed wire, a wire ring, a rope, a leather belt, a brush, a fern leaf, a steel strip, a string, a toothpick, a carrot, a dead mouse, a live rat, and a live guinea-pig. The only "non-equivalent" object found may be a live snake.

Whether we are dealing with the problem of "equivalence" in tool use, dreams, symbols, processes of thinking, or reactions to the sensory world, the behaviors met with always require an analysis of abilities or tendencies to "isolate," "identify," "select," or "abstract" one property or set of properties in heterogeneous situations. An equivalence of heterogeneous stimuli or events cannot be understood, it seems, without assuming that they are in some way "similar." "Similarity" is one of those fundamental concepts that has engaged the attention of thinkers from Aristotle to Freud and Scheler, not to mention modern logicians and psychologists. For Freud, for instance, the factor of similarity was of paramount importance in the formation and structuring of dreams. Similarities may serve as a basis for relating, ordering, and classifying the most diverse elements, objects, and events. It may be said, therefore, that there are no unique or specific properties of objects but only properties a given object shares with other objects.[89] Reactions to "unique" objects cannot be understood without knowing the classificatory or ordering principles and the similarities involved.

Such considerations cannot easily be ignored in our search for relevant brain mechanisms in perception, recognition, memory, and other psychological functions. The statement that a given item is or is not perceived, recognized, remembered, etc. is of little value as long as the pertinent similarities effective in ordering the phenomena are not stated at the same time. If a "circle," for instance, was not responded to or not recalled we want to know whether it was a circle in a "curvilinearity" series or in some other series differently categorized. Recent attempts to elucidate storage, transfer, and readout of "information" in terms of molecular biology should not ignore the fact that items cannot be "stored" without "storing" at the same time the relevant ordering principles. To assume "specific" memory traces or engrams is equivalent to assuming relata without relations. Psychologically or behaviorally there is always an interdependence of relations and relata[74,78,80] and only a suggestion that under exceptional circumstances relata without relations may occasionally exist. Unfortunately, the number of possible similarities basic for different relations between relata and, therefore, for ordering principles is overwhelmingly large: ". . . there is no end to the possible kinds of similarity," to quote Popper.[138] There is, in fact, a "lawless revelry of similarity," as William James long ago insisted. Furthermore, the character or characteristics in terms of which psychologically or behaviorally effective similarities become established are so widely different that in man, for instance, we may have—to confine ourselves to visual phenomena only—ordering principles as diverse as those in terms of "color," "shape," "size," "angularity," "asymmetry," and "physiognomic characters" (such as "graceful," "restless," "sad," "melancholy," and "gloomy").[80]

Any serious attempt at relating the kind of psychological phenomena Jaspers had in mind to brain mechanisms must cope with *a large number of diverse and even unstable, that is, rapidly changing, ordering principles*. The fact that the identification and experimental demonstration of different ordering principles as associated with different dimensions of similarity is often a difficult and time-consuming procedure should not blind us to the fact that in ongoing behavior such principles may rapidly change. In "thinking," for instance, we

may constantly shift from one property or one complex of characteristics to another in "isolating" or "abstracting" one aspect in a set
of widely different items. The same flux of ordering principles is
characteristic of many other psychological activities.[81] We constantly
shift dimensions and thereby the ordering principles; we go from one
form of equivalence to another, thereby "destroying" similarities and
constantly "creating" new ones. It should not be overlooked that the
similarities we are concerned with do not exist in the external world
but only with reference to an organism and certain conditions and
processes within the organism. Similarities and dissimilarities in the
environment are not simply projected into the organism and passively
registered there. Unfortunately, psychologists have been satisfied with
merely introducing distinctions such as that between a "passive" and
an "active" attention in trying to do justice to such facts. The active
role of the organism has often been overlooked and consequently little
progress has been made even in the description and identification of
psychological functions operative in this active role. (It is of interest
in this connection that our anatomical and physiological knowledge of
cortico- and centrifugal systems has also remained rather slight.[143])

Such considerations become relevant even in the interpretation of
currently available neuropsychological data. For instance, if a cortically
injured animal has lost a previously established positive (or negative)
response to one of several sensory stimuli it may be readily concluded
that the cortical ablation has temporarily produced an amnesia for
certain sensory (visual, auditory, etc.) properties. In studying the fate
of previously established differential reactions to various kinds of
visual, auditory, and weight stimuli in cortically injured monkeys, I
reached the conclusion that the ablations produced a disturbance of
the ability to "relate" and "compare" sensory items rather than an
amnesia for the sensory items themselves. The elimination of the "comparison behavior" as a primary result of the cortical ablations was
discovered when using sensory stimuli which could be correctly responded to only by comparing and relating them *successively,* such as
auditory and weight stimuli.[74,80] With the "spontaneous" restitution of
comparison behavior the correct responses immediately reappeared. It
may be said then that the cortical damage affected non-sensory rather
than sensory functions. These observations, however, do not exclude the
possibility of definite relations between non-sensory and sensory functions. In fact, my experimental findings in this area of research support the view that there is generally an interdependence of sensory and

non-sensory functions or, more generally speaking, of relations and relata. Any theory trying to specify psychologically and behaviorally relevant brain mechanisms will have to cope with this interdependence.

The problems discussed here have reached such a level of complexity that a final remark may be in order. In an age of "wet" and "dry" biophysics the "blood, sweat, and tears" (all of them wet!) approach to the brain should perhaps be abandoned for the drier climate of cybernetics, information theory, and the world of self-organizing systems. For the time being, however, there is no clear evidence that the "dry" approaches have reduced the complexities of the brain as they present themselves in the light of older approaches. What is rather needed is perhaps the commodity recommended by the famous Dutch microbiologist A. J. Kluyver[59] when he addressed the National Academy of Sciences in this country 10 years ago, namely, "brains": meaning "the type of brain fertile from the point of view of scientific discovery." Kluyver called attention to a truly great scientific genius, the first Nobel Prize winner for chemistry, J. H. van't Hoff, who, on being appointed to the chair of chemistry at the University of Amsterdam, delivered a remarkable talk on "Imagination in Science." It was van't Hoff's contention that scientific progress has been chiefly due to a strong power of imagination acting as a driving force not only in the scientific field but also manifesting itself in artistic talents, poetry, love of literature, etc. He tried to document such a thesis—and did it convincingly, in Kluyver's opinion—by an analysis of the biographies of 200 eminent scientists. No doubt, the type of scientist van't Hoff had in mind belongs to what Ostwald has called the "romantic" type. Apparently he was prejudiced in favor of this kind of scientist since he himself seemed to be a "romantic" in Ostwald's sense. When still a student of Kekulé, van't Hoff issued his first publication, namely a four-page English poem entitled "Elegy on the Death of a Lady Student at Bonn" and in the same year, on returning to Holland, wrote and published a brilliant paper which made him the father of stereochemistry. It may be argued, of course, that for further progress scientists with "classical" brains, to use Ostwald's expression, are as badly needed as those with "romantic" brains. Unfortunately, it is often overlooked that sciences are in a constant flux and that the psychological aptitudes and interests, whether characteristic of "classical," "romantic," or other kinds of brains, required for making progress at a particular stage in a particular science today may not necessarily be the same kind of aptitudes and interests required tomorrow. To relate the structure of science to the psychological structure of its famous discoverers requires, I believe, the qualifications of a competent psychologist combined with those of an outstanding chemist, physicist, mathematician, etc. Since there is little danger that such a combination will appear on the horizon of the scientific world, it is likely that a reliable history of the great scientific advances in psychological terms—at least large chapters of it—will forever remain unwritten. Although there is no reason for being unduly pessimistic, there is no good reason either for going beyond the hope that particular problems in a particular stage of brain research will find the particular "brains" needed for making great advances. It has been said that physics is a science which can "predict" everything except its own future history; it is difficult to believe that brain research will do better than physics in predicting its own future.

ACKNOWLEDGMENT

Grateful acknowledgment is made for grants from the National Institute of Mental Health (MH-01981), United States Public Health Service; the Commonwealth Fund; the Committee for Research in Dementia Praecox founded by the Supreme Council, Thirty-third Degree, Scottish Rite, Northern Masonic Jurisdiction, U.S.A.; and the Dr. Wallace C. and Clara A. Abbott Memorial Fund of the University of Chicago which have made possible much of the author's work reported in this presentation.

REFERENCES

1. ADEY, W. R.: The sense of smell. In J. Field, H. W. Magoun, and V. E. Hall (Eds.): Handbook of Physiology. Sect. 1: Neurophysiology, pp. 535-548. Washington, D.C.: Amer. Physiol. Soc., 1959.
2. AHLENSTIEL, H., AND KAUFMANN, R.: Vision und Traum. Stuttgart, Enke Verlag, 1962.
3. AKERT, K., et al.: Klüver-Bucy syndrome in monkeys with neocortical ablations of temporal lobe. Brain 84: 480-498, 1961.
4. ALAJOUANINE, P. T. (Ed.): Les grandes activités du rhinencéphale. Vol. 1: Anatomie du rhinencéphale. Vol. 2: Physiologie et pathologie du rhinencéphale. Paris, Masson, 1961.
5. ALLISON, A. C.: The morphology of the olfactory system in the vertebrates. Biol. Rev. 28: 195-244, 1953.
6. ANAND, B. K.: Structure and functions of the limbic system ("visceral brain"); a review. Indian J. Physiol. Pharmacol. 1: 149-184, 1957.
7. ——: Functional importance of the limbic system of brain. Indian J. Med. Res. 51: 175-222, 1963.
8. ANDY, O. J., AND STEPHAN, H.: The Septum of the Cat. Springfield, Charles C Thomas, 1964.

9. ANASTASOPOULOS, G.: Hypersexualität, Schlafstörungen und akute Demenz bei einem Tumor des rechten Schläfenlappens. Psychiat. Neurol. *136:* 85-108, 1958.

10. ——: Zur Symptomatologie des rechten Schläfenlappens und seiner Tumoren. Wien. Z. Nervenheilk. *16:* 131-161, 1959.

11. ——, DIAKOYIANNIS, A., AND ROUTSONIS, K.: Three cases of temporal lobe epilepsy with endocrinopathy. J. Neuropsychiat. *1:* 65-76, 1959.

12. ——, AND KOKKINI, D.: Transient bulimia-anorexia and hypersexuality following pneumoencephalography in a case of psychomotor epilepsy. J. Neuropsychiat. *4:* 135-142, 1963.

13. BENTE, D., AND KLUGE, E.: Sexuelle Reizzustände im Rahmen des Uncinatus-Syndroms. Ein klinischer Beitrag zur Pathophysiologie und Pathobiologie des Archicortex. Arch. Psychiat. Nervenkr. *190:* 357-376, 1953.

14. BODAMER, J.: Die Prosop-Agnosie. (Die Agnosie des Physiognomieerkennens.) Arch. Psychiat. Nervenkr. *179:* 6-53, 1947.

15. BORNSTEIN, B.: Zur Physiologie und Pathologie des Rhinencephalon. Schweiz. Arch. Neurol. Psychiat. *67:* 264-273, 1951.

16. BÖRNSTEIN, W.: Über den Geruchsinn. Deutsch. Z. Nervenheilk. *104:* 55-91, 173-207, 1928.

17. BRADY, J. V.: The paleocortex and behavioral motivation. *In* H. F. Harlow and C. N. Woolsey (Eds.): Biological and Biochemical Bases of Behavior, pp. 193-235. Madison, Univ. of Wisconsin Press, 1958.

18. BUCY, P. C., AND KLÜVER, H.: Anatomic changes secondary to temporal lobectomy. Arch. Neurol. Psychiat. *44:* 1142-1146, 1940.

19. ——, AND ——: An anatomical investigation of the temporal lobe in the monkey (*Macaca mulatta*). J. Comp. Neurol. *103:* 151-252, 1955.

20. BUDDENBROCK, W. VON: Vergleichende Physiologie. Vol. I: Sinnesphysiologie. Basel, Birkhäuser, 1952.

21. COBB, S.: Observations on the comparative anatomy of the avian brain. Perspect. Biol. Med. *3:* 383-408, 1960.

22. CORDEAU, J. P.: Quelques données récentes sur la physiologie du lobe temporal. Evaluation actuelle du syndrome de Klüver et Bucy. Un. Méd. Canada *89:* 963-975, 1960.

23. CRAGG, B. G., AND HAMLYN, L. H.: Some commissural and septal connexions of the hippocampus in the rabbit. A combined histological and electrical study. J. Physiol. *135:* 460-485, 1957.

24. CRITCHLEY, M.: The Parietal Lobes. London, Arnold, 1953.

25. DELAFRESNAYE, J. F. (Ed.): Brain Mechanisms and Consciousness. Springfield: Charles C Thomas, 1954.

26. DE JONG, H. L.: Experimental Catatonia. Baltimore, Williams & Wilkins, 1945.

27. DOWNER, J. L. DEC.: Interhemispheric integration in the visual system. *In* Mountcastle, V. B. (Ed.): Interhemispheric Relations and Cerebral Dominance. Baltimore, Johns Hopkins Press, 1962.

28. DRABKIN, D. L.: Metabolism of the hemin chromoproteins. Physiol. Rev. *31:* 345-431, 1951.

29. ——: Imperfection: biochemical phobias and metabolic ambivalence. Perspect. Biol. Med. *2:* 473-517, 1959.

30. DRACHMAN, D. A., AND OMMAYA, A. K.: Memory and the hippocampal complex. Arch. Neurol. *10:* 411-425, 1964.
31. ETTLINGER, G.: Visual discrimination following successive temporal ablations in monkeys. Brain *82:* 232-250, 1959.
32. FALCONER, M. A. et al.: Treatment of temporal-lobe epilepsy by temporal lobectomy. Lancet *i:* 827-835, 1955.
33. FLORIDA, F. A. DE, AND DELGADO, J. M. R.: Lasting behavioral and EEG changes in cats induced by prolonged stimulation of amygdala. Amer. J. Physiol., *193:* 223-229, 1958.
34. FREEMAN, W., AND WILLIAMS, J. M.: Human sonar; the amygdaloid nucleus in relation to auditory hallucinations. J. Nerv. Ment. Dis. *116:* 456-462, 1952.
35. FREUD, S.: Das Unbehagen in der Kultur. *In* Gesammelte Schriften, vol. 12, pp. 27-114. Wien, Intern. Psychoanal. Verlag, 1954.
36. GLEES, P., AND GRIFFITH, H. B.: Bilateral destruction of the hippocampus (cornu ammonis) in a case of dementia. Mschr. Psychiat. Neurol. *123:* 193-204, 1952.
37. GLOOR, P.: Electrophysiological studies on the connections of the amygdaloid nucleus in the cat. EEG Clin. Neurophysiol. *7:* 223-264, 1955.
38. ——: Amygdala. *In* J. Field, H. W. Magoun, and V. E. Hall (Eds.): Handbook of Physiology. Sect. 1: Neurophysiology, pp. 1395-1420. Washington, D.C., Amer. Physiol. Soc., 1960.
39. GODDARD, G. V.: Functions of the amygdala. Psychol. Bull. *62:* 89-109, 1964.
40. GORBMAN, A. (Ed.): Comparative Endocrinology. New York, Wiley, 1959.
41. GREEN, J. D.: The function of the hippocampus. Endeavour *22:* 80-84, 1963.
42. ——: The hippocampus. Physiol. Rev. *44:* 561-608, 1964.
43. ——, CLEMENTE, C. D., AND GROOT, J. DE: Rhinencephalic lesions and behavior in cats; an analysis of the Klüver-Bucy syndrome with particular reference to normal and abnormal sexual behavior. J. Comp. Neurol. *108:* 505-545, 1957.
44. GRÜNTHAL, E.: Über das klinische Bild nach umschriebenem beiderseitigem Ausfall der Ammonshornrinde. Ein Beitrag zur Kenntnis des Ammonshorns. Mschr. Psychiat. Neurol. *113:* 1-16, 1947.
45. ——: Über den derzeitigen Stand der Frage nach den klinischen Erscheinungen bei Ausfall des Ammonshorns. Psychiat. Neurol. (Basel) *138:* 145-159, 1959.
46. GUERRERO-FIGUEROA, R., AND HEATH, R. G.: Evoked responses and changes during attentive factors in man. Arch. Neurol. *10:* 74-84, 1964.
47. HALLERSTEIN, V. H. v.: Zerebrospinales Nervensystem. *In* L. Bolk et al. (Eds.): Handbuch der vergleichenden Anatomie der Wirbeltiere, vol. 2, part 1, pp. 1-318. Berlin, Urban Schwarzenberg, 1934.
48. HARRIS, G. W.: Neuroendocrine relations. Res. Publ. Ass. Res. Nerv. Ment. Dis. *40:* 380-405, 1962.
49. HAYWARD, J. N., AND SMITH, W. K.: Influence of limbic system on neurohypophysis. Arch. Neurol. *9:* 171-177, 1963.
50. HEATH, R. G.: Electrical self-stimulation of the brain in man. Amer. J. Psychiat. *120:* 571-577, 1963.
51. HENNING, H.: Der Geruch. Leipzig, Barth, 1924.

52. HERRICK, C. J.: The functions of the olfactory parts of the cerebral cortex. Proc. Nat. Acad. Sci. USA *19:* 7-14, 1933.

53. IBAYASHI, H. et al.: Effect of electrical stimulation of the limbic system on pituitary-adrenal function: anterior and posterior cingular gyrus. Endocrinology *73:* 816-818, 1963.

54. ISAACSON, R. L. (Ed.): Basic Readings in Neuropsychology. New York, Harper & Row, 1964.

55. JASPER, H. H. et al. (Eds.): Reticular Formation of the Brain. Boston, Little, Brown & Co., 1958.

56. JASPERS, K.: General Psychopathology. Chicago, Univ. of Chicago Press, 1963.

57. JELGERSMA, H. C.: Ein Fall von juveniler hereditärer Demenz vom Alzheimer Typ mit Parkinsonismus und Klüver-Bucy-Syndrom. Arch. Psychiat. Nervenkr. *205:* 262-266, 1964.

58. KAADA, B. R.: Cingulate, posterior, orbital, anterior insular and temporal pole cortex. *In* J. Field, H. W. Magoun, and V. E. Hall (Eds.): Handbook of Physiology. Sect. 1: Neurophysiology, pp. 1345-1372. Washington, D.C., Amer. Physiol. Soc., 1960.

59. KAMP, A. F. et al. (Eds.): Albert Jan Kluyver, His Life and Work. New York, Interscience Publ., 1959.

60. KELLER, H. A.: The World I Live In. New York, Century Co., 1920.

61. KLEIN, R.: Beitrag zur Frage der hemianopischen Halluzinationen. Mschr. Psychiat. Neurol. *92:* 131-149, 1936.

62. KLING, A., AND HUTT, P. J.: Effect of hypothalamic lesions on the amygdala syndrome in the cat. Arch. Neurol. Psychiat. *79:* 511-517, 1958.

63. ——, ORBACH, J., SCHWARTZ, N. B., AND TOWNE, J. C.: Injury to the limbic system and associated structures in cats. Arch. Gen. Psychiat. *3:* 391-420, 1960.

64. KLINGLER, J., AND GLOOR, P.: The connections of the amygdala and of the anterior temporal cortex in the human brain. J. Comp. Neurol. *115:* 333-369, 1960.

64a. KLOOS, G.: Das Realitätsbewusstsein in der Wahrnehmung und Trugwahrnehmung. Leipzig, Thieme, 1938.

65. KLÜVER, H.: An experimental study of the eidetic type. Genet. Psychol. Monogr. *1:* 71-230, 1926.

66. ——: Mescal visions and eidetic vision. Amer. J. Psychol. *37:* 502-515, 1926.

67. ——: Visual disturbances after cerebral lesions. Psychol. Bull. *24:* 316-358, 1927.

68. ——: Studies on the eidetic type and on eidetic imagery. Psychol. Bull. *25:* 69-104, 1928.

69. ——: Mescal. London, Kegan Paul, 1928.

70. ——: Fragmentary eidetic imagery. Psychol. Rev. *37:* 441-458, 1930.

71. ——: The equivalence of stimuli in the behavior of monkeys. J. Genet. Psychol. *39:* 3-27, 1931.

72. ——: The eidetic child. *In* Carl Murchison (Ed.): A Handbook of Child Psychology, pp. 643-668. Worcester, Clark Univ. Press, 1931. *Entitled* Eidetic Imagery, in 2nd ed., pp. 699-722.

73. ——: Eidetic phenomena. Psychol. Bull. *29:* 181-203, 1932.

74. ——: Behavior Mechanisms in Monkeys. Chicago, Univ. of Chicago Press, 1933. *Also in* Phoenix Sci. Series, Univ. of Chicago Press, 1961.

75. ——: The eidetic type. Res. Publ. Ass. Res. Nerv. Ment. Dis. *14:* 150-168, 1933.

76. ——: A tachistoscopic device for work with subhuman primates. J. Psychol. *1:* 1-4, 1935.

77. ——: An analysis of the effects of the removal of the occipital lobes in monkeys. J. Psychol. *2:* 49-61, 1936.

78. ——: The study of personality and the method of equivalent and non-equivalent stimuli. Character & Personality *5:* 91-112, 1936.

79. ——: Certain effects of lesions of the occipital lobes in macaques. J. Psychol. *4:* 383-401, 1937.

79a. ——: Visual functions after removal of the occipital lobes. J. Psychol. *11:* 23-45, 1941.

80. ——: Functional significance of the geniculo-striate system. Biol. Symposia *7:* 253-299, 1942.

81. ——: Mechanisms of hallucinations. *In* Studies in Personality, pp. 175-207. New York, McGraw-Hill Book Co., 1942.

82. ——: Porphyrins, the nervous system, and behavior. J. Psychol. *17:* 209-228, 1944.

83. ——: On naturally occurring porphyrins in the central nervous system. Science *99:* 482-484, 1944.

84. ——: On a possible use of the root nodules of leguminous plants for research in neurology and psychiatry (preliminary report on a free porphyrin-hemoglobin system). J. Psychol. *25:* 331-356, 1948.

85. ——: On naturally occurring porphyrins in the root nodules of leguminous plants. Fed. Proc. *7:* 66, 1948.

86. ——: Isolation of legcoproporphyrin. Fed. Proc. *8:* 86-87, 1949.

87. ——: Functional differences between the occipital and temporal lobes with special reference to the interrelations of behavior and extracerebral mechanisms. *In* L. A. Jeffress, (Ed.): Cerebral Mechanisms in Behavior, pp. 147-199. New York, Wiley, 1951.

88. ——: Discussion. Trans. Seventh Conference on Cybernetics, 1950, pp. 226-227. New York, Josiah Macy, Jr. Foundation, 1951.

89. ——: Introduction. *In* F. Hayek: The Sensory Order, pp. xv-xxii. Chicago, Univ. of Chicago Press, 1952.

90. ——: Brain mechanisms and behavior with special reference to the rhinen-cephalon. Journal-Lancet (Minneapolis) *72:* 567-574, 1952.

91. ——: Porphyrins in relation to the development of the nervous system. *In* H. Waelsch (Ed.): Biochemistry of the Developing Nervous System, pp. 137-144. New York, Academic Press, 1955.

92. ——: "The temporal lobe syndrome" produced by bilateral ablations. *In* G. E. W. Wolstenholme and C. M. O'Connor (Eds.): Ciba Foundation Symposium on the Neurological Basis of Behaviour, pp. 175-182. Boston, Little, Brown & Co., 1958.

93. ——: Psychological specificity—does it exist? *In* F. O. Schmitt, (Ed.): Macromolecular Specificity and Biological Memory, pp. 94-98. Cambridge, M.I.T. Press, 1962.

94. ——, AND BARRERA, E.: A method for the combined staining of cells and fibers in the nervous system. J. Neuropath. Exp. Neurol. *12:* 400-403, 1953.

95. ——, AND ——: On the use of azaporphin derivatives (phthalocyanines) in staining nervous tissue. J. Psychol. *37:* 199-223, 1954.

96. ——, AND BARTELMEZ, G. W.: Endometriosis in a rhesus monkey. Surg. Gynec. & Obst. *92:* 650-660, 1951.

97. ——, AND BUCY, P. C.: "Psychic blindness" and other symptoms following bilateral temporal lobectomy in Rhesus monkeys. Amer. J. Physiol. *119:* 352-353, 1937.

98. ——, AND ——: An analysis of certain effects of bilateral temporal lobectomy in the rhesus monkey, with special reference to "psychic blindness." J. Psychol. *5:* 33-54, 1938.

99. ——, AND ——: A preliminary analysis of the functions of the temporal lobes in monkeys. Trans. Amer. Neurol. Ass. pp. 170-175, 1939.

100. ——, AND ——: Preliminary analysis of functions of the temporal lobes in monkeys. Arch. Neurol. Psychiat. *42:* 979-1000, 1939.

101. KOIKEGAMI, H.: Amygdala and other related limbic structures; experimental studies on the anatomy and function. Acta Med. Biol. (Niigata) *10:* 161-277, 1963; *12:* 73-266, 1964.

102. ——, FUSE, S., AND KAWAKAMI, K.: Bilateral destruction experiments of hippocampus or amygdaloid nuclear region. Neurol. Medicochir. (Tokyo) *2:* 49-55, 1960.

103. ——, ——, YOKOYAMA, T., WATANABE, T., AND WATANABE, H.: Contributions to the comparative anatomy of the amygdaloid nuclei of mammals with some experiments of their destruction or stimulation. Folia Psychiat. Neurol. Japonica *8:* 336-370, 1955.

104. KRELLENBERG, P.: Über die Herausdifferenzierung der Wahrnehmungs und Vorstellungswelt aus der originären eidetischen Einheit. Z. Psychol. *88:* 56-119, 1922.

105. KRIES, J. VON: Allgemeine Sinnesphysiologie. Leipzig, Vogel, 1923.

106. LESSE, H. ET AL.: Rhinencephalic activity during thought. J. Nerv. Ment. Dis. *122:* 433-440, 1955.

107. LEUNER, H.: Die experimentelle Psychose. Monogr. Neurol. Psychiat. (Berlin) vol. 95. Berlin, Springer, 1962.

108. LIDDELL, D. W., AND NORTHFIELD, D. W. C.: The effect of temporal lobectomy upon two cases of an unusual form of mental deficiency. J. Neurol. Neurosurg. Psychiat. *17:* 267-275, 1954.

109. LISSÁK, K., AND ENDRÖCZI, E.: Die neuroendokrine Steuerung der Adaptationstätigkeit. Budapest, Ungar. Akad. Wissensch., 1960.

110. LÓPEZ, IBOR, J.: Psychiatrie und Neurologie am Kreuzwege. Nervenarzt *35:* 145-148, 1964.

111. LOCKE, S., ANGEVINE, J. B., AND YAKOVLEV, P. I.: Limbic nuclei of thalamus and connections of limbic cortex. Arch. Neurol, *4:* 355-364, 1961.

112. LONGMAN, J., AND VALENTE, M. I.: Distúrbios neuropsiquiátricos por lesões bilaterais do lobo temporal. Síndrome de Klüver e Bucy. Arq. Neuropsiquiat. *15:* 46-57, 1957.

113. McLARDY, T.: Hippocampal formation of brain as detector-coder of temporal patterns of information. Perspect. Biol. Med. *2:* 443-452, 1959.

114. MacLean, P. D.: The limbic system with respect to self-preservation and the preservation of the species. J. Nerv. Ment. Dis. *127:* 1-11, 1958.

115. ———: Contrasting functions of limbic and neocortical systems of the brain and their relevance to psychophysiological aspects of medicine. Amer. J. Med. *25:* 611-626, 1958.

116. ———: Psychosomatics. *In* J. Field, H. W. Magoun, and V. E. Hall (Eds.): Handbook of Physiology. Sect. 1: Neurophysiology, pp. 1723-1744. Washington, D.C., Amer. Physiol. Soc., 1960.

117. Mason, J. W.: Plasma 17-hydroxycorticosteroid levels during electrical stimulation of the amygdaloid complex in conscious monkeys. Amer. J. Physiol. *196:* 44-48, 1959.

118. ———, Nauta, W. J. H., Brady, J. V., Robinson, J. A., and Sachar, E. J.: The role of limbic system structures in the regulation of ACTH secretion. Acta Neuroveg. *23:* 4-14, 1961.

119. Meyer, J. E.: Die Entfremdungserlebnisse. Stuttgart, Thieme, 1959.

120. ———:Dreamy states and depersonalisation. Arch. Psychiat. Nervenkr. *200:* 12-18, 1959.

121. Morsier, G. de: Etudes sur les dysraphies crânio-encéphaliques. Schweiz. Arch. Neurol. Psychiat. *74:* 309-361, 1954.

122. Mourgue, R.: Neurobiologie de l'hallucination. Bruxelles, Lamertin, 1932.

123. Nalbandov, A. V. (Ed.): Advances in Neuroendocrinology. Urbana, Univ. of Illinois Press, 1963.

124. Narabayashi, H., et al.: Stereotaxic amygdalotomy for behavior disorders. Arch. Neurol. *9:* 1-16, 1963.

125. Nauta, W. J. H.: Hippocampal projections and related pathways to the mid-brain in the cat. Brain *81:* 319-340, 1958.

126. ———: Neural associations of the amygdaloid complex in the monkey. Brain *85:* 505-520, 1962.

127. Orbach, J. Milner, B., and Rasmussen, T.: Learning and retention in monkeys after amygdala-hippocampus resection. Arch. Neurol. *3:* 230-251, 1960.

128. Ostow, M.: A psychoanalytic contribution to the study of brain function. Psychoanal. Quart. *24:* 383-423, 1955.

129. Pampiglione, G., and Falconer, M. A.: Electrical stimulation of the hippocampus in man. *In* Handbook of Physiology. Sect. 1: Neurophysiology, pp. 1391-1394. Washington, D.C., Amer. Physiol. Soc., 1960.

130. Pasik, T. et al.: Factors influencing visual behavior of monkeys with bilateral temporal lobe lesions. J. Comp. Neurol. *115:* 89-102, 1960.

131. Physiologie de l'hippocampe. Colloque International No. 107 held at Montpellier. Paris, Centre National de la Recherche Scientifique, 1962.

132. Pilleri, G.: Orale Einstellung nach Art des Klüver-Bucy-Syndroms bei hirnatrophischen Prozessen. Schweiz. Arch. Neurol. Psychiat. *87:* 286-298, 1961.

133. Ploog, D.: Verhaltensforschung und Psychiatrie. *In* H. W. Gruhle, R. Jung, W. Mayer-Gross, and M. Müller (Eds.): Psychiatrie der Gegenwart, vol. I/1B, pp. 291-443. Berlin, Springer, 1964.

134. ———: Vom limbischen System gesteuertes Verhalten. Nervenarzt *35:* 166-174, 1964.

135. POECK, K.: Die klinische Bedeutung des limbischen Systems. Nervenarzt *35:* 152-161, 1964.
136. POIRIER, L. J., AND CORDEAU, J. P.: Effect of hypothalamic lesions on the responses to cold and immobilization in the monkey. Amer. J. Physiol. *191:* 148-152, 1957.
137. ——, ——, LEMIRE, A. P., AND AYOTTE, R. A.: Blood picture of spinal and bitemporal monkeys under the influence of immobilization. Amer. J. Physiol. *187:* 193-198, 1956.
138. POPPER, K. R.: The Logic of Scientific Discovery. New York, Science Editions, 1961.
139. POWELL, T. P. S., COWAN, W. M., AND RAISMAN, G.: Olfactory relationships of the diencephalon. Nature *199:* 710-712, 1963.
140. PRIBRAM, K. H., AND KRUGER, L.: Functions of the "olfactory brain." Ann. New York Acad. Sci. *58:* 109-138, 1954.
141. RAMEY, E. R., AND O'DOHERTY, D. S. (Eds.): Electrical studies of the unanesthetized brain. New York, Hoeber, 1960.
142. RIMINGTON, C.: Suggestions concerning the biochemical defects in the different porphyrin diseases. Panminerva Med. *4:* 307-311, 1962.
143. ROSSI, G. F., AND ZANCHETTI, A.: The brain stem reticular formation; anatomy and physiology. Arch. Ital. Biol. *95:* 199-435, 1957.
144. ROTH, R., AND HARPER, M.: Temporal lobe epilepsy and the phobic anxiety-depersonalization syndrome. Part II: Practical and theoretical considerations. Compr. Psychiat. *3:* 215-226, 1962.
145. SAWA, M., MARUYAMA, N., HANAI, T., AND KAJI, S.: Regulatory influence of amygdaloid nuclei upon the unitary activity in ventromedial nucleus of hypothalamus. Folia Psychiat. Neurol. Japonica *13:* 235-256, 1959.
146. ——, UEKI, Y., ARITA, M., AND HARADA, T.: Preliminary report on the amygdaloidectomy on the psychotic patients, with interpretation of oral-emotional manifestation in schizophrenics. Folia Psychiat. Neurol. Japonica *7:* 309-329, 1954.
147. SCHARRER, E., AND SCHARRER, B.: Neuroendocrinology. New York, Columbia Univ. Press, 1963.
148. SCHILDER, P.: Psychoanalyse und Eidetik. Z. Sex.-Wiss. *13:* 56-61, 1926.
149. ——: Mind: Perception and Thought in Their Constructive Aspects. New York, Columbia Univ. Press, 1942.
150. SCHLOETH, R.: Zur Psychologie der Begegnung zwischen Tieren. Behaviour *10:* 1-80, 1956.
151. SCHREINER, L., AND KLING, A.: Effects of castration on hypersexual behavior induced by rhinencephalic injury in cat. Arch. Neurol. Psychiat. *72:* 180-186, 154.
152. SCOVILLE, W. B., AND MILNER, B.: Loss of recent memory after bilateral hippocampal lesions. J. Neurol. Neurosurg. Psychiat. *20:* 11-21, 1957.
153. SHEER, D. E. (Ed.): Electrical Stimulation of the Brain. Austin, Univ. of Texas Press, 1961.
154. SOLOMON, P. ET AL. (Eds.): Sensory Deprivation. Cambridge, Harvard Univ. Press, 1961.
155. SPERLING, E., AND CREUTZFELDT, O.: Der Temporallappen. Zur Anatomie, Physiologie und Klinik (mit Ausnahme der Aphasien). Fortschr. Neurol. Psychiat. *27:* 295-344, 1959.

156. STANLEY-JONES, D.: Posture and the rhinencephalon. J. Nerv. Ment. Dis. *125:* 591-598, 1957.

157. STARBUCK, E. D.: The intimate senses as sources of wisdom. J. Religion *1:* 129-145, 1921.

158. STEPIEN, L. S., CORDEAU, J. P., AND RASMUSSEN, T.: The effect of temporal lobe and hippocampal lesions on auditory and visual recent memory. Brain *83:* 470-489, 1960.

159. STRAUS, E.: Die Ästhesiologie und ihre Bedeutung für das Verständnis der Halluzinationen. Arch. Psychiat. Neurol. *182:* 301-332, 1949.

160. ——: The Primary World of Senses. New York, Macmillan Co. (Free Press of Glencoe), 1963.

161. TEUBER, H. L.: Physiological psychology. Ann. Rev. Psychol. *6:* 267-296, 1955.

162. TERZIAN, H.: Observations on the clinical symptomatology of bilateral partial or total removal of the temporal lobes in man. *In* M. Baldwin, and P. Bailey (Eds.): Temporal Lobe Epilepsy, pp. 510-529. Springfield, Charles C Thomas, 1958.

163. ——, AND ORE, G. D.: Syndrome of Klüver and Bucy reproduced in man by bilateral removal of the temporal lobes. Neurology *5:* 373-380, 1955.

164. TURNER, E. A.: The future of psychosurgery. A review of the thymencephalon. Birmingham Med. Rev. *18* (n.s.) : 85-102, 1953.

165. ——: Cerebral control of respiration. Brain *77:* 448-486, 1954.

166. ULE, G.: Über das Ammonshorn. Fortschr. Neurol. Psychiat. *22:* 510-530, 1954.

167. VAN REETH, P. C., DIERKENS, J., AND LUMINET, D.: L'hypersexualité dans l'épilepsie et les tumeurs du lobe temporal. Acta Neurol. Belg. *58:* 194-218, 1958.

168. VICTOR, M. ET AL.: Memory loss with lesions of hippocampal formation. Arch. Neurol. *5:* 244-263, 1961.

169. VIGOUROUX, R. P.: Physiologie du rhinencéphale non olfactif. Thèse de Sciences, Marseille, 1959.

170. WALKER, A. E.: Recent memory impairment in unilateral temporal lesions. Arch. Neurol. Psychiat. *78:* 543-552, 1957.

171. WEBER, W. C., AND JUNG, R.: Über die epileptische Aura. Z. ges. Neurol. *170:* 211-265, 1940.

172. WEST, L. J., (Ed.) : Hallucinations. New York, Grune & Stratton, 1962.

173. WHITTY, C. W. M., AND LEWIN, W.: Vivid day-dreaming: an unusual form of confusion following anterior cingulectomy. Brain *80:* 72-76, 1957.

174. WILLIAMS, J. M.: The amygdaloid nucleus. Confin. Neurol. *13:* 202-221, 1953.

175. WOLSTENHOLME, G. E. W., AND O'CONNOR, C. M., (Eds.) : Ciba Foundation Symposium on the Neurological Basis of Behaviour. Boston, Little, Brown & Co., 1958.

176. WOOLLARD, H. H.: An outline of Elliot Smith's contributions to neurology. J. Anat., *72:* 280-294, 1938.

177. YAKOVLEV, P. I. et al.: Limbic nuclei of thalamus and connections of limbic cortex. Arch. Neurol. *3:* 620-641, 1960; *5:* 364-400, 1961.

178. ZUCKERKANDL, E.: Die Riechstrahlung. Arb. Neurol. Inst. Wien. Univ. *11:* 1-28, 1904.

2

A NEUROPHYSIOLOGICAL APPROACH TO PERCEPTUAL PSYCHOPATHOLOGY

by CHARLES SHAGASS, M.D.*

HISTORICALLY, THE MODERN ERA of scientific psychology was initiated by perceptual studies, and perception was long regarded as the basic problem of experimental psychology.[1] The early workers attempted to explain perceptual experiences primarily in the structure of the prevailing field, the stimulus situation. They attempted to determine lawful relationships between the physical environment on the one hand and subjective experience on the other. This is exemplified by the famous Weber-Fechner law, which gave rise to the psychophysical methods.

The neurophysiological approach to the problem appears to have predated experimental psychology. Johannes Muller came out with his theory of specific nerve energies in 1826. According to Boring, Muller insisted that the nerves of each of the five senses has its own peculiar neural quality, and noted that the specificity may lie not in the nerve itself, but in its central termination. This early suggestion of sensory brain centers became well accepted toward the end of the nineteenth century, following the demonstrations of cerebral localization by Broca, Fritsch and Hitzig, and Ferrier, Munk and Goltz. As Boring remarks, "Even a function seems better established if it occurs in some particular place."[1,p.675] Although experimental psychology and neurophysiology did not move forward in a unified manner in the study of perception, psychology quickly incorporated neurophysiological findings into its textbooks.

In recent years, a new approach to the experimental study of perception has become increasingly productive. This approach is obviously influenced by dynamic and differential psychology. Ittleson[15]

*Department of Psychiatry, College of Medicine, and Psychopathic Hospital, State University of Iowa, Iowa City, Ia.

The research discussed in this paper was supported (in part) by a grant (MY-2635) from the National Institute of Mental Health, U.S. Public Health Service.

compares it with the earlier approach in terms of two questions. The old stimulus determination approach asks, "What does the environment do to the perceiver?" The new motivational approach asks, "What does the perceiver do to the environment? What is actually done by the individual when he perceives?" Perceiving, from the latter view, becomes an active process rather than a passive reaction. As a corollary, the measurable attributes of perceptual functioning are seen as windows to the personality. The application of perceptual techniques to the study of psychopathological states becomes a logical next step. Pursuit of this approach, as exemplified by the groups led by Witkin[41] and Ittleson,[15] has already contributed an impressive body of literature.

Coincident with the introduction of a dynamic approach to perceptual problems, neurophysiology has undergone its own dynamic revolution. New experimental findings have forced revision of many long-accepted concepts. The all-or-none principle was shown not applicable to dendrites.[5] The integrating and modulating role of the mid-brain and thalamic reticular formations on a large variety of brain functions was discovered and elaborated.[17] Central control of afferent inputs was demonstrated.[21] The Papez hypothesis of a circuit for emotional responses was found to have a basis in fact, and the concept of the "visceral brain" was elaborated.[24] Cerebral areas capable of producing positive and negative reinforcements of behavioral responses were found.[23] Over the span of a few years the telephone-exchange model of brain activity had to be discarded, and new models sought. In keeping with the times, the favorite model is the computer. However, as Grundfest pointed out, providing neurophysiological evidence to support the inferences of the mathematician, von Neumann, the brain seems to combine and intermix both the analogue and digital types of computers, a formidable engineering job.[14]

Modern neurophysiology has thus acquired techniques and concepts which endow observable neuronal activities with the complexity potential required to understand behavior. Satisfactory application of these to behavioral phenomena has hardly begun. One would, for example, suppose that the data of neurophysiological and psychological observation should meet most agreeably in the area of this symposium, perceptual functioning. The neurophysiologist applies stimuli which we can readily agree are sights, sounds, touches, etc., and records electrical responses in the nervous system. Must not such responses provide the physical basis of sensory experience? However, although the activity of the visual afferent system is essential if we are to see anything, visual experience is not confined to light flashes. Much is known about the effects of light flashes, but it is still not possible to describe, in neurophysiological terms, how the letters M-A-N come to be perceived as designating the male of our species. We have some good ideas about the transport of information into the brain, but so far we don't know very much about the coding, decoding, information correlation, and information utilization processes which must be involved in perception.

It appears then that the established neurophysiological correlates of perception are confined to a rather primitive level of perceptual functioning. Consequently, it should be clear that, currently, the potential neurophysiological correlates of perceptual psychopathology must similarly be limited. However, such a limitation is no reason to refrain from investigation of this area until more is learned about normal perception. The new motivational approach to perception supports such a positive attitude. Its basic question, "What does the perceiver do to the stimulus?," implies that the stimulus interacts with a pre-existing neural state, determined by the personality, previous experience, and current wishes and feelings of the perceiver. Individual differences in response to a standard stimulus should thus be heavily determined by personality and motivational factors; among these, psychopathological processes should be important. Now, it is known that there is considerable intra- and inter-individual variability in cerebral responses to even simple stimuli, such as brief electrical pulses or light flashes, when these are studied in unanesthetized subjects. Does this variability of cerebral response depend upon personality factors related to psychopathology? This question is amenable to experimental answer. One has but to measure cerebral responsiveness to sensory stimulation and determine whether and how individual differences relate to psychopathology. The research program in our laboratory has been devoted to this approach for several years. Some of our main findings will be described after consideration of methodological problems.

Recording and Interpretation of Cerebral Sensory Responses in Man

It is easy to measure cerebral responses to sensory stimulation in animals by recording evoked electrical potentials. Not many humans, however, will consent to having holes placed in their cranium, at least not for experimental purposes. No prior surgery is needed to record the electroencephalogram (EEG), but the usual EEG rarely reveals evoked potentials. These are so small that they are obscured by the "spontaneous" brain rhythms. Fortunately, it is possible to record evoked potentials from scalp recordings by means of the averaging principle introduced by Dawson.[8] He administered multiple stimuli and averaged the EEG effects. This procedure resulted in cancellation of the "spontaneous" brain rhythms, which are not time-locked to the stimulus, while, at the same time, the time-locked evoked potential was clearly brought out. Several types of instrumentation for achieving au-

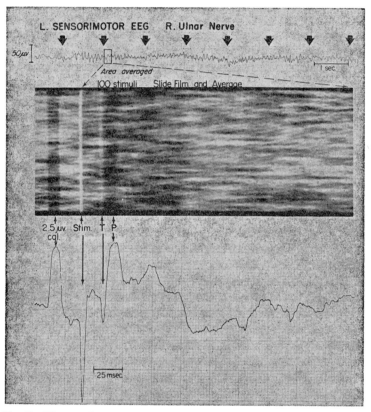

FIG. 1.—Photographic averager technique. Upper trace: EEG during ulnar nerve stimulation (arrows); note difficulty in observing any response. Middle portion of figure contains enlarged Polaroid transparency, with effect of 100 stimuli, corresponding in time to XY-plotter trace below. Relative positivity of sensorimotor electrode gives upward deflection. Trough (T) is maximum negativity and peak (P) is maximum positivity of initial evoked response component. For further description, see text.

tomatic averaging have by now been developed. The one we have used most extensively in our work so far is a photographic average, built for us by Shipton[38] and similar to the one described by Koshevnikov.[19] Figure 1 shows how this instrument works and also illustrates why averaging is required.

The upper tracing of figure 1 shows the EEG from the left sensori-motor area during periodic stimulation of the right ulnar nerve through electrodes placed over the skin at the wrist. The stimuli were brief (0.1 msec.) electrical pulses, of sufficient intensity to elicit a visible twitch in the little finger, but not painful. Note that there was no discernible effect of this stimulus on the EEG. The averaging process is confined to the brief period of time following the stimulus indicated by the little rectangle; in this instance it was about 250 msec. The major component in the photographic system is a cathode ray oscillo-scope, modified in such a way that each sweep of the beam is horizontal. The usual vertical deflection, which indicates amplitude, is displayed as a fluctuation in brightness of this horizontal line. With each successive stimulus, the vertical position of the beam is systematically shifted by a raster, and the successive sweeps are photographed on a continuously exposed Polaroid transparency. The middle portion of the figure shows an enlarged Polaroid transparency obtained in this way. Now, since brightness fluctuates as a function of amplitude, any changes in ampli-tude which are time-locked to the stimulus will cause consistent light or dark vertical bands on the film. The record so obtained is then converted into a conventional tracing by passing the film across a slit through which a beam of light shines on a photosensitive device, whose output is then recorded by means of an XY-plotter. The tracing below the Polaroid film represents the optical analysis of this film. Note that the major events following the stimulus in the film are consistent in time and constantly present. This means that we were extracting by averaging not just an occasional event, but one which was always there. From right to left, the succession of bands on the film, corresponding to major deflections in the tracing, are: a 2.5 microvolt calibration signal, placed on every tracing; the artifact generated by the electrical stimulus; the initial, downward-going, negative component of the somatosensory evoked potential (T); the initial, upward-going, positive component (P); a series of later com-ponents, which are somewhat irregular in this particular tracing. We have used three other averaging instruments in our laboratory, and believe that our latest is superior to the photographic in several respects.

However, most of our own data which will be presented have been collected with the photographic averager.

What can be learned from the scalp-recorded evoked potential? First, it is important to note that the temporal characteristics of the deflections appear quite similar to those obtained in recordings from electrodes placed directly on brain tissue. Our somatosensory responses correspond well with those recorded by Jasper, Lende, and Rasmussen[16] during neurosurgical operations. The characteristics of the averaged scalp-recorded response to light flash also agree with those recorded from electrodes implanted in the visual cortex of man.[2,39,40] As might be expected from recordings at a distance, and from evidence that the scalp acts as an averager of electrical activity from the multiple underlying cortical areas,[10] responses at the scalp are much less precisely localized than those recorded directly from brain. Nevertheless, using phase reversal technique with closely spaced electrodes, we have found the initial components of the somatosensory response to be quite sharply localized to an area which corresponds roughly with the contralateral post-central gyrus. Cobb and Dawson[7] have similarly localized the primary visual response components to the expected occipital region. On the other hand, the later components of evoked responses may be recorded from widespread areas and are not restricted to the contralateral hemisphere. Evidence from implanted electrode studies in man suggests that some of these later electrical changes are not modality specific.[39]

In an attempt to relate the somatosensory response components to specific neurophysiologic events, Goff et al.[12] have suggested that the initial component (mainly negativity in our records) represents potentials in pre-synaptic thalamo-cortical fibers of the primary somatosensory projection pathway, and that the succeeding positive component represents corresponding post-synaptic potentials. The next positive component they thought might reflect extra-lemniscal activity, perhaps mediated by reticular formation. The later electrical events, with their widespread distribution and relative non-specificity may involve little or no sensory information. It may be speculated that they represent electrical signs associated with information processing mechanisms set in motion by any sensory stimulus. This would be consistent with observations that the later components are more susceptible to change with alterations of awareness, as in sleep, and by centrally acting drugs, such as anesthetics.[2] However, the non-specific qualities of the later components should not be emphasized at the expense of recognizing the existence of major differences between modalities. For example, records A and B of figure 2 are somatosensory and visual responses from the same subject. The responses are different in duration and complexity.

Additional evidence suggesting modality-specific relations of later evoked activity comes from observations of the so-called "ringing" phenomenon, which seems to be particularly associated with visual responses. This consists of rhythmic oscillations, starting at least 300 msec. after a light flash and sometimes continuing for long periods. Record C of figure 2 gives an example. Walter[40] claims to have recorded "ringing" for several seconds. He reports that it is augmented by attention to the stimulus and by inhalation of CO_2, and that voluntary hyperpnea attenuates it; these characteristics distinguish it from "spontaneous" alpha rhythm, which reacts in an opposite manner to

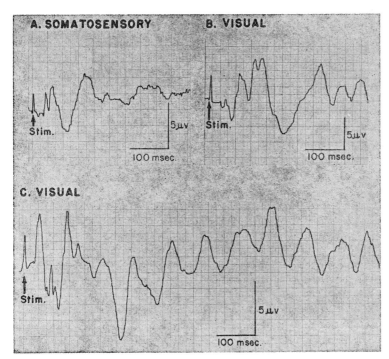

FIG. 2.—A, B, somatosensory and visual responses from same subject. Note longer duration and greater complexity of visual response. C, visual response from another subject to illustrate "ringing." Relative positivity at presumably active lead gives upward deflection in this and subsequent records.

such manipulations. The topographic observations of Perez-Borja et al.[25] support this distinction. In patients with multiple electrode implants in the occipital lobe they found evoked responses to flash, sometimes followed by "ringing," to be limited to discrete areas near the calcarine region, whereas rhythmic activity, including alpha, was recorded from widespread areas. Walter's suggestion about the significance of "ringing" seems worthy of quotation in the present context: ". . . it is a true reverberatory effect, preserving information about the stimulus as a significant event, by activation of diffuse projection mechanisms through delay circuits which can sustain an oscillation with adequate stability to avoid runaway or dispersion."[40, pp. 243-244]

Although the cortical responses to brief, simple stimuli can obviously be very complex, it seems possible, for conceptual purposes, to divide them into two portions. One may distinguish between the initial events, which represent the arrival of sensory information, and the later ones which are likely concerned with preserving and interpreting this information. The exact point of demarcation between the initial and later events is not certain, and one may question whether any clear point exists. Parenthetically, one is reminded here of the attempts to distinguish between sensation and perception, a distinction now regarded as academic, as it is almost impossible to conceive of one without the other. *A priori*, one might expect personality variables to stand a better chance of being reflected in the later, elaborative, aspects of the evoked potential than in the early ones. While it is true that the initial components are more stable and less subject to experimental alteration,[40] they are not, however, invariable. Indeed they have been shown to be subject to marked change by experimental manipulations, such as reticular formation stimulation.[22] Consequently, it seems appropriate to keep an open mind as to which portion of the evoked potential ought to be studied in relation to psychopathology. In our own program, we have so far devoted most of our attention to the initial components of the somatosensory potential. However, this was due mainly to technical difficulties in studying the visual response and the later portions of the somatosensory, and is not to be construed as a preference based on evidence. The technical difficulties are now being overcome, and we expect to expand our scope of observation in the future.

Some Experimental Findings

1. Sensory Threshold and Somatosensory Cortical Responses

In our initial study of somatosensory responses, we explored the relationship between stimulus intensity and response amplitude.[29] As might be expected, amplitude was found to increase with greater intensity (fig. 3). Somewhat unexpected was the finding that the first evidence of an evoked response is obtained with a stimulus intensity corresponding to sensory threshold, i.e., when the subject first reports awareness of the stimulus. This close relationship between psychological and physiological thresholds was also observed by Dawson[9] and has been confirmed repeatedly in our laboratory.[35] Parallel findings for auditory responses were reported by Geisler et al.,[11] although there is now some uncertainty about the nature of the responses which they recorded; they were certainly not primary auditory potentials.

We then conducted experiments on cats to determine whether peripheral nerve and cortical response thresholds were the same or different.[28] The superficial radial nerve was stimulated distally and simultaneously recordings were made from the proximal nerve and cortex. Nerve and cortical response thresholds were found to be identical both in anesthetized and flaxedil-immobilized, unanesthetized animals. These animal experiments supported the conclusion that a stimulus capable of exciting an afferent nerve will produce a cortical response. Taken together with the human results, the findings showed that a cortical response is a necessary, although not sufficient, condition for sensory awareness. These data define the physiological limit for the phenomena designated as "subliminal perception," in which an unreported stimulus exerts behavioral effects.[13] Obviously, a stimulus which is subliminal in the physiological sense cannot affect behavior, because it does not affect the nervous system. Subception appears to depend mainly on the relationship between perception and attention.

2. Somatosensory Intensity-Response Function and Psychiatric Illness

As illustrated in figure 3, considerable variation was noted between subjects in the relationship between stimulus intensity and amplitude of the somatosensory cortical response. In some subjects response amplitude rose sharply as stimulus intensity increased, whereas in others the rise was much more gradual and amplitude was low even at the highest intensity available to us. The psychiatric correlates of this response difference were examined in 111 subjects, of whom 87 were a heterogeneous group of patients and 24 were nonpatients.[34,35] Sensory threshold was used as a physiological "zero" point for the intensity scale and curves were plotted which related stimulus voltage increments above threshold to the amplitude of the primary component (T to P

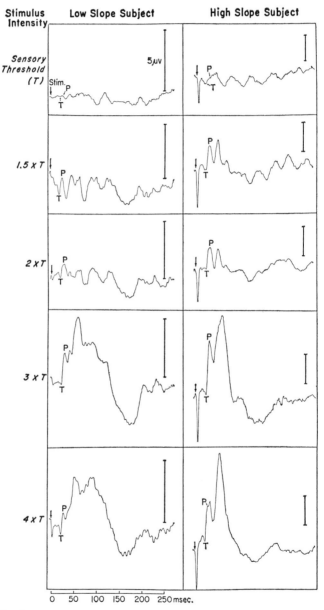

Fig. 3.—Somatosensory responses at different stimulus intensities in two subjects, one with slow and the other with rapid rate of amplitude increase. Note change in configuration between two and three times threshold. Amplitude measured from T to P for intensity-response curves.

in fig. 3). These curves had the shape of a decelerating growth function (fig. 4). They could be made linear if plotted in terms of the logarithm of stimulus intensity; the slopes of such linear transforms were also calculated.

The results demonstrated a significant difference between patients and nonpatients. Amplitudes at all intensities were greater for patients; their rate of amplitude increase, as given by the slope, was also significantly higher. Breakdown of the patient sample by psychiatric diagnosis revealed that only one sizeable group gave intensity-response curves indistinguishable from nonpatients. This group could be described as "dysthymic" neurotics; it consisted of patients with diagnoses of anxiety, depressive, obsessive-compulsive, or psychophysiologic reactions. Figure 4 shows the mean intensity-response curves obtained by combining nonpatients and dysthymics into one group and all remaining patients into another. All intensity points, even those at threshold, were statistically significantly different. The

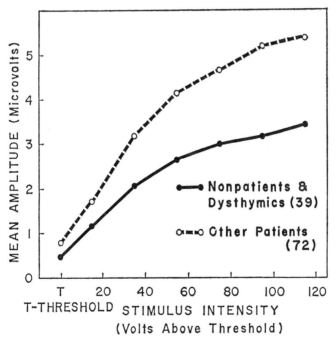

Fig. 4.—Mean curves, relating somatosensory response amplitude to stimulus intensity, in voltage increments above threshold. Note higher amplitudes at all stimulus intensities in patients other than dysthymics.

major diagnostic groups, apart from dysthymics, did not differ significantly from one another. They included patients with diagnoses of: schizophrenia, psychotic depression of all types, various kinds of personality disorder, conversion reaction, and adjustment reaction.

It could be concluded that the intensity-response function separates the psychiatric population into two groups. Dysthymics are placed with nonpatients in a low response amplitude group, while all other patients, except possibly those with brain syndromes, are placed in a high amplitude group. The statistical, and not absolute, nature of this distinction should be noted, as there was overlapping between the two groups. Repeat studies in several patients with psychotic depressions revealed a shift from high to low amplitude curves following successful drug or electrotherapy.[37] Proper neurophysiological interpretation of the intensity response findings is not yet possible. They suggest that some mechanism, which normally operates to restrict the amplitude of response in aggregates of cortical neurones, is impaired in a large variety of psychiatric disorders. Multiple mechanisms may ultimately be implicated if, as is possible, the cortical effect is a "final common path."

3. Somatosensory Cortical Recovery Function and Psychiatric Illness.

Another measure of cerebral responsiveness, or excitability, may be gained by administering paired stimuli, separated by varying intervals. This procedure resembles the classical method of studying nerve excitability by applying paired "conditioning" and "test" stimuli; it differs in that we used supramaximal rather than threshold intensities. By comparing the relative amplitude of response to the two stimuli of a pair, it is possible to plot the cycle of recovery of responsiveness. Figure 5 illustrates the kind of recovery cycle findings which we have come to expect in normal individuals.[30] As shown in the curve on the right, the early portion of the recovery cycle for the primary somatosensory response tends to be biphasic in form. The first phase of recovery occurs very early, the amplitude of the second response equaling that of the first, or exceeding it, before 20 msec. There is then a phase of diminished responsiveness, followed by a longer phase of full recovery, usually reaching a peak at about 100 to 130 msec.

As will be noted in the tracings on the right of figure 5, the response to the second stimulus, particularly at brief separations, takes place at the same time as later components of the first response. To estimate the actual amplitude of the second response it was necessary to correct for the effects of the first stimulus which were occurring at the same time. Responses to single, unpaired stimuli were used as the reference for such correction. The equipment which we are now using incorporates a device which makes this correction automatically and continuously. Data so far obtained with new equipment confirm our description of the biphasic somatosensory recovery pattern, although it appears that the initial recovery peak may actually occur earlier and the amount of facilitation may be greater than our previous data indicated. The rapid initial phase of recovery was a somewhat surprising finding, insofar as available information concerning somatosensory recovery cycles, which was derived from animal data, showed no such early peak.[4] Similar biphasic shapes, have, however, been described for cortical recovery cycles obtained by stimulation of the optic radiation in animals with chronically implanted electrodes.[27]

In our first systematic study of the recovery function, we compared the findings in 13 nonpatients and in a heterogeneous sample of 92 psychiatric patients.[30] Figure 6 shows the mean curves. The major difference occurred in the amount of recovery taking place before

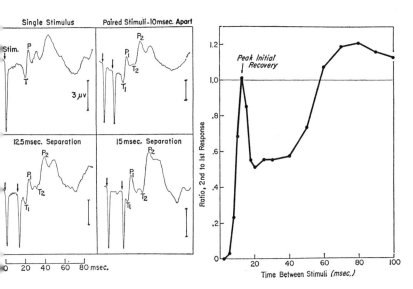

Fig. 5.—Somatosensory recovery function. Tracings at left illustrate responses to paired stimuli separated by varying intervals. Amplitude measured from T to P. Curve at right shows first 100 msec. of recovery cycle. Ratio of 1.00 indicates that $R_2 = R_1$. R_2 measurements compensated for the late effects of R_1. Curve is arithmetically smoothed. Note biphasic shape.

20 msec., i.e., in the early recovery phase. The patient group exhibited significantly less recovery than the nonpatients. As with the intensity response function, the recovery results in dysthymic patients did not differ significantly from those of nonpatients.[31] Particularly deviant results were found in patients with diagnoses of schizophrenia, psychotic depression, and personality disorder. For purposes of statistical analysis, a convenient single numerical index, characterizing the recovery data, was the ratio indicating the peak amount of recovery by 20 msec. Figure 7 shows the distribution of these peak early recovery ratios for a sample of 207 subjects. These were divided into three groups: nonpatients; patients with personality disorder, schizophrenia, or psychotic depression; all other patients. The recovery ratios in the

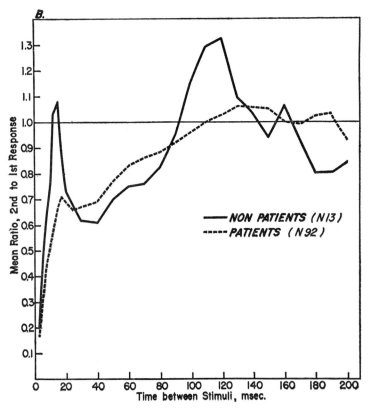

Fig. 6.—Mean somatosensory recovery curves in 92 psychiatric patients and 13 nonpatients. Note greater initial recovery, before 20 msec., in nonpatients.

"functional" psychoses and personality disorders differed significantly from those of the other two groups.[36]

The fact that personality disorders resembled functional psychoses in their recovery findings was particularly interesting as there is considerable disagreement about whether the personality disorders should be considered to be more like psychoneuroses or like psychoses.[6,18] Figure 8 shows the distribution of peak recovery ratios by 20 msec. in four subject groups, all of about equal mean age.[33] The distribution of ratios in the personality disorders is identical with that in the schizophrenic patients, and both of these groups differed significantly from the normals and dysthymics. Thus, at least as far as this physiological index is concerned, the evidence places the personality disorders more in the realm of psychosis than neurosis. Most of the patients in our personality disorder group were classified either as personality trait disturbances or as sociopathic personality disturbance, antisocial reaction. No significant difference in recovery

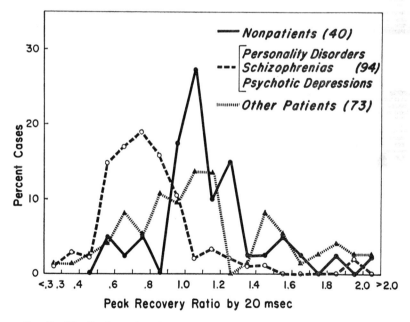

FIG. 7.—Distributions of peak initial somatosensory recovery ratios in 40 nonpatients, and 167 psychiatric patients divided into two groups. Note preponderance of low ratios in patients with diagnoses of personality disorders, schizophrenia or psychotic depression.

function was found between these subgroups, but the sample was relatively small.

We were able to demonstrate the reversibility of deviant recovery curves accompanying psychopathology by carrying out serial studies in 16 patients with psychotic depressions.[32] These were mainly diagnosed as manic depressive, depressed, although a few involutional and psychotic depressive reactions were included. Following successful treatment of depression, the recovery curves returned to the normal pattern. Similar results followed both electrotherapy and drug remissions. However, these treatments probably do not affect either of our measures of somatosensory responsiveness directly. This was indicated by the findings obtained by giving an anti-depressant in therapeutic dose for several weeks to two nonpatient volunteers.[37] The changes observed were in the direction of greater abnormality.

It will have been noted that the clinical differentiations provided by our two somatosensory measures were quite similar. However, in 44 subjects for whom both measures were obtained, the correlation between them was found to be quite low. It appeared that the differen-

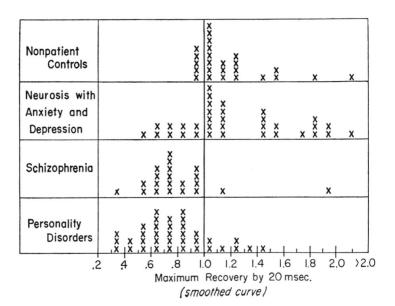

Fig. 8.—Distributions of peak initial somatosensory recovery ratios in 25 nonpatients, 34 psychoneurotics, 21 schizophrenics, and a mixed group of 36 personality disorders.

tiation between clinical groups was independently achieved by each measure.[35]

4. Visual Cortical Responses

We have recently begun to study the recovery function of the visual evoked potential. It was impossible to do this, at least for the first

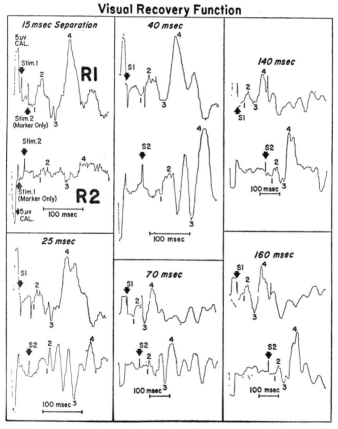

Fig. 9.—Sample tracings from visual recovery function determination in one subject, using Mnemotron computer and automatic subtractor. R_1 trace is average response to 50 single flashes. R_2 trace is residual of 50 single and 50 double flashes. R_1 and R_2 taken in same 100 stimulus sequence, single and double flashes alternating every two stimuli. 1, 2, 3, 4 indicate sequential components in R_1, presumably duplicated in R_2. Note early, minimal, evidence of R_2 by 15 msec., and complexity of R_2 at 25, 40 and 70 msec. separations. At 160 msec., R_2 and R_1 are similar.

100 msec., without an automatic subtracting device. This was because the latency and form of responses to the second of a pair of light flashes differ from those to the first. We are not yet able to report any correlations with psychopathology, although the findings of other workers with critical flicker fusion[20] and double flash discrimination[26] suggest that significant relationships should be present. However, in connection with the earlier discussion of visual response complexity, some indication of the complexity added by a second stimulus may be of interest. Figure 9 shows sample tracings from the recovery function of one subject. Note the great differences between responses to the first and second flashes. During the earlier phases of recovery the second response contains additional components, and latencies are considerably longer, even though the amplitude of the initial component is quite great. Besides demonstrating how much more complex the visual response becomes when a second light flash is added, figure 9 indicates the major problem we face in attempting to quantify the visual recovery function. When components of first and second responses differ in latency and form, it is difficult to be sure that they correspond to one another.

Concluding Remarks

There is an immense volume of literature which can be considered relevant to the neurophysiology of perception. In this paper, emphasis has been placed upon observations of cerebral sensory responses in man. This emphasis, which reflects the writer's research interests, seems justifiable in relation to the topic of this symposium. Verbal report of subjective experience remains our main source of data for identifying psychopathological states in man. This is particularly true in the area of perception. Even though psychopathology has been produced experimentally in lower animals, we cannot be sure to what extent it replicates human psychiatric illness. To demonstrate that a physiological change accompanies psychopathology, observations in man are essential. Proven physiological correlates may then be used as a guide to more extensive research in animals, and such research can more confidently be considered relevant to human psychopathology.

In presenting some of our own research findings, the main aim was to illustrate an approach which is feasible and which gives promise of yielding important information. Although the data represents the work of several years, they should clearly be regarded as preliminary, rather than definitive. Progress in this area of investigation has been highly dependent upon developments in instrumentation. The instruments we are using today can give us information which is more reliable and detailed than that yielded by those we used last year. It will take quite a while to learn what they are able to tell us, even though we can be sure that this is no more than a tiny fraction of what must be going on in the brain. It is highly likely that the future will see development of instruments capable of yielding more information and of a different kind.

Although instrumentation is crucial, its application to psychopathological problems will depend upon conceptual and technical developments of a psychological nature. Our significant correlations with psychiatric diagnosis are somewhat remarkable, when one considers the nature of current nosology. One can hope that more precise correlations will emerge when relevant psychological variables are identified, and defined with sufficient precision to permit adequate tests to be developed. However, even if specific techniques change completely, the general experimental approach to neurophysiological investigation of psychopathology outlined above should continue to be of use.

ACKNOWLEDGMENTS

Dr. Marvin Schwartz has been a constant collaborator in the research program considered in this paper. His critical reading of the manuscript is also gratefully acknowledged.

REFERENCES

1. BORING, E. G.: A History of Experimental Psychology, 2nd Ed. New York, Appleton-Century-Crofts, 1950.
2. BRAZIER, M. A. B.: Normal and abnormal oscillatory phenomena in the electrical activity of the brain. In Grenell, R. G. (Ed.) ; Neural Physiopathology. New York, Hoeber, 1962, pp. 258-265.
3. ——: Studies of evoked responses by flash in man and cat. In Jasper, H. H., Proctor, L. D., Knighton, R. S., Noshay, W. C., and Costello, R. T. (Eds.) ; Reticular Formation of The Brain. Boston, Little, Brown & Co., 1958, pp. 151-168.
4. CHANG, H.-T.: The Evoked Potentials. In J. Field (Ed.) ; Handbook of Physiology. Washington, American Physiological Society, 1959, Vol. 1, pp. 299-313.
5. CLARE, M. H., AND BISHOP, G. H.: Properties of dendrites; apical dendrites of the cat cortex. Electroenceph. clin. Neurophysiol., 7: 85-98, 1955.
6. CLECKLEY, H.: Psychopathic states. In Arieti, S. (Ed.) ; American Handbook of Psychiatry, pp. 567-588. New York, Basic Books, 1959.

7. Cobb, W. A., and Dawson, G. D.: The latency and form in man of the occipital potentials evoked by bright flashes. J. Physiol., *152:* 108-121, 1960.

8. Dawson, G. D.: A summation technique for the detection of small evoked potentials. Electroenceph. clin. Neurophysiol., *6:* 65-84, 1954.

9. ——: The relative excitability and conduction velocity of sensory and motor nerve fibres in man. J. Physiol., *131:* 436-451, 1956.

10. DeLucchi, M. R., Garoutte, B., and Aird, R. B.: The scalp as an electroencephalographic averager. Electroenceph. clin. Neurophysiol., *14:* 191-196, 1962.

11. Geisler, C. D., Frishkopf, L. S., and Rosenblith, W. A.: Extracranial responses to acoustic clicks in man. Science, *128:* 1210-1211, 1958.

12. Goff, W. R., Rosner, B. S., and Allison, T.: Distribution of cerebral somatosensory evoked responses in normal man. Electroenceph. clin. Neurophysiol., *14:* 697-713, 1962.

13. Goldiamond, I.: Indicators of perception: 1. Subliminal perception, subception, unconscious perception: An analysis in terms of psychophysical indicator methodology. Psychol. Bull. *55:* 373-411, 1958.

14. Grundfest, H.: Discussion. *In* Jasper, H. H., Proctor, L. D., Knighton, R. S., Noshay, W. C., and Costello, R. T. (Eds.); Reticular Formation of the Brain, Boston, Little, Brown & Co., 1958, pp. 473-487.

15. Ittleson, W. H., and Kutash, S. B.: Perceptual Changes in Psychopathology. New Brunswick, N. J., Rutgers University Press, 1961, Chapt. 1.

16. Jasper, H., Lende, R., and Rasmussen, T.: Evoked potentials from the exposed somatosensory cortex in man. J. Nerv. Ment. Dis., *130:* 526-537, 1960.

17. Jasper, H. H., Proctor, L. D., Knighton, R. S., Noshay, W. C., and Costello, R. T. (Eds.); Reticular Formation of the Brain, Boston, Little, Brown and Co., 1958.

18. Karpman, B.: The Sexual Offender and His Offenses. New York, Julian Press, 1954.

19. Koshevnikov, V. A.: Photo-electric method of selecting weak electrical responses of the brain. Sechenov. J. Physiol., *44:* 801-809, 1958.

20. Krugman, H. E.: Flicker fusion frequency as a function of anxiety reaction. An exploratory study. Psychosom. Med., *9:* 269-272, 1947.

21. Livingston, R. B.: Central control of afferent activity. *In* Jasper, H. H., Proctor, L. D., Knighton, R. S., Noshay, W. D., and Costello, R. T. (Eds.); Reticular Formation of the Brain, Boston, Little, Brown and Co., 1958, pp. 177-185.

22. Long, R. G.: Modification of sensory mechanisms by subcortical structures. J. Neurophysiol., *22:* 412-427, 1959.

23. Olds, J.: Self-stimulation experiments and differentiated reward systems. *In* Jasper, H. H., Proctor, L. D., Knighton, R. S., Noshay, W. C., and Costello, R. T. (Eds.); Reticular Formation of the Brain, Boston, Little, Brown and Co., 1958, pp. 671-687.

24. Papez, J. W.: The visceral brain, its components and connections. *In* Jasper, H. H., Proctor, L. D., Knighton, R. S., Noshay, W. C., and Costello, R. T. (Eds.); Reticular Formation of the Brain, Boston, Little, Brown and Co., 1958, pp. 591-605.

25. PEREZ-BORJA, C., CHATRIAN, G. E., TYCE, F. A. AND RIVERS, M. H.: Electrographic patterns of the occipital lobe in man: A topographic study based on use of implanted electrodes. Electroenceph. clin. Neurophysiol., 14: 171-182, 1962.

26. ROTH, A. C.: The effect of experimentally induced stress on perceptual measures. In Ittleson, W. H. and Kutash, S. B. (Eds.); Perceptual Changes in Psychopathology, New Brunswick, N. J., Rutgers University Press, 1961, Chapt. 9.

27. SCHOOLMAN, A., AND EVARTS, E. V.: Responses to lateral geniculate radiation stimulation in cats with implanted electrodes. J. Neurophysiol., 2: 112-129, 1959.

28. SCHWARTZ, M. AND SHAGASS, C.: Physiological limits for "subliminal" perception. Science, 133: 1017-1018, 1961.

29. SHAGASS, C. AND SCHWARTZ, M.: Evoked cortical potentials and sensation in man. J. Neuropsychiat., 2: 262-270, 1961.

30. —— AND ——: Reactivity cycle of somatosensory cortex in humans with and without psychiatric disorder. Science 134: 1757-1759, 1961.

31. —— AND ——: Excitability of the cerebral cortex in psychiatric disorders, in Roessler, R. and Greenfield, N. S. (Ed.); Physiological Correlates of Psychological Disorder, U. Wisconsin Press, Madison, 1962, pp. 45-60.

32. —— AND ——: Cerebral cortical reactivity in psychotic depressions. A.M.A. Arch. gen. Psychiat. 6: 235-242, 1962.

33. —— AND ——: Observations on somatosensory cortical reactivity in personality disorders. J. Nerv. Ment. Dis. 135: 44-51, 1962.

34. —— AND ——: Psychiatric disorder and deviant cerebral responsiveness to sensory stimulation. Recent Advances in Biological Psychiatry, Vol. 5. New York, Plenum Press, 1963, pp. 321-330.

35. —— AND ——: Cerebral responsiveness in psychiatric patients. A.M.A. Arch. gen. Psychiat. 8: 177-189, 1963.

36. —— AND ——: Psychiatric correlates of evoked cerebral cortical potentials. Am. J. Psychiat. 119: 1055-1061, 1963.

37. —— —— AND AMADEO, M.: Some drug effects on evoked cerebral potentials in man. J. Neuropsychiat., 3: S49-S58, 1962.

38. SHIPTON, H. W.: Photographic averaging for the study of evoked cortical potentials in man. In C. N. Smyth (Ed.); Medical Electronics. London, Illiffe & Sons, 1960, pp. 186-187.

39. WALTER, W. G.: Where vital things happen. Am. J. Psychiat., 116: 673-694, 1960.

40. ——: Spontaneous oscillatory systems and alterations in stability. In Grenell, R. G. (Ed.); Neural Physiopathology, New York, Hoeber, 1962, pp. 222-257.

41. WITKIN, H. A., LEWIS, H. B., HERTZMAN, M., MACHOVER, K., MEISSNER, P. B., AND WAPNER, S.: Personality Through Perception. New York, Harper, 1954.

3

THE PSYCHOPATHOLOGY OF
INTEROCEPTIVE STIMULATION

by GREGORY RAZRAN*

L ET ME, FIRST, define the scope of my concern and the source of
my evidence. The scope extends only to what might be called
specific primary interoceptive stimulation; that is, direct delivery of
specific mechanical, chemical, thermal, and electrical stimuli to
specific portions of the interior of the digestive, urogenital, vascular,
and respiratory systems. Secondary or feedback interoceptive stimulation resulting from primary exteroceptive and direct intracranial and
pharmacal stimulations does of course exist; and, I suppose, also, that
it is legitimate to infer the operation of interoceptive stimulation, both
primary and secondary, in drives and motives. However, these must
obviously be anchored to our experimental knowledge of what specific
primary interoceptive stimulation is and does. I should not like to
put, so to speak, the cart of what is inferred before the horse of what
is observed. Again, as a psychologist—and here also as psychopathologist—I am naturally more interested in the general organismic effects
than in the local-reflex characteristics of this stimulation.

More specifically, I will concern myself here primarily with two
aspects of interoception: *a*) the unconditioned aspect or, better, interoception as a sense modality—What is special about it? *b*) the conditioned aspect—interoception as a category of learning or of acquired
behavior, its existence and special existence. Being a continual built-in
activity of the organism, the interoception inflicts more complications
than does exteroception on experimental separations of unconditioned
from conditioned aspects. But, on the other hand, interoception is,
as you will see, but little deranged by matters of cognition, which makes
its animal and human experimentation much more interchangeable

*Queens College of The City University of New York.
Research supported by Grant MH 02196 of the National Institute of Mental
Health, National Institutes of Health, Public Health Service, United States De-
partment of Health, Education, and Welfare.

than that of exteroception. When Ecclesiates said: "Man has no pre-eminence over beast," he was no doubt thinking of interoception.

Experimental evidence on specific primary interoceptive stimulation, in the aspects that I am going to discuss, is almost a Russian or Soviet monopoly. As you no doubt suspect, the technique of this stimulation involves, in animals, fistulation of vessels and viscera, their exterioza-tion, or both; and, in humans, utilization of subjects with existing

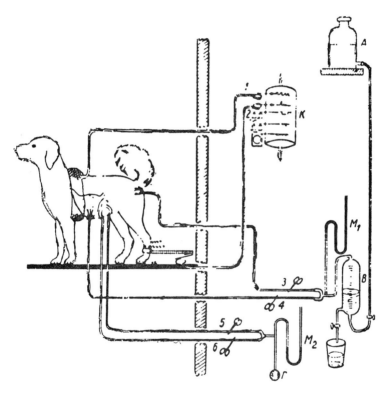

Fig. 1.—Conditioning of dogs in Ayrapetyants' laboratory. (Salivary fistula and general arrangement for exteroceptive food conditioning not shown. A, water reservoir; B, graduated vessel; M_1, manometer to measure intragastric pressure; M_2, manometer to measure pressure in ileocecal region; Γ , bulb to inflate the ileocecum; K, kymograph; 1, tube connecting respiratory cuff with Marey tam-bour; 2, tube connecting apparatus registering paw movement with Marey tam-bour; 3, tube for inflating rectum; 4, tube for inflating the balloon in the dog's stomach; 5, 6, tubes connecting manometer M_2 with the balloons in the ileocecal region, one balloon on the ileal side of the ileocecal valve and one on the cecal side.)

fistulas or subjects swallowing of tubings. The Russians have been "fistulators" for a long time, since Pavlov and even earlier; and, while I am not sure that the Russians have more fistulated patients than we do, they do seem to have more of them that "volunteer" for experiments, and—to carry my comparison further—I might say that the Russians seem to be more willing to swallow things than we are.

I shall not trouble you with details of techniques, but should, perhaps, mention that Thiry-Vella loops and Pavlov pouches are common in gastrointestinal fistulations; that spleens are exteriorized to the abdominal wall; that gall bladders are either exteriorized or fistulated; that uteri are, as a rule, both exteriorized and fistulated, with glass or plastic funnels fitted into the tops of the horns' opening to keep out possible secondary exteroceptive stimulation; that urinary bladders are often removed and urethral orifices sutured to the skin[1,2,14,16]—and that, in general, modern educators of educated Pavlov dogs would hardly be welcomed by our SPCA as good-will ambassadors. Here is a dog with five fistulas: a gastric, ileal, cecal, rectal, plus a salivary fistula which is old hat and not shown in the diagram (fig. 1[10]).

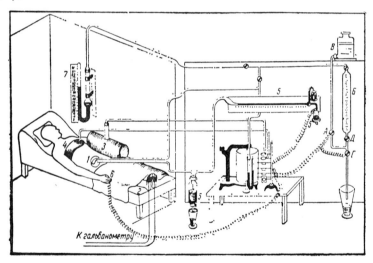

Fig. 2.—Apparatus for interoceptive conditioning of human subjects with urinary bladder fistulas. (1, urinary bladder fistula; 2, PGR electrodes; 3, plethysmograph; 4, respiratory cuff; 5, registration of urination; 6, subject's report of sensations; 7, manometer watched by subject; Б, graduated cylinder; B, water vessel regulating pressure; A, Г , Ц, valves. Russian words at lower left mean "leading to galvanometer.")

Soviet innovations in human experimentation might be called "poly-effector polytechnicalization"; that is, they record now a swarming multitude of effectors and not just the traditional one effector of salivation or paw-withdrawal. Here is a "volunteer" with a urinary-bladder fistula (fig. 2).

What goes in the bladder is a rubber balloon which inflates it with air or water or water varying in temperature. What gets out and gets recorded is: the contraction of the *detrussor urinae* registered on a manometer; urination which is both collected and recorded by a drop counter; respiration, blood volume, and *GSR;* and last, but not least, the subject's graphic signalization of his sensations—that "he's got to go." In addition, there are of course bells and buzzers and metronomes

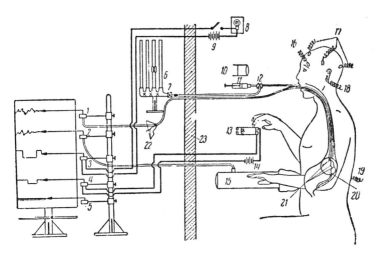

Fig. 3.—Swallowing technique for the study of conditioned and unconditioned interoception and their effects on EEG, volume of blood vessels, blinking, and visual sensitivity in human subjects. (1, record of gastric movements; 2, record of arm plethysmogram; 3, marker of light stimulus; 4, subject's report of interoceptive and/or visual sensations; 5, time; 6, burettes to introduce solutions into stomach through opening of stopcocks 7 and 12; 8, electric bulb; 9,14, accumulators; 10, disc of Makarov optic chronaximeter, measuring visual sensitivity; 11, syringe to draw out liquid contents of stomach; 13, key to signal gastric or visual sensations; 15, plethysmograph; 16, electrical registration of blinks; 17, EEG electrodes; 18, indifferent EEG electrode; 19, indifferent electrode for electrical stimulation of the stomach; 20, gastric balloon; 21, electrodes and leads of balloon; 22, terminal of balloon lead; 23, partition between experimenter and subject. Swallowing technique has also been used to study interaction between interoception and respiration, cardiac action, and galvanic skin reflex.)

and, interestingly, also experimenter's instructions to watch the manometer, the scale value of which becomes in time a significant *CR* parameter. And here is an almost riotous array of recordings (fig. 3) in college students, swallowing gastric and duodenal balloons, to which positioned electrodes and burettes with chemicals are attached; undergoing, at the same time, tests of EEG's, visual sensitivity, blinking, and plethysmographic changes; and reporting interoceptive and, this time also, exteroceptive sensations.

I

So much for techniques. As I indicated, I shall discuss, first, data on the unconditioned or general sense modality characteristics of interoception. Three main attributes need to be considered. First, there is the crucial attribute of conscious sensitivity. When and to what extent does interoception become a reportable conscious event? And what, if any, is the specific nature of the event? Second, comes the just as important attribute of organismic reactivity and interactivity of interoception, distal (rather than the proximal or local) effects. *a*) How does interoception affect, or interact with, ongoing distal, both vital and stimulus-evoked, organismic reactions? *b*) To what extent does interoception by itself evoke such distal organismic reactions, as its stimulus values increase? Terming part *a*) the effect of interoception on ongoing activities, a *correcting* effect, the way the Russians do, seems as yet premature—just interacting effects, for the present. Third, follows the problem of reaction stability as reflected in adaptability or habituability. Recent evidence indicates rather clearly that the ease of the habituation of a reaction upon repetition is a very important determinant of the nature of its conditionability which alone is, of course, a matter of basic organismic import. Incidentally, it should be obvious that interoception must be compared, not with distance, but with contact exteroception, i.e., with what is conventionally known as skin or cutaneous or dermal reception or stimulation.

Table 1, which is just a translation of several Russian tables,[9] will provide, I think, considerable information on interoceptive-exteroceptive differences in conscious reportability and, in a restricted sense, also distal reactivity. It is quite clear from the table that the threshold of verbal reportability of electrical stimulation of the interior of the stomach is very much higher than that for the hand or middle finger. Yet, with respect to the *GSR*, a distal reaction, hand and stomach hardly seem to differ: low threshold for both. The high threshold of interoceptive visceral conscious sensitivity will, I assume, not surprise you in view of the fact that in the past American interospective experimental psychologists such as Titchener and Boring[4] doubted altogether its existence. What may surprise you, however, is the next Figure (fig. 4)[8] which shows that, at supra-threshold stimulus values, conscious information from the stomach is strikingly precise. The data are means from four subjects who swallowed balloons equipped with

TABLE 1.—GSR Magnitudes and Verbal Reports of Sensations of Subject O. S. Whose Pyloric Region of the Stomach and Hand Immersed in a Physiological Solution Were Stimulated Electrically.

Electrical Units	PGR Scale Deviations in mm.		Verbal Report of Sensations	
	Hand	Stomach	Hand	Stomach
10	7	2	None	
20	10	5	Faint sens.	
40	20	12		
50	25	17	Sensations	No sensation
70	35	25	increase in intensity	reported
80	40	25		
90	90	35		
100	140	50	Pain	
110	150	50		
120	170	55	Pain	
130	170	65	increases	Faint sens.
140	Not tested	70	Intense	Not tested
170	190	80	pain	Unpleasant
220	250	Not tested	Not tested	
230	280	Not tested	Not tested	Pain

1. Unit lower threshold of verbal report of electrical stimulation of interior of stomach in 24 subjects (48 tests):

	Mean	Range
Pyloric region	118.3	90-140
Cardial region	129.0	90-160
Medial region	59.6	90-180

2. Unit lower threshold of verbal report of electrical stimulation of middle finger in five subjects: mean, 34; range, 20-50.

electrodes positioned in the stomach 8 cm. apart. As the electrical stimuli increased in intensity and the pre-sensation period passed, the two points were stimulated at intervals ranging from several to 200 microseconds. As you may see, three stages were observed. When the intervals were less than 50 msec., the two stimulations were not at all discriminated, either in time or in space: subjects reporting a single sensation in a single medial locus. Between 50 and 105 msec., there was temporal but not spatial discrimination, i.e., two successive sensations in a medial spot—while with intervals greater than 105 msec., both spatial and temporal discrimination set in, discrimination becoming in the end very precise indeed. (The author of the study, Professor Makarov, is one of the most careful Soviet experimenters in the area, a member of Ukhtomsky Physiological Institute of the Leningrad University, perhaps the most sophisticated group in Soviet psychophysiology.)

The low *GSR* threshold for interoceptive electrical gastric stimulacion seen in table 1, is paralleled by an experiment[11] in which distention of the intestinal walls of four human subjects with existing intestinal fistulas was experienced with. There, too, *GSR*s were obtained at 10 mm. of pressure on a mercury manometer, while 40 to 50 mm.

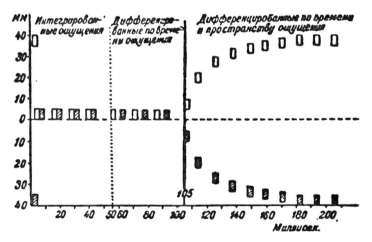

Fig. 4.—Two-point threshold in electrical stimulations of the gastric mucosa of human subjects. (From left to right, Russian words mean: "integrated [fused] sensation," "temporal discrimination," "spatial discrimination." Units on abscissa are interstimulation intervals in milliseconds; units on ordinate are distances between stimulation points in millimeters.)

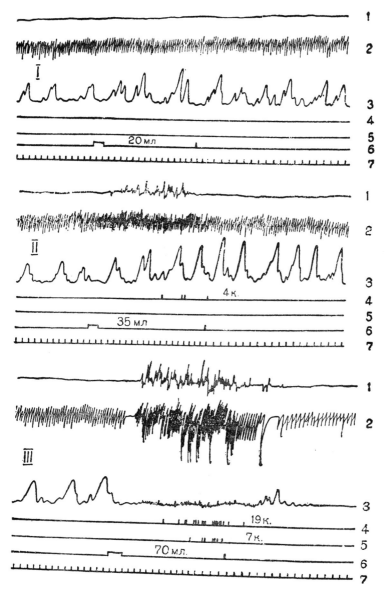

FIG. 5.—Reactions of dog Tuzik to increasing interoceptive distentions of his gall bladder—distentions at 20, 35 and 70 ml. of pressure. (1, head movements; 2, respiration; 3, gastric contractions; 4, submaxillary salivation; 5, parotid salivation; 6, ml. of pressure; 7, time.)

of pressure were needed for the subjects to report a felt sensation. Relative thresholds of a specific-distal reaction are, however, less important than the general scope of such reaction, illustrated to a limited degree in this figure (fig. 5).[5] The fistulated gall bladder of a dog was distended, at various times, at 20, 35, and 70 mm. of pressure. Reading downwards, the five top lines in each of the three sections of the figure are: head movements, respiration, gastric contraction, submaxillary salivation, and parotid salivation. And you may see that 20 mm. hardly did anything; that 35 mm. produced some changes in respiration and initiated some head movements and salivation; and that 70 mm. of pressure stirred up profoundly all the five recorded distal activities.

Space prevents my multiplying figures in an area in which Russian experiments are in the hundreds, except to say that reported evidence leaves no doubt that the scope of distal organismic reactivity and interactivity of interoceptive stimulation is very wide, encompassing the organism's total unfolding repertoire. And the encompassment is by all tokens a gradual orderly monotonic function of stimulus value and not, as in exteroceptive stimulation, just a matter of nociception, emotionality, or emerging perception. A portion of this interoceptive encompassment is no doubt due to "natural" conditioning, that is, to the fact that interoceptive stimulations, being constant companions of all living and acting, become natural conditioned evokers of a good deal that is done in living and acting. Most of the effects appear, however, to be inherent in the very nature of interoception, as a system in commerce with the organism itself rather than with the organism's environment, the way exteroception is. That is to say, while, on the one hand, interoception is largely an unconscious hinterland, in the periphery of conscious and/or verbal control and organization, it is, on the other hand, very much of an organismic forefront, in the very center of the organism's own control and organization—the fulcrum of its vital mechanics, so to speak. So that one might say that man—and to some extent, higher animals—is really a "bicentral" organism, under control of two separate centers: a) an exteroceptive, largely conscious, organism-external environment center; and b) an interoceptive, largely unconscious, organism-internal environment center—a formulation which in a general philosophical way is, I suppose, not unlike what was said a hundred years ago by Herbert Spencer. Or, if you want, you could relate it, to, William James, and, even, to Sigmund Freud.

I shall summarize the habituatory aspect of interoception in one statement, namely, that interoceptively-produced reactions are much more resistant to habituation than are comparable exteroceptively-produced ones.[16] Not only local but also comparable distal reactions are so: a *GSR* produced by stretching the intestine is about 10 times less habituable than is a *PGR* produced by visual, auditory, tactile, and,

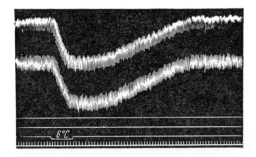

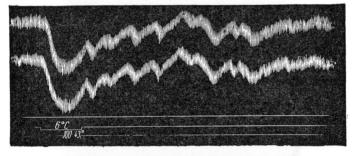

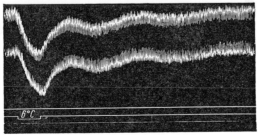

Fig. 6.—Arm plethysmogram of human subjects when warming their gastric mucosa at 43°C. succeeds by a few seconds cooling their epigastric region at 6°C. (Upper figure: the plethysmogram in response to the cooling prior to its combination with the warming; middle figure—the cooling and the warming combined, note fluctuation; lower figure: cooling after a number of cooling-warming combinations.)

even, gustatory and olfactory stimuli.[11] This relative "unhabituation" may account, I think, for evidence on the dominance of interoceptive over equal but opposite exteroceptive reactions in conditioning-like situations, illustrated in the next two figures (figs. 6 and 7).[14] The epigastric region of a human subject was cooled by a circular 6°C. "thermode" producing arm vasoconstriction (upper section of figure), and this exteroceptively-produced vasoconstriction was then juxta-posited with a vasodilation of the arms produced interoceptively

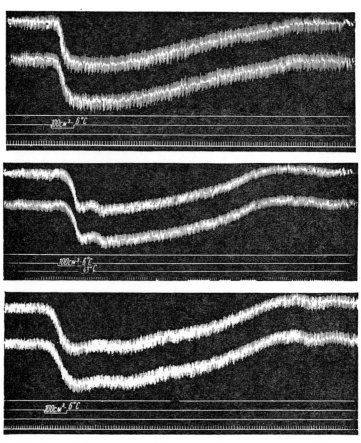

Fig. 7.—Arm plethysmograms of human subjects when cooling their gastric mucosa at 6°C. precedes by a few seconds warming their epigastric region at 43°C. (Upper figure: the plethysmograms in response to the cooling prior to its combination with the warming; middle figure—the cooling and the warming combined; lower figure: cooling after a number of cooling-warming combinations.)

through pouring into subject's gastric balloon 100 cc. of warm water at 43°C. (middle section of figure). As you see, the exteroceptive vaso-constriction had difficulty maintaining itself *vis-a-vis* the interoceptive vasodilation (middle section) which persisted even after its warming stimulus was no longer there (lower section of figure). Indeed, the experimenter states that eventually the vasoconstriction was totally replaced by the vasodilation, that is to say, the exteroceptive stimulus became classically conditioned to the interoceptive reaction. But now, look at figure 7 in which the manner of interaction is reversed so that interoceptive cooling *precedes* and is juxtaposited with exteroceptive warming. Note the middle section of the figure: the interoceptive re-action holds its own, is little effected by the opposing exteroceptive one, and, when the exteroceptive stimulus is removed, the interoceptive vasoconstrictive reaction is in full bloom (lower section). In other words, whether interoceptive reaction precedes or succeeds a compar-able exteroceptive reaction, the interoceptive dominates the exterocep-tive reaction. Indeed, since the experimenter states that the interocep-tive reaction may even become strengthened through continual subse-quent juxtaposition with the exteroceptive one, there is the tempting speculation to relate this type of learned modification to operant con-ditioning (in contrast to the preceding type which by all tokens illus-trates classical conditioning).

II

The interoceptive-exteroceptive interaction of opposing reactions, dis-closed in figures 6 and 7, was conditioning-like, but really not typical conditioning—either interoceptive or exteroceptive—where, as you

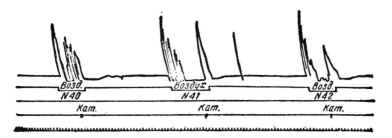

Fig. 8.—Conditioned withdrawal of a female dog's paw upon stimulation of her uterus. (Lines from above: paw-withdrawal; conditioned stimulus, stimula-tion of uterus with a jet of air; ordinal number of application of conditioned stimulus; unconditioned stimulus, electric shock; time in seconds.)

know, the conditioned and unconditioned reactions are neither equal nor as a rule antagonistic. Let me show you now several figures of typical interoceptive conditioning. The upper line in figure 8 is the record of a female dog's paw-withdrawal; the second line, of stimulation of the interior of her fistulated uterus with a jet of air; the third line, of the number of pairings of the intrauterine stimulation with an electric shock to the dog's paw, producing withdrawal; the fourth line is the record of unconditioned shock stimulus. As you may see, the dog invariably lifted its paw upon the uterine stimulation prior to the administration of the shock.[7] And here is a comparison of interoceptive and exteroceptive conditioned stimuli when food was the unconditioned stimulus and salivation, measured to one-tenth of a drop, the unconditioned reaction (table 2).[6] You see in the first column, the

TABLE 2.—Magnitudes of Salivary Reflexes of Dog *Osa* to One Conditioned Exteroceptive Stimulus and Two Conditioned Interoceptive Stimuli in Normal State, during Estrum, and during Estrum Nine Months after Ablation of the Motor Cortex.

Conditioned Stimulus (applied for 20 sec.)	Units of Salivation (1 unit = 0.1 drop)		
	Normal State (182d session)	Estrum (92d session)	Estrum + Ablation (240th session)
Metronome, 120 beats per min.	145	135	145
Tactile stimulation of intestinal mucosa, 120 per min.	110	45	20
Tactile stimulation of intestinal mucosa, 60 per min. (not reinforced previously)	50	40	45
Metronome, 120 beats	130	30	130
Intrauterine irrigation, continuous stream for 1 min.	60	60	80
Intrauterine irrigation, intermittent stream for 1 min. (not reinforced previously)	45	20	40
Metronome,, 60 beats (not reinforced previously)	25	70	40
Metronome, 120 beats	110	125	140

sound of a metronome was a more effective conditioned stimulus than the rhythmic intestinal taction which, in turn, was more effective than continuous intrauterine irrigation, and the differentiability of the conditioning followed the same order of efficacy. However, in the second column you note that, when the animal was in heat, the uterine conditioning gained differentiability, while the metronome and the intestinal stimulation lost both differentiability and magnitude. And in the third column you observe that the ablation of the motor cortex seems to have affected only the conditioning of the intestinal stimulations.

The statistics of the differential conditioning in the preceding figures could be questioned. But here is a differential record that could not be (fig. 9). The dog had two fistulas, a cecal and ileal on both sides of the ileocecal valve, with rubber balloons in each. Distention of the cecal region at 30 mm. Hg pressure was paired with shock to the paw; distention of the ileal region at the same pressure was administered without shock. In the figure, trials 210, 211, 212, 213, and 215 are positive cecum-distention trials; trials 26 and 27 are negative ileum-distention ones—and you see the clear-cut differences. The top line is a record of paw-withdrawal; the second line of respiration. And here

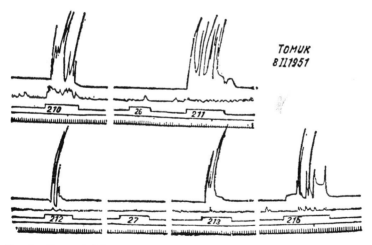

Fig. 9.—Ileocecal differential conditioning. (Dog showing paw-withdrawal when cecum next to ileocecal valve is distended at 30 mm. Hg, but no withdrawal when ileum next to valve is similarly distended. No. 210-216 are positive cecal trials, whereas No. 26-27 are negative ileal trials. Lines from above: paw-withdrawal, respiration, conditioned stimuli, unconditioned stimuli, time in seconds.)

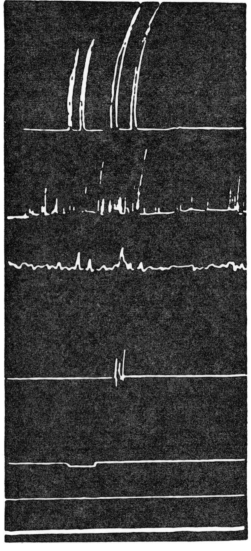

Fig. 10.—Second-order interoceptive paw-withdrawal conditioning in dogs. (CS₁ interoceptive, CS₂ exteroceptive. Lines from above: movement of conditioned left-hind paw; movement of nonconditioned right-hind paw; respiratory changes; first-order conditioned stimulus, distention of intestine with 30-40 cc. of air; second-order conditioned stimulus, sound of buzzer; unconditioned stimuli; time in seconds.)

is second-order interoceptive conditioning (fig. 10).[13] Lines from above are: movement of the conditioned left-hind paw; movement of nonconditioned right-hind paw; respiratory changes; first-order conditioned stimulus, distention of intestine with 30-40 cc. of air; second-order conditioned stimulus, the sound of a buzzer. The buzzer had never been paired with the electric shock, only with the intestinal distention; but, as you see, it came to evoke the desired conditioned reaction.

Let me now match the four cited animal-experiments with figures of four human experiments. Here is a record of a "volunteer" with a urinary bladder fistula and technique described at the beginning of the article (fig. 11).[1] The black lines from above are the subject's pneumogram, GSR, intrabladder pressure, and report of urinary urge all conditioned to the rising and falling white line, the conditioned stimulus of the experimenter's moving upward and downward the readings of the manometer which originally had been paired a number of times with the unconditioned stimulus of actually distending the bladder (horizontal white line). Note the differences in the rise and fall in the conditioning of the various types of reactions: the conscious urge —lowest horizontal black line—seems to appear last and disappear first, and the change in intrabladder pressure, second black line from bottom, seems most dramatic. And here is a case of interoceptive verbal

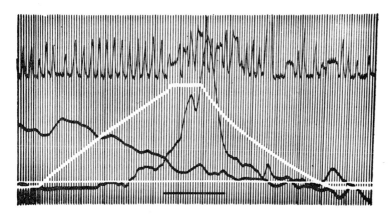

FIG. 11.—Interoceptive urinary conditioning in man. (Black lines from above: pneumogram, PGR intrabladder pressure, subject's report of urinary urge. Upper white line is the conditioned stimulus—the experimenter's moving upward the readings of the manometer. The lower white line is for the unconditioned stimulus—filling the bladder with air; not used in the test, bladder empty.)

conditioning (fig. 12).[14] Vasoconstriction of the subject's arms, elicited by pouring 100 cc. of water at 6°C. into his gastric tube, is conditioned to the flash of a blue light and then to the experimenter's mere saying, "I am flashing on a blue light." The upper section of the figure shows the pairings of the light with the cold water; the middle section, the conditioning to the light; and the lower section, the conditioning to the experimenter's statement.

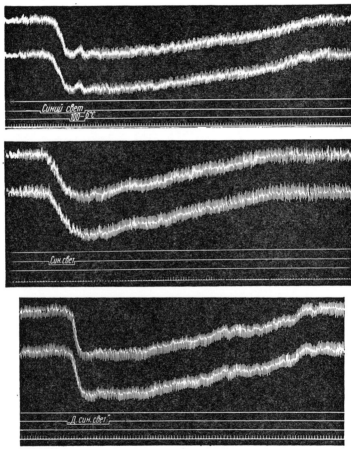

Fig. 12.—Conditioned vasoconstriction of the blood vessels of the arms of human subjects to the flash of a blue light after the light had been combined a number of times with cooling the subjects' gastric mucosa with water at 6°C. on even trials of the same CR stereotype. (Upper figure: record when the flash was, after a few seconds, reinforced by the cooling; middle figure: flash applied alone; lower figure: experimenter saying "I am flashing on a blue light.")

Finally, this figure (fig. 13)[12] demonstrates a rather complex mechanism of "natural" interoceptive verbal conditioning. The left section shows that, when a subject is told to inhale, there occurs not only a change in his pneumogram but also in his arm plethysmogram, the latter being supposedly a viscerovisceral reflex. Now, on the right side, the experimenter instructs the subject not to inhale when he is told to inhale and then says "inhale." The subject does not inhale: his pneumogram is regular, but the change in the plethysmogram persists. Presumably, the plethysmographic change was verbally conditioned to the word "inhale" but not to the opposing verbal instructions. And more than that, here is a case of a vascular neurosis, produced through disrupting a sequence in what is called a dynamic stereotype—specifically here, applying a conditioned vasoconstrictive stimulus in a position in a sequence in which another stimulus produced vasodilation, and vice versa. The experimenter assures us that such vascular neuroses are accompanied by subjective symptoms of headaches and sensory distortions (fig. 14).[13] Space forbids further summaries of individual experiments. Let me thus just state that to date approximately 130 such experiments have been reported, and finish with four short general summary sentences:

1. Interoceptive conditioning is by and large readily formed and is obviously largely a recurrent built-in unconscious conditioning of vital functions.

2. Interoceptive conditioning clearly multiplies threefold the incidence of conditioning: conditioning not only from outside in, but also from inside out, and inside to inside.

3. Interoceptive conditioning follows well Pavlovian-discovered laws

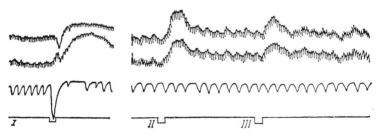

FIG. 13.—Conditioned interoceptive vascular changes in human subjects. (Plethysmograms and pneumograms to the sound of the word "inhale" when a) the subjects were told to inhale—left portion of figure—and when b) they were told *not* to inhale when they heard the word "inhale"—right portion of figure.)

of extinction, generalization, differentiation, higher order conditioning, and the like; indeed, these laws seem to manifest themselves more regularly in interoceptive conditioning than in Pavlov's own exteroceptive visceral conditioning.

4. There is some evidence that interoceptive conditioning forms a special dimension of conditioning which, as a rule, conflicts and does not summate with related exteroceptive conditioning, the way two different modalities of related exteroceptive conditioning summate with each other.

I have not said anything as yet pertaining specifically to the psychopathology of interoception, and I have no space left to begin saying it now. I assume, however, that the general psychopathologic implications of the article are quite immanent and discernible. Consider: *a*) the largely unconscious—largely conscious dichotomy of interoception-

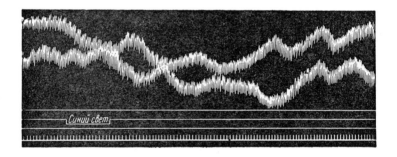

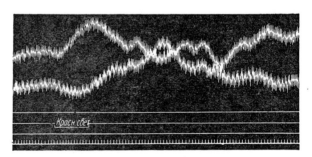

Fig. 14.—Marked vascular fluctuation ("vascular neurosis") in response to the flash of the blue light when the cooling and the warming are no longer regularly alternated and the CR-stereotype is thus disrupted (upper figure). Lower figure shows similar results of an experiment in which the flash of a red light was the conditioned stimulus, the epigastric region was cooled and the gastric mucosa was warmed.

exteroception; *b*) the further organic dichotomy—the evidence that interoception is, with respect to concomitant action and learning modifiability, not just another modality but a different dimension conflicting with exteroception as such and tending to dominate it through relative inertness; *c*) the statistical or incidence differentiae between interoceptive and exteroceptive stimulations, one admittedly recurrent, regular, periodic, the other largely adventitious, circumstantial, and aperiodic, and also, *d*) the pure algebraic fact that interoceptive conditioning multiplies conditioning threefold: not only, let us say, may feelings of anxiety become conditioned stimuli to produce, let us say, constipation, but sensations of constipation or rectal distention may be conditioned to bring about anxiety, and conditioned to produce asthma or gout or angina pectoris or what not.

Likewise, with respect to perception—the second word of this symposium—interoception could, I posit, be of considerable significance in highlighting inchoate groundings of the process, whatever it is. Information provided by a toothache differs, I believe, in its very essence, from that supplied by perceiving a person or a building or a melody.

My very final sentence will be a pragmatic note, the need to duplicate and verify Russian results. American culture has sometimes been classed as adolescent. If so, present-day Russian culture appears to me to be pubescent, and I would not, for all its fumblings and errors, underestimate the energy and imagination of the pubescent.

REFERENCES

1. AYRAPETYANTS, E. SH.: Higher nervous activity and the receptor of internal organs. Moscow: Akad. Nauk SSSR, 1952.
2. —— AND TEL'BERBAUM, I. M.: Methods of studying interoceptive conditioned reflexes: the uterine fistula. Fiziol. Zh. SSSR, *37*: 240-243, 1951.
3. ——, LOBANOVA, L. V., AND CHERKASOVA, L. S.: Materials on the physiology of the internal analyzer in man. Trud. Inst. Fiziol. Pavlova, *1*: 3-20, 1952.
4. BORING, E. G.: The sensations of the alimentary canal. Amer. J. Psychol., *26*: 1-57, 1915.
5. BULYGIN, I. A.: The study of the laws and mechanisms of interoceptive reflexes. Minsk: Akad. Nauk SSSR, 1959.
6. LEBEDEVA, L. I.: Dynamics of uterine signalization in different stages of the sexual cycle of dogs. Trud. Instit. Fiziol, Pavlova, *8*: 268-272, 1959.
7. LOTIS, V. I.: Conditioned interoceptive uterine reflexes. Akush. Ginekol., No. 6, 15-19, 1949.
8. MAKAROV, P. O.: Pre-excitation and presensation. Uchen. Zap. Leningr. U., Ser. Biol., *22(123)*: 369-399(a), 1950.

9. ——: The neurodynamics of man. Leningrad: Medgiz, 1959.

10. MOISEYEVA, N. A.: The effect of gastric mechanoreceptors on higher nervous activity. Trud. Instit. Fiziol. im. Pavlova, *1:* 95-102, 1952.

11. MYSYASHCHIKOVA, S. S.: The extinction of vegetative reactions during the stimulation of the peripheral apparatus of various analyzers. *In* K. M. Bykov (Ed.) ; Voprosy fiziologii interotseptsii. Moscow: Akad. Nauk SSSR, 1952. pp. 411-427.

12. OKHNYANSKAYA, L. G.: A study of the conditioned respiratory-vasomotor reflexes: Respiration as the stimulus of vaso-motion. Fiziol. Zh. SSSR, *39:* 610-613, 1953.

13. PAUPEROVA, G. F.: Formation of a secondary exteroceptive conditioned reflex on the basis of a primary interoceptive one. *In* K. M. Bykov (Ed.) ; Voprosy fiziologii interotseptsii. Moscow: Akad. Nauk SSSR, 1952, pp. 437-442.

14. PSHONIK, A. T.: The cerebral cortex and the receptor functions of the organism. Moscow: GIZ, 1952.

15. RAZRAN, G.: The observable unconscious and the inferable conscious in current Soviet psychophysiology: Interoceptive conditioning, semantic conditioning, and the orienting reflex. Psychol. Rev., *68:* 2, 81-147, 1961.

16. ——: Unconditioned interoception. Unpublished.

17. SPERANSKAYA, E. N.: Operative methods and the conduct of chronic physiological experiments in dogs. Moscow: Akad. Nauk SSSR, 1953.

4

INFORMATION SYSTEM ANALYSIS OF THE ORGANIZATION OF MOTOR ACTIVITY

by RICHARD ALLEN CHASE, M.D.*

W E HAVE STUDIED THE SYSTEMS which control movement in man in an attempt to define the critical functional operations of this control system. We have designed techniques, and structured experiments to help us gain some concept of the broad categories of functional operations which underly the organization and control of movement.[6,7,8,9,10,11,12] These investigations have provided partial illumination of some of the information processing functions of the central nervous system.† Since generalizations about central nervous system information processing are relevant to the understanding of many of the higher functions of the nervous system, a review of some of our thinking, as it has emerged in the study of movement, seems pertinent to a discussion of perception.

*Assistant Professor, Department of Psychiatry, and Director, Neurocommunications Laboratory, Department of Psychiatry, The Johns Hopkins University School of Medicine, Baltimore, Maryland. At the time this manuscript was prepared, the author was Director of the Neurocommunications Unit. Clinical Neuropharmacology Research Center, National Institute of Mental Health, St. Elizabeths Hospital, Washington, D. C., and Clinical Instructor in Neurology, George Washington University School of Medicine, Washington, D. C.

†The experiments on sensory feedback reported in this paper were initiated at Columbia University College of Physicians and Surgeons and the Department of Biometrics Research, New York State Department of Mental Hygiene, in collaboration with Dr. Samuel Sutton, Dr. Joseph Zubin, Dr. Edmund P. Fowler, Jr., Dr. Isabelle Rapin, Dr. Susan Standfast and Dr. Seth Harvey. This research is now being continued at the Neurocommunications Unit of the Clinical Neuropharmacology Research Center, National Institute of Mental Health at Saint Elizabeth's Hospital. Current collaborators include Mr. John K. Cullen, Jr., Dr. Joseph Openshaw, Dr. Joel Elkes, Mr. Donald Harvey and Mr. Scott A. Sullivan. The instrumentation for our current studies has been developed by Mr. Robert Laupheimer, Mr. John K. Cullen, Jr., and Mr. Paul Dirlik. In addition to major experimental contributions, the above collaborators have provided persistent stimulating dialogue which provided the context within which many of the ideas discussed in this paper were born.

Figure 1 shows the general architecture of an organization of functional operations involved in the processing of sensory information for the control of movement. At the input end of our flow-diagram the receptor systems are represented. These comprehend all of the structures which are specialized for the transformation of energy into forms which are utilizable for information processing functions. The arrow leading to this region from the bottom indicates the feedback pathway along which the motor response is represented through its sensory accompaniments. The arrow leading from the top indicates the capability of the central nervous system to influence the patterns of afferent activity generated at receptor sites. Although many sensory channels are activated in the course of any movement, there is probably a synthesis of inputs available at any point in time which can be utilized by two major central processing functions, noted as "error detection" and "error correction programming." The error detection operation consists of some type of matching of the pattern of sensory feedback against some standard corresponding to a correct pattern of motor activity. Error in motor activity is registered as a mismatch of the sensory feedback pattern and the afferent pattern which serves as a standard. If a mismatch, or error is detected, there must be some mechanism able to program a pattern of neural activity, which, when transmitted to the effector system, results in a change in motor activity resulting in a closer approximation to the desired end-state.

The information processing operations which we shall focus upon are indicated by circled numbers. We shall initially discuss ways in

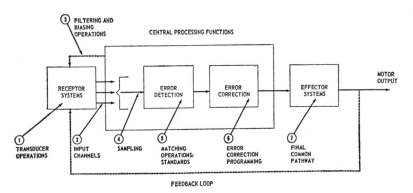

Fig. 1.—Flow diagram of a functional system for the control of movement.

which the receptor systems can be analyzed in terms of the type of information which they transduce energy into. We shall consider ways in which classes of sensory input channels function in the role of information transmission lines. The capabilities of the central nervous system to affect its input patterns by filtering and biasing operations will be noted. We shall speculate about the sampling operations which might be functioning when sensory input is utilized for error detection, and the fundamental operations of matching and the organization of appropriate standards will be examined.

The final event effected by the systems which organize and control movement consists of the contraction of skeletal muscle. The most precise information which might be utilized to inform the nervous system about movement would be expected to result from specialized receptor systems directly in skeletal muscle or its attachments. These receptor systems consist of Golgi tendon organs, and the muscle spindles.[2] Synaptic relationships in the spinal cord between muscle spindle afferents and alpha motoneurones, and the known ability of muscle spindle efferent activity to affect the pattern of muscle spindle afferent activity, define the essential capabilities of a peripheral servo-system for the control of the length of skeletal muscle.[28,33] It is appreciated, however, that the pattern of spindle afferent activity is affected not only by the length of the extrafusal fiber system, but by its rate of change of length.[20] The anatomical complexity of the muscle spindle and the identification of numerous regions of the central nervous system which receive inputs from the muscle spindles and which affect their activity,[18] suggest the probability of far more complex information processing functions than are comprehended in models of the muscle spindles as part of a servo-system for the control of muscle length.

The progressive refinement of our understanding concerning central nervous system information requirements and information processing operations should liberate the study of sensory receptor physiology from the circumscribed search for the ways in which simple stimulus parameters are coded into neural events. Understanding of central information requirements and the mechanisms by which these requirements permit biasing of receptor and transmission systems to provide the elements of these information requirements should permit us to "listen in" to the same patterns of neural activity which seem so enigmatic in terms of stimulus representation, and to observe in these messages elements in the synthesis of more complex information units.

The amazing morphological and functional complexity of biological transducers, and the fact that their outputs enter almost immediately into highly organized interactions with other neural units suggest vast potentialities for the peripheral receptor apparatus to function not only as a system of energy transducers, but as the apparatus for the synthesis of information in complex form.[3,19,32]

The nervous system is apparently capable of rejecting portions of its sensory inputs. We shall refer to the systematic rejection of certain portions of sensory input patterns and the acceptance of others as "filtering."[27]

It has been shown that if a subject is asked to attend to speech presented through earphones to one of his ears while other spoken messages are simultaneously presented to the other ear, the subject will not be able to identify important aspects of the competing message, such as details of semantic content or even the language spoken.[13] Somehow this information has been lost to subjective registration, probably as an integral part of the attention being given to the messages presented to the test ear.

The ability to alter the sensitivity of a receptor to the same stimulus is referred to as "biasing." A good example of the manner in which the central nervous system might bias a receptor so as to effect a particular pattern of sensory input is provided by examination of the muscle spindle system. As the extra-fusal fibers contract, tension on the muscle spindle is reduced, and spindle afferent activity is reduced. When the extra-fusal fibers are stretched, tension on the muscle spindle is increased, and there is a corresponding increase in spindle afferent activity. However, stimulation of the gamma efferent fibers which innervate the muscle spindles, results in contraction of the intra-fusal fibers and corresponding increases in spindle afferent activity.[33] The frequency of spindle afferent discharge accompanying a specific amount of passive stretch is increased progressively as a function

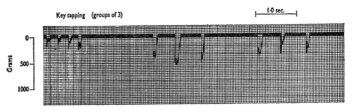

FIG. 2.—Patterns of key-tapping associated with delayed auditory feedback of clicks.

of the frequency of stimulation of gamma efferent fibers supplying the spindle.[21] Since the activity of gamma efferent fibers can be influenced by a wide variety of central nervous system structures,[18] the capability of central control of the pattern of spindle afferent activity accompanying a specific state of the extra-fusal fiber system is clear.

There is a way in which the central nervous system can significantly alter patterns of sensory input independent of its capabilities of altering receptor and other peripheral sensory processing operations. This is accomplished by issuing motor command patterns which will result in the generation of the sensory information needed.

Figure 2 shows the pattern of key-tapping which we observed from a subject who had been trained to tap in groups of three taps each at a fixed rate and amplitude.[7] A click was provided through the subject's earphones simultaneously with each tap. After a short time, the clicks were presented at a fixed delay of 350 msec. after the tap. This figure shows the pattern of motor activity which resulted at the time the delayed clicks were first presented. Note that there is an initial confusion of number; the subject taps 4 times instead of 3. We then observe a return to the correct number of taps in each group, but a marked increase in amplitude and decrease in rate of tapping are observed. The increased amplitude of tapping will result in a markedly increased input from receptors in skin, muscle and joints in the

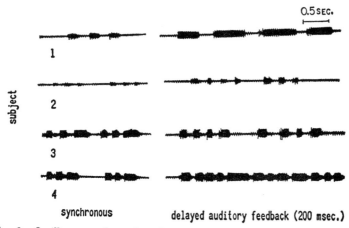

Fig. 3.—Oscillograms of speech under synchronous and delayed auditory feed-back. Subjects are repeating the speech sound "b" as in book in groups of three sounds each.

subject's finger and forearm, and it might be argued that the increased amplitude of tapping has been effected specifically to increase the sensory input passing through these channels. The temporally-distorted sensory information entering via the auditory system might thereby be more effectively counterbalanced by an increase in sensory information passing through normally-functioning input channels.[7,8]

The effects of delayed sensory events in different modalities on motor control provides information about channel equivalence for information transmission. It is well known that a delay in air-conducted auditory feedback results in marked and characteristic changes in speech.[4,11,35] The major speech changes consist of: 1) increased mean sound pressure level, 2) increased phonation time, 3) decreased rate and 4) repetitive errors. These changes are apparent in the set of oscillograms shown in figure 3. On the left side of this figure you see the oscillograms of four subjects who are repeating the sound "b" as in "book" in groups of three sounds each. The subjects are trying to repeat the sounds of constant amplitude and rate. On the right side of the figure you see the effects of a delay in air-conducted auditory feedback of 244 msec. on the pattern of speech. In the extreme case shown by subject (4), there is total disintegration of the patterning of speech activity.

We attempted to parallel some of the delayed auditory feedback experiments on speech for another motor system. We selected simple

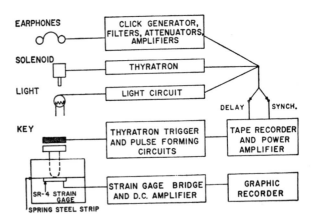

Fig. 4.—Schematic diagram of equipment used to provide synchronous and delayed feedback of clicks, light flashes and tactile pulses in association with key-tapping responses.

key-tapping responses of the index finger.[6,7] Subjects were trained to tap in groups of three taps each, and were requested to maintain constant rate and amplitude of tapping. The key which the subjects tapped deformed a spring steel strip with a strain gage attached, and the output of the strain gage bridge was used to obtain an analog record of the time and amplitude of tapping. Each time the subject tapped on the key he activated a trigger and pulse forming circuit which resulted in the presentation of a click through earphones. The instrumentation used for this experiment is schematically represented in figure 4. When the click was systematically delayed about 200 msec. we observed changes in key-tapping which were analogous to all of the qualitative changes noted in speech under delayed auditory feedback, as shown in figure 5.

It is therefore clear that a delayed sensory event presented through the same channel, in this case the auditory pathways, can have qualitatively similar effects upon the output of different motor systems.

We investigated the effects of delaying sensory events of different modalities on the pattern of key-tapping responses.[8] It was observed that a delayed light flash and a delayed tactile pulse also resulted in increased amplitude of tapping, decreased rate, increased time of pressing on the key, and repetitive errors; just as had been observed with a delayed click. These results show that a delayed sensory event has the same qualitative effects on key-tapping independent of the

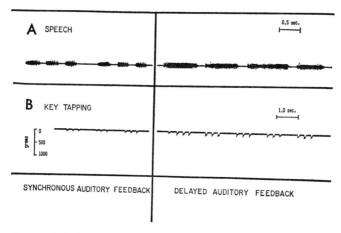

Fig. 5.—Parallel changes in speech and key-tapping under conditions of synchronous and delayed auditory feedback.

channel through which the sensory event enters the nervous system. We must conclude that some of the information processing operations of the central nervous system that operate upon sensory input to control movement operate independently of the sensory channels utilized. This equivalence of input channels with respect to the effect of delayed sensory events on motor activity calls our attention to the probability that the nervous system is able to operate upon its inputs as information, utilizing common *formal* properties and not simply unique properties determined by differences in transducers or the geography of specific primary sensory projection pathways. In this case all of the delayed sensory events probably represent common misinformation about the temporal aspects of the motor activity, and therefore result in a common impairment of control.

Patterns of sensory feedback must be sampled to obtain information essential to the detection of departures of the motor output from some desired standard. It is not clear what the characteristics of such sampling operations might be. However, studies with delayed sensory events have taught us something about the critical time periods within which the sensory accompaniments of a motor response must return to the nervous system for appropriate processing. It is now well known that delays in air-conducted auditory feedback as short as 30 msec. result in impairment of speech, and that this disturbance of speech control increases as a function of the delay time up to a maximum at delays about 200 msec.[35,44] We have speculated elsewhere that the disturbing effects of delayed auditory feedback on motor control might result from a discrepancy in information between the delayed auditory component of sensory feedback, and the remainder of the normal pattern of sensory accompaniments of the motor activity which results when the delayed feedback overlaps the normal feedback pattern in time. Such a concept suggests that the curve of disturbance in motor control as a function of the delay time of a sensory event should vary as a function of the size of the units of motor output under study, and the rate at which they are effected. In support of such a prediction we now know that key-tapping responses, unlike speech, show progressive impairment of control as the delay time of clicks accompanying the taps is increased from 0 to 1000 msec. in 100 msec. steps.[30]

Direct control of the temporal quanta of visual feedback information has been obtained in our work on compensatory tracking of index finger position utilizing visual displays.[12] In these experiments the subject is seated in front of a dual-beam oscilloscope. The index finger of his dominant hand is placed in a cup attached to a pulley system, and the lower shaft of the pulley system is attached to a rotary motion potentiometer. A photograph of the instrumentation is shown in figure 6. Movement of the finger results in the generation of a voltage from the potentiometer, and this signal is displayed on the oscilloscope. The transducer system is adjusted so that the output of the potentiometer, presented as a horizontal bar on the oscilloscope, will coincide with another horizontal bar which remains fixed on the oscilloscope screen. This fixed visual display is the reference signal, which corres-

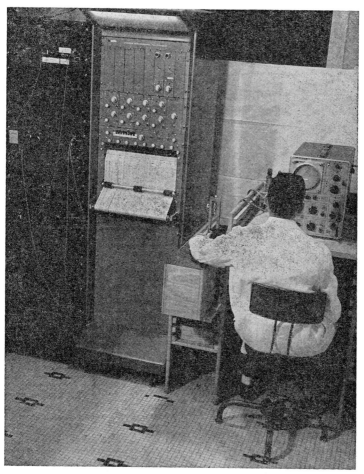

Fig. 6.—Photograph of instrumentation used for visual feedback in monitoring of finger position tracking tasks.

ponds to the point in space which the finger would be at if extended parallel to the ground. The visual display which represents the output of the potentiometer functions as error-signal information, informing the subject about the position of his finger in space with respect to the reference position in space. In a typical experiment, the subject is asked to keep the two lines on the oscilloscope superimposed. He is told that one line will always remain stationary, and that the movement of the other line is controlled by the movement of his finger. We have the ability to present the visual error-signal information in a variety of forms, and in varying amounts. We control the amount of information inflow by presenting the visual feedback display as an intermittent pulse. These capabilities permit the presentation of error signal information in discrete packets, or quanta, presented at a controlled rate. We thereby impose sampling limitations on the sensory input directly, and hope that study of the effects of the intermittent signals on performance will permit inferences about central nervous system sampling and processing operations.

Figure 7 shows the effects of intermittent presentation of visual feedback on finger movement. The portion marked "A" shows the pattern of finger movement which appears when a subject uses a low-gain, proportional error signal for tracking. The reference position is drawn as a straight horizontal line, and the movements of the finger

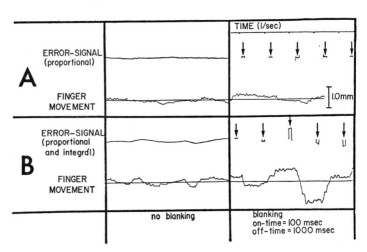

Fig. 7.—The effects of intermittent visual-feedback display of proportional and mixed proportional and integral error signals on the pattern of finger movement in a tracking task.

above and below this line represent the departures of the subject's finger from the reference position. The left-hand box, labeled "A" shows the pattern of movement corresponding to utilization of a continuously presented signal. The adjacent right-hand box shows the moderate impairment of control which results when the proportional error signal is presented in 100 msec. pulses, with intervening periods of 1000 msec. during which there is no error signal display. The small arrows mark each pulse of visual feedback display. The portion of the slide marked "B" shows the pattern of finger movement which results when the same subject utilizes a visually-presented error signal which represents a mixture of proportional and integral transforms of his departure from the reference position. Note that intermittent presentation of this error signal results in much more marked impairment of motor control than was the case for a proportional error signal alone. This experiment indicates that the sampling requirements for the sensory feedback control of movement should be expected to vary as a function of the kind of information being sampled. The tracking technique permits quantitative exploration of these interactions between kind and amount of information.

Figure 8 shows the complex changes which result in the pattern of finger movement as a result of progressive decrease in the time during which the error-signal is available for monitoring. In the portion labeled "A" you see the pattern of finger movement resulting from continuous utilization of a mixed proportional and integral error signal. The portions marked "B", "C" and "D" represent progressive decreases in the on-time of the visual display from 800 to 100 msec. Note the corresponding changes in finger movement pattern, which are labeled 1-4. There is a clear appearance of a progressively higher-amplitude, lower-frequency activity as a function of decreasing on-time of the visual display. It would appear that the alteration in display conditions is acting as a "forcing function," serving to generate an orderly progressive change in output.

In the early stages of learning it is likely that frequent sampling of sensory feedback is necessary in order to control the large errors in output which characterize new motor performances. During the course of learning, there is progressive improvement in the motor performance, and the possibility presents itself that the nervous system is now able to sample the corresponding sensory feedback more intermittently than at earlier stages in learning. We might speculate that motor learning involves progressively more accurate central programming of a motor command pattern such that errors in output become progressively more infrequent; and that, as a consequence, the sampling of sensory feedback for error detection operations becomes progressively less necessary and therefore progressively more intermittent. It is possible to conceive of some highly learned motor sequence operating essentially independently of sensory feedback utilization. In the terms of control system theory, we are suggesting that learning might involve the progressive change of closed-loop control into open-loop control via progressive improvement in the central programming of motor command patterns.

The *sine qua non* of a control system which utilizes feedback information is error detection. The system must be able to compare the representation of its output, provided in the feedback information, with some representation of the desired output of the system. The discrepancy which is detected by this matching operation constitutes

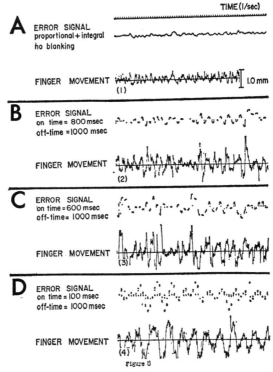

FIG. 8.—The effects of decreasing on-time of intermittent visual-feedback displays on the pattern of finger movement in a tracking task.

the error of the system, and control of the system output is achieved when this error is corrected by an appropriate modification of the motor command presented to the effector components of the system. We shall refer to the neural representation of the desired output of the system against which the feedback pattern is matched as a "standard."

Some categories of learning have been noted to occur very rapidly, within strictly limited periods in development. Such observations suggest that in some cases, the standards which define the correctness or incorrectness of patterns of motor activity may be rapidly incorporated into functional neural architecture in highly organized forms, and not slowly fashioned through successive trial and error sequences.

Consider the complexity of the standards which are utilized to monitor speech. The acoustic patterns which are represented in the standards utilized for error detection and control of speech motor activity could most economically be translated into patterns of neural organization by incorporating the complex acoustic inputs provided by other individuals who have already learned the vocal motor activity in question. The study of vocalization in birds has provided some very pertinent observations concerning this possibility. It has been observed for many species that the fully developed species-specific song patterns do not develop in birds which are hand-reared in separation from other members of their species.[22,38] If birds are reared with members of other species they will frequently incorporate parts of the vocalization pattern of the other species into their own repertoire of vocalization patterns. In support of the position that complex, sensory inputs might be rapidly incorporated into the organization of standards, or other critical functional components of central processing operations, are the observations that the actual expression of vocal patterns acquired from other birds may not occur until many months after the exposure, without any subsequent exposures being made available.[22,38] The idea that there can be critical time periods in development during which highly complex sensory inputs can be rapidly integrated into the architecture of central processing operations which determine the vocal behavior of the animal derives from the observation that no further vocal learning occurs in most bird species after the first year.[22,38] Not only is the development of new vocal activity strictly limited in time, but the patterns of vocal activity acquired during the first year of life remain the patterns of vocal activity which that bird shows the rest of his life in remarkably stereotyped fashion.[22,38]

There is another mechanism by which standards for central error detection operations might be generated. This mechanism involves generation of the standard as an antecedent or concommitant of the initiation of the activity in question. The same patterns of neural activity which are considered to underly the initiation of movement are considered to be simultaneously involved in the generation of standards for the error detection operations which will take place in the subsequent monitoring of that movement.

A model for the generation of patterns of neural activity which might function as standards for the error-detection operations underlying the control of movement is suggested by Anokhin in his discussion of the physiological architecture of conditioned reflexes.[1] Anokhin considers that central and peripheral afferent activity compound to form an "afferent synthesis" which constitutes the neural substrate of the "idea," "intention" or "aim" to perform a given act. The afferent synthesis is therefore the necessary antecedent of any motor response, but it is also conceived to simultaneously constitute the pattern of neural activity against which the afferent return which accompanies the response is compared for error-detection operations.

It becomes important to establish what the critical information input requirements for the construction of standards and other components of central processing operations are.[5,31] Clarification of these information input requirements might be potentially more valuable in the solution of some of our clinical problems of sensory prosthesis than understanding of the equivalence of sensory channels for information flow. This would seem to apply particularly to the classes of congenital sensory deficits.

An effective control system must be able to detect errors, or departures of its output from some desired standard; but error detection is not sufficient for control. There must also exist the capability of correcting for the error detected. We have therefore indicated this error correction capability as a separate element on our flow diagram of a system for the control of movement (fig. 1).

The error correction system operates upon the information about departure of the output of the system from a desired end state which results from the matching operations of the error detection system. It then programs an appropriate pattern of motor command, which, when transmitted to the lower motor neurone pools, results in a change in motor output which appropriately corrects for the error previously detected.

We have made some observations in the course of our studies on human tracking performance which are pertinent to an understanding of the effector capabilities of the human motor control system. In these studies, a subject is seated in front of an oscilloscope and the index finger of his dominant hand is fixed in the motion transducer described earlier. One horizontal beam of the oscilloscope is fixed in the middle of the oscilloscope screen, and this reference line corresponds to the point in space which the subject's finger contacts when fully extended parallel to the ground. The other horizontal beam on the oscilloscope screen moves above or below the reference beam as the subject's finger moves above or below the reference position in space. This beam gives error signal information, and the subject utilizes this information in his attempt to keep his finger fixed at the reference position in space, and thereby to keep the two lines on the oscilloscope screen superimposed. We have studied the effects of varying the amplification of the error signal display on the ability to control movement in such a task.

The amplification of the error signal is varied by changing the amount of separation of the error signal from the fixed reference line on the oscilloscope for a given actual displacement of the finger from the reference point in space. As an example, consider the case in which the subject's finger is 1 mm. above the reference point in space. If we present the error signal line 1 mm. above the reference line on the oscilloscope screen, then this condition is referred to as unity amplification of the error signal. However, if we represent the same actual finger displacement by presenting the error signal 2 or 4 mm. above the reference line, then we have presented the error signal at 2 and 4 times amplification respectively. These relationships are schematically represented in figure 9.

Figure 10 shows portions of the polygraph record of a subject who is monitoring finger position at error signal amplifications of 2, 4 and 10 times. Examination of the finger movement channel shows progressive attenuation of a high-amplitude, low-frequency "hunting" activity and the appearance of predominantly high-frequency activity centered accurately about the reference line as the amplification of the error signal increases. The progressive decrease in size of the lines on the "integrated absolute error" channel indicates progressive decrease in the area traced out by the subject's finger above and below the reference line per sample period. The increasing density of dots and bars on the "zero-crossing" channel indicates progressive increase in

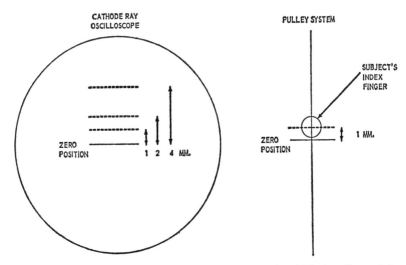

FIG. 9.—Schematic representation of an experiment in which the effects of increasing gain of a proportional visual-feedback display on patterns of finger movement tracking are studied.

the frequency with which the subject's finger passes through the reference position in space per sample period.

It is clear that the motor control system is utilizing increasing amplification of a proportional error signal to obtain progressively more accurate control of movement; and that this increase in the accuracy of motor control is characterized by the elimination of low-frequency, high-amplitude movement with the appearance of predominantly high-frequency activity precisely centered about the reference position in space. At 20 and 40 times amplification, no further decrease in absolute error or increase in zero-crossings was noted. It appears that there is a limit beyond which the motor control system can no longer utilize increasing amplification of an error signal to effect further control of movement. Whether this is due to limits in the capabilities of error correction programming or other central processing operations, or limits imposed by the physical characteristics of the peripheral components of the motor system are matters of conjecture at this time.

As our discussion has evolved, we have distinguished several classes of information input requirements for the initiation and control of movement. We have considered that the programming of standards for the matching operations which constitute error detection are dependent upon organized stimulus inputs. We are now aware that significant decreases in the energy of sensory inputs from the environment, or alterations in the patterns of sensory inputs, may have marked effects on cognition, perception, social and other types of behavior.[36,41,43] The ability of such alterations in the sensory environment to profoundly affect behavior and subjective experience, even in the adult, and even after fairly brief exposures, suggests that there are information input requirements necessary for the maintenance of the neural organizations which underly the central information processing functions of the organism.[5]

In addition to the investigation of the critical information input requirements for the construction, maintenance and operation of central processing operations, we must consider whether there might not also be critical information input requirements for the *initiation* of movement.[1,29,39,40] A partial lesion involving dorsal roots and dorsal columns, such as is found in tabes dorsalis, results in impaired control of movement. However, complete section of all of the dorsal roots supplying an extremity results in complete inability to initiate voluntary

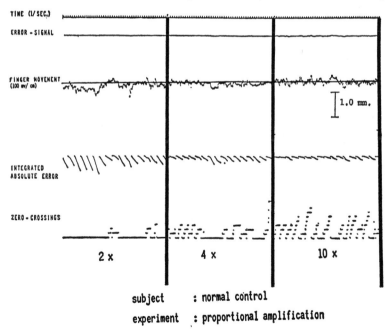

Fig. 10.—The effects of increasing the amplification of proportional visual feedback displays on patterns of finger movement in a tracking task.

movement in the monkey and dog.[16,17,23,24,25,26,34] A wide variety of lesions involving sensory transmission and projection systems will result in impaired motor activity,[23,24,34] but the striking observation of paralysis following dorsal root section confronts us squarely with the question of whether there might not be unique information input requirements necessary for the initiation of movement.[1,29,39,40]

It is potentially rewarding to consider the apraxias as specific deficits in information processing operations constituting the antecedents of movement. The inability of an apraxic patient to pretend to drink a glass of water while maintaining the ability to drink from a glass of water spontaneously[14] suggests that specific information input deficits might account for the patient's localized inabilities to initiate movements.

Our conception of the system for control of movement is one of a complex, yet plastic organization of information generating and processing functions. We have considered the potentialities for incorporating organization from the stimulus environment, and the potentialities for complex information processing of sensory information at or near the peripheral receptor sites. We have considered the equivalence of sensory channels for information flow, and the central nervous system filtering, biasing and sampling capabilities which result in the presentation of organized information patterns to error detection, error correction and other central processing functions which organize the motor command patterns that mix at the lower motor neurone pools and result in organized patterns of skeletal muscle activity. During the course of such a discussion, one cannot help but become aware of the present inadequacies of the language of the biological sciences to comprehend the formal properties of complex neurophysiological processes which we have been discussing in metaphor and by allusion. We need new symbolic systems which will permit descriptive and quantitative reference to the complex patterns of neurophysiological organization which underly the organization of behavior and subjective experience.[15]

We must be reminded however that new languages are invented, not discovered; and that they are invented in the context of concrete necessities. Newton did not discover the calculus. He developed it in parallel with his development of a mechanics, and we are reminded that it remained an inexact, semiphysical formulation for over 150 years after its inception.[42]

The development of new symbolic systems for the study of behavior and subjective experience awaits more precise clarification of the requirements of such a language. It is hoped that continued formal characterization of the information processing functions of the nervous system will contribute to this clarification.

REFERENCES

1. ANOKHIN, P. K.: A new conception of the physiological architecture of conditioned reflex. *In* Brain Mechanisms and Learning, Oxford, Blackwell Scientific Publication, 1961, p. 213.

2. BARKER, D.: The structure and distribution of muscle receptors. *In* Barker, D. (Ed.); Symposium on Muscle Receptors. Hong Kong, Hong Kong University Press, 1962, pp. 227-240.

3. BARLOW, H. B.: Possible principles underlying the transformation of sensory messages. *In* Rosenblith, W. A. (Ed.): Sensory Communication. New York, John Wiley & Sons, Inc., 1961, pp. 217-234.

4. BLACK, J. W.: The effect of delayed sidetone upon vocal rate and intensity. J. Sp. Hearing Res., *16:* 56-60, 1951.

5. BRUNER, J. S.: The cognitive consequences of early sensory deprivation. *In* Sensory Deprivation. Cambridge, Harvard University Press, 1961, pp. 195-207.

6. CHASE, R. A., HARVEY, S., STANDFAST, S., RAPIN, ISABELLE, AND SUTTON, S.: Comparison of the effects of delayed auditory feedback on speech and key-tapping. Science, *129:* 903-904, 1959.

7. ——, ——, ——, ——, AND ——: Studies on sensory feedback I: Effect of delayed auditory feedback on speech and keytapping. Quart. J. Exper. Psychol., *13:* 141-152, 1961.

8. ——, RAPIN, I., GILDEN, L., AND SUTTON, S.: Studies in sensory feedback II: Sensory feedback influences on key-tapping motor tasks. Quart. J. Exper. Psychol., *13:* 153-167, 1961.

9. ——, SUTTON, S., AND FIRST, D. A.: Developmental study of changes in behavior under delayed auditory feedback. J. Genetic Psychol., *99:* 101-112, 1961.

10. ——, ——, FOWLER, E. P., JR., FAY, T. H. AND RUHM, H. B.: Low sensation level delayed clicks and key-tapping. J. Sp. Hearing Res., *4:* 73-78, 1961.

11. ——, ——, AND RAPIN, I.: Sensory feedback influences on motor performance. J. Auditory Research, *3:* 212-223, 1961.

12. ——, AND CULLEN, J. K., JR.: Experimental studies on motor control systems in man. Am. J. Med. Electronics. In press.

13. CHERRY, E. C.: Some experiments on the recognition of speech, with one and with two ears. J. Acoust. Soc. Amer. *25:* 975-979, 1953.

14. DENNY-BROWN, D.: The nature of apraxia. J. Nerv. & Ment. Dis., *12:* 9-32, 1958.

15. ELKES, J.: Subjective and objective observation in psychiatry. Harvey Lecture delivered before the Harvey Society, New York Academy of Medicine, February 15, 1962.

16. GORSKA, T., AND JANKOWSKA, E.: The effect of deafferentation on the in-

strumental conditioned reflexes established in dogs by reinforcing passive movements. Bull. Acad. Polonaise Sci., CL. II, *8:* 527-530, 1960.

17. ——, AND JANKOWSKA, E.: Instrumental conditioned reflexes of the deafferentated limb in cats and rats. Bull. Acad. Polonaise Sci., CL, VI, *7:* 161-164, 1959.

18. GRANIT, R.: Receptors and Sensory Perception. New Haven, Yale University Press, 1955, Ch. 7.

19. HARTLINE, H. K.: Vision-Introduction. *In* Handbook of Physiology, I: Neurophysiology, I, Washington, D. C., American Physiological Society, 1959.

20. JANSEN, J. K. S., AND MATTHEWS, P. B. C.: The central control of the dynamic response of muscle spindle receptors. J. Physiol., *161:* 357-378, 1962.

21. KUFFLER, S. W., HUNT, C. C., AND QUILLIAM, J. P.: Function of medullated small-nerve fibers in mammalian ventral roots: efferent muscle spindle innervation. J. Neurophysiol. *14:* 29-54, 1951.

22. LANYON, W. E.: The ontogony of vocalization in birds. *In* Lanyon, W. E., and Tavolga, W. N. (Eds.): Animal Sounds and Communication. Washington, American Institute of Biological Sciences, 1960, pp. 321-347.

23. LASSEK, A. M.: Potency of isolated brachial dorsal roots in controlling muscular physiology. Neurology, *3:* 53-57, 1953.

24. ——: Inactivation of voluntary motor function following rhizotomy. J. Neuropath. & Exper. Neurol., *12:* 83-87, 1953.

25. ——, AND MOYER, E. K.: An ontogenetic study of motor deficits following dorsal brachial rhizotomy. J. Neurophysiol., *16:* 247-251, 1953.

26. ——: Effect of combined afferent lesions on motor functions. Neurology, *5:* 269-272, 1955.

27. MARLER, P.: The filtering of external stimuli during instinctive behavior. *In* Thorpe, W. H., and Zangwill, O. L. (Eds.): Current Problems in Animal Behavior. Cambridge University Press, 1961, pp. 150-166.

28. MERTON, P. A.: Speculations on the servo-control of movement. *In* Symposium on the Spinal Cord. Ciba Foundation Symposium, London, Churchill, 1953, 247-260.

29. PAILLARD, J.: The patterning of skilled movements. *In* Handbook of Physiology I: Neurophysiology, III, Washington, D. C., American Physiological Society, 1960.

30. RAPIN, ISABELLE, COSTA, L. D., MANDEL, I. J., AND FROMOWITZ, A. J.: Effects of varying delays in auditory feedback on key-tapping in children. Perc. Mot. Skills, *16:* 489-500, 1963.

31. RIESEN, A. H.: Plasticity of behavior: Psychological aspects. *In* Harlow, H. F., and Woolsey, C. N. (Eds.): Biological and Biochemical Bases of Behavior. Madison, The University of Wisconsin Press, 1958, pp. 425-450.

32. ROSENBLITH, W. A., AND VIDALE, E. B.: A quantitative view of neuroelectric events in relation to sensory communication. *In* Koch, S. (Ed.): Psychology: A Study of a Science, Vol. 4, Biologically Oriented Fields: Their Place in Psychology and in Biological Science. New York, McGraw-Hill, 1962, 334-379.

33. RUCH, T. C., PATTON, H. D., WOODBURY. J. W., AND TOWE, A. L.: Neurophysiology. Philadelphia, Saunders, 1961, pp. 188-194.

34. SHERRINGTON, C. S., AND MOTT, S. W.: Experiments upon the influence of sensory nerves upon movement and nutrition of the limbs. Proc. Roy. Soc., *57:* 481-488, 1895.
35. SMITH, K. U.: Delayed Sensory Feedback and Behavior. Philadelphia, Saunders, 1962.
36. SOLOMON, P., et al. (Eds.): Sensory Deprivation. Cambridge, Harvard University Press, 1961.
37. SPRAGUE, J. M., CHAMBERS, W. W., AND STELLAR, E.: Attentive, affective and adaptive behavior in the cat. Science, *133:* 165-173, 1961.
38. THORPE, W. H.: Sensitive periods in the learning of animals and men: A study of imprinting with special reference to the induction of cyclic behavior. *In* Thorpe, W. H., and Zangwill, O. L. (Eds.): Current Problems in Animal Behavior. Cambridge, Cambridge University Press, 1961, pp. 194-224.
39. TWITCHELL, T. E.: Sensory factors in purposive movement. J. Neurophysiol., *17:* 239-252, 1954.
40. VANDERWOLF, C. H.: Medial thalamic functions in voluntary behavior. Canad. J. Psychol., *16:* 318-330, 1962.
41. VERNON, J., MARTON, T., AND PETERSON, E.: Sensory deprivation and hallucinations. Science *133:* 1808-1812, 1961.
42. VON NEUMANN, J.: The mathematician. *In* The World of Mathematics, Vol. 4, New York, Simon & Schuster, 1956, p. 2056.
43. WHEATON, J. L.: Fact and Fancy in Sensory Deprivation Studies. Air University, School of Aviation Medicine, USAF, Brooks AFB, Texas, August, 1959 (Review 5-59).
44. YATES, A. J.: Delayed auditory feedback. Psychol. Bull. *60:* 213-232, 1963.

Discussion

by H. E. LEHMANN, M.D.

H AVING TO DISCUSS four scientific presentations in a few minutes is a challenging task. The four papers have a common theme of course, namely perception, but I searched for still another unifying image to bring all of them together in the same perspective.

And it occurred to me that one might compare this afternoon's search for the features of the perceptual process to an attack of modern physical research on the nature of certain nuclear processes.

Staying for a moment with this analogy, we could see Dr. Lhamon's study* of time judgment as delving into the nature of what the physicists today call plasma, that is a strange and extremely elusive medium—neither solid nor liquid nor gas—in which fundamental processes are operating. Time, St. Augustine has said, is something I know very well if you don't ask me about it, but that eludes me when I try to define it. Time is, to be sure, the psyche's only proper dimension and the only thing we can quantify phenomenologically without having to refer to an external criterion.

Still stretching our analogy, we may then look at Dr. Shagass' paper on the neurophysiological measures of perception as an investigation of the material substrate of nuclear physics, of the varied particles, if you want, that can be photographed and demonstrated with lawful regularity.

Finally, we may regard Dr. Razran's and Dr. Chase's studies on the psychopathology of interoception and the organization of motor functions as an attack on the field forces which structure the events we are observing.

And here this most artificial analogy definitely ends. Why did I concoct it in the first place? Perhaps to get right from the start over the atavistic tendency to visualize everything psychological in terms of physical science, to get this inclination to the line of least epistemological resistance out of my system, so to speak.

However, any processes we are studying must be considered in their substrate, in the relationships that govern them and in the medium in which they take place.

---

*Dr. Lhamon's study appears on p. 164.

Dr. Lhamon and his co-workers are convinced that the process of temporalisation can be rendered understandable through the ground rules of science. They are well aware of the tremendous conceptual complexity which characterizes any experimental study of time judgment. Taking the stand that the socially acquired units of our surroundings, including the units of time experience, constitute our instrumentarium for judging the testing of reality, they have examined the development of time judgment as a criterion of mental maturity and found that this specific ability consistently makes its first appearance at 8 years of age and then remains remarkably stable until about 60 years. Psychiatric illness interferes with the experiencing of passing time and so do the effects of certain psychotropic drugs.

Rather than simply employ a procedure of comparing two stimuli where the subject would act as an "organic meter," they have their subjects compare one stimulus with a personally held concept.

They found that the inner-directed, autistic and the schizophrenic person tend to overestimate time, when clock-time comparison is excluded. In other words, the schizophrenic tends to overestimate short durations and will therefore equate, e.g., 0.44 second with 1.00 second while the healthy individual will require 0.78 second for this personal equation. This difference between schizophrenics and controls holds only for the acute and subacute patients. It disappears in the chronic schizophrenic and is reversed in the schizophrenic in remission. Manic patients, on the other hand, tend to underestimate time. (They equate 1.36 seconds with 1.00.)

An interesting finding is that the sense mode is an important factor in judging time. Tactile stimuli are estimated to last longer than auditory and auditory longer than visual. (Might one say that the more distance or space the sense mode of the stimuli is taking in, the less time it is filling for the individual?)

However, these intersensory differences of time judgment are possibly reduced in schizophrenics who experience difficulty in adapting to the complexity of immediate focal and background influences versus internally held concepts. The authors observed—like others before them—that sedative drugs slow down internal events that make external events apparently speed up, whereas stimulants speed up internal events and make the external events apparently slow down. The same effect as with stimulants is produced by hyperthyroidism and hyperthermia, namely a speeding up of internal and a slowing down of external events. However, while drug effects on time judgment are sensitive to

changes in the psychophysical method of detecting them, hyperthyroidism and fever alter time judgment independently of the measuring method. With psychotomimetic drugs their subjects' ability to
compare with an internal time concept was severely disturbed qualitatively as well as quantitatively.

One is impressed with the authors' careful and methodical approach
to the bewildering problem of time experience. They have spent 8 years
on it and have worked with 5,000 subjects. No other psychological
laboratory could match these qualifications. Their findings are often
rather startling, and probably of considerable importance. What do
they mean?

Asking this question as a discussant, I shall take advantage of my
limited responsibility and take a leap from the authors' solid data into
the outer space of free-flight speculation.

To begin with, we too in our laboratory in Montreal have been able
to show the specific differential effects of psychotropic drugs on time
estimation. We have also observed phenomena in the temporal discrimination of acute and chronic schizophrenics which correspond to the
results of Lhamon, Goldstone and Goldfarb. And this is the theory we
have constructed:

Human consciousness or awareness, the medium for all perceptual
processes of varying structure and modality, is not a continuum but
rather a set of discontinuous time-space events. Much of the meaning,
quality and affective tone of our experiences is the cumulative resultant
of these discontinuous units of experience which vary in length between
different persons and may vary in the same person under different
conditions. There comes to mind the analogy of the discontinuous
energy of quanta of the physical sciences, but the essential difference
lies in the assumption that in mental phenomena, it is not the intensity
or "energy" of experience which is discontinuous but the very medium
in which the experience occurs. In other words, there may be in
psychological science not a time-space continuum such as the quantum-
physicist has at his disposal but instead little moments, blocks or bits
of experience of varying length. (Quantum refers to energy, 'bit' to
information and the word moment has too many meanings. We even
have a new name to propose for them: oligons; oligon is the Greek
word for 'bit'.) Different human experiences might conceivably be the
result of different "spectral distributions" of oligon lengths, or oligon
frequencies. The range of oligon durations probably lies between 10
and 100 msec.

For instance, this theory postulates that shorter oligons are produced by stimulant drugs, hyperthyroidism, and hyperthemia as well as by acute schizophrenia and this would account for more input moments of experience per clock time unit, resulting in the phenomenon of the subject being stimulated and eventually being pushed into psychotic jamming of central processing.

Conversely, sedative drugs may exert their inhibiting effect by increasing the length of the oligon—the postulated irreducible unit of experience—and in this way they reduce the number of oligons, of input or output moments, per clock-time unit. External time then seems to pass faster.

I should like to ask Dr. Lhamon whether he also interprets his findings in this discontinuous fashion or whether he prefers to view them as the expressions of judgments on continua of varying length. In other words, does he visualize the central nervous system as a digital or as an analog computer when it comes to time judgment?

More trivially, I also wonder whether he would indicate to us which of his varied observations he considers to be the most firmly established since in the data I have seen the statistical level of confidence has not been indicated.

Dr. Chase applies the comparatively recent methodology of information theory to the study of perception which he defines as the capacity to extract and shape neural events from amorphous inputs. Analyzing the systems of error detection and error correction programming, he notes the capacity of the CNS to affect its input patterns by filtering and biasing operations. The scale of stimuli intensities and the subjective intensity of sensation correspond as a power function relationship which may be common to most sensory channels. The intensity of visual stimuli seems to be encoded as a pulse frequency.

Experimenting with delayed auditory feedback, Dr. Chase observed that this can have qualitatively similar effects upon the output of different motor systems amounting to a certain sensory channel equivalence for information transmission. But in sampling the environment, does the CNS depend on informational or temporal quanta? This important question can not yet be answered. However, Dr. Chase was able to take a close experimental look at the time periods of sensory feedback necessary for appropriate processing.

He considers the probability that in addition to trial and error learning there are conceptual schemata implicated in the organization of standards for error detection and matching operations. While the vulnerability of a particular subject to disturbance of speech control under delayed auditory feedback conditions is a stable feature of this subject's motor control system, such disturbance is not an invariant feature of the performance of an individual in other motor functions besides speech.

Dr. Chase raises the significant question which classes of learning occur not through slow trial and error procedure but as a very rapid process at certain critical times of the individual's development. When are these critical times and of what kind are the stimulus configurations that may so rapidly be acquired as neural templates for error detection operations? Is one not reminded of the old trial—error versus gestalt learning controversy, only now being given a new look through the introduction of critical time periods which have been so dramatically demonstrated in the imprinting experiments of the ethologists?

I should like to ask Dr. Chase whether he can see the application of some of the sampling experiments, for instance, to the technology of learning and possibly even to the techniques of psychotherapy—or are we reasonably close to new insights about the role of critical periods in the development of the human psychic apparatus?

Dr. Razran has reported on some fascinating experiments on interoception which, as he points out, is little deranged by cognition and therefore makes animal and human experimentation more interchangeable than is the case with experiments involving exteroception. There is a much higher threshold of verbal reportability for interoceptive stimuli than for exteroceptive, but for distal reactions not involving awareness, as for instance PGR or vascular reactions, the thresholds for interoceptive and exteroceptive stimuli are not much different.

Russian investigators have shown that interoceptive simulation more than exteroceptive seems to result in gradual, orderly, monotonic representation in the CNS. It is a system in commerce with the organism itself rather than with the organism's environment, a fulcrum of its vital mechanics, as Dr. Razran calls it.

While the exteroceptive system is mainly functioning at the conscious level, the interoceptive system is mainly unconscious. It is interesting that interoceptively produced reactions are more resistant to habituation than exteroceptively produced ones. Is this, I wonder, related to the clinical fact that psychosomatic neuroses tend so often to be chronic? Quite consistently, interoceptive reactions dominate exteroceptive. Interoceptive conditioning is readily formed, more readily, in fact, than exteroceptive conditioning; and interoceptive conditioning,

Dr. Razran concludes, constitutes a special dimension of conditioning which as a rule conflicts with exteroceptive conditioning.

This last statement I find rather puzzling and I wonder whether it is a theoretical extrapolation of experimental data or based on actual observations. No doubt, there must be a frightening amount of conflicting stimulation occurring many times in the course of a day in any one's life leading to power struggles of the various stimulus values and perhaps even to temporary experimental "organ neuroses"—but would this not be true on the level of competing exteroceptive stimuli alone as well as for the competition between exteroceptive and interoceptive systems?

Are we really exposed to a never ending bitter sibling rivalry between our vital reactions and those of the second signaling system which we proudly claim as our special human heritage?

Dr. Shagass has measured cerebral responsiveness to sensori-motor stimuli as manifested in basic time constants and ratios. He has recorded evoked brain potentials by averaging methods and has found that the normal recovery cycle following a single electrical stimulus is altered in patients diagnosed as suffering from schizophrenia, psychotic depression or personality disorders. In such subjects the recovery of evoked potentials is delayed.

Another measure of cerebral responsivity, the stimulus intensity-response amplitude gradient was observed to be less steep in subjects with no psychiatric disorder or with neurotic so-called dysthmic syndromes than in patients with other psychiatric diagnoses.

It seems to me that Dr. Shagass' research has multiple implications of significance. One is the fact that he has discovered certain basic time relationships between events in consciousness and events in its neurophysiological substrate. If there is such a thing as an "oligon," this kind of experimental research will be required to reveal its nature. The time range for the recovery cycle of evoked potentials seems to go from 10 to 100 msec. as Dr. Shagass has shown.

Then, there is the possibility that eventually this method may provide us with some objective indices of pathology and criteria of change in the central nervous system—things we badly need today.

Furthermore, as Dr. Shagass has pointed out himself, the whole muddy question of our psychiatric nosology may receive a clarifying impetus from this type of experimental approach. While I for one— as Dr. Shagass knows—do not see much sense in introducing *ad hoc* formulated and grouped new diagnostic categories based on questionable theoretical simplifications, I would certainly welcome as a helpful system any new psychiatric classification that is firmly based on consistent objective data, particularly if these data consist of reductions to the neurophysiological level. Does he think such a new nosological system based on electro-physiological responsiveness of the CNS is in the offing?

Finally, Dr. Shagass was able to establish definitely that cortical representation of an event is a necessary prerequisite of all awareness. This gives me a certain amount of personal pleasure for the following reason: my friend Dr. Zubin has been pulling my scientific leg ever since he heard me profess that I believed there were things in the mind that are not in the brain! I still believe that, but I am also happy to go on record acknowledging Dr. Shagass' finding that there are no things in awareness that are not in the cortex!

Part II: Psychopathology of Pain, Taste and Time

5

QUANTIFICATION OF THE SUBJECTIVE PAIN EXPERIENCE

by HENRY K. BEECHER, M.D.*

PROBABLY THE MOST ANCIENT REASON for the development of the physician was the symptom of pain. Of all the ills man is subjected to, pain seems to be the one most urgently requiring treatment. Since pain has such ancient origins and connotations, this may be the reason pain and its treatment are encumbered by more folklore than anything else in medicine. The many exciting advances in specific therapeutics of recent years should not draw our attention from the fact that a very large part of the practice of medicine consists still in the relief of symptoms.

It became possible some years ago to deal with pain in a quantitative manner in terms of the percentage of individuals who present certain arbitrary criteria (i.e., pain "half gone" at both 45 and 90 minutes after a drug or placebo injection).[4,8,17,18,19,35,36] As a consequence of the quantitative approach, it has been possible to cut through and discard much of the confusing folklore in this important field. As Lord Kelvin said:

> "I often say that when you can measure what you are speaking about, and express it in numbers, you know something about it; but when you cannot measure it, when you cannot express it in numbers, your knowledge is of a meagre and unsatisfactory kind; it may be the beginning of knowledge, but you have scarcely, in your thoughts, advanced to the stage of *Science* whatever the matter may be."

For years I have been an ardent follower of this point of view.

Psychopharmacology has its roots deeply buried in sensation and in alterations in sensation produced by drugs. One could place at 200

---

*Anaesthesia Laboratory of the Harvard Medical School at the Massachusetts General Hospital, Boston, Mass.

years ago the beginnings of a modern interest in sensation with Haller's *Elementa physiologiae* (1757-1766). In this he discussed fully the senses; however, I would much prefer to place the beginnings at Charles Bell's discovery in 1811, and its confirmation 11 years later by Magendie, that there are two kinds of nerves—sensory which lead to the posterior roots of the spinal cord and motor from the anterior roots. This discovery 150 years ago ". . . reminded the physiologists that the mind's sensations were as much their business as the muscles' movements." Motor conduction could be studied a hundred years ago since the motor nerve has a muscle at its end. "At the end of the sensory nerve there was only introspection. . . ." I do not suppose anybody holds the belief that there is any such thing as a pure sensation. We have perceptions, that is, modified sensations, certainly modified at both a cortical and subcortical level, modified by drugs at sites and levels about which we know only a little.

Present gaps in fundamental knowledge need not oblige us to remain at a purely descriptive level. We can now proceed from descriptive words alone to numbers in many instances in psychopharmacology and I think it is urgent to do so whenever this is possible.

The beginnings of what Lord Kelvin might have called a scientific approach to these problems can be found in 1846 when Ernst Heinrich Weber became interested in separating pain from the sensation of touch. Four years later, in 1850, Fechner saw in Weber's studies on intensity of sensory experience, ". . . a way for writing quantitative relations between mind and body, or, more particularly, between sensation and its stimulus." At the moment we are not interested in whether Fechner's "logarithmic law" is the correct expression of such matters or, as Stevens believes[49] that Plateau's "power law" is the correct representation.

Before I give you practical evidence that one can indeed work with pain in quantitative terms, I should like to introduce a caution.

Since the quantification of subjective response is of first concern here, it is, in a broad sense,[41] an exercise in psychophysics. Yet those who look for what is sometimes called the "psychophysics of pain" will find no elaborate presentation of this subject. The reason is simple: enough dependable data are not as yet available. This is not to dismiss thoughtlessly the painstaking work on the "dol," an earnest attempt to establish the "psychophysics of pain" on a basis comparable to that already developed for vision and for hearing. (This work has been given a reasonably full discussion by Beecher[9]). The failure of other careful investigators to confirm much of that work on pain leaves its precise meaning in doubt. If the psychophysics of pain is ever to be established in an orderly way, much of the material in the following pages will have to be drawn into the formulation. The complexity of the problem makes it seem unlikely that it will prove possible to describe the psychophysics of pain in a definitive manner, except perhaps in some limited experimental situations where the pain aroused may have little relation to the pain experienced in disease. A definitive psychophysics of vision, of hearing, perhaps of taste, smell, and touch, yes, for these sensations can be turned on and off by stimulus control. But the task of developing the psychophysics of significant pain would be like that of studying the "psychophysics" of emotion or of anxiety, experiences whose stimulus correlates are only to be guessed at. There is indeed reason to believe that anxiety constitutes one of the basic elements in the pain process. We are not likely to make an effective attack on the psychophysics of pain of pathological origin until a host of elusive variables have been brought under control.

Many investigators seem grimly determined to establish—indeed, too often there does not seem to have been any question in their mind —that for a given stimulus there must be a given response; that is, for so much stimulation of pain endings, so much pain will be experienced, and so on. This fundamental error has led to enormous waste. If this paper does no more than to point clearly to this, it will have succeeded in one of its major purposes. This mistake has been common in laboratories where principal attention has been devoted to techniques of producing experimental pain in man. Work presented here makes it clear that there is no simple relationship between stimulus and subjective response. It is also made evident that the reason for this is the interposition of conditioning, of the processing component, of the psychic reaction. It is evident that this component merits and must have extensive consideration. It must be taken into account not only for pain but probably for all subjective responses.

In years gone by I have been asked why one whose primary orientation is in the field of research in anesthesia should spend so much time on the problem of pain and its treatment. There is more than one good answer to this question, I believe. Rather obviously the anesthetist's entire life is concerned with the amelioration, or the avoidance, or the suppression of pain. I believe one must agree that basically—broadly —the anesthetist's interests are founded on the factors which diminish irritability. At least this is true at a cellular level. At a cellular level one must conclude that any factors which diminish the irritability of a single cell are within the anesthetist's province. Cellular irritability and the factors which determine it constitute the central problem of all biology; for that matter, they constitute the central problem of life itself.

There is another good reason why the anesthetist can quite properly be interested not only in pain and its relief but in other broadly associated fields; let me illustrate this in the following way: There are five major classes of drugs of particular interest to the pharmacologist, drugs which have as their primary purpose the alteration of subjective responses. There are sedatives and hypnotics (sleep-producing agents), analgesics (pain-relieving agents), ego depressants (used by psychiatrists to probe disturbed patients' minds) and, finally, the anesthetics. One can, by the simple expedient of administering a barbiturate, produce sedation. A small increase in the dose of the same agent and it becomes a hypnotic; further increase in the dose and analgesia is produced. A still further increase and ego depression occurs. Still more of the drug and anesthesia ensues. It is impossible for me to believe that nature is aware of boundaries between any of these pairs of arbitrarily designated conditions. Since one can by the simple expedient of increasing the dose of a given drug move from the mild state of sedation, through hypnosis, analgesia, ego depression and into profound anesthesia, it seems most likely that there are mechanisms held in common in the production of all five of these states. One would expect to find stimulating cross fertilization of ideas and new approaches to the study of anesthetics, for example, by studying hypnotics. One would expect to gain insight into ego depression by studying sedation, and so on. I shall give you some evidence for such cross fertilization from our own work over the past 20 years.

Twenty years ago we started with the supposition that pain was pain, that it varied in duration, quality and intensity but that however produced it was pretty much the same thing, varying only in the qualities just mentioned. We knew that pain had been experimentally contrived in the laboratory in many ways, by skin pricks, by electric shocks to teeth, by chemicals placed in blisters, by tourniquets, by physical pressure, by cold, by heat. In the beginning we had no doubt that all of these methods were useful, for indeed they did produce pain. That was unquestionable. So we set out to use one of the methods which had been carefully worked out by Hardy, Wolff and Goodell.[37] With our interest in quantification, this method was particularly attractive, for it presented a means of measuring accurately the amount of heat thrown on an area of the skin, usually the forehead. Since we wished to study pain in man, this seemed to be a fine approach. To cut short a long and painful period, it was a rude shock for us to find that with this beautifully worked out method we could not distinguish between a large dose of morphine (15 mg.) and 1 ml. of normal saline. Of course both of these agents were administered as unknowns to subject and to observer. (This double unknowns technique is a requirement for studies in this field.) We turned then to a man who had had a great deal of experience with this Hardy-Wolff-Goodell method and, again to shorten a long story, he was quite unable, notwithstanding his early successes with the method (when he had not worked with the double unknowns technique), to distinguish between a large dose of morphine and a little table salt in solution.

As the years have gone by, some 15 groups in England and America have now utterly failed to demonstrate any dependable relationship in man between the relief of experimentally contrived pain, called the pain threshold, and great doses of narcotic. This refers to the methods generally used at present. It may be possible in the future to devise experimental methods wherein the pain threshold will respond in dependable fashion to graded doses of narcotic. These matters have all been dealt with extensively and the proper references made elsewhere in my book.[9] This need not be documented further here.

When one takes into account the fact just mentioned of the failure of experimentally produced pain in man to respond dependably to even large doses of narcotic agents, when one places this fact alongside the universally observed fact that pain arising from disease or injury, what we shall call pathological pain from here on, *always* responds in greater or lesser degree to even small doses of morphine and similar narcotics, then one must conclude that our original assumption that pain was pain whatever its origin simply does not hold. There is some fundamental and mysterious difference between pain produced in the laboratory, even severe pain produced there, and the pain produced by disease or injury.

In fairness to Hardy, Wolff and Goodell, and other originators of experimentally produced pain studies, I should like to say at once that experimentally contrived pain surely does have its uses in man. For example, the classic work of Gasser, Erlanger, Heinbecker, Bishop, and others in which they identified pain pathways, has very often depended upon experimentally produced pain. One must add also that experimental pain in animals is a useful approach to certain kinds of important studies. The Hardy-Wolff-Goodell method works beautifully when a small quantity of heat is thrown on a rat's tail, as applied by D'Amour and Smith.[16] I suspect that all pain is to an animal serious and significant. It does not seem like a reckless assumption to assume that an animal is quite unable to distinguish between experimental pain and pathological pain. Indeed, there may be a clue in this statement to a very significant factor in the pain situation. Later on evidence will be given to indicate that the meaning of the pain sensation is the factor which determines the suffering from it. We all know that a small ache in a finger may be a trivial annoyance, easily disregarded, whereas the same duration and intensity of an ache beneath the sternum, if it connotes the possibility of sudden death from heart failure, may be a wholly unsettling experience. The implications contained in these statements are of such importance I should like to deal with them in some detail.

It long ago became apparent from study of the world's literature on pain that this subjective experience is one surrounded by many pitfalls to trap the unwary. It early became apparent that sound design of study was to be of paramount importance.

Many workers beside myself have made contributions to this area. For example, the Keeles[35,36] in England long ago understood the requirements for study here. Many important contributions have been made by colleagues in our laboratory, to name a few: Denton, Lasagna, Keats and Smith. The contributions of many others besides our own have been described in my book.[9] I should like to mention, however, in a few words the essentials of sound design in the study of the pain experience. (These remarks apply to other subjective responses as well.) As I indicated a moment ago, an individual's bias may be a crippling matter in such studies. The subject's and the observer's bias must therefore be eliminated. This is done by the use of the double blind approach where neither subject nor observer knows what has been administered in a given case. It is also essential to insert placebos into the situation, also as unknowns. The word placebo means "I shall please." A placebo is a substance inert in its ordinary biological sense, which is given to the subject with the subject's belief that it is or may be an active drug. As we shall see later on, situations can have placebo effects also, the concept of a placebo as only something that pleases has to be modified to include effects and situations produced by placebos which may be unpleasant. We must have the double blind approach, the use of placebos, randomization of the placebos and drugs studied, isolation of one subject from another so they cannot compare and discuss the effects experienced, and mathematical validation of supposed differences encountered. It is necessary to have a sufficient number of subjects, usually not fewer than 25, for work on pain. In studying postoperative wound pain, for example, one has to rely on the subject's statement that he is having pain of a given degree —none, slight, moderate or severe. In our own work we chose to record whatever the fact was, severe pain for example, administer an unknown solution which might be an active drug or which might be a placebo; a neutral technician visits the patient 45 minutes later and again 90 minutes after the drug was administered. For a positive result we arbitrarily require that a patient say his pain is at least half gone on both occasions. If he says it is all gone on one occasion and not half on another, it is arbitrarily recorded as a negative result. There are many ways of approaching this problem. This one has worked well in our hands. It may seem as though the "one-half gone" decision was a difficult one to make, but actual experience has shown that patients have found this judgment easy to make and to reproduce. We then take the number of individuals in a given group whose result was "positive" and calculate their percentage. This makes it possible to fulfill Lord Kelvin's requirement of placing significant numbers in front of meaningful items. We can thus compare a new agent with a standard, usually morphine, or a placebo, in studies of pain.

You may say, what actual evidence do you have that one can deal in a quantitative manner here? I can refer you to some data obtained in this laboratory.[33] We had an outside individual make up two series of flasks, six flasks in Series A and six in Series B. We did not know what either series contained, but assumed that one series contained a pain-relieving agent. When we had completed the study, using postoperative wound pain, and broke the code, we found that both series of flasks had contained morphine. In Series A there was always 10 mg./ml. In Series B there were different concentrations of morphine in each flask. On graphing the data we constructed the two lines shown in figure 1.[33] Where the two graphs crossed, there is equivalence of analgesic action: we had equated 10 mg. morphine to 10.8, an 8 per cent error. As any statistician knows, these are not truly lines that cross but bands that cross, and one must calculate the regression lines, and this was done under the guidance of Professor Frederick Mosteller, without whom none of our work would have been possible. (As a mathematician, he has kept us from many errors.) These calculations required that we add 2 per cent more to the 8 per cent error and gives a total error of 10 per cent. We are thus able to work quantitatively in the elusive field of subjective responses. I submit that this 10 per cent error is about as accurately as one measures most objective things in man (except for perhaps chemical determinations in a sample of blood) such as blood pressure, cell counts, and so on.

Another observation which gave us reason to believe that we were working in a satisfactorily dependable manner was the reproducibility and agreement from time to time of the data obtained, not only in our own laboratory but by others. For example, Houde and Wallenstein are two of the ablest workers in this field, working usually with the pain from cancer, presumably the pain from smooth muscle and periosteum; they found also that 10 mg. morphine relieved 65 per cent of the individuals, as shown in table 1.[27,37,38] While it is true that such isolated data do not prove anything, they are contributing evidence that we were on the right track. They also gave some reason for the cautious generalization that pain from pathological origin was very much alike in that it responded in the same way to a given dose of pain-relieving agent.

Quantitative studies have led to some very practical results of a dependable sort. For example, with the great tensions in the world situation, with China fairly cut off from the Western world, we have lost that source of opium from which morphine is made. It is quite conceivable that other sources of opium, such as the Middle East and India, may become suddenly unavailable. We need have no fear that this will result in our being without adequate pain-relieving agents. For example, a considerable family of methadones,[18,19] which are made rather simply from substances common to the world of commerce, the

TABLE 1.—Pain Relief Effected by 10 mg. Morphine and by a Placebo in Two Independent Laboratories

Investigators	Studies	No. of Patients	Per cent Relieved Morphine 10 mg. s.c.	Placebo
Lasagna and Beecher	1952	66	65.8	
Postoperative wound pain	1953	56	69.3	39.0*
Houde and Wallenstein	1952-	67	65.0	42.0
Chronic pain in cancer patients	1953			

*Averaged data from Lasagna, Mosteller, von Felsinger and Beecher, 1954.[46]

nitriles, can be made into agents just as effective as morphine for pain relief. Several of these methadones are milligram for milligram the equivalent of morphine. Unfortunately, they are milligram for milligram equivalent to morphine in undesirable effects as well. They produce just as much depression of the respiration, just as much addiction, and so on. There is reason to believe, from our work, that the levo-iso-methadone has less nausea associated with it for an equal degree of pain relief than is true of morphine.

The quantitative approach I have just mentioned lends itself very well to a comparison of new agents designed to relieve pain. Unfortunately, pain-relieving agents must be measured against two yardsticks. There is the pain-relieving yardstick and there is the side-effect yardstick, and so what Lasagna and I[37] like to call the optimal dose of morphine, or the optimal dose of any other pain-relieving agent, is determined from placing both yardsticks where we can see them and arriving somewhat arbitrarily at the most advantageous dose of agent to use, taking into account the agent's rather accurately determined pain-relieving power per milligram and also its undesirable side effects per milligram.

It is our hope that the use of the technique referred to will make it possible eventually to find an agent which will relieve pain but not have the sometimes devastating side effects that powerful pain-relieving agents have at the present time.

An Old Concept Newly Applied

In 1894, a philosopher, Marshall, wrote a book, *Pain, Pleasure and Aesthetics,* in which he almost made a crucial assumption.[48] He did in fact lay the background for an assumption which was made the next year by Strong.[42] This assumption said, in effect, that an experience like suffering has two major components, the original sensation and the processing component, or what I like to call the psychological reaction component. So far as I have been able to discover, neither Marshall nor Strong had any factual evidence for this concept. It seems to have been simply one of those brilliant intuitive insights which have been so rewarding in medicine over the centuries. We have been able to gain, however, considerable supporting evidence for this Marshall-Strong concept and I should like to tell you about it because this evidence has given us some rather far-reaching insights not only into the origins of pain and the control of pain but also into other subjective responses and their modification by drugs in man.

THE REACTION COMPONENT

In the immediately preceding section, I mentioned that an experience such as suffering consists of two elements, the original sensation and the reaction component. I also described, in the preceding section on "Pain," that pain as now commonly contrived experimentally does not respond in man in a dependable fashion to even large doses of narcotics. Then I made the working hypothesis that the original sensation was not the site of action of drugs such as morphine. It is surely true that there is no such thing as pure sensation, all sensations having been modified, probably at a subcortical level before they erupt into consciousness and certainly modified after erupting into consciousness by conditioning, significance, meaning. If such agents as narcotics are without effect, as seems to be the case, on the original sensation or the nearest approximation to the original sensation, then the site of action must be the reaction component. At least we can take this as a working hypothesis and then see how pertinent data relate to the concept. I should now like to present evidence that this is in truth the case, that the reaction component has vast influence on our lives. First, I should like to present in support of this thesis the effect of placebos.

PLACEBO

It was only after I had worked in this field for some years that I realized we usually had a very high average degree of effectiveness of placebos in treating postoperative wound pain and other conditions as well. Following this realization I then looked around amongst the papers of other individuals and was struck by the beautiful study of Evans and Hoyle[23] in England. In this pioneer and now classic study they found that the pain of angina pectoris was relieved by placebos just about as often as we later found for the pain of postoperative wounds. The paper of Evans and Hoyle marks a considerable milestone in clinical sophistication in studies of subjective responses. With this much material in hand, I then made quite a search of the literature for other comparable findings. This material is summarized in table 2, which I first presented in a paper called "The Powerful Placebo."[5] One must call attention to the fact that the data presented in table 2 are *average* figures.

I have obtained a good deal of data, some better than others, that the effectiveness of a placebo is very much greater when stress is severe than when it is not. For example, I found[7] that when pain was very severe following surgery, the usual dose of morphine relieved not the usual 65 per cent of individuals but now only 52 per cent. At the same time a placebo relieved 40 per cent. If one considers that the 52 per cent relievable by the morphine represents roughly the maximum amount of pain relievable by chemical agents, then the 40 per cent is actually 77 per cent of 52 per cent, and we see that the placebo effectiveness is twice as great as one had found on the average. When the pain diminished in severity the same dose of morphine then relieved 89 per cent of individuals, but curiously the placebo effect had fallen to 26 per cent. Twenty-six per cent of 89 per cent, is now 29 per cent compared with the earlier 77 per cent, only about one-third as much as it had been. It is true, as some have pointed out, that this may represent a special situation and one can find conflicting data. Less easily open to challenge, however, are the following data.[9] As I have pointed out, the average effectiveness of placebos when dealing with pathological pain is 35 per cent, the average effectiveness of placebos with experimentally contrived pain is only 3.2 per cent. In other words, the placebo is *10 times* more effective in relieving pain of pathological origin than it it is in relieving pain of experimentally contrived origin. These data, I believe, are difficult to get around; they illustrate my point. There is, it is true, a mild assumption involved here but one I do not believe anybody would have difficulty in accepting, that there is more anxiety associated with pain from disease than there is in pain experimentally contrived in the laboratory. Consider the example of the finger pain and the sub-sternal pain mentioned above. This assumption seems to be so far removed from the possibility of adequate challenge that it need not be discussed further. When stress is severe, placebos are more effective than when stress is less or absent.

I mentioned earlier that morphine was not dependably effective in man in relieving experimentally contrived pain as usually produced, but was always effective in greater or lesser degree in relieving pain of pathological origin. Thus one can, I believe, state a new principle of drug action: some drugs are effective only in the presence of an appropriate mental state.

Much more could be said about chemical agents as placebos but before we leave this section I should like to point out that situations can also have placebo effects—the surgical situation, for example. In 1939 it was suggested, in Italy, that the pain of angina pectoris could be greatly lessened by ligation of the internal mammary arteries. Eventually this suggestion was adopted in America and rather spectacularly favorable results were obtained. Not only were the objective results impressive,

TABLE 2.—Therapeutic Effectiveness of Placebos in Several Conditions (From Beecher, 1955[5])

Condition	Study	Placebo Agent	Route	Source of Data	Number of Patients	Per Cent Satisfactorily Relieved by a Placebo
	Keats and Beecher (1950)	Saline	I.V.		118	21
	Beecher, Deffer, Fink and Sullivan (1951)	Saline	S.C.		29	31
Severe	Keats, D'Allesandro and Beecher (1951)	Saline	I.V.		34	26
Postoperative	Beecher, Keats, Mosteller and Lasagna (1953)	Lactose	P.O.		52 36 44 40	40 26 } 33 34 32
Wound Pain	Lasagna, Mosteller, von Felsinger and Beecher (1954)	Saline	S.C.		14 20 15 21 15 15	50 37 53 } 39 40 40 15
Cough	Gravenstein, Devloo and Beecher (1954)	Lactose	P.O.		22 23	36 } 40 43
Drug-induced Mood Changes	Lasagna, von Felsinger and Beecher (1955)	Normal Saline	S.C.	Normals Post-Addicts	20 30	30 30

Pain from	Reference	Agent	Route	Number	Average Relieved
Angina Pectoris	Evans and Hoyle (1933)	Sodium Bicarbonate	P.O.	66	38
	Travell, Rinzler, Bakst, Benjamin and Bobb (1959)	"Placebo"	P.O.	19	26
	Greiner, Gold, Cattell, Travell and ten colleagues (1950)	Lactose	P.O.	27	38
Headache	Jellinek (1946)	Lactose	P.O.	199	52
Seasickness	Gay and Carliner (1949)	Lactose	P.O.	33	58
Anxiety and Tension	Wolf and Pinsky (1954)	Lactose	P.O.	31	30
Experimental Cough	Hillis (1952)	Normal Saline	S.C.	1 (Many Scores of Experiments)	37
Common Cold	Diehl (1933)	Lactose	P.O.	Cold acute 110	35
				Subacute chronic 48	35
				1082 Total Patients	35.2 ± 2.2% Average Relieved

the patients said they felt better and the objective evidence supported this: there was great reduction in the number of nitroglycerine pills taken, exercise tolerance was greatly increased; for example, a patient could take only 4 minutes of standardized exercise until intolerable pain stopped him and the T-waves in his electrocardiogram inverted in an ominous way. After the operation this individual could exercise for 10 minutes without pain on the exercise steps and his T-waves did not invert. Several individuals[1,15,21,24] began to wonder if this might not be a placebo effect. They went to their patients, explained the situation and told them they would like to carry out a study where the patients would not know what had been done, nor would the observers know until the study was completed. They told their patients that half of them would have the internal mammary arteries exposed and ligated and the other half would simply have them exposed but not ligated. These studies were carried out and in the case I mentioned above, the individual who had had intolerable pain after 4 minutes of exercise and who after the operation could stand 10 minutes of exercise had had only the sham operation. Many similar examples indicated that ligation had no real effect beyond that of a placebo effect. You may say, what is wrong with this? Our aim is to relieve often and to cure when we can. The difficulty in the present situation was that even though the operation was innocuous in concept, individuals with angina pectoris are in a vulnerable state—one patient died during the procedure and another had a further severe myocardial infarction. Even this simple procedure was not without real hazard. This hazard might have been tolerable if the placebo effects had been lasting, but unfortunately, placebo effects usually last from days to weeks to months at best. Thus we have here an example of a situation rather than a chemical agent acting as a placebo. We should all make a searching examination of our present procedures to see what surgical operations or medical activities at the present time may possibly be nothing more than placebo procedures.[10,11] Placebo effects however produced surely are to be construed as evidence for the existence of a powerful reaction component.

SUFFERING AND THE SIGNIFICANCE OF THE WOUND

Another type of support for the reaction component is the finding that the significance of the wound seems to have great influence on the amount of pain resulting from a given injury. In a study of men wounded in battle[3] I was astonished to find in some 215 seriously wounded men that only 25 per cent had enough pain to want anything done about it and so stated in response to a direct question which reminded them that they could have a narcotic if they wanted it. Three quarters simply did not need such help. There were 50 men in each of four groups: serious wounds of the extremities (compound and comminuted fractures or traumatic amputations), extensive soft tissue wounds, penetrated chests, penetrated abdomens, and a final group of 15 with penetrated cerebrums. Only those individuals were included in the study who were clear mentally, with normal blood pressure, not in shock. In many cases they had had no narcotic at all but in no case had they had one within 4 hours. This study was repeated in civilian life where the injury was merely a surgical wound, made under anesthesia. In this latter case the ratio was reversed. More than 80 per cent of such individuals had enough pain to want something done about it. This comparison is described in a paper on the significance of the wound.[7] The wounded soldiers were studied principally on the Anzio beachhead where shelling never stopped day or night for months and where every individual realized that the possibility of death was not a remote thing even for himself. When such men were struck down, the wound meant that the war was suddenly over for the individual; it was a ticket to the safety of the hospital and then home. In the early hours the wound seemed to be construed as a good thing. On the other hand, in the civilian experience the necessity for surgery is uniformly considered to be a disaster by normal individuals. I believe that the significance of the wound, the meaning of the wound in this case, determines the suffering therefrom. I had thought in the beginning that this was an original observation, but found this not to be the case. For example, Guthrie, writing about the Peninsular Wars in Europe in 1827, said that of two individuals suffering the same decrement from the wound, one will smile with contempt whilst the other writhes in pain.[28] Dupuytren, the leading surgeon of his time in France, said almost precisely the same thing. A small boy injured in a fist fight may have been quite severely bruised or cut and felt no pain while emotion was high. We all know that distraction can block pain, that emotion can block pain. It has always seemed puzzling to me that the wise Lord Adrian could have believed that pain dominates the central nervous system: ". . . pain messages are clearly more potent than any others . . . in capturing the attention," he said.[2] This simply is not the case. Emotion can dominate the central nervous system. One hardly needs to emphasize that fact to this group. So also can counterirritation, distraction, attention to other things—all of these can dominate the central nervous system and block the perception of pain. Pain often does not dominate. These matters reflect the power and importance of the reaction component.

*   *   *

All of these things, the fact that emotion can block pain, that the significance of the wound seemingly determines the presence or absence of suffering, the powerful action of placebos and increased effectiveness of placebos with increased stress, and the same for some active drugs— all of these things add up to strong evidence that the psychological processing of the original sensation, the reaction component, is the site of action of drugs which modify subjective responses. This also surely is the site of action of the many nonspecific forces which can modify disease and its treatment.[11]

Measurement in the field of sensations and mood presents an area of significance in human behavior. This work is relevant to the behavioral sciences. The behavioral sciences must, if they are to be soundly established, move onward from the present state which in many areas is largely one of description to one of measurement. Measurement depends upon the recognition and precise definition of variables and their relationships, and the development of tools and techniques for working with them in quantitative terms. As in all sciences eventually there must be possibility of prediction. Implicit in this not only is the necessity to recognize elements that can be measured, but to understand the existence and nature of the essential safeguards, the controls, of observations made. One goal of science is rules ("laws") and the more invariable these rules are, the better it is. We seek to predict from given situation to certain effect. In the complex field of the behavioral sciences in man, observations have, as mentioned, so far largely been descriptive. The basic purpose of these comments is to show that a quantitative approach to sensation ("feeling") is possible and rewarding. Sensation as used here and mood are often controlling factors in behavior and as such are elementary considerations in the development of the behavioral sciences.

REFERENCES

1. ADAMS, R.: Internal-mammary-artery ligation for coronary insufficiency, evaluation. New Engl. J. Med. *258:* 113-115, 1958.
2. ADRIAN, E. D.: Pain and its problems. I. The physiology of pain. Practioner *158:* 76-82, 1947.

3. BEECHER, H. K.: Pain in men wounded in battle. Ann. Surg. *123:* 96-105, 1946.

4. ——: Experimental pharmacology and measurement of the subjective response. Science *116:* 157-162, 1952.

5. ——: The powerful placebo. J.A.M.A. *159:* 1602-1606, 1955.

6. ——: Evidence for increased effectiveness of placebos with increased stress. Amer. J. Physiol. *187:* 163-169, 1956a.

7. ——: Relationship of significance of wound to the pain experienced. J.A.M.A. *161:* 1609-1613, 1956b.

8. ——: Measurement of Subjective Responses: Quantitative Effects of Drugs. New York, Oxford University Press, 1959.

9. ——: Increased stress and effectiveness of placebos and "active" drugs. Science *132:* 91-92, 1960.

10. ——: Surgery as placebo. J.A.M.A. *176:* 1102-1107, 1961.

11. ——: Nonspecific forces surrounding disease and the treatment of disease. J.A.M.A. *179:* 437-440, 1962.

12. ——, DEFFER, P. A., FINK, F. E., AND SULLIVAN, D. B.: Field use of methadone and levo-iso-methadone in a combat zone (Hamhung-Hungnam, North Korea). U.S. Forces med. J. *2:* 1269-1276, 1951.

13. ——, KEATS, A. S., MOSTELLER, F., AND LASAGNA, L: The effectiveness of oral analgesics (morphine, codeine, acetylsalicylic acid) and the problem of placebo "reactors" and "non-reactors." J. Pharmacol. *109:* 393-400, 1953.

14. BORING, E. G.: Sensation and Perception in the History of Experimental Psychology. New York, Appleton-Century-Crofts, 1942.

15. COBB, L. A., THOMAS, G. I., DILLARD, D. H., MERENDINO, K. A., AND BRUCE, R. A.: Evaluation of internal-mammary-artery ligation by double-blind technic. New Engl. J. Med. *260:* 1115-1118, 1959.

16. D'AMOUR, F. E., AND SMITH, D. L.: A method for determining loss of pain sensation. J. Pharmacol. *72:* 74-79, 1941.

17. DENTON, J. E., AND BEECHER, H. K.: New Analgesics. I. Methods in the clinical evaluation of new analgesics. J.A.M.A. *141:* 1051-1057, 1949a.

18. ——, AND ——: New Analgesics. II. A clinical appraisal of the narcotic power of methadone and its isomers. J.A.M.A. *141:* 1146-1148, 1949a.

19. ——, AND ——: New analgesics. III. A comparison of the side effects of morphine, methadone and methadone's isomers in man. J.A.M.A. *141:* 1148-1153, 1949c.

20. DIEHL, H. S.: Medicinal treatment of common cold. J.A.M.A. *101:* 2042-2049, 1933.

21. DIMOND, E. G., KITTLE, C. F., AND CROCKETT, J. E.: Evaluation of internal mammary artery ligation and sham procedure in angina pectoris. Circulation *18:* 712-713, 1958.

22. DUPUYTREN, quoted by LESCELLIÈRE-LAFOSSE, F. G.: Histoire de la cicatrisation, de ses modes de formation, et des considérations pathologiques et thérapeutiques qui en découlent, Montpellier, France, Castel, 1836, p. 29.

23. EVANS, W., AND HOYLE, C.: The comparative value of drugs used in the continuous treatment of angina pectoris. Quart. J. Med *2:* 311-338, 1933.

24. FISH, R. G., CRYMES, T. P., AND LOVELL, M. G.: Internal-mammary-artery

ligation for angina pectoris; its failure to produce relief. New Engl. J. Med. *259:* 418-420, 1958.

25. GAY, L. M., AND CARLINER, P. E.: The prevention and treatment of motion sickness. Johns Hopkins Hosp. Bull. *84:* 470-487, 1949.

26. GRAVENSTEIN, J. S., DEVLOO, R. A., AND BEECHER, H. K.: Effect of antitussive agents on experimental and pathological cough in man. J. appl. Physiol. *7:* 119-139, 1954.

27. GREINER, T., GOLD, H., CATTELL, McK., TRAVELL, J., BAKST, H., RINZLER, S. H., BENJAMIN, Z. H., WARSHAW, L. J., BOBB, A. L., KWIT, N. T., MODELL, W., ROTHENDLER, H. H., NESSELOFF, C. R., AND KRAMER, M. L.: A method for the evaluation of the effects of drugs on cardiac pain in patients with angina of effort. Amer. J. Med. *9:* 143-155, 1950.

28. GUTHRIE, G. J.: A Treatise on Gunshot Wounds. London, 1827, p. 3.

29. HARDY, J. D., WOLFF, H. G., AND GOODELL, H.: Pain Sensations and Reactions. Baltimore, Williams & Wilkins, 1952.

30. HILLIS, B. R.: The assessment of cough suppressing drugs. Lancet *1:* 1230-1235, 1952.

31. HOUDE, R. W., AND WALLENSTEIN, S. L.: A method for evaluating analgesics in patients with chronic pain. Drug Addiction & Narcotics Bull., Appendix F: 660-682, 1953.

32. JELLINEK, E. M.: Clinical tests on comparative effectiveness of analgesic drugs. Biomet. Bull. *2:* 87-91, 1946.

33. KEATS, A. S., BEECHER, H. K., AND MOSTELLER, F. C.: Measurement of pathological pain in distinction to experimental pain. J. Appl. Physiol. *1:* 35-44, 1950.

34. KEATS, A. S., D'ALESSANDRO, G. L., AND BEECHER, H. K.: A controlled study of pain relief by intravenous procaine. J.A.M.A. *147:* 1761-1763, 1951.

35. KEELE, C. A.: The assay of analgesic drugs on man. Analyst *77:* 111-117, 1952.

36. KEELE, K. D.: The pain chart. Lancet *2:* 6-8, 1948.

37. LASAGNA, L., AND BEECHER, H. K.: The optimal dose of morphine. J.A.M.A. *156:* 230-234, 1954.

38. LASAGNA, L., MOSTELLER, F., VON FELSINGER, J. M., AND BEECHER, H. K.: A study of the placebo response. Amer. J. Med. *16:* 770-779, 1954.

39. ——, ——, AND ——: Drug induced mood changes in man. I. Observations on healthy subjects, chronically ill patients, and "post-addicts." J.A.M.A. *157:* 1006-1020, 1955.

40. MARSHALL, H. R.: Pain, pleasure, and aesthetics. Macmillan, London, 1894.

41. STEVENS, S. S.: Measurement and man. Science *127:* 383-389, 1958.

42. STRONG, G. A.: The psychology of pain. Psychol. Rev. *2:* 329-347, 1895.

43. TRAVELL, J., RINZLER, S. H., BAKST, H., BENJAMIN, Z. H., AND BOBB, A. L.: Comparison of effects of alpha-tocopherol and a matching placebo on chest pain in patients with heart disease. Ann. N.Y. Acad. Sci. *52:* 345-353, 1949.

44. WOLF, S., AND PINSKY, R. H.: Effects of placebo administration and occurrence of toxic reactions. J.A.M.A. *155:* 339-341, 1954.

6

THE PERCEPTION OF TASTE: SOME PSYCHOPHYSIOLOGICAL, PATHOPHYSIOLOGICAL, PHARMACOLOGICAL AND CLINICAL ASPECTS*

by ROLAND FISCHER, FRANCES GRIFFIN
and BENJAMIN PASAMANICK†

> "My substitute, then, for your problem of describing the nature of the universe which we experience, would be the problem of forming a description of a universe which makes sense of our experience."—*H. Dingle*

ANIMALS PICK UP DIFFERENT KINDS of stimulus information in accordance with their peculiar way of life and characteristic for the species. Analogously, humans can display intraspecies individuality by the kind and amount of stimulus information they are able to pick up. As examples, genetically governed differences in taste thresholds and differences in drug responsivity[57] can be mentioned. To be more specific and to develop our point farther, let me quote in this context the "Fair Gourmand," Brillat-Savarin (in 1883): "The sensation of taste is a chemical process, . . . that is the sapid molecules must be dissolved in some fluid, in order to be thereupon absorbed by the nervous projections . . ."[9]

"What we perceive," says Klüver[15] "are never specific or unique properties of individual objects but only properties which such objects share with" . . . . "other objects." We may say, therefore, that what quinine molecules, e.g., share with the receptor phase, represents an informational relationship, resulting in bitter taste sensation. Since

---

*A short version of this paper was presented at the 53rd Annual Meeting of the American Psychopathological Association, Feb. 22-23, 1963, New York City.

†Research Division, Department of Psychiatry, Medical College, Ohio State University, Columbus, Ohio.

quinine is a typical drug, we may regard bitterness as a sensory expression of drug‡ activity. Moreover—as we shall indicate later— quantitative taste thresholds for quinine or for certain other drugs may be indicators of pharmacogenetic, psychophysiological and patho- physiological peculiarities. From this point of view, the study of drug activity includes the study of drug responders.

From Taste Formation to Information

Although the bitter taste sensation of quinine is somewhat removed from the "total reality" of the chemical, it represents vital information about quinine molecules in their relation to the drug (taste) responder. How do we conceptualize the transformation and transmission of this information? The affinity of a drug implies its sorption to the receptor membrane protein.[22,23] This affinity can also be equated with an energy input modifying the molecular configuration of the receptor and hence its permeability. Through this transconformation[79] the protein performs the function of a transducer. The resulting "sodium pump" is then regarded as the source of an action potential which may be registered within 30 msec. after the chemical stimulus reaches the surface of the tongue.[4] Modulation of the time sequence of successive signals carry the information. Depolarization is followed by hyperpolarization and other processes occurring in the dendrite. This must be followed then by a discussion of spatial aspects of nerve impulse reception in the brain, the filtration of signals and the increase of contrast. How, finally, these phenomena give rise to taste sensation is not known.

Clark[12] made a few experiments with varying constants to see how many different formulae could be used to interpret the same set of figures which depict relations between concentration and action if a variation of $\pm$ 5 per cent were allowed. Interestingly, Langmuir's formula expressing the drug-receptor absorption equilibrium, and the well known Weber-Fechner law,* are both within limits, strikingly similar exponential functions, large portions of the two curves even being identical. We may add that processes with slower time rates of change than perception, i.e., learning,[77] forgetting,[38] growth,[76] aging,[52]

---

‡Our special definition for drugs in this paper is: nitrogenous bases (a) water soluble in a concentration of at least 1×10^{-6} M; (b) bitter tasting in concentra- tions up to 1.5×10^{-3} M; (c) to tasters, that is subjects who taste quinine sulfate or 6-n-propylthiouracil as bitter in concentrations of at least 1.2×10^{-5} M and 9.4×10^{-5} M respectively.

*or Stevens' (1961) power law function.

and evolution[65] are also exponential phenomena. It would seem that our laws which describe drug-receptor interaction are mirror images of those psychophysical laws which deal with the sensory representation of biological activity.

Of particular interest here is the taste receptor site[7] and the way in which an influx of K^+ and efflux of Na^+—via active transport[58]—may be linked to a phosphoprotein as the transporting system.[48,55] The spatial distribution of such a phosphoprotein membrane area accessible for excitation is assumed to fluctuate randomly with time.[60] This fluctuation is the result of the affinity† of the chemical to the membrane. Bitterness, incidentally, is that taste quality which is elicited with fewer molecules of a chemical than are necessary for the production of other taste qualities. One needs approximately a 2000 times higher concentration of sucrose to taste its sweetness than that necessary to taste the bitterness of quinine. Teleologically, it might be said that the bitter taste quality is evidently carrying information of the highest survival value for the organism, especially in view of the bitterness of most of the poisons and drugs naturally occurring as well as synthetic. The hydrogen bonded quinine molecules—or other drug molecules—elicit the active transport of Na^+ against the concentration and electrical gradients in the receptor membrane. Branson[8] calculated a model for the squid axon which transports 20 $\mu\mu$moles/ cm.² sec. of Na^+. Inserting this value in equation $H = 7.3 \times 10^{13}$ bits/cm.² sec., where H stands for information or negentropy, it can be assumed that the information units, the bits, appearing in the equation are identical with those used in discussing the information content of the printed page. In terms of a familiar example, taking the information content of a single printed page as 10^4 bits, the equation requires that the cm.² of nerve surface produce information equivalent to that contained in a library of 7.3 million volumes of a 1000 pages each second—this is over half the number of books in the Library of Congress. This value is not inordinate in comparison with the estimates of the information content of biological objects, where for man the value is of the order of 10^{25} bits.

We will proceed now 1) to factors, local and systemic, which relate to, and are an expression of, differences in taste thresholds between certain individuals, i.e., between sensitive and insensitive ("non"-)

---

†For quantitative expressions of affinity and intrinsic activity, see Ariens;[2] for a discussion whether the active transport system should be regarded as an enzymatic or non-enzymatic mechanism, see Christensen.[11]

tasters and 2) with certain normal behavioral traits and pathological states associated with high taste thresholds for certain drugs and other compounds.

DIFFERENCES IN SALIVARY COMPOSITION BETWEEN SENSITIVE TASTERS* OF 6-N-PROPYLTHIOURACIL (*PROP*) AND QUININE AND VERY INSENSITIVE ("NON"-) TASTERS OF PROP AND QUININE†

The classical hypothesis of "non-tasting" or "taste-blindness" refers to the inability to taste the bitter phenylthioureas, and is based on homozygosity for simple Mendelian recessive alleles.[27] Most of the published studies on the genetics of taste thresholds, however, have been carried out with phenylthiourea (PTC), a toxic, impure and odorous compound. It is not surprising, therefore, that the literature abounds with discrepancies apparently based on the utilization of defective techniques which have not provided reliable data.[33,34,61] Instead we advocate the use of another thiourea-type (taster-"non"-taster) differentiator compound, 6-n-propylthiouracil (PROP) because it is an *odorless* structural analog of PTC and the *least toxic* of the phenylthioureas.

Our taste-test method is a modification[36] of the Harris-Kalmus[47] double blind placebo procedure including the final sorting out technique with a range of variability 0 to −1. That PROP is at least as good a differentiator as PTC can be shown, as we have, e.g., by determining the taste thresholds of 66 college age subjects for both compounds. We used the Harris-Kalmus procedure with our modifications —i.e., the use of glass distilled water instead of tap water and a distilled water rinse between each cup—and obtained a high positive correlation (r = +0.873). See table 1.

Previously we reported[28,46] that in very insensitive ("non"-) tasters, the spectrophotometrically determined salivary oxidation rate of PROP and of other H—Ṅ—Ċ = S type goitrogens, measured as the so-called "8 min △ O.D." effect, is twice as fast as in sensitive tasters. Twenty-

---

*That is, subjects who can differentiate 9.38 x 10^{-5} M concentrations of PROP or less (solution No. 8) from distilled water. These subjects who constitute about 20-25 per cent of a Caucasian population can also differentiate 5.86 x 10^{-6} M solutions of quinine, or less (solution No. 4).

†That is, subjects who can only differentiate half saturated solutions (No. 13 = 3.00 x 10^{-3} M) or higher concentrations of PROP from distilled water. These subjects who constitute about 10 per cent of a Caucasian population, also can not differentiate less than 4.69 x 10^{-5} M quinine solutions corresponding to solution No. 7.

TABLE 1

PROP Solution No.	PTC Solution No.																Total Subjects
	16	15	14	13	12	11	10	9	8	7	6	5	4	3	2	1	
14	2																2
13	1	2	1	1		1		1									7
12			4		1			1									6
11		2	3							1							6
10								1	4								5
9									2	7	3						12
8								2	10	3							15
7									1	2	6	1					10
6														1			1
5														1			1
4															1		1
3																	
Total Subjects	3	4	8	1	1	1		5	17	13	9	1		2	1		66

TABLE 1.—Distribution of Taste Thresholds—Measured by our Modified Harris-Kalmus Procedure—of 66 College Students for 6-n-Propylthiouracil (PROP) and Phenylthiourea (PTC). Each Solution Is Double the Concentration of the Next Lower Solution, e.g., No. 16 = 2.4 x 10^{-2} M and No. 15 = 1.2 x 10^{-2} M. A Solution Number Represents an Identical Molar Concentration for each Compound. Note That Our Ascending Series of Solution Numbers Expresses Increasing Concentrations, Whereas That of Harris and Kalmus Does Not.

There is a high positive correlation ($r = + 0.873$) between the taste thresholds of 66 subjects for PROP and PTC.

minute samples of mixed morning saliva were used in these studies. Very insensitive ("non"-) tasters, it should be mentioned, display about twice as low a salivary flow rate than do sensitive tasters, which makes the just mentioned observation about their twice as fast salivary oxidation rate even more significant. Subsequently we reported[31] that other compounds chemically unrelated to the thioureas, are also oxidized faster in the mouth of an insensitive ("non"-) taster of PROP and quinine than in that of a sensitive taster. An example: from 5 cc. of an aqueous .235 μM chlorpromazine solution kept in the mouth for 5 seconds, approximately 28 per cent will be oxidized by very insensitive ("non"-) tasters, whereas only half as much is oxidized by sensitive tasters. The differential disappearance of chlorpromazine can be measured at $\lambda \, \frac{H_2O}{max.} = 254$ mμ with a spectrophotometer ("Spectracord 4000A" Perkin-Elmer). Chlorpromazine has only been chosen to illustrate a general phenomenon.

At this point we should like to give a summary report of new data related to the above difference in salivary oxidation rate. Firstly, the meaning of the "8-min $\triangle$ O.D." effect should be clarified. Recently,[28] it was reported that dialysis tubing—among other things—removed the ability of saliva to display the "8-min. $\triangle$ O.D." effect. In the meantime we found that dialysis tubing contains a reducing factor also discovered by Lilly and Owen-Vallance[59] and described as an insulin antagonizing sulfur compound. According to Dr. J. Gander (Columbus, Ohio) the reducing compound apparently is glutathion. If Visking tubing is washed in water until the washing water stops decolorizing potassium permanganate, the tubing is freed from its reducing impurity. Saliva dialyzed with such tubing no longer shows the "8 min. $\triangle$ O.D." effect. Addition of the dialyzate to the dialyzed saliva restores the effect. We therefore conclude that the "8 min. $\triangle$ O.D." effect is produced by a water-soluble, easily reducible and dializable factor of low molecular weight. It is also inferred that the factor is likely to be reduced by compounds such as the thioureas, certain imidazoles, and other reducing antithyroid drugs containing the $H—\dot{N}—\dot{C} = S$ grouping.

Likely candidates for the factor among salivary constituents are iodine,[62] hydrogen peroxide and possibly ferrichloride.[54] If centrifuged saliva, more specifically its supernatant, as processed by Griffin and Fischer[46] and Fischer and Griffin,[29] is incubated for 3 minutes with 0.3 mg./ml. beef liver catalase (Worthington chemicals) at 17° C. and 27° C. prior to the addition of PROP, the "8-min. $\triangle$ O.D." effect is abolished. We conclude therefore, that the "8-min. $\triangle$ O.D." effect which is at least twice as large in very insensitive ("non"-)tasters than in sensitive tasters of PROP and quinine and is an expression of the greater salivary oxidation rate of PROP, is largely produced by hydrogen peroxide.

It is not possible, however, to lower by more than one solution number the taste threshold of a very insensitive ("non"-)taster of PROP by asking him to taste PROP—in a concentration which is one solution number (threshold) below his actual threshold—dissolved in about 1 mg./5 cc. beef liver catalase. The tasted total volume = 5 cc.; the respective placebo contained only the enzyme.

It is evident, therefore, that although hydrogen peroxide is largely responsible for the twice as high salivary oxidation rate displayed by very insensitive ("non"-) tasters of PROP and quinine, the difference in the magnitude of the "8-min △ O.D." effect can not account for more than one threshold—that is, a twofold concentration difference—between very insensitive ("non"-) tasters and sensitive tasters. Another line of experimentation leads to the same conclusion. When 3, 4, 5-trihydroxybenzoic acid (i.e., propylgallate; Tenox PG), a water-soluble antioxidant and PROP are simultaneously administered in an equimolecular ratio at the highly resolved* so-called "fine" threshold of a subject for PROP: the resulting lowering of taste threshold (increase in sensitivity) for PROP is not greater than one threshold in both the very insensitive ("non"-) tasters and sensitive tasters.

PHYSICO-CHEMICAL DIFFERENCES BETWEEN THE RECEPTOR SITE OF SENSITIVE TASTERS OF 6-N-PROPYLTHIOURACIL AND QUININE, AND INSENSITIVE ("NON-") TASTERS

Up to now and in terms of differential salivary oxidation rates, we were able to account for only one threshold difference between very insensitive ("non"-) tasters and sensitive tasters of PROP and quinine. An 8-16-fold threshold difference is, therefore, still in need of interpretation. Under these circumstances we resorted to the operational assumption, that *at threshold the available sites of the receptor phase are occupied by PROP and quinine molecules.*

Historically, adsorption as a factor in taste perception has already been implied by Cameron.[10] It has been discussed explicitly by Ferguson and Lawrence;[20] Beidler[5] expressed the relationship between concentration and taste intensity through Freundlich- or Langmuir-type equations. Beidler[6] recently proposed a Lineweaver-Burk-type equation for the possibility of a theoretical prediction of "the intensity of sensation reported by a human subject to certain mixtures of two taste substances of similar taste quality."

Since the taste threshold of a drug can be regarded as pharmaco-sensory expression of drug-receptor interaction, we subjected taste thresholds for PROP and quinine to a biophysical interpretation.

Method

Taste thresholds for quinine sulfate, U.S.P. or N.F. (Mallinckrodt, St.

---

*Highly resolved means ten-fold increase in sensitivity (resolution) as compared to our modification of the Harris-Kalmus[47] procedure.

Louis), and for 6-n-propylthiouracil U.S.P. (Mann, New York), were determined in healthy, normal, trained subjects by the Harris-Kalmus[47] procedure as modified by Fischer and Griffin.[29] This method was used during the subject's training period which consisted of one to two threshold determinations per week for at least 3 weeks.

For this procedure, the solution numbers represent powers of two, that is, each number denotes a doubling of the concentration, e.g., solution number 5 is twice as concentrated as number 4. To increase the resolution of the taste threshold determination, finer concentration intervals based on fractional powers of 2 were prepared, e.g., the range between solution number 4 and 5 was subdivided into continuous intervals of $2^{1/10}$. With this modification "fine" taste thresholds for series of binary mixtures of quinine and PROP were determined. The concentration of one compound was held constant while the concentration of the second was decreased in $2^{2/10}$ steps until a taste threshold was reached. Then the accuracy of the taste threshold was further increased by the application of the same procedure but using concentration intervals of $2^{1/10}$ steps. This procedure was repeated reversing the order of the compounds. For each subject approximately 120 combinations of the compounds were tested on two occasions within a 5-day period. A subject's "rough" threshold and then his "fine" thresholds for quinine and PROP (in this order) were determined on each experimental day and used as a baseline prior to the collection of data for that test day. Although there may occur fluctuations in the baseline of a subject—up to one solution number—from one day to another, the precision of our method is within the limits of a $2^{1/10}$ interval, whereas its accuracy is half as great for each test day. This constancy of the units of concentration relative to the values of the particular baseline of the subject on the test day enables us to collect and plot data from subjects daily over periods of 2 to 3 weeks. The characteristic pattern of a plot or part of it obtained in this manner can be replicated at any future testing session. Above all, discrete values can be replicated irrespective of the order of the presentation of the concentrations.

Results

The most important finding *is the discontinuous pattern in the taste sensation of certain subthreshold concentrations of binary mixtures of PROP and quinine.*

Our data can easily be visualized through pictorial presentation of

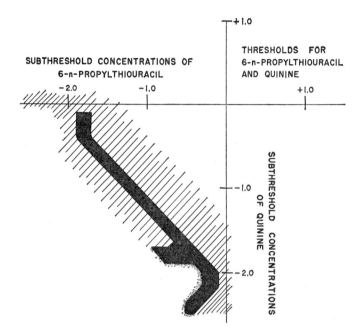

FIG. 1.—Tasted (hatched area) and non-tasted (shaded area) concentrations of binary mixtures of 6-n-propylthiouracil (PROP) and quinine for a typical insensitive ("non"-)taster of PROP. Concentration intervals are powers of 2; the intersection of the ordinate and abscissa represents the taste thresholds of the subject for PROP and quinine alone. Negative numbers denote subthreshold concentrations of PROP (abscissa) and quinine (ordinate) in the binary mixtures. The discontinuity of taste sensation is not proportional to the concentration of the components in the binary mixture. Examples: (a) subthreshold concentration –1.9 PROP and –1.0 quinine are a tasted combination; (b) –1.0 PROP and –1.2 quinine (in the shaded area) are not tasted; (c) the still lower concentration of –1.0 PROP and –1.4 quinine, however, is a tasted combination.

the tasted and non-tasted concentrations of the binary mixtures of PROP and quinine for a typical insensitive ("non"-)taster of PROP. In figure 1 the taste threshold of the subject on the experimental day for the single compound was: quinine* $= 1.77$ x 10^{-5} M and PROP $= 1.98$ x 10^{-3} M. The intersection of the ordinate and abscissa represents the subject's threshold for quinine and PROP, i.e., the baseline. Left of the intersection on the abscissa, subthreshold concentrations of PROP appear as negative numbers; below the intersection on the

---

*Although quinine sulfate (U.S.P.) crystals were used to prepare the solutions, their molarity (fig. 1) refers to that of the free base.

ordinate, subthreshold concentrations of quinine appear as negative numbers. The numbers denote concentration intervals based on powers of 2; for example: —1 indicates 2^{-1}, that is, ½ of the concentration at the baseline; —2 indicates 2^{-2}, that is, ¼ of the concentration at the baseline.

Interpretation of our data can be facilitated by transposing the exponential plot of figure 1 into a linear representation (see figure 2).

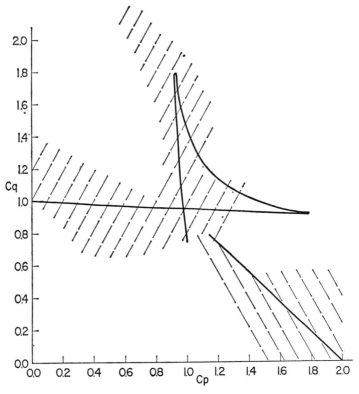

Fig. 2.—Isothermal taste diagram for binary mixtures of quinine and 6-n-propyl-thiouracil (PROP) at room temperature for a typical insensitive ("non"-) taster of the compounds. In contradistinction to the exponential representation in fig. 1, this figure is a linear representation of the same data supplemented with additional results. $C_q = 1.0$ represents the quinine threshold of the subject, whereas $C_p = 1.0$ represents ½ of the PROP threshold. This adjustment makes it possible to superimpose experimental data and theoretical curve. Representative quinine and PROP threshold concentrations for a typical ("non"-) taster correspond to 1.55 x 10^{-5} M (solution No. 5.4) and 1.31 x 10^{-3} M (solution No. 11.8), respectively.

In figure 2 the taste threshold concentrations of a typical insensitive ("non"-) taster for quinine and PROP are represented as concentrations of quinine (C_q) plotted against the concentrations of PROP (C_p). All concentrations have been adjusted by a constant factor so that the feature of interest appears at values of C_p near 1.

The hatched areas represent those concentration combinations of quinine and PROP which are not tasted by the subject. The white areas (with the exception of the area near the origin) represent concentration combinations of the two drugs which are tasted. Forty combinations were found to be sufficient to define the no-taste areas. Between 60 and 80 measurements were necessary to cover the important features of the areas representing tasted combinations.

The boundary between tasted combinations and non-tasted ones defines a phase diagram for the taste phenomenon. Figure 2, in fact, resembles quite closely an isothermal solubility diagram of a pair of salts having an ion in common, both of which are dissolved in a fixed amount of solvent.[21]

Discussion

If drug-receptor interaction is considered as an equilibrium process in taste perception, we can regard the water solution as one of the phases and the taste receptor as the other phase of our system. The two components of this system are the two drugs or possibly their positive ions which may combine with sites in the receptor phase and be associated with anions in the solution phase. Further assumptions were, firstly, that dilution effects by saliva are negligible since the volume of a taste test solution is approximately 5 ml., whereas the average volume of saliva secreted during each step of a taste test is approximately 0.04 to 0.18 ml. Secondly, that the receptor phase does not significantly alter the concentration of the compounds in the water solution phase. Thirdly, it was assumed that at threshold all available sites of the receptor phase are occupied by PROP and quinine molecules.

In order to deal with the taste phenomenon in terms of an isothermal diagram, we have resorted to the regular solution theory of Porter,[69] Heitler,[49] Hildebrand[50] and Hildebrand and Scott.[51] We determined the boundary (thresholds) theoretically and compared it to the envelope separating the experimentally determined non-tasted combinations from the tasted ones. The mathematical treatment of these assumptions has been published elsewhere.[70]

An examination of figure 2 reveals a qualitative correlation between the leaf-like shape of the theoretical threshold curve and the dividing envelope in the region of high quinine concentrations (e.g., those greater than 0.6). The qualitative agreement between the theoretical curve and the experimentally obtained envelopes allows us to make the following conclusions. At threshold a certain number of sites in the receptor are occupied by either quinine molecules or an unknown compound formed from quinine and PROP. The attraction forces between quinine molecules or the attraction forces between the molecules of the new unknown compound are greater than forces of attraction between molecules of quinine and the new compound. This type of interaction gives the leaf-like threshold envelope as long as there are some quinine molecules in the receptor phase. The energy of interaction denotes the degree of electrostatic attraction—or repulsion—between molecules. A comparison of the C_p values of a typical insensitive ("non-") taster with that of a typical sensitive taster of PROP (see page 2, Rubin, Griffin and Fischer, 1962) shows a 6.5-fold difference. Energy of interaction, on the other hand, is inversely proportional to the distance between receptor sites and is lower in a typical insensitive ("non-") taster than in a typical sensitive taster of PROP. Therefore we infer that the receptor sites per unit receptor volume are probably farther apart in a typical insensitive ("non-") taster than in a typical sensitive taster of PROP.

At high PROP concentrations (e.g., those greater than 1.0) the dividing envelope is a diagonal straight line pointing toward and including the PROP threshold (see lower right portion of curve in figure 2). This area, we postulate, corresponds to a receptor phase free of quinine molecules. It is not unreasonable, then, to assume that the net attraction forces are zero and the theoretical curve becomes a diagonal straight line corresponding to a perfect solution mixture of PROP and the unknown compound in the receptor phase.

The qualitative correlation between the theory of regular solutions applied to the phase rule and experimental evidence allows us to regard the taste threshold of a drug or of a mixture of drugs as a specific state of part of the receptor with a given number of receptor sites occupied by drug molecules. Taste threshold concentrations of a subject for various compounds depend then upon the number of available sites as well as the magnitudes of the partition coefficients.[70] Since the values of the partition coefficients in the gel of the receptor phase differ for insensitive ("non"-) tasters from those of sensitive tasters on the one hand and partition coefficients are implicitly temperature dependent on the other, we are now involved in investigating the influence of variations in temperature in relation to the structure of the taste diagram of the receptor phase.

TASTE THRESHOLDS AND DRUG RESPONSE

A. General Aspects

The isothermal taste diagram (fig. 2) actually illustrates a dose-response curve for binary mixtures of quinine and PROP. Taste (white) or non-taste (hatched) areas represent certain combinations of the two drugs giving rise to phenomena which can be interpreted as positive or negative synergism in the terminology of Gaddum,[41] as discussed by Schueler.[73]

Such an interpretation may also help to account for the apparent synergism produced by binary mixtures of PROP (or quinine) and certain thyroxine precursors.[36,46] Such mixtures containing each compound in *sub*-threshold concentrations produce bitter taste in concentrations substantially lower than the original threshold of a subject.

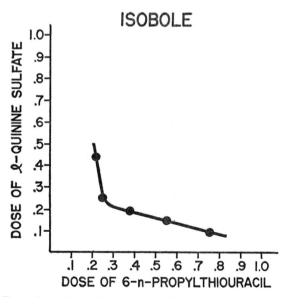

FIG. 3.—Taste threshold as drug response. Isobole indicating coalitive synergism for certain binary mixtures of PROP and quinine in a subject whose fine taste threshold for PROP and quinine is 6.8 and 5.8 respectively.

We can also plot the taste thresholds of certain molar ratios of PROP and quinine so that 1.0 represents on the abscissa the threshold of a subject for one of the components of the binary mixture, while 1.0 on the ordinate stands for the other component. The resulting isobole depicts coalitive synergism—see figure 3—if drug activity and drug threshold are treated as analogous biological responses and the response is only obtainable with the combination of the two components of the mixture but not with either of the compounds alone.

Such an isobole is only one of several possible types[16] and may be interpreted as a characteristic systemic response of a particular subject to the binary mixture. In our preliminary experiments, sensitive and insensitive drug responders produce characteristically different isoboles for the same pair of drugs.

The response in figure 3 is greater than additive since the sum of fractional doses for each PROP-quinine mixture is less than 1.0. For example, the taste threshold for the molar ratio PROP over quinine $= 2$, occurs at 0.25 dose of quinine and 0.25 dose of PROP.

B. Specific Aspects

In the following it is intended to illustrate differences in fine

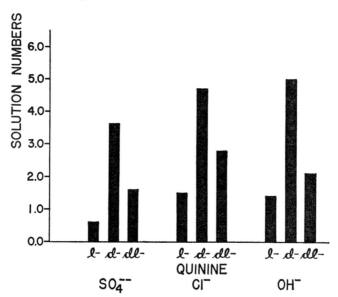

Fig. 4.—Fine taste thresholds of a sensitive taster of PROP (8) and quinine (3) for d-quinine and l-quinine and their racemates for sulfate, chloride and free base respectively.

thresholds between quinine—the *l*evorotatory form of the drug—and quinidine, the *d*extrorotatory isomer, for a sensitive taster (fig. 4) and a very insensitive ("non"-) taster (fig. 5) of PROP and quinine. The free bases, the sulfates and chlorides of both the d- and l-quinine as well as their racemates have been tested.

These data—the results of three experiments—show that our sensitive taster (fig. 4) displays low thresholds for l-quinine and higher thresholds for d-quinine for the sulfate, chloride and free base. There is a difference of about three thresholds between the l- and d-forms. Our very insensitive ("non"-) taster (fig. 5)—a PROP 14 subject—displays, although with high thresholds, a pattern similar to that of the sensitive taster with one exception. The l-quinine chloride threshold in our very insensitive ("non"-) taster (fig. 5), is higher than that for d-quinine chloride, whereas the opposite was true in a sensitive taster (fig. 4).

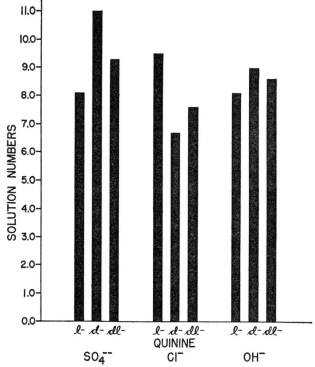

FIG. 5.—Fine taste thresholds of a very insensitive ("non"-) taster of PROP (14) and quinine (8) for l-quinine, d-quinine, and their racemates for sulfate, chloride and free base respectively.

It is too early to make generalized conclusions in relation to the above difference. PROP 13-14 subjects are relatively rare—they represent about 10-12 per cent of a Caucasian population—and we need to collect more data about them. It may well turn out that they fall into two classes: one with relatively low d-quinine chloride thresholds, like our subject in figure 5, and one with relatively high d-quinine chloride thresholds. However, our present finding—if duplicated— could be interpreted as a major stereospecific difference in the fine structure of the receptor site between sensitive tasters and certain very insensitive ("non"-) tasters.

We have seen that taste thresholds for all d-forms are higher —especially in sensitive tasters[*]—than for l-forms. This indicates— in our terms—that l-quinine is a more potent systemic drug than d-quinine. In other words, low thresholds are indicative of greater biological (re) activity for both the subject and the drug. Indeed, the l-form is described as displaying higher antimalarial activity[82] than the d-form of quinine; in addition, the systemic reactivity of the drugs— in terms of toxicity—also displays the same relationship: the oral LD_{50} of the l-form is 214.8 $\pm$ 25.1 mg./kg. for the mouse,[67] whereas the corresponding value for the d-form is 535 mg./kg.[71] In summary then, an approximately twofold difference in toxicity is reflected in a threefold difference in taste thresholds in sensitive tasters. We empha- size, however, that only *systemic reactivities* should be related to taste thresholds; isolated organ preparations—i.e., isolated and electrically stimulated rat ventricle strips[63]—will show no difference in activity between l-quinine sulfate and d-quinine sulfate in concentrations of 5×10^{-6} to 3×10^{-5} M which are incidentally also taste threshold con- centrations for an average quinine taster. It would appear that lower taste thresholds may be indicators of higher *systemic* reactivity only.

Another pair of isomers also illustrates the same relationship. The LD_{50}, after very slow intravenous injection (1.0 cc. in 2 min.) of L-amphetamine, is 79.2 $\pm$ 8.5 mg./Kg. in the mouse, whereas that of the 16 times more active D-amphetamine is 5.0 $\pm$ 1.3 mg./Kg.[80] The coarse taste thresholds for the same two drugs correspond to a fourfold concentration difference in an insensitive ("non"-) taster of PROP and quinine, whereas a sensitive taster displayed a twofold concentration difference. In both subjects the more active D-amphetamine had the lower threshold in comparison with the L-amphetamine.

---

[*]About three thresholds corresponding to a $2^3 = 8$-fold concentration difference.

Other drugs—not only stereoisomers—also conform to this relationship. Desmethylimipramine (Geigy 35020), the "active metabolite"[44] of imipramine (Tofranil, Geigy), and Ensidon (Geigy 33040) are both tasted in twofold lower concentrations by sensitive tasters and insensitive ("non"-) tasters alike than the parent compound Tofranil. Desmethylimipramine as well as Ensidon are accordingly described as more active antidepressant drugs, as is Tofranil.[3] The same relationship holds for chlorpromazine (i.p. LD_{50} in the mouse = 190 mg./Kg.) and its sulfoxide (LD_{50} in the mouse = 163 mg./Kg.). The latter is more toxic; however, for other reasons this mildly sedative drug of very short duration is of no pharmaceutical interest.[64] The systemic toxicity values of the two drugs, on the other hand, are again related to their taste thresholds; specifically the more toxic sulfoxide displays the lower taste thresholds in both sensitive tasters and insensitive ("non"-) tasters.

Interestingly, larger doses of imipramine are required—according to Herr, Stewart and Charest—than of chlorpromazine if a given degree of effect is to be obtained on a particular test (such as potentiation of hexobarbital and alcohol narcosis, decrease of body temperature, etc.). The taste threshold of imipramine, the less potent compound, is accordingly higher, we find, than that of chlorpromazine.

These examples were cited in order to call attention to a general relationship. No particular emphasis was laid on the numerical values of the "coarse" taste thresholds. Only the quinine data were measured as highly resolved "fine" thresholds.

To answer another question, whether or not the fine thresholds for certain dl-quinine mixtures are additive in relation to their respective d- and l-thresholds, our data have been treated analogously to the diagrammatical representation of drug interaction, according to Gaddum[41] as interpreted by Schueler.[73] The details of these calculations will be published elsewhere; it should suffice to remark, however, that they allow the tentative prediction that a dl-mixture of quinine free base, e.g., may be a drug displaying positive synergism if compared to the activity of the d- or l-form alone.

Two Ranges of Taste Sensitivity

Two years ago we made the incidental observation that a very insensitive ("non"-) taster of PROP and quinine was unable to taste chlorpromazine solutions below solution number 12. We then determined the coarse taste thresholds for chlorpromazine of 17 subjects using the Harris-Kalmus procedure with our modifications and employing fresh chlorpromazine hydrochloride solutions, prepared just prior to each concentration step of the taste testing. Age, sex and smoking habits have been matched for both groups, the very insensitive ("non"-) tasters of PROP and quinine and the rest of the sample.[31] Figure 6 illustrates the results showing that the insensitive group displays higher chlorpromazine thresholds (solution No. 10-12) than the rest of the subjects—with PROP threshold 12 and below and quinine 2 to 6—who are tasters—with low thresholds (solution No. 7-9) of chlorpromazine.

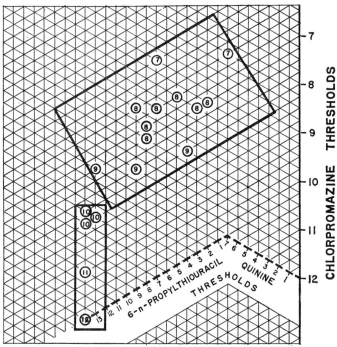

FIG. 6.—Taste threshold correlation diagram for 6-n-propylthiouracil (PROP), quinine and chlorpromazine for 17 subjects. Insensitive ("non"-) tasters of PROP (threshold 13-14) and quinine (7 and above) are also insensitive tasters of chlorpromazine (10-12), whereas sensitive tasters of PROP and quinine are also sensitive tasters of chlorpromazine (7-9). Taste thresholds are marked as solution numbers using 14 concentrations ranging from taste solution $2 = 1.46 \times 10^{-6}$ M to $14 = 6 \times 10^{-3}$ M, each numbered step representing a doubling of the concentration. The dotted line indicates by way of example the method by which one subject's data have been plotted; his thresholds are quinine 7, PROP 14 and chlorpromazine 12.

Our next relevant observation was made during the administration of psilocybin to subjects whose fingertappings were recorded prior, at the peak, and 24 hours after a psilocybin experience.[26] It was noted that one of our volunteers tasted the aqueous 1.13 x 10⁻³ M (No. 11.6) solution of psilocybin administered orally, whereas the other did not. Incidentally the psilocybin "non"-taster reacted minimally to the drug while the psilocybin-taster had a full blown "model psychosis."[24,25]

We then determined the taste thresholds for a variety of compounds of three insensitive ("non"-) tasters versus seven sensitive tasters of PROP and quinine. The first six compounds tested were $H — \overset{.}{N} — \overset{.}{C} = S$ type goitrogens, whereas the other compounds constituted a variety of drugs and chemicals (see table 2 and 3 and figure 7). It is evident from the comparison of thresholds between the two taste-groups that they display two characteristically different ranges of taste sensitivity for a large variety of compounds. It should be emphasized that we did not employ *very* insensitive ("non"-) tasters of PROP and quinine for these comparative studies. We wished to show that it is sufficient

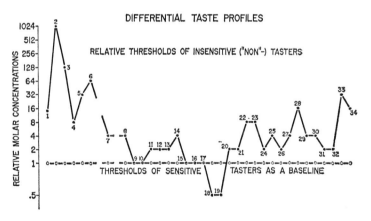

FIG. 7.—Taste thresholds for 34 compounds of sensitive tasters of 6-n-propyl-thiouracil and quinine as a baseline (N = 3). The threshold of these subjects was No. 3 for quinine and No. 8 for 6-n-propylthiouracil. Taste thresholds for the same compounds of insensitive ("non"-) tasters of 6-n-propylthiouracil and quinine (N = 7) are plotted in relation to the baseline. A typical insensitive ("non"-) taster in this group of seven subjects displays taste threshold No. 6 for quinine and No. 12 for 6-n-propylthiouracil. The relative difference in taste thresholds between sensitive tasters and insensitive ("non"-) tasters is plotted on the ordinate in relative molar concentrations.

TABLE 2.—Taste Thresholds and Relative Taste Thresholds for 34 Compounds as in Figure 7

Compounds		Thresholds				Relative Thresholds	
Name	Number of Compound	Sensitive Tasters		Insensitive ("Non"-) Tasters		Solution Number	Molar Ratio
		Solution Number	Molarity 1×10^5	Solution Number	Molarity 1×10^5		
6-n-propylthiouracil	1	8	9.4	12	150.0	4	16
phenylthiourea	2	6	2.3	16	2400.0	10	1024
thioacetamide	3	9	18.8	16	2400.0	7	128
thiourea	4	11	75.0	14	600.0	3	8
2-mercapto imidazole (Lily 00416)	5	8	9.4	13	300.0	5	32
2-mercapto-5-carbomethoxy imidazole (Lily 00415)	6	5	1.2	11	75.0	6	64
L-ergothioneine*	7	10	37.5	12	150.0	2	4
Chlorpromazine* (Smith, Kline & French)	8	8	9.4	10	37.5	2	4
Mellaril* (Sandoz)	9	8	9.4	8	9.4	0	1
Trifluopromazine* (Squibb)	10	8	9.4	8	9.4	0	1
methylene blue* C.I. No. 922	11	7	4.7	8	9.4	1	2
Chlorpromazine sulfoxide* (Smith, Kline & French)	12	4	0.6	5	1.2	1	2
Geigy 31002*	13	9	18.8	10	37.5	1	2
Ensidon* (Geigy 33040)	14	8	9.4	10	37.5	2	4
Geigy 21169*	15	9	18.8	9	18.8	0	1
Tofranil* (Geigy)	16	9	18.8	9	18.8	0	1
desmethylimipramine*	17	8	9.4	8	9.4	0	1

		11	75.0	10	37.5	−1	.5
19	2-mercapto-4 (or 5)-imidazole carboxylic acid (Lily 07882)						
20	acetamide	18	9600.0	19	19200.0	1	2
21	urea	17	4800.0	18	9600.0	1	2
22	L-phenylalanine	14	600.0	17	4800.0	3	8
23	DL-phenylalanine	13	300.0	16	2400.0	3	8
24	D-amphetamine sulfate	8	9.4	10	37.5	2	4
25	L-amphetamine sulfate	8	9.4	9	18.8	1	2
26	β-(3,4-dihydroxyphenyl)-L-α-alanine (DL-Dopa)	11	75.0	12	150.0	1	2
27	sucrose	15	1200.0	17	4800.0	2	4
28	sodium chloride	12	150.0	16	2400.0	4	16
29	potassium chloride	13	300.0	15	1200.0	2	4
30	hydrochloric acid	10	37.5	12	150.0	2	4
31	n-propyl ester of 3,4,5-trihydroxy benzoic acid (Eastman Tenox PG)	12	150.0	13	300.0	1	2
32	Niamid* (Pfizer)	9	18.8	10	37.5	1	2
33	Antistine* (Ciba)	4	0.6	9	18.8	5	32
34	quinine sulfate	3	0.3	6	2.3	3	8

*Hydrochloride.

Acetamide, reagent grade; potassium chloride, C.P.; sodium chloride, reagent grade; thioacetamide, reagent grade and urea, reagent grade were purchased from J. T. Baker Chemical Company, Phillipsburg, N.J.; sucrose, U.S.P. and thiourea, CfP from California Corp. for Biochemical Research, Los Angeles, Calif.; DL-amphetamine, D-amphetamine, U.S.P.; L-amphetamine, M.A.; DL-Dopa, M.A.; L-phenylalanine, M.A. and 6-n-propylthiouracil, U.S.P. from Mann Research Laboratories, Inc., N.Y.; Phenylthiourea; MP 153-154°C. from Eastman Organic Chemicals, Rochester, N.Y.; DL-phenylalanine from Nutritional Biochemical Corp., Cleveland; hydrochloric acid, C.R. from Fisher Scientific Co, Pittsburgh; quinine, U.S.P. from Mallinckrodt Chemical Works, St. Louis; and methylene blue, first edition, C.I. No. 922, from National Aniline Div., Allied Chemical Dye Corp., New York.

TABLE 3.—Chemical Structure of Certain Compounds

Tofranil (Imipramine)
Desmethylimipramine (Geigy 35020)

R = H if desmethylimipramine
R = CH$_3$ if imipramine

Geigy 31002

Ensidon (Geigy 33040)

Geigy 21169

Geigy 34586

to compare insensitive ("non"-) tasters* with sensitive tasters of PROP and quinine in order to demonstrate the existence of two characteristically different ranges of taste sensitivity for a large variety of compounds.

We tried to discover at least one compound which does not show the above relationship and succeeded in finding that very insensitive ("non"-) tasters of PROP and quinine who are all insensitive tasters of other compounds, also can be either sensitive or insensitive tasters of hydrochloric acid. Our finding is based on the re-evaluation of data obtained in 48 mainly college aged subjects.[29,30] At that time we observed that all PROP "non"-tasters (subjects with thresholds above the antimode, *viz*, solution No. 9, which divides "tasters" from "non"-tasters) can be "high" or "low" for quinine and that those subjects who are "high" for quinine are also "high" for sodium chloride, hydrochloric acid and sucrose. The low quinine subjects, accordingly, were found to be also low for the other three compounds. We know now that the very insensitive ("non"-) tasters of PROP (No. 13-14) are a separate group with quinine thresholds 7 and above† and that it is this group whose members are "high"—insensitive—for most compounds (with the exception of some for hydrochloric acid). The detailed evaluation of these and other data is intended to be published elsewhere. Here it can be emphasized, however, that hydrochloric acid thresholds (in our 48 subjects), are independent of the PROP taster phenotype, the "non"-taster genotype and also independent of a subject's taste threshold for quinine, sodium chloride and sucrose. It appears, therefore, that at least *three* genetic loci may exist for taste: one for PROP-like substances, another for quinine-like which also includes taste competence for sodium chloride and sucrose, and a separate locus for hydrochloric acid and related substances.

The two characteristically different ranges of taste sensitivity, as shown in figure 7, are consistent with and constitute a corollary of the findings described in the previous sections of this paper: the differences in salivary oxidation rate, the difference in partition coefficients of the receptor phase, the stereospecific differences in the receptor site and the

---

*That is, subjects who can differentiate 7.50 x 10^{-4} M (No. 11) and 1.50 x 10^{-3} M (No. 12) concentrations of PROP from distilled water. These subjects, who constitute about 13 per cent of a Caucasian population, can also differentiate 1.77 x 10^{-5} M concentrations or 2.34 x 10^{-5} M (No. 6) solutions of quinine.

†Quinine thresholds conform to a Gaussian distribution in an unselected population, of which the median is solution No. 5.

relation between higher biological (re) activity of man (or drug) and lower taste thresholds. With these considerations in mind, the treatment of taste thresholds for drugs as sensory representation of pharmacological (re) activity, enables us to think along pharmacogenetic lines in approaching the 1) design of new, potent and non-toxic drug combinations from components each of which alone is neither necessarily active nor toxic, and 2) the determination of dose-response relationships for drugs which, like most of the psychotropic drugs, are either administered on a trial and error basis or prescribed on a rather crude dose-body weight basis.

Taste Thresholds and Food Dislikes

Two bitter drugs, PROP—a goitrogen with bimodally distributed taste thresholds—and quinine, the thresholds of which display a Gaussian distribution, were used as parameters to differentiate subjects who display "high" and "low" taste-sensitivities for a wide variety of compounds. Would subjects with high taste thresholds for both compounds differ in their food preferences from subjects with low thresholds for the two drugs?

Forty-eight subjects checked food dislikes on an alphabetical listing of 120 foods previously tested on a college-age Ohio population. Excluding foods unfamiliar or never sampled by each subject, the percentage of familiar foods disliked was used as the individual score. Scores ranged from 0 to 55 per cent; the median was 10 per cent, as in the standard population.

In another report we have already discussed the relevant details and statistical analyses of our data.[35] Dislike for foods could not be significantly related to a subject's sensitivity to, or taste thresholds for, sucrose, sodium chloride, or hydrochloride acid. However, taste threshold for PROP and quinine show a relation to percentage of food dislikes. Specifically the correlation between per cent of food dislikes and thresholds for quinine is statistically highly significant. The linear regression of percentage of food dislikes versus concentrations of quinine is $Y = 23.167 - 2.03 X$. The probability that our sample came from a population of linear regression of zero is 0.001 using Student's t test.

The correlation between percentage food dislikes and quinine concentrations is $+ 0.272$. Although this accounts for only 7.5 per cent of the variance, it is significant at the 0.001 level of confidence. The evidence indicates that taste-acute individuals have more food dislikes or that the number of foods disliked grows in proportion as the taste threshold for bitter compounds decreases.

Actually for 25 per cent of the subjects on one end of the Gaussian distribution, with high taste thresholds (7 to 8 and above) for quinine, a low amount—or no—food dislikes can fairly well be predicted. Similarly, for 25 per cent of the subjects on the other end of the Gaussian distribution, with low quinine thresholds (4 and below), it is easy to predict that they will dislike quite a number of foods. It is indeed only for these discriminating people that the "Great Gourmand", Brillat-Savarin wrote his *Physiologie du Goût* in 1883. For subjects with quinine thresholds 4-7 who constitute the 50 per cent middle range of the Gaussian distribution curve, no prediction can be made as to amount of foods disliked in relation to taste thresholds. In this group cultural, social and idiosyncratic variables will probably decide[19,75] the matter of food aversions.

Taste Thresholds and Smoking

Fordyce[39] reported recently that tests on 147 persons provided no evidence of an association between cigarette smoking and acuity of smell. Through smoking, however, a variety of bitter tasting drugs, e.g., nicotine and other bases*[81] are being dissolved in the saliva and thus tasted. Taste acute individuals could then be expected to dislike cigarettes more than insensitive tasters.

Coarse taste thresholds for quinine sulfate, U.S.P. and PROP, U.S.P. were, therefore, determined twice in 127 subjects, mostly college students. The Harris-Kalmus[47] procedure, with our modifications, was used and the data analyzed in relation to the smoking habits of the same individuals. The detailed presentation of data and their analysis have been published elsewhere by Fischer, Griffin and Kaplan.[37] The summary conclusions are as follows: The proportion of smokers is lower among sensitive tasters of quinine than among insensitive ("non"-) tasters. The converse relation similarly holds. Interestingly this relation is analogous to that observed between high food dislikes and low (sensitive) taste thresholds for quinine (see previous section of this paper). Krut et al. (see[37]) also found a similar correlation between smoking and high taste thresholds for bitter compounds. Moreover,

---

*Namely, 6 aldehydes, 8 ketones, 20 organic acids, 17 alcohols, 18 alkaloids, such as nicotine, anabasine, α-, β-, and γ-socratine, cotinine, etc., 12 pyrrole and pyridine type nitrogenous bases, 30 hydrocarbons, 15 amines and amino acids as well as 20 other organic and inorganic solid constituents.

the report of Krut et al. indicates no correlation between smoking and taste thresholds for sweet, sour and the salty. This is again analogous to our previously described findings describing no correlation between amounts of foods disliked and taste thresholds for sucrose, hydrochloride acid and sodium chloride. Apparently the amount of foods disliked and amount of cigarettes smoked are analogously related to the four "classical" taste qualities.

HIGH TASTE THRESHOLDS IN PARENTS OF CHILDREN AFFECTED WITH DOWN'S SYNDROME (MONGOLISM)

Could the insensitive ("non"-)tasting trait, as an indicator of systemic reactivity and in conjunction with another genetic factor express "predisposition," that is greater risk of developing certain syndromes?

We have investigated, therefore, the possibility of a relationship between "non"-tasting and Down's syndrome. Taste thresholds for quinine sulfate (U.S.P.) and 6-n-propylthiouracil (U.S.P. Mann) were determined in 19 pairs of parents of children affected with Down's syndrome. The double blind placebo and final sorting out procedure of Harris and Kalmus[47] was employed, with our modifications.[29,30] Each subject was tested in the morning at 10:00 A.M. The data are summarized in table 4. They support the observation by Penrose[66] of a maternal age-related dichotomy. The age distribution of mothers in our sample, i.e., age at birth of affected child, is bimodal and with an antimode in the age range from 30 to 35. The fathers belonging to the aforementioned maternal groups are characterized by median ages of 28 and 40, respectively.

The dichotomy between sensitive tasters and insensitive ("non"-) tasters in the general population occurs at threshold 5 for quinine; and for 6-n-propylthiouracil the antimode is at threshold 9.[29,30,35,36]

In our sample of mothers the median quinine threshold (No. 7), although it is two thresholds higher than in an unselected Caucasian population, does not differ in the two age groups, whereas the median PROP threshold is 2 thresholds higher (No. 10) in the older than in the younger (No. 8) age group.[32]

Our figures of a four-fold concentration difference in taste thresholds for PROP, between younger and older mothers of children affected with Down's syndrome, derive from subjects spanning 7-year and 6-year age-ranges. There is no present basis for assuming a measurable

Proband Number	Maternal Quinine Threshold	Maternal 6-n-propyl-thiouracil Threshold	Maternal Age When Child Born	Maternal Age When Tested	Paternal Quinine Threshold	Paternal 6-n-propyl-thiouracil Threshold	Paternal Age When Child Born	Paternal Age When Tested
1	7	9	22	37	8	12	25	40
2	7	8	23	34	9	9	26	37
3	7	7	24	44	8	12	21	41
4	8	7	25	35	6	13	28	37
5	5	8	26	41	7	10	28	43
6	8	7	27	34	8	9	28	35
7	8	9	28	39	6	9	46	57
8	7	8	29	40	8	12	30	41
9	6	11	29	38	9	14	38	47
10	7	7	30	37	13	14	26	33
Median	7	8	26.5	37.5	8	12	28	40.5
11	6	10	35	35	7	14	35	35
12	8	9	36	45	9	11	40	49
13	8	9	36	49	7	11	41	54
14	10	13	36	52	8	13	40	56
15	7	10	36	43	9	14	35	42
16	6	13	37	44	8	13	40	47
17	8	12	38	43	8	13	37	42
18	7	7	39	51	5	7	37	49
19	7	9	40	41	8	10	44	45
Median	7	10	36	44	8	13	40	47

deterioration of taste threshold within such a small age-range. Using the Mann Whitney U test for rank data,[74] U $=$ 16 which indicates that the difference between the taste thresholds of the younger mothers and the older ones is significant at p $<$ 0.02 for a two-tailed test. This is a conservative estimate, because it does not correct for ties.[33] In our sample of fathers, with the exception of one subject, all fathers are insensitive ("non"-)tasters of PROP.

Generally speaking, the entire parent-sample displays a lack of very sensitive quinine tasters (threshold 4 and below). Indeed 81 per cent of the parents are characterized by very high thresholds for quinine (7 and above). For a detailed analysis of our data, see Fischer, Griffin and Kaplan.[34]

One may speculate about the possible significance of an increased incidence of high quinine thresholds among the parents of mongoloids. Ek's[18] data appear to be related to our findings; he reports the serum-protein-bound iodine of the mothers of mongoloids to be definitely higher (7.1 γ/100 ml.) than in controls. We have mentioned earlier in another paper an association between high thresholds for PROP and quinine on the one hand and hyperthyroid activity on the other.[29,30] Higher than normal thyroid hormone levels may increase the frequency of chromosomal non-disjunction;[40] this frequency also increasing with maternal age, leading to the presence of an extra V_h chromosome in the egg that is to develop into a mongol. An abnormally high quinine threshold in our parents of mongols might then be regarded as an indicator of hyperthyroid metabolism, which may exert its damaging influence during early phases of spermatogenesis, öogenesis or onto-genesis in general. Such a hypothesis is not inconsistent with the available evidence on the effect of thyroid hormone on teeth and bone formation[68] and the finding of an incidence of 96 per cent periodontal disease with severe alveolar bone loss[14] among mongoloid children.

A tentative comment about the epidemiological significance of our data. Mongolism occurs in 3 per 1000 live births but is 5 times as common in the children of women over 40, the ratio being one in 64. If the quinine findings can be replicated, we can combine the factors of age and quinine taste thresholds to estimate the risk for women, with and without these characteristics, of delivering a mongoloid child. By also considering the paternal PROP and quinine taste threshold characteristics, it may be possible to predict with sufficiently high precision when to recommend avoidance of pregnancy or abortion in couples with the combination of characteristics in question.

The involvement of the non-tasting trait in the frequency of Down's syndrome is also supported by observed population differences. For example, only about 7 per cent of Japanese are non-tasters of PTC, compared to about 30 per cent in Caucasians.[1] The respective frequencies of Down's syndrome are about 0.84 per cent in Japan, compared to about 0.16 per cent in Caucasians.[33,34]*

A SELECTIVE ASPECT OF THE "NON" TASTING TRAIT

A few words only about the possible selective value of the tasting phenotype and the "non"-tasting genotype. Clements[13] describes the following general pattern of a sudden appearance and then a gradual disappearance of goiter in newly-settled lands. The usual procedure, when new lands are settled, is for the cows and stock to first be grazed on the indigenous grasses. At the same time, land is cultivated for crops. Later, when this land is allowed to lie fallow, it quickly becomes infested with varieties of weeds, e.g., *Raphanus raphanistrum* and *Brassica campestris*, which contain significant concentrations of bitter tasting goitrogenic compounds.[45,56]

Epidemiological studies of seasonal thyroid enlargement in children 7-10 years of age have strongly suggested the etiologic involvement of goitrogens present in milk.[43] In fact, Clements' data[13] show seasonal peaks of incidence for visible goiter* in Australia, each peak occurring in the months of August-September. Interestingly, the susceptible children develop goiter each year whereas others do not. It could well be that there is a relation between taste thresholds, ingested goitrogens and development of visible goiter. This hypothesis, of course, has still to be tested. Meanwhile, further evidence has accumulated in support of the above hypothesis: (1) A fourfold prevalence of non-tasters, in comparison to tasters, was found in 962 goitrous Israeli subjects (Brand, N.: Ann. Human Genet. *26*:321, 1963). (2) In the endemic area of Brazil, nodular goiter proved to be significantly elevated among non-tasters of PTC; implying that goiter in non-tasters is more likely to evolve in the nodular form (Azevedo, E., et al.: Am. J. Human Genet. *17*:87, 1965).

---

*In a recent study (conducted with Kaplan, A. R., Zsakó, S., Griffin, F., and Glanville, E. V.: Acta Genet. Med. Gemell. [in press]) in the Akron-Cleveland area (1963-64), after carefully controlling the factors of age, sex and smoking habits affecting taste sensitivity in 142 parents of children with trisomy-21-syndrome, it was found that the parents did not differ from the control population in their taste sensitivity for quinine.

Taste Thresholds and Personality Traits

We have examined the possibility of a relation between taste thresholds for PROP and quinine and certain behavioral characteristics. The complete Wechsler Adult Intelligence Scale (W.A.I.S.) was administered to 27 college aged subjects whose taste thresholds for quinine and PROP (in this order) were at least twice determined with our modification of the Harris-Kalmus[47] procedure.†[29,30]

The subjects consisted of groups characterized by the most frequently encountered taste threshold combinations of PROP and quinine; half of the subjects represented the non-tasting genotype whereas the rest, the tasting phenotype.

The taste threshold determinations as well as the calculations of the W.A.I.S., performed by Dr. David Saunders, Princeton, N.J., followed a double blind technique. We find a correlation of the order of +.40 between Digit Symbol Performance and taste thresholds. The scores used represent deviations of the individual's Digit Symbol score from his average level of performance on the test. Additional findings: the insensitive and very insensitive ("non"-) tasters of PROP and quinine (N = 4) show a pattern of scores on the W.A.I.S. known as "compensated"; in other words, these seem to be subjects who easily maintain contact with other individuals. Another extreme group, the sensitive tasters of quinine in our sample (N = 5), show a W.A.I.S. pattern best described as "internalization."[72]

Evidently our pilot data need extension and further validation. In the meantime it should be added that Dr. Saunders (in personal communication) reports that in monozygotic twins, a high consistency exists between members of each pair with respect to their "primitive" personality profile on the W.A.I.S. and also between the deviations from the Digit Symbol score. This profile has been shown to have close genetic relationships. In this context it should also be mentioned that with our modification of the Harris-Kalmus method, taste thresholds for PROP and quinine in 41 pairs of monozygotic twins show a correlation of 1.00 within a single threshold.

Taste has also other than *scientific* aspects. Our daily language habits illustrate well the poetic-symbolic relation between systemic reactivity and gustatory competence. We usually say in praise, "he has taste," meaning that he has a very characteristic approach, a definite type of

---

*Not iodine deficiency goiter.

†Partially supported by the Human Ecology Fund, N.Y.

systemic reactivity, a style according to which he patterns his responses in relation to the stimuli of the outer world. That this systemic style is a very individual one is pointedly illustrated by the French *Chacun a son gout!* and the Latin *De gustibus non est disputandum! Artistic* taste probably means the fusion of creative systemic style with the taste of the time, the style of environment, the *Zeitgeist.* "To reject or ignore any of the aspects of the whole" . . . says Hinshelwood,[53] ". . . is to impoverish it: without poetry it loses color, without art immediacy and without science it loses structure and coherence."

Summary

The bitter taste sensation elicited by drugs is regarded as a sensory manifestation of pharmacological activity. Formation and information content of bitterness are described in terms of affinity, "sodium pump" and electrical aspects of nerve impulse reception.

Differences in salivary oxidation rate, a difference in partition coefficients of the receptor phase and stereospecific differences in the receptor site are described for insensitive ("non"-) tasters and sensitive tasters. It is shown that subjects who are genotypically insensitive ("non"-) tasters of bitter, thiourea-type goitrogens, are also insensitive ("non"-) tasters of a large variety of chemically unrelated compounds. Taste profiles for 34 compounds are presented to illustrate the observation that differential taste sensitivity is not restricted to the phenylthioureas. At least three genetic loci are reported to exist for taste: one for 6-n-propylthiouracil and related compounds, another for quinine-like compounds also including taste competence for sucrose and sodium chloride, and a separate locus for hydrochloric acid and related substances.

A relation between high biological (re) activity of man (or drug) and lower taste thresholds is demonstrated and a pharmacogenetic approach for designing new drug mixtures and calculating effective doses is postulated.

An abnormal congregation of high taste thresholds for 6-n-propylthiouracil and quinine exists in parents of mongoloid children and is interpreted as an expression of genetic predisposition. Factors of age and taste thresholds in parents of children affected with Down's syndrome may be combined to estimate the risk for women of delivering a mongoloid child.

A selective aspect of taste polymorphism is discussed. Taste thresholds for PROP and quinine are compared with certain characteristics of the Wechsler Adult Intelligence Scale. A positive correlation is found between Digit Symbol Performance and taste thresholds.

ACKNOWLEDGMENTS

Ciba Pharmaceuticals Inc., Summit, N.J. generously supplied us with pure antistine; Eastman Chem. Products Inc., Kingsport, Tenn., with Tenox PG; Geigy Pharmaceuticals, Basel, with Tofranil, desmethylimipramine (G35020), Ensidon (G33040), G34586, G21169, and G31002; The Lilly Research Laboratories, Indianapolis, with the imidazole derivatives 00416, 00415 and 07882; Chas. Pfizer & Co., Inc., Groton, Conn., with Niamid; Sandoz Pharmaceuticals, Hanover, N.J., with Mellaril; Smith, Kline & French Laboratories, Philadelphia; with chlorpromazine and chlorpromazine sulfoxide; E. R. Squibb & Sons, New Brunswick, N.J., with triflupromazine. These studies were supported by Grants M-2731, M-4694 and 42071 of the National Institutes of Health, U.S. Public Health Service. We are indebted to Mrs. Mae Moyer, Miss Barbara A. Henker, to Drs. Wm. B. McIntosh, H. L. Plaine and D. H. Stanbery, Columbus, Ohio and Mr. Sam England, Raleigh, N.C. for their most helpful cooperation.

REFERENCES

1. ALLISON, A. C., AND BLUMBERG, B. S.: Human Biology *31:* 352, 1959.
2. ARIENS, E. J., AND SIMONIS, A. M.: Acta Physiol. Pharmacol. Neerland, *11:* 151, 1962.
3. AZIMA, H., SILVER, A., AND ARTHURS, R. N.: Canad. M.A.J. *87:* 1224, 1962.
4. BEIDLER, L. M.: J. Neurophysiol. *16:* 595, 1953.
5. ——: J. Gen. Physiol., *38:* 133, 1954.
6. ——: The physiological basis of flavor. *In* Flavor Research and Food Acceptance. (Sponsored by Arthur D. Little, Inc.) Reinhold Publishing Corp., New York, 1958, pp. 3-28.
7. ——: Taste receptor stimulation. *In* Progress in Biophysics and Biophysical Chemistry, Pergamon Press, Oxford, 1961, p. 107.
8. BRANSON, H.: Some membrane phenomena from the point of view of information theory. *In* Symposium on Information Theory in Biology, Pergamon Press, New York, 1958, p. 197.
9. BRILLAT-SAVARIN, J. A.: The Physiology of Taste, or Meditations on Transcendental Gastronomy, Dover Publ., Inc., New York, 1960, p. 24.
10. CAMERON, A. T.: Can. J. Res., *23:* E, 139, 1945; *see* pp. 159-160.
11. CHRISTENSEN, H. N.: Advances in Protein Chemistry *15:* 245, 1960.
12. CLARK, A. J.: The Mode of Action of Drugs on Cells. Baltimore, The Williams & Wilkins Co., 1933, p. 4.

13. CLEMENTS, F. W.: Brit. Med. Bull. *16:* 133, 1960.
14. COHEN, M. M., et al.: Oral Surg., Oral Med. & Oral Pathol. *14:* 92, 1961.
15. KLÜVER, H.: Psychological specificity; does it exist? *In* Schmitt, F. O. (Ed.): Macromolecular Specificity and Biological Memory. Cambridge, M.I.T. Press, 1962, p. 95.
16. DE JONGH, S. E.: Isoboles. *In* DeJonge, H. (Ed.): Quantitative Methods in Pharmacology, North Holland Publ. Co., 1961, p. 318.
17. DINGLE, H.: *In* A Threefold Cord, Philosophy, Science, Religion, A discussion between Viscount Samuel and Prof. H. Dingle. London, G. Allen & Unwin, Ltd., 1961, p. 17.
18. EK, J. K.: Acta Paediat. Uppsala, *48:* 33, 1959.
19. EPPRIGHT, E. S.: Iowa State Res. Bull. 376, 1950.
20. FERGUSON, L. N., AND LAWRENCE, A. R.: J. Chem. Educ., *35:* 436, 1958.
21. FINDLAY, H.: The Phase Rule, 8th Ed. New York, Longmans, Green & Co., 1938.
22. FISCHER, R.: Affinity for wool as an indicator of neuropharmacological activity. Grenell, R. G., and Mullins, L. J. (Eds.): *In* Molecular Structure and Functional Activity of Nerve Cells, Sympos. A.I.B.S., Washington, 1956, p. 63.
23. ———: Selection on the molecular level; biological role of drug-protein interaction! 3rd Interntl. Symposium on Basic Questions in Biology; Sept. 1960, Berlin, Veb. G. Fischer Verlag, Jena, 1962.
24. ———: Ann. New York Acad. Sci. *96:* 92, 1962.
25. ———: Bull. Atom. Sci. *18:* 36, 1962.
26. ———, AND ENGLAND, S.: Paper delivered at the 8th Internatl. Conference on Biological Rhythms, Hamburg, Sept. 9-11, 1963.
27. ———, AND GRIFFIN, F.: Experientia *15:* 447, 1959.
28. ———, AND ———: Journ. Heredity *51:* 182, 1960.
29. ———, AND ———: Biochemical Genetic Factors in Taste Polymorphism. Proc. IIIrd World Congr. Psychiatry, June 6-10, Montreal, Univ. of Toronto Press, Vol. 1, 1961, p. 542.
30. ———, AND ———: Experientia *17:* 36, 1961.
31. ———, ———, AND MEAD, E. L.: Med. Exptl. *6:* 177, 1962.
32. ———, ———, AND KAPLAN, A. R.: Lancet *ii:* 992, 1962.
33. ———, ———, AND ———: Lancet *1:* 393, 1963.
34. ———, ———, AND ———: Am. J. Ment. Deficiency, *67:* 849, 1963.
35. ———, ———, ENGLAND, S., AND GARN, ST.: Nature, London *191:* 1328, 1961.
36. ———, ———, ENGLAND, S., AND PASAMANICK, B.: Med. Exptl. *4:* 356, 1961.
37. ———, ———, AND KAPLAN, A. R.: Med. Exptl. *9:* 151, 1963; and Nature, London, *202:* 1366, 1964.
38. FOERSTER, H., AND POETZL, O.: Das Gedächtnis. Wien, Franz Deuticke, 1948.
39. FORDYCE, I. D.: Brit. J. Indust. Med. *18:* 213, 1961.
40. FRASER, C.: *In* Warkany, J.: J. Pediat. *56:* 412, 1960.
41. GADDUM, J. H.: Trans. Faraday Soc. *39:* 323, 1943.
42. GANDER, J.: Private communication.
43. GIBSON, H., HOWELER, J., AND CLEMENTS, F. W.: Med. J. Australia, *1:* 875, 1960.
44. GILETTE, J. R., DINGELL, J. V., et al.: Experientia *17:* 417, 1961.

45. GREER, M. A., AND WHALLON, J.: Proc. Soc. Exper. Biol. & Med. 107: 802, 1961.
46. GRIFFIN, F. AND FISCHER, R.: Nature, London 187: 417, 1960.
47. HARRIS, H., AND KALMUS, H.: Ann. Eugen. 15: 24, 1949.
48. HEALD, P. J.: Nature, London 193: 451, 1962.
49. HEITLER, W.: Ann. der Physik., 80: 629, 1926.
50. HILDEBRAND, J. H.: Am. Chem. Soc., 51: 66, 1929.
51. ——, AND SCOTT, R. L.: Regular Solutions, Prentice-Hall, Inc., Englewood Cliffs, N. J., 1962.
52. HINCHCLIFFE, R.: J. Gerontol. 17: 45, 1962.
53. HINSHELWOOD, C.: The Vision of Nature. Cambridge, Cambridge Univ. Press, 1961.
54. HOFMANN, K.: Imidazole and Its Derivatives, Part. I. New York, Interscience Publ., Inc., 1953, p. 89.
55. JUDAH, J. D., AND AHMED, K.: Nature, London 194: 382, 1962.
56. JUKES, T. H., AND SHAFFER, C. B.: Science, 132: 296, 1960.
57. KALOW, W.: Pharmacogenetics. Philadelphia, W. B. Saunders Co., 1962.
58. KEYNES, R. D.: The mechanism of active transport of ions in nerve and muscle fibres. In Biochemie des aktiven Transports. Berlin, Springer Verlag, 1961, p. 145.
59. LILLEY, M. D., AND OWEN-VALLANCE, J.: Nature, London 190: 1196, 1961.
60. LOEWENSTEIN, W. R.: Excitation and inactivation in a receptor membrane. In Current Problems of Electrobiology, Ann. New York Acad. Sc. 94: 511, 1961.
61. MERTON, B. B.: Acta Genet. Statist. Med. 8: 114, 1958.
62. MILLER, W. H., ROBLIN, R. O., AND ASTWOOD, E. G.: J. Am. Chem. Soc. 67: 2201, 1945.
63. MOLINENGO, L., AND SEGRE, G.: Journ. Pharmacy & Pharmacol. 13: 625, 1961.
64. OPITZ, K.: Arzneimittelforschung. 12: 333, 1962.
65. PALMER, L. S.: Man's Journey Through Time. London, Hutchinson Scient. & Technical Co., 1957, p. 147.
66. PENROSE, L. S.: Ann. New York Acad. Sci. 57: 494, 1954.
67. PFEIFFER, C. C.: Science 124: 29, 1956.
68. PITT-RIVERS, R., AND TATA, J. R.: The Thyroid Hormones. London and New York, Pergamon Press, 1959, p. 71.
69. PORTER, A. W.: Trnas. Faraday Soc., 16: 336, 1920.
70. RUBIN, T. R., GRIFFIN, F., AND FISCHER, R.: Nature, London 195: 362, 1962.
71. SCHALLEK, W.: J. Pharmacol. Exptl. Therap. 105: 291, 1952.
72. SCHUCMAN, H., SAUNDERS, D. R., AND THETFORD, W. N.: An application of syndrome analysis . . .; paper read at the Am. Psychol. Assocn. Ann. Meeting, St. Louis, Mo., Sept. 3, 1962.
73. SCHUELER, F. W.: Chemobiodynamics and Drug Design. New York, McGraw-Hill Book Co., 1960.
74. SIEGEL, S.: Nonparametric Statistics for the Behavioral Sciences. New York, McGraw-Hill Book Co., 1956.
75. SMITH, W., POWELL, E. K., AND ROSS, S. J.: J. Abnorm. Soc. Psychol., 50: 101, 1955.
76. STAHL, W. R.: Science 137: 205, 1962.

77. STEVENS, J. C., AND SAVIN, H. B.: J. Exptl. Anal. Behavior 5: 15, 1962.
78. STEVENS, S. S.: Science 133: 80, 1961.
79. UNGAR, G., AND ROMANO, D.: J. Gen. Physiol. 46: 267, 1962.
80. VERNIER, V. G.: Personal communication to Dr. Carl C. Pfeiffer, Emory University, Georgia, 1954.
81. WERLE, E., AND SCHIEVELBEIN: Arzneimittelforschung, 11: 1011; 1149; 1961; 12: 202, 1962.
82. WILSON, A., AND SCHILD, H. O.: Applied Pharmacology (Cook). Boston, Little Brown & Co., 1959.

7

THE PSYCHOPATHOLOGY OF
TIME JUDGMENT*

by WILLIAM T. LHAMON†, SANFORD GOLDSTONE
and JOYCE L. GOLDFARB‡

> "Close your eyes and simply wait to hear some-
> body tell you that a minute has elapsed. The
> full length of your leisure with it seems in-
> credible. You engulf yourself into its bowels as
> into those of that interminable first week of an
> ocean voyage, and find yourself wondering that
> history can have overcome many such periods in
> its course . . ."—*W. James*

INTEREST IN THE EXPERIMENTAL STUDY of the judgment of time is
as old as the science of psychology,[51] and no student of behavior
is permitted to forget that a "personal equation" in regard to time
judgment, not incompetence, resulted in the famous dismissal of the
assistant Kinnebrook by the Astronomer Royal, Maskelyne, at Green-
wich in 1796.

The process of temporalization that permits people to resolve stimuli
into duration and succession, and provides the basis for a rich appreciation of an historical past, an operational present and a moderately
predictable future has been a traditional source of fascination and
speculation for the philosopher, theologian, artist and physical scientist. However, the task of the behavioral scientist precludes the luxury
of assigning human timing behavior to the realm of metaphysical and
metapsychological discourse. The experimental psychologist and psychopathologist must adhere to the conviction that man's basic experiences and his reality can be rendered understandable through the
ground rules and methods of science.

Supported by U.S.P.H.S. Grant MH 01121.
†Cornell University Medical College, New York, N. Y.
‡Baylor University College of Medicine and Houston State Psychiatric Institute.

All behavior involves a temporal component; all behavior exists within a temporal context. The capacity of people to harness duration into increasingly refined communicable and measurable units of experience provides a background for interpersonal, cultural and scientific transactions of remarkable conceptual complexity. The taken-for-granted ability to conceptualize a *yesterday, today,* and *tomorrow,* and the capacity to compare temporal experiences with those of others permits an otherwise impossible level of socialization. The experimental study of time judgment is of obvious interest to the student of ordered and disordered behavior.

The fact that people can provide incredibly sensitive, accurate and precise responses to the temporal properties of their world is part of the same mystery as their equally remarkable ability to demonstrate severe disruptions of time judgments. The abundance of anecdotal accounts of a paradoxic "time sense" that was both accurate and distorted, stable and capricious, acted as a frustrating deterrent to the experimental psychopathologist. The classical psychophysicist studied accuracy and error within narrow laboratory conditions, and the experience of time was left largely for philosophic discussion.

The failure to regard time judgment as a complex mental process dependent upon conditions of stimulation and states of the organism produced contradictory findings, ambiguous terminology,[6] and discouraged extensive experimentation. Investigators spoke of a "time sense" as if temporalization could be divorced from the adaptive interaction between the organism and its sensory mechanisms, and stimulating conditions. The judgment of time should be included within a theoretical and experimental schema that acknowledges a temporal response as an integration of focal and background stimulation, and, momentary and permanent states of the organism.[31,32]

This realization has led to increased interest in reducing terminologic ambiguity, and renewed and vigorous research in the area of time judgment.[18,20,52]

TIME AND PSYCHOPATHOLOGY

The minute that seems like hours, or the hour that has the apparent duration of a minute, dependent upon circumstances, mood, drug state, fatigue, and psychopathology has long been recognized by laymen and scientists. Alteration of time judgment is a common symptom of mental dysfunction whether of specific organic origin, or in functional disorders. Temporal orientation is a major consideration in the mental status examination of the psychiatrist who has traditionally considered the sensorium a key to the diagnosis of mental disease. This examination emphasizes a clinically useful concept of *reality* which may be operationally defined in terms of the status of sensory attributes as observed through the judgment process. A patient is asked to scale cultural norms in accordance with accepted limits of judgment. Stimuli within specific contexts are compared with these internal standards and the response is appraised with respect to appropriateness and accepted range. Shared standards are necessary for socialized behavior, and the culturally accepted units of experience such as seconds, inches and ounces, with their learned concepts, may be considered a psychophysical definition of reality. The comparison of stimuli with these concepts and the ability to make corrections for momentary contextual and organismic changes permits the standardization of perceptual responses and interpersonal relations. Alterations or defects in the learning or comparison processes should accompany social impairment and mental disease. The diagnostic assessment of orientation with respect to time, place, and person involves a patient's ability to make absolute judgments of his surroundings in relation to acquired units accepted socially as *reality*.

From an experimental point of view, norms or social units may be assumed to vary along subjective scales that can be studied with measures of central tendency and variability. These internal scales shift with external anchoring conditions and organic states.

Lewis[36] and Schilder[45] reviewed many cases of mental disturbance and time judgment. They recognized the importance of time concepts but focused upon the subjective or symbolic aspects of the dysfunctions.

The attempts to attack experimentally the problem of time judgment and psychopathology produced few consistent results.[14,15,16,39] The complexity of this area requires a large scale assault and not an occasional, isolated study.

In 1955 two of the authors (W.T.L. and S.G.) initiated several experiments regarding time judgment and psychopathology. The earliest finding that schizophrenic patients overestimated the duration of auditory stimuli more than healthy subjects[37] led to continued investigation of the effects of various organismic and contextual factors upon time judgment. Each experiment increased the scope of the problem area, and after 8 years and 5000 subjects, the writers are left with healthy respect for the complex processes that lead to ordered and disordered temporal behavior. This program of research did not fulfill the investigators' dream of quickly unraveling the mysteries of human time judgment but increased their conviction that man's temporal experience could be systematically explored with the methods and traditions of the laboratory.

This presentation will review some of the findings and ideas that emerged from these experiments, emphasizing the relationship between time judgment measures and mental illness, intoxication and metabolic alteration.

The "Second Estimation Point"

The fact that people show remarkably sensitive and accurate time judgments under certain conditions while demonstrating marked alterations under others is particularly evident in psychopathologic states. The schizophrenic patient may report temporal immobility in a world of the present where "time stands still" and yet perform tasks that require adaptation to succession and change. This patient may offer judgments about the clock and calendar that reveal altered temporal orientation and yet conform to the work, feeding and sleep schedules of a hospital. The depressed patient may report that "time is dragging and the day appears like an eternity" and yet provide an accurate representation of his temporal world in clock and calendar units.

An experimental program that seeks to expose an ever-existing, all-pervasive defect in time judgment accompanying psychopathology is overlooking clinical facts. Research must emphasize organism and judgment circumstances to determine the details of conditions that accompany ordered and disordered temporal behavior within the same population.

It is probable that the method of single stimuli is the most effective experimental approach to the psychopathology of time judgment. The method of absolute judgment where a person compares a stimulus with a concept is more likely to reveal temporal conceptual disturbance than a simple comparison procedure where the subject acts as an organic meter.

Schizophrenic and healthy subjects were asked to compare auditory durations with their concept of a social temporal unit, one clock second. This essential, communicable norm is learned and should be available within specific acceptance-rejection limits unless the conceptualization process is disordered. A short unit was selected to minimize the use of multiple exteroceptive and proprioceptive cues that might serve to correct for, and obscure judgment defects.

Healthy controls and serially selected schizophrenic patients were provided alternating runs of ascending and descending auditory durations with a step interval of 0.1-sec. starting 1.0-sec.[37] Subjects judged each duration as *more* or *less* than one clock second. The duration reported *more* and *less* 50 per cent of the time was derived from these judgments and was designated the Second Estimation Point (SEP). The mean log SEP for the schizophrenic group (.31-sec.) was smaller than that of the healthy group (.56-sec.). Information regarding the identity of the clock second using a comparison procedure eliminated the patient-control difference.

The SEP measure was sensitive to clinical observations of the inner-directed, autistic person's tendency to overestimate temporal events based upon external occurrences when the only available standard was a concept. When a standard for comparison was offered, the schizophrenics provided normal temporal judgments.

Alone, this finding does little more than confirm clinical observations of occasional disruptions in temporal judgment accompanying schizophrenia. What of the circumstances that promote this disruption? When is this disruption evident?

Parametric studies that modified the temporal context in various ways and included additional attention to the definition of the schizophrenic populations as well as other psychopathologic states and organismic alterations were undertaken. These parameters were selected because of their possible relevance to the judgment of time and its relationship to psychopathology.

POPULATIONS

Much has been said about the wisdom of using the classification schizophrenia in investigative work.[17,50] There are those who question intrainstitutional reliability of diagnosis, whereas others emphasize interinstitutional differences in defining this mental illness, and still others deny the fruitfulness or existence of any single classification of a wide variety of disordered behaviors.

Healthy control populations are equally vulnerable to sampling and definition criticism. Is the college student coerced and uncoerced, a sensible control when studying mental disorder? Can the volunteer, paid and unpaid, be considered a representative sample of a non-sick population? The investigating psychopathologist usually recognizes the problem and defines patient and control populations in terms of available sources, letting results speak for themselves. Although care is taken to point out that patient-control differences must be cautiously interpreted within the populations studied, it is hoped that the results might be verified with other samples. Groups of subjects are used to cope with the problem of reliability of the classification, and it is presumed that *the schizophrenic group is more schizophrenic than the normal group.* Unfortunately, duplication with other samples is rare, and subsequent negative findings serve to dismiss earlier results without sufficient emphasis upon possible population differences or diagnostic idiosyncrasies.

The present investigators sampled several populations to explore similarities and differences among groups similarly classified as schizophrenic and healthy. Three sources of schizophrenic subjects were defined: 1) a receiving hospital for less chronic illnesses in people who were considered good candidates for remission after short, intensive treatment (M); 2) a state hospital (T) that cares for more chronic problems; 3) a veteran's hospital that emphasizes short-term treatment for both acute and chronic patients (V). Table 1 summarizes the characteristics of T, M, and V. Patients with other disorders emphasizing affective excesses such as anxiety, depression and mania were also studied. The healthy subjects were younger but did not differ in educational level.

CONTEXTUAL PARAMETERS

1. Psychophysical Method

Although several writers[6,13,20] have emphasized the need for considering the nature of the judgmental context in understanding the results

TABLE 1.—Characteristics of the Schizophrenic Populations: Median Age, Education, Duration of Illness from Initial Onset, and Duration of Current Hospitalization

Hospital	Age: Mdn	Education: Mdn Grade Years	Illness Duration: Mdn Years since Onset	Duration Present Hospitalization: Mdn Years
T (Chronic)	44	10.5	7.2	2.9
M (Less Chronic)	36	12.2	2.9	0.4
V (Veterans' Hospital)	35	12.2	3.4	0.2

of time estimation experiments and comparing findings among investigations, this basic question is often dismissed with only casual reference to its presence. Different judgmental responses under different conditions are expected and care must be taken not to generalize unless results are verified across several representative methods. Four psychophysical procedures that differed in the nature of the task, available cues, and level of difficulty were employed.

The *method of limits* using ascending and descending presentations was chosen as a starting point because it provided flexibility in determining appropriate ranges of inputs, approximate organismic sensitivity and ease of instrument construction and experimental delivery. The classical method was modified so that the subject was partially responsible for the range of durations presented. This procedure offered the subject some measure of self-determination since he and not the examiner arranged for a less predictable environment. Studies with healthy subjects indicated the reliability of this procedure across samples, and studies with children showed that the ability passively to estimate duration emerged between seven and eight.[21,47,58]

The *constant method* provides a fixed environment for a subject where his responses do not influence his contextual destiny. He is at the mercy of the examiner and subsequent inputs do not depend on previous behavior. The constant method should be less difficult for passive people who prefer a structured world and avoid acting upon their surroundings. People who are acted upon by their environment and have trouble adjusting to a life that requires instrumental conceptual behavior should be less able to deal with a method of limits than a constant stimuli situation. Schizophrenic subjects should manifest more conceptual impairment with the more flexible, demanding method of limits. Studies with healthy subjects indicated differences between this method and the method of limits. Subjects adapted within the programmed range of durations after quickly developing a reference scale in a simpler context.[28a,34a,54]

The *method of production* required subjects to tap or count at a rate comparable with a temporal concept; an instrumental muscle response was identified with the concept.

The distance senses that passively receive inputs are less likely to be the basic factors in accurately interpreting social temporal units than a more instrumental proprioceptive mode. SEPs derived from counting should be more accurate than those obtained from passive estimation of distance modes in healthy populations and there should be a disruption of the connection between kinesthetic cue and concept with schizophrenia. Studies with healthy subjects demonstrated the remarkable accuracy and precision of counting or tapping seconds. This capacity emerged between ages 7 and 8 and deteriorated with aging.[23] Blind subjects demonstrated that interruption of one mode decreased the accuracy of kinesthetic estimates, which suggests that accurate temporal judgment is a multisensory function.

The *method of adjustment* required subjects to alter the period of an auditory metronome in accordance with a temporal concept. The proprioceptive mode was involved but did not define the concept as with the production method.

Since the subject is dealing with a continuous source of information while adjusting a repeating interval, he should be better able to mobilize his resources for temporal conceptualization than when he must passively estimate a single duration. Studies with healthy subjects indicated very accurate and precise judgments of one second periods.

2. Temporal Standard

Subjective judgments of longness or shortness are more a function of foreground and background contextual influences than judgments based upon social, learned concept residuals. A person can use the same yardstick when scaling along a longness-shortness continuum with two non-overlapping series of durations. While private units may yield gross individual differences of experienced apparent duration, judgment in terms of social units permits temporal standardization, communication and interaction among people.

With the *social temporal standard,* subjects were required to estimate, produce or adjust durations in accordance with their concept of one clock second. Healthy subjects from similar learning backgrounds with similar emphases upon temporal standards should demonstrate judgmental similarities under a variety of experimental parameters, and disordered socialization due to mental illness or intoxication should be accompanied by an analogous, predictable and measurable disorder of this norm. With the *subjective temporal standard,* subjects were required to judge durations along a multi-category scale of longness-shortness. Studies with healthy subjects using the constant method indicated a consistent tendency to adapt higher within a given range of durations for the subjective than social standards.[28a]

3. Stimulus Series and Step Interval

After almost one hundred years of psychophysical research on the relationship between physical continua and judged magnitude, behavioral scientists cannot offer general laws that permit immediate derivation of a series of stimuli that are separated by equal judgment units. The classical psychophysicist emphasized the physical scale in an absolute fashion, and sensitivity measures such as the just-noticeable-difference were seen as error values. It is easy to lose sight of the fact that objective physical scales are socially agreed upon yardsticks; sensory, perceptual and conceptual distances are equally valid points of departure.

The convenient and usual arithmetic series does not approximate an equal interval psychophysical series since the lower end is separated by the most psychological distance. Possible intraseries effects determined by unequally spaced stimuli made this a problem worthy of consideration. Studies with healthy subjects using the method of limits and constant method yielded no SEP differences between arithmetic and geometric stimulus spacing.[58]

4. Subjective Scale

The nature of a judgment task and its conceptual complexity is not just a function of stimulus dimensions. The characteristics of response requirements are of fundamental importance. Passive categorization may not be equivalent to the instrumental production, adjustment and fractionation responses even though the internal standard is constant. A yes-no categorization may differ in kind or complexity from a more-less or n category magnitude scale. Furthermore, judgments will partly depend upon the values and costs of the judgments that are made.[49]

Psychopathology should be more dramatically reflected in judgments that require complicated conceptual responses. Daily life requires absolute judgments involving scales with fine discriminations. Only a custodial, protecting institution offers an existence where simple yardsticks permit adaptation by individuals who are not able to conceptualize socially essential nuances through a more elaborate scaling process. Few schizophrenic patients would be in error in identifying maleness and femaleness from anatomical considerations, but these concepts become socially complex, demanding finely categorized and scaled discriminations that are impaired in this patient group. Studies indicated that healthy subjects took advantage of the width of open-ended, multicategory response scales thereby presenting remarkably sensitive judgments.[28a,54]

5. Anchor Effects

The extent to which a subjective scale shifts with background influences, distractions or irrelevant stimuli is of importance to the psychopathologist. These anchor effects provide considerable information on the status of a concept or internal scale.

Weight lifting[44] and constancy[41,42,55] experiments suggest weaker or less vivid concepts and greater anchor effects in schizophrenic patients indicating that they are less able to mobilize past conceptual resources in judgment situations to ward off background noise. This might be considered a psychophysical analogue to a primary symptom of the illness, passivity.

Schizophrenic patients should be more affected by immediate anchors than healthy subjects when judging temporal concepts, and show less pooling of recent and remote anchors in making these judgments. That is, recent anchors will influence their judgments more while past anchors will have less influence. Studies with healthy subjects demonstrated anchoring effects upon judgments based upon social and subjective scales, arithmetic and geometric intervals, and, the constant method, method of limits and method of adjustment.[22,28a,53]

6. Intersensory Factors

Intersensory differences are of more than passing concern to the psychopathologist who has long been confronted with the mysterious hallucination. Experiments with healthy subjects have demonstrated a curious auditory-visual difference in time judgment that is independent of stimulus characteristics, temporal standard, psychophysical method, step interval and stimulus range.[2,3,24,25,28a] Longer visual filled durations were judged equivalent to internal temporal norms than those received through the auditory mode. Tactile durations were judged longer than auditory inputs.[38]

PSYCHOPATHOLOGY, DRUG EFFECTS AND PHYSIOLOGIC CHANGE

Findings will be summarized according to psychophysical method, and details regarding instrumentation, experimental design and statistical operations will be sacrificed in this presentation.

Method of Limits

Psychopathology. Early studies additionally explored the previously determined shorter SEP of a schizophrenic group by varying two contextual factors, sense mode and step interval, and examining similarly diagnosed patients from three hospitals (M, V, and T). Table 2 provides a composite of median SEP values obtained from the various populations under different sensory and step interval conditions using the method of limits procedure.

Statistical analysis indicated the following: 1) Schizophrenic patients of V and M verified the shorter SEP with auditory durations that were arithmetically spaced. This result was not obtained for T. 2) The auditory SEPs of schizophrenic patients did not differ from those of healthy controls with geometric spacing.[58] 3) Depressed, anxious and physically disabled patients did not provide shorter auditory, arithmetic SEPs.[27] 4) A small group of manic patients provided the longest auditory, arithmetic SEPs. 5) Schizophrenic patients in remission provided longer auditory SEPs than healthy controls when .10-sec. arithmetic and 10 per cent geometric step intervals were used. This

TABLE 2.—Median Second Estimation Point (SEP) in Seconds for Auditory and Visual, Arithmetic and Geometric Step Interval Groups Using the Method of Limits Anchored at One Second

Population	N	Sense Mode	Step Interval	Mdn SEP
Healthy	125	Aud.	.10 Sec., Arith.	.62
Healthy	163	Aud.	10%, Geometric	,66
Healthy	40	Aud.	.18 Sec., Arith.	.75
Healthy	40	Aud.	18%, Geometric	.78
Healthy	84	Vis.	.10 Sec., Arith.	1.07
Healthy	82	Vis.	10%, Geometric	1.06
Schizophrenia (M)	36	Aud.	.10 Sec., Arith.	.47
Schizophrenia (M)	36	Aud.	10%, Geometric	,61
Schizophrenia (M)	39	Aud.	.18 Sec., Arith.	.44
Schizophrenia (M)	39	Aud.	18%, Geometric	.55
Schizophrenia (V)	53	Aud.	.10 Sec., Arith.	.53
Schizophrenia (V)	51	Vis.	.10 Sec., Arith.	.90
Schizophrenia (T)	51	Aud.	.10 Sec., Arith.	.80
Schizophrenia (T)	50	Vis.	.10 Sec., Arith.	.89
Schizophrenia-Remission (M)	18	Aud.	.10 Sec., Arith.	1.08
Schizophrenia-Remission (M)	18	Aud.	10%, Geometric	.93
Schizophrenia-Remission (M)	28	Aud.	.18 Sec., Arith.	.55
Schizophrenia-Remission (M)	26	Aud.	18%, Geometric	.58
Depression (V)	35	Aud.	.10 Sec., Arith.	.54
Anxiety (V)	10	Aud.	.10 Sec., Arith.	.77
Physically Disabled (V)	35	Aud.	.10 Sec., Arith.	.63
Manic	8	Aud.	.10 Sec., Arith.	1.36

was not found with .18-sec. or 18 per cent increments. 6) Visual SEPs are longer than those obtained through auditory judgments. This intersensory difference was most marked for the control group and least evident with schizophrenic patients from T.[58] 7) No schizophrenia-healthy differences were obtained with visual judgments.

Although the earliest finding of greater overestimation of short durations by schizophrenic patients was replicated, this was dependent upon population and contextual characteristics.

The elimination of the schizophrenia-control differences with a geometric step interval is not difficult to understand in terms of the psychopathology of these patients and the psychophysical characteristics of the two series. It is probable that the greater psychophysical asymmetry of the arithmetic series provided more potent short anchors, resulting in increased overestimation of the presented durations.

The reduced intersensory difference with schizophrenia has been discussed[26] as a possible factor in determining hallucinatory experiences. This population may be less able to conceptualize intersensory distinctions, interpreting adequate inputs to one mode in terms of another.

The long SEPs obtained from schizophrenics in remission and manics, and the lack of a patient-control difference with the most chronic patients indicates the importance of population considerations.* The possibility that schizophrenics in remission and manics may compensate for excessive anchor vulnerability or possess an "input hunger" should be studied further.

The number of alternating responses in the continuous ascending and descending presentation, and the number of suddent shifts in transition zone indicated greater variability in judgment with all schizophrenic populations.

Sociometric measures of medical student subjects with the most and least accurate auditory, arithmetic SEPs were compared.[24a] The ability to accurately judge time in clock units is associated with more choices and fewer rejections for prestige and friendship. As a related sidelight, schizophrenic patients elected as ward representatives to hospital government in population M had more accurate SEPs than their voting constituents.

Another contextual parameter involves the range of durations

---

*A similar difference between chronic and acute patients was obtained in a study of pupil responses.[29]

emphasizing the extreme magnitudes. These anchors were presented as the first stimulus and the series ascended from a short duration (.1-sec.) or descended from the long anchor (2.0-sec.). Subjects were presented alternate short and long anchor series with order controlled to study the successive pooling of these effects.

Table 3 summarizes the median SEP values obtained from healthy and schizophrenic subjects. A ratio of long anchor SEP/short anchor SEP was obtained for each subject as an indicant of anchor effect and successive pooling. Unfortunately the auditory patients were drawn from a less chronic population than the visual schizophrenics limiting the interpretation of findings. Considering the restrictions upon generalizations across populations, the following results were obtained: 1) The expected downward pulling effect of the short anchor and the upward pulling effect of the long anchor was demonstrated with all populations. 2) The healthy population provided the anticipated auditory-visual difference. This is also seen between the two different schizophrenic populations. 3) The less chronic population demonstrated shorter auditory, arithmetic SEPs than the healthy controls. The intraserial anchor effects were more potent with this group than the extreme stimuli. The more chronic group with visual durations showed greater effects due to extreme anchors than to intraserial anchors. Additional research will determine whether this was a function of population or sense mode factors. 4) The healthy groups demonstrated a residual effect of the initial anchor upon subsequent judgments of the alternate anchor series. This successive pooling, or influence of past experience was

TABLE 3.—Median Second Estimation Points (SEP) in Seconds of Healthy and Schizophrenic Group with Alternate Short (.1 sec.) and Long (2.0 sec.) Anchors: Arithmetic Series: Method of Limits

Population	N	Sense Mode	Anchor: 1st Series	Mdn SEP	Anchor: Alternate Series	Mdn SEP	Mdn Long/ Short Ratios
Healthy	40	Aud.	Long	.71	Short	.55	1.14
Healthy	40	Aud.	Short	.40	Long	.55	1.29
Healthy	40	Vis.	Long	1.30	Short	1.02	1.22
Healthy	40	Vis.	Short	.66	Long	.76	1.14
Schiz.*	23	Aud.	Long	.38	Short	.30	2.30
Schiz.*	23	Aud.	Short	.28	Long	.58	1.94
Schiz. T	17	Vis.	Long	1.60	Short	.83	1.55
Schiz. T	20	Vis.	Short	.52	Long	.73	1.45

*A less chronic state hospital population similar to M.

less evident with the schizophrenic groups.[56] Schizophrenic patients were more vulnerable to immediate anchors and less influenced by anchors from past experience than healthy subjects. Additional investigation will determine the relationship between anchor vulnerability and schizophrenia on the one hand, and the nature of the anchoring context on the other.

Anchor studies have relevance to schizophrenia since these patients are especially subject to behavioral alteration associated with background noise and are less able to mobilize conceptual resources derived from past learning to instrumentally and appropriately deal with the flood of immediate stimulation. These studies provide a psychophysical analogue to the clinical passivity of these patients and may help to determine the kinds of stimuli and the conditions of stimulation that lead to pathologic judgment.

Drug effects. An increased auditory, arithmetic SEP was obtained with 0.2 Gm. of secobarbital, a decreased SEP with 15 mg. of dextroamphetamine and no significant change with a placebo.[22,23] These results conform to those obtained by others[20,48] and are consistent with the observation that sedatives slow down internal events while making external events appear to speed up, and stimulants speed up internal events while making the outside appear to slow down.

Although alcohol should act as a depressant, no significant increase in the auditory, arithmetic SEP was obtained.[34] Half of the subjects reported that time appeared to "drag" and depressed affect, while others reported acceleration and euphoria. This lack of a predictable alteration due to alcohol was also found by Laties and Weiss[35] and suggests that future research should consider individual tolerance and type of affective response.

Increased variability was obtained with 100 μg. of LSD. As with alcohol, the SEP changes seemed to be more a function of the subject's individual response to the drug. SEP determinations were accompanied by increased response time. Subjects would occasionally hesitate for several minutes before responding to an input, reporting that the internal standard was temporarily lost. This modification of conceptual availability was the most consistent finding with LSD and probably accounted for the increased variability.

Ditran* in 2.5 mg. to 10.0 mg. doses produced an initial period

---

*N-ethyl-3-piperidyl-phenylcyclopentyl glycolate is an anticholinergic substance similar to atropine in its autonomic properties and was initiated as a possible mood elevator.

of withdrawal and stupor followed by a highly productive toxic psychosis. The delirium lasted 6 to 48 hours during which time the subjects were confused, out of contact with the investigators, and enjoyed vivid visual hallucinations. Attempts to test the subjects during the delirium failed. When the psychosis terminated, the subjects were able to provide decreasingly variable SEPs. The first "contact" was with misused conceptual responses such as *strong, white, right,* and *average.* Later, the correct responses *more* and *less* were used with gradually decreasing variability.

Sernyl† in sub-anesthetic doses of 5.0 mg. produced temporary nausea, minimal ideation and an almost aphasic-like spontaneous word finding difficulty. Subjects appeared to be in contact although spontaneous verbalization was rare. There seemed to be a detachment of proprioception from ideas of muscle movement so that one subject could not determine whether he was thinking about getting out of bed, or actually getting out of bed. Subjects tried to make SEP judgments but could not; apparently they had lost the concept of one second. After about 6 hours, judgment was impaired only by slight increased variability. All subjects were familiar with the SEP test prior to the drug study, and yet could not compare the auditory input with their concept.

Physiologic change. Certain physiologic changes are accompanied by an increased rate of body rhythms and a comparable speeding of ideomotor activity, whereas others are associated with a slowing of body rhythms, and mental and muscular responses. If temporal appreciation is related to the comparison of the rate of internal with external events mediated by a social concept, modification of the internal event rate should produce an alteration in temporal experience.

A "speeding" internal clock should result in relative overestimation of the social unit; hyperthyroid patients should experience time as dragging. The hyperthyroid patient, as with the subject under a stimulant, may have a speeding internal event rate so that the former event rate-social norm calibration should be in error in the direction of increased overestimation; the SEP should become shorter. This result was obtained in a study using hyperthyroid patients and non-hyperthyroid patients as controls.[34a]

The shorter SEPs of the hyperthyroid group verify the notion of a speeded internal clock along with increased overestimation of external

---

†1-(1-phenylcyclohexyl) piperidine was used as an intravenous anesthetic agent.

events. Studies with a geometric series and other psychophysical methods should indicate if this is a function of the context or is a general measure of altered time judgment.

Constant Method

Psychopathology. The method of constant stimuli presents a different judgment circumstance than the method of limits, and facilitates the use of multicategory scales, and social and subjective standards. At first 11 auditory durations from .15-sec. to 1.95-sec. in 28 per cent increments were randomized and judged as *more* or *less* than one second. Long (2.0-sec.) and short (.1-sec.) anchors were paired with each duration and subjects judged the second duration excluding the anchor. Long and short anchor series were alternated with order controlled and the long anchor SEP/short anchor SEP ratio was obtained as before. Table 4 summarizes the results of this experiment which suggests the following: 1) Although anchor effects were obtained with the constant method, these effects were not as profound as with the method of limits even though the anchor appeared more frequently with the randomized procedure. This is most evident for the healthy groups. 2) T schizophrenics did not differ from the healthy group under the no anchor procedure. This T schizophrenia-healthy result was also obtained with the method of limits. However, another study with V schizophrenia provided no arithmetic series, constant stimuli, patient-control difference.[54] The short schizophrenic auditory, arithmetic SEP is *not* a characteristic of the constant method where the subject adapts within a restricted, structured range of inputs regardless of

TABLE 4.—Median Auditory Second Estimation Point (SEP) Measures of Healthy and Schizophrenic Groups with No Anchor, Long Anchor and Short Anchor: Geometric Series: Constant Method

Population	N	Anchor: 1st Series	Mdn SEP	Anchor: Alternate Series	Mdn SEP	Mdn Long/ Short Ratios
Healthy	20	No Anchor	.71	—	—	—
Healthy	25	Long	.66	Short	.56	1.10
Healthy	26	Short	.61	Long	.81	1.22
Schizophrenic V	21	Long	.78	Short	.64	1.26
Schizophrenic V	19	Short	.49	Long	.78	1.42
Schizophrenic T	45	No Anchor	.69	—	—	—
Schizophrenic T	22	Long	.87	Short	.64	1.33
Schizophrenic T	23	Short	.66	Long	.86	1.60

conceptual strength. The differential complexity of the two psychophysical methods is additionally demonstrated by fewer testing failures with the constant method. 3) V and T were more influenced by the long anchor than the control group and V showed a trend toward greater alteration due to the short anchor.* 4) Less successive pooling of anchor effects by schizophrenic subjects was suggested.

This study indicates that the short SEP obtained with the method of limits is in part a function of psychophysical method, and greater immediate anchor effects are associated with schizophrenia using a two category judgment scale and repeated extreme stimulation.

A shorter auditory, arithmetic SEP was *not* obtained with V schizophrenia with the constant method when subjects judged durations along a nine point scale from *very much less than a second* to *very much more than a second*.[54] The fact that no differential effect due to long and short anchors was obtained between V schizophrenia and healthy controls[53] when nine judgment categories were used indicates the relevance of the response scale in patient-control differences. Schizophrenic subjects consistently used fewer response categories than healthy controls under this condition.

The altered estimates of a clock second obtained earlier with schizophrenic subjects are a function of sense mode, step interval, and psychophysical method. The increased immediate anchor effects accompanying schizophrenia are a function of psychophysical method and the response scale. These differences in temporal judgment are not general pervasive properties of the schizophrenic illness, but clearly relate to specific contextual factors.

Drug effects. The constant method did not provide the SEP changes with secobarbital and dextroamphetamine obtained with the method of limits. Psychophysical method is a relevant variable in measuring altered time judgment due to drugs.

The constant method was sensitive to the increased variability associated with 4, 7, and 12 μg. of LSD,[9] indicating the likelihood that this finding is independent of psychophysical method.

Physiologic change. Francois[19] and Hoagland[33] showed that artifically and naturally induced hyperthermia was accompanied by overestimation of time using a method of production. It was possible that these findings reflected a change in the rate of psychomotor performance

---

*Bevan, Reed, and Pritchard[5] found low intensity auditory anchors less effective than an intensity above the series.

rather than altered time judgment. Auditory, arithmetic, constant method SEPs were obtained from subjects before and after their body temperature was raised 1.8° to 3.6°F. with hot, moist air.[34a] Reduced SEPs were provided by the heated subjects while no such change was found with a control group, verifying earlier work with fever and suggesting that altered time judgment due to such physiologic changes as hyperthyroidism and hyperthemia is independent of psychophysical method.

Method of Production

Psychopathology. Table 5 shows the remarkable accuracy of SEPs obtained from subjects age 8 through young adult who counted seconds aloud and silently. This accuracy was not present at ages 6 and 7, or past 60. V schizophrenic subjects also demonstrated impairment in their ability to instrumentally communicate a temporal concept via the proprioceptive mode.

It is probable that accurate social time perception is a complex multisensory enterprise. The cues available from several senses contribute to the learning and calibration of socialized temporal experience. Since considerable accuracy in judging seconds was obtained with the counting method, it is likely that the proprioceptive mode is basic for social temporal conceptualization. Younger children and older adults were less able to display this accuracy in counting seconds. The counting procedure involves kinesthetic cues, and we might assume that the learning of this short standard unit of time is at least in part muscular.

TABLE 5.—Median SEP for All Counting Groups

Population: Age Groups	N	Silent Count: Mdn SEP	N	Aloud Count: Mdn SEP
6	20	.61	19	.59
7	20	.63	20	.61
8	20	.99	20	1.06
9	20	1.00	20	1.25
10	20	.92	20	1.09
11	20	1.06	20	1.11
12	20	.96	20	1.04
13	20	.98	20	1.08
14	30	.93	30	1.06
Young Adult	20	1.01	20	1.06
Older Adult	20	.81	20	.80
V-Schiz.	26	.55	26	.76

The method of limits, auditory method where no motor production was involved, resulted in a shorter SEP. At about age 8, kinesthetic cues become associated with standard temporal concepts providing for temporal conceptualization and consistent experienced duration. This cut-off point at 8 suggests this age as the approximate level of maturation which would permit temporal learning based upon discriminated concepts of magnitude.

Further evidence of kinesthetic primacy in learned temporal units was suggested by the younger children's difficulty in counting silently. Many of them violated instructions and made manifest muscle movements, as though temporal concepts were in the process of being learned and needed the kinesthetic accompaniment. It seems that 6 or 7 year olds have not established a stable relationship between the social concept and muscle cues, whereas older adults and schizophrenics apparently lost this relationship.

Drug effects. No effects due to secobarbital and dextroamphetamine were obtained with this method.

Method of Adjustment

Psychopathology. Although studies have been undertaken where subjects vary a steady or changing period auditory metronome to their concept of a second, no patients have been examined. This method permits a continuous recording of the temporal judgment process simultaneous with psychophysiologic measures and holds promise for investigations of time judgment and psychopathology within a changing and stressful context.

Drug effects. SEP measures obtained from subjects under secobarbital and dextroamphetamine who adjusted the variable metronome to their concept of a second have not provided consistent results. One study found no effect due to the stimulant and depressant, while another obtained a longer SEP under secobarbital. It was suggested that exercise and fatigue produced a shorter adjustment SEP. These results are tentative and this method needs further exploration.

Sensori-Motor Synchrony

Psychopathology. A different timing behavior procedure required subjects to tap in synchrony with a steady period, continuous auditory metronome, and maintain the same tapping rate when the inputs were removed. The taps of V schizophrenic subjects passively followed the inputs while the healthy and physically handicapped controls instrumentally anticipated the inputs.No patient-control difference was found in the ability to maintain the concept during the free-tapping period.[1]

Drug effects. Secobarbital and dextroamphetamine did not alter sensori-motor synchrony although psychomotor performance under the free-tapping condition accelerated with the stimulant.[27]

NEXT STEPS

The future requires similar exploration of new stimulus parameters that alter time judgment in predictable ways with healthy and psychopathologic groups. The relevant contextual factors already determined have been partially investigated and only a few have been studied in relation to mental illness, physiologic change and intoxication. Much remains to be accomplished.

Other psychophysical methods are readily available for study. The methods of comparison, reproduction and fractionation will provide information regarding time judgment under new circumstances, and the method of adjustment with a regular and changing period auditory and visual metronome deserves considerable attention. The use of unfilled durations, rhythms and different ranges of durations will expand the scope of experimental conditions, and intramodal and cross-modal anchor studies that plot the limits of these effects using more extreme and less relevant background stimuli are of obvious importance in the understanding of healthy and disordered time judgment.

Of immediate interest is additional research into the auditory-visual-tactile time judgment difference in psychopathologic groups. Are these intersensory differences reduced with schizophrenia regardless of experimental conditions? Is there a reduction in the successive pooling of intersensory differences with schizophrenia similar to that found with alternately presented anchors? Do these intersensory differences change with intoxication? Is there a relationship between these intermodal differences and the presence or absence of hallucinations? Developmental studies will determine whether intersensory differences in time judgment emerge suddenly or develop slowly with learning.

It is also desirable to learn if the differences in time judgment obtained using various internal temporal standards exist with psychopathologic populations.

Parallel research involving dimensions other than time is necessary if results are specific to temporal judgment or represent more general phenomena. Limited exploration of this issue using spatial judgments[9,11,11a] has highlighted the importance of this consideration.

Undoubtedly, excursions into these areas will provide increased understanding while continuing to broaden the scope and complexity of the problem. If the past may be used for prediction, each new piece that fits into the puzzle will create many additional pieces that require exploration. This state of affairs is not discouraging but is rather viewed as consistent with the natural course of scientific events.

Discussion

It is clear from clinical observation and these experiments that the context can differentially modify temporal judgments when considering various psychopathologic populations. These contextual factors are not sources of experimental error, but provide essential data about the determinants of judgment alterations. In this instance negative findings are as important as positive results.

It is clear that the simplest measure of absolute threshold involves a complex process determined by an interaction of many organismic and contextual parameters. Perceptual studies usually involve some variation of the absolute method where the standard *and* the response are both concepts.

The sensory process involves an exciting adequate stimulus and a nerve impulse which offers inexplicit information that a more central decoder must translate.[26] Research must determine the kinds of information included in and excluded from the judgment process. When producing a solution to a problem about duration, what kinds of data are selected and rejected? How does the organism's capacity to integrate stimulation and conceptual residuals develop, and what defects within the system determine the mental illness or drug induced errors?

The approach to date has been largely empirical and normative since it was initially necessary to gather facts about time judgment. However, the accumulation of large amounts of data without attempts at systematization leads to research without direction and a chaotic collection of unrelated information.

From a theoretical point of view, Helson's[31,32] adaptation-level schema offers the most useful point of departure. This approach to the concept *adaptation* has proven useful in basic psychophysical research[40] and has been extended into the areas of motivation and learning,[4] social psychology,[7,43] clinical judgment,[12] intelligence,[30] and personality and psychopathology.[28a] This schema views an adjustment response as an integration of focal, background and residual factors that can be defined and measured experimentally. When the contribution of these focal and background stimuli, and the organismic residuals have been determined, one should be able to predict the response or adaptation level. This has been successfully accomplished under laboratory and social situations.

The results of time judgment research with its abundance of focal and background contextual influences, as well as with different organismic states involving altered concept residuals may be ordered within an adaptation-level schema. The differential effects of controlled experimental parameters such as step interval, psychophysical method, anchor durations and sense mode upon the time judgments of healthy and psychopathologic subjects may provide information regarding altered concept residuals. The pooling of present input with concept residuals that reflect previous encounters with similar classes of stimuli is basic to time judgment research and the general problems of psychopathology.[26,28a]

Another useful point of departure was suggested by the studies with drugs and physiologic change. People may be viewed as event producing and counting units with variations in a standard event-rate resulting in predictable changes in judged duration. Increased event-rate accompanying high fever or stimulation results in overestimation of the duration of inputs, while sedation results in underestimation.[19,22,23,33,34a] This model has been useful when it was necessary to coordinate psychologic and physiologic variables.

Finally, the point of view and experimental techniques of decision theory[49] may offer a fruitful approach to the effects of personality, psychopathology, and outcome contingencies on temporal judgment.

These remarks were occasioned by only one program of research emphasizing an orientation to the experimental study of time judgment that mushroomed from "the Second Estimation Point" 8 years ago. Research in this area is only in its infancy. Instruments, methods and conceptual framewords are increasingly available that should permit the continued progress of work on the experimental psychopathology of time judgment.

REFERENCES

1. ABELL, A.: Sensory-motor synchrony: a study of temporal performance. Unpublished doctoral dissertation, University of Houston, 1962.

2. BEHAR, I., AND BEVAN, W.: Analysis of the prime psychophysical judgment. Percept. mot. Skills, *10:* 82, 1960.

3. ——, AND ——: The perceived duration of auditory and visual intervals: cross-modal comparison and interaction. Am. J. Psychol., *74:* 17-26, 1961.

4. BEVAN, W., AND ADAMSON, R.: Reinforcers and reinforcement: their relation to maze performance. J. Exp. Psychol., *59:* 226-232, 1960.

5. ——, REED, W. G., AND PRITCHARD, J. F.: Single-stimulus judgments of loudness as a function of presentation-interval. Tech. Rep. #3, Nonr-3290 (01), Project NR 142-155, 1961.

6. BINDRA, D., AND WAKSBERG, H.: Methods and terminology in studies of time perception. Psychol. Bull., *53:* 155-159, 1956.

7. BLAKE, R. R., ROSENBAUM, M., AND DURYEA, R. A.: Gift giving as a function of group standards. Human Relations, *8:* 61-73, 1955.

8. ——, MOUTON, J. S., AND HAIN, J. D.: Social forces in petition signing. Southwestern soc. sci. Quart. *36:* 385-390, 1956.

9. BOARDMAN, W. K., GOLDSTONE, S., AND LHAMON, W. T.: Effects of lysergic acid diethylamide (LSD) on the time sense of normals. Arch. Neurol. & Psychiat., *78:* 321-324, 1957.

10. ——, ALDRICH, R. C., REINER, M. L., AND GOLDSTONE, S.: The effects of anchors on apparent length. J. Gen. Psychol., *61:* 45-49, 1959.

11. ——, GOLDSTONE, S., REINER, M. L., AND FATHAUER, W. F.: Anchor effects, spatial judgments, and schizophrenia. J. Abnorm. & Soc. Psychol. *65:* 273-276, 1962.

11a. ——, ——, ——, AND HIMMEL. In press.

12. CAMPBELL, D. T., HUNT, W. A., AND LEWIS, N. A.: The effects of assimilation and contrast in judgment of clinical materials. Am. J. Psychol. *70:* 347-360, 1957.

13. CLAUSEN, J.: An evaluation of experimental methods of time judgments. J. exp. Psychol., *40:* 756-761, 1950.

14. COHEEN, J.: Disturbances in time discrimination in organic brain disease. J. Nerv. Ment. Dis., *112:* 121-129, 1950.

15. COHEN, S. I., AND MEZEY, A. G.: The effect of anxiety on time judgment and time experience in normal persons. J. Neurol. Neurosurg. Psychiat., *24:* 266-268, 1961.

16. DOBSON, W. R.: An investigation of various factors in time perception as manifested by various nosological groups. J. Gen. Psychol., *74:* 27-35, 1954.

17. EYSENCK, H. J., GRANGER, G. W., AND BRENGELMAN, J. C.: Perceptual processes and mental illnesses. Maudsley Monographs 2, New York, Basic Books, 1957.

18. FRAISSE, P.: Psychologic du temps. Paris, Press Universitaires, 1957.

19. FRANCOIS, M.: Contribution a l'étude de sens du temps. La temperature intérne comme facteur de variation de l'appréciation subjective des durées. L'année Psychol., *28:* 186-204, 1927.

20. FRANKENHAEUSER, M.: Estimation of Time. Stockholm, Almquist & Wiksell, 1959.

21. GOLDSTONE, S., LHAMON, W. T., AND BOARDMAN, W. K.: The time sense: Anchor effects and apparent duration. J. Psychol., *44:* 145-153, 1957.

22. ——, BOARDMAN, W. K., AND LHAMON, W. T.: Effect of quinal barbitone,

dextro-amphetamine, and placebo on apparent time. Brit. J. Psychol., *49:* 324-328, 1958.

23. ——, ——, ——: Kinesthetic cues in the development of time concepts. J. Genet. Psychol., *93:* 185-190, 1958.

24. ——, ——, ——: Intersensory comparisons of temporal judgments. J. Exp. Psychol., *57:* 243-248, 1959.

24a. ——, ——, ——, FASON, AND JERNIGAN. In press.

25. ——, JERNIGAN, C., LHAMON, W. T., AND BOARDMAN, W. K.: A further note on intersensory differences in temporal judgment. Percept. mot. Skills, *9:* 252, 1959.

26. ——: Psychophysics, reality and hallucinations. *In* West, L. J. (Ed.) : Hallucinations. New York, Grune & Stratton, 1962.

27. ——, AND GOLDFARB, J. L.: Time estimation and psychopathology. Percept. mot. Skills, *15:* 28, 1962.

28. ——, ——, STRONG, J., AND RUSSELL, J.: Replication: Effect of subliminal shock upon judged intensity of weak shock. Percept. mot Skills, *14:* 222, 1962.

28a. ——, AND ——: In press.

29. HAKEREM, G.: Instrumentation for research in pupillography. Psychopharm. Serv. Cent. Bull. *2:* 11-14, 1962.

30. HEIM, A. W.: Adaptation to level of difficulty in intelligence testing. Brit. J. Psychol., *46:* 211-224, 1955.

31. HELSON, H.: Adaptation-level as a frame of reference for prediction of psychophysical data. Am. J. Psychol., *60:* 1-29, 1947.

32. ——: Adaptation-level theory. *In* Koch, S. (Ed.) : Psychology: A Study of a Science, Vol. I., New York, McGraw Hill, 1959.

33. HOAGLAND, H.: The physiologic control of judgment of duration. Evidence for a chemical clock. J. Gen. Psychol., *9:* 267-287, 1933.

34. KIRKHAM, J., GOLDSTONE, S., LHAMON, W. T., BOARDMAN, W. K., AND GOLDFARB, J. L.: Effects of alcohol on apparent duration. Percept. mot. Skills, *14:* 318, 1962.

34a. KLEBER, LHAMON, W. T., AND GOLDSTONE, S.: Hyperthermia, hyperthyroidism, and time judgment. J. Comp. Physiol. Psychol. *56:* 362-365, 1963.

35. LATIES, V. G., AND WEISS, B.: Effects of alcohol on timing behavior. J. Comp. Physiol. Psychol., *55:* 85-91, 1962.

36. LEWIS, A.: The experience of time in mental disorder. Proc. Roy. Soc. Med., *25:* 611-620, 1932.

37. LHAMON, W. T., AND GOLDSTONE, S.: The time sense: Estimation of one second durations by schizophrenic patients. Arch. Neurol. & Psychiat., *76:* 625-629, 1956.

38. ——, EDELBERG, R., AND GOLDSTONE, S.: A comparison of tactile and auditory time judgment. Percept. mot. Skills, *14:* 366, 1962.

39. MEZEY, A. G., AND COHEN, S. I.: The effect of depressive illness on time judgment. J. Neurol. Neurosurg. Psychiat., *24:* 269-270, 1961.

40. MICHELS, W. C., AND HELSON, H.: A quantitative theory of time-order effects. Am. J. Psychol., *67:* 327-334, 1954.

41. RAUSH, H. L.: Perceptual constancy in schizophrenia. J. Person., *46:* 131-141, 1951.

42. REYNOLDS, G. A.: Perceptual constancy in schizophrenics and normals. Unpublished doctoral dissertation, Purdue Univ., 1953.
43. ROSENBAUM, M., AND BLAKE, R. R.: Volunteering as a function of field structure. J. Abnorm. & Soc. Psychol., *50:* 193-196, 1955.
44. SALZINGER, K.: Shift in judgment of weights as a function of anchoring stimuli and instructions in early schizophrenics and normals. J. Abnorm. & Soc. Psychol., *55:* 43-49, 1957.
45. SCHILDER, P.: Psychopathology of time. J. Nerv. Ment. Dis., *83:* 530, 1936.
46. SMYTHE, E. J.: A normative, genetic study of the development of time perception. Unpublished doctoral dissertation, University of Houston, 1956.
47. ——, AND GOLDSTONE, S.: The time sense: A normative genetic study of the development of time perception. Percept. mot. Skills, *7:* 49-59, 1957.
48. STEINBERG, H.: Changes in time perception induced by an anaesthetic drug. Brit. J. Psychol., *46:* 273-279, 1955.
49. SWETS, J. A., TANNER, W. P., AND BIRDSALL, T. G.: Decision processes in perception Psychol. Rev. *68:* 301-340, 1961.
50. SZASZ, T. S.: A contribution to the psychology of schizophrenia. A.M.A. Arch. Neurol. & Psychiat., *77:* 420-436, 1957.
51. VIERORDT, K.: Der Zeitsinn nach Versuchen. Tubingen, H. Laupp, 1868.
52. WALLACE, M. AND RABIN, A. I.: Temporal experience. Psychol. Bull., *57:* 213-236, 1960.
53. WEBSTER, F. R.: Studies in time perception: Contextual factors and psychopathology. Unpublished doctoral dissertation, Vanderbilt University, 1962.
54. ——, GOLDSTONE, S., AND WEBB, W. W.: Time judgment and schizophrenia: Psychophysical method as a relevant contextual factor. J. Psychol., *54:* 159-164, 1962.
55. WECKOWICZ, T. E.: Size constancy in schizophrenic patients. J. Ment. Sci., *103:* 475-486, 1957.
56. WEINSTEIN, A. D., GOLDSTONE, S., AND BOARDMAN, W. K.: The effect of recent and remote frames of reference on temporal judgments of schizophrenic patients. J. Abnorm. & Soc. Psychol., *57:* 241-244, 1958.
57. WOODROW, H.: Time perception. *In* Handbook of Experimental Psychology. New York, Wiley, 1951.
58. WRIGHT, D. J., GOLDSTONE, S., AND BOARDMAN, W. K.: Time judgment and schizophrenia: Step interval as a relevant contextual factor. J. Psychol., *54:* 33-38, 1962.

Discussion

by JOSEPH ZUBIN, Ph.D.

THE TWO PAPERS THIS MORNING deal with two of the less studied and less quantified senses—pain and taste. While all sensation occurs through the excitation of sensory receptors within the organism (or on its surface), pain and taste, unlike the distance senses (the visual and auditory), are referred to locations on or within the skin of the organism in the case of pain, and on the tongue in the case of taste, rather than to the world outside the organism. For this reason, perhaps, their measurement has lagged behind the other senses. In the case of pain, it has remained a private event not readily open to public scrutiny. To some extent this also holds true of taste. On the other hand, while vision and audition also are basically private events, they can be more readily controlled and triangulated from the outside and thereby become more open to public scrutiny.

Pain is not only the origin for medicine, but it is probably also the beginning of consciousness, the beginning of self as differentiated from the environment. Psychopathology can hardly be imagined without the presence of pain. Why then has its measurement lagged? The only answer that I can offer is that, unlike the other sense modalities in which one can relate percepts to external criteria, pain is still a self-referred sense. Warmth too is a self-referred internal event, but in the course of time it became possible to obtain external criteria for gauging the degree of warmth present. History records that the initial steps in the direction of the measurement of warmth came in the form of rating scales ranging from the hottest day of summer to the coldest day of winter with two intervening subdivisions. The first break-through in relating subjective warmth and its measurement probably occurred when it became possible to modulate the source of warmth so as to increase or decrease the subjective feeling. The objective measurement of vision was more easily developed because the relation between vision and light was much more readily felt, and control and measurement of the objective source of light was more easily obtainable. The same holds true of the relation between hearing and sound. But in the case of pain it is taking a longer time and is more difficult to determine the adequate stimulus for pain, and to measure it against

189

external criteria. We have not yet found the best way of doing it today.

In measuring the response to a light stimulus we observe that the response can be detected on several levels: the physiological, sensory, perceptual, psychomotor or conceptual. The same may be said to hold true of the response to stimuli which evoke pain. But it is debatable whether the usual meaning of the term pain refers to its physiological, sensory, perceptual, psychomotor or conceptual aspect. It may very well be that the conceptual component of pain, the stored memories of previous pain experiences, are far more important in the response to a painful stimulus than is the stimulus itself. Evidence for this comes from the studies of Hebb and his students, in which animals who had been prevented from being exposed to painful stimuli in their early development found it very difficult to learn how to respond adequately to painful stimuli later. Perhaps early experience with pain is the only way in which an animal can develop the proper response to pain, and hence the conceptual component developed from past experience is very important.

Dr. Beecher in his paper draws attention to the distinction between the psychophysical approach to pain provided by Hardy, Wolff and Goodell and the method of titrating pain by 15 mg. of morphine through the measurement of the half-life of painful experience (when the pain is subjectively reduced to half of what it had been initially). The first is a laboratory technique; the second deals with the measurement of pain in situ—namely, in the pathological conditions.

It is no wonder at all that the two methods do not always lead to the same results since in the first method the conceptual component is probably not nearly as important as in the second, naturalistic approach. When a person is suffering from an illness he has anticipations of pain which would produce a result that would hardly parallel the laboratory situation where no anticipation of pain resulting from illness is to be expected.

The evidence of sensory physiology continues to leave unresolved the question of whether pain may be considered as a separate sensory system with its own receptors and fibers or whether pain results from a special mode of activation of fibers which also respond to mechanical, thermal or other stimuli.[4] If the controversy is resolved in favor of the latter alternative, there is a sense in which one might consider pain not as a sensation with which affective and conceptual components may be associated, but rather as a conceptual component from the very outset.

In any case, whenever the response to a stimulus depends heavily on past experience, as in the case of pain, it is possible for the response to become emotionally toned. By this we mean that there are other elements besides the stimulus itself which account for the eventual response and that the level of the sensory threshold is hardly sufficient for explaining the kind of response obtained. From this point of view pain may be regarded as an emotion, since it is heavily laden with past experience. Thus any methods which will attempt to reduce pathological pain by eliminating anxiety and similar expectations will have results which cannot be paralleled by the experimental approaches to pain. This is essentially what Dr. Beecher has been arguing for. That the conceptual component operates also in the case of experience with pain in animals is demonstrated by the investigation of Hill, Bellevielle and Wikler.[1] They demonstrated that an animal which has learned to respond to a warning signal for an impending shock by reducing its bar pressing will ignore the warning signal after being injected with morphine and continue its bar pressing rate as if no warning signal had been given. Thus the effect of morphine is to interfere with the memory of the previous experience or with the attitude towards it; and when the effects of morphine have worn off, the effectiveness of the warning signal returns and the animal reduces its rate of bar pressing again during the warning signal. On the other hand, Verhave[2] demonstrated that the injection of 10 mg. of morphine per kg. of body weight tends to eliminate avoidance responses but not escape responses. Is it possible that the escape response is so closely attached to the painful stimulus that it depends less on previous memory while the avoidance response must depend basically upon stored memories?[3]

Another example of the conceptual component in pain arises from the consideration of intractable pain. An examination of the degree of pain as measured by the number of doles indicates that intractable pain is of a rather low order of pain and the only reason why it is so unbearable is not the intensity of the pain but its duration and unavoidability—a conceptual component. It is further interesting to note that frontal lobotomy will relieve the pain though it doesn't alter the sensory threshold for pain. This indicates that it is the anxiety of the pain that is reduced and not the sensory level.

Dr. Fisher and Pasamanick present a very good case for exploring the sense of taste as a probe for personality and disease indicators. Since taste sensitivity is a more subtle characteristic than some of the other behavioral indicators, it probably suffers less change induced by cultural and social factors. Furthermore, it seems to have, at least in the case of taste, for some substances, a rather high genetic loading. This permits the use of this modality as a basis for developing personality types as well as disease-prone types. It is quite likely that such psychochemical investigations may prove to be a greater source of knowledge about behavior and personality than psychophysical investigations. Since most of the psychophysical experiments hardly touch the surface of the receptors, their effect in eliciting basic behavior may be very mild compared to psychochemical influences, and psychochemistry may replace psychophysics as a more powerful tool in behavioral investigations.

One wonders, however, whether the single positive correlation between taste threshold and the digit-symbol test found by Fisher and Pasamanick is to be regarded seriously. One would like to know how many other correlations with the Wechsler-Bellevue subscores were computed before the deviation score was selected. Was this a single chance finding or does it represent a serious result? If so, one would have to provide some rationale for the relationship between digit-symbol substitution and taste threshold.

REFERENCES

1. HILL, H. E., BELLEVIELLE, R. E., AND WIKLER, A.: Motivational determinants in modification of behavior by morphine and pentobarbital. A.M.A. Arch. Neurol. Psychiat. 77: 28-35, 1957.
2. VERHAVE, T., OWEN, J. E., JR., AND ROBBINS, E. B.: The effect of secobarbital and pentobarbital on escape and avoidance behavior. Psychol. Repts. 3: 421-428, 1957.
3. ZUBIN, J., AND KATZ, M. M.: Psychopharmacology and personality. In Worchel, P., and Byrne, D. (Eds.): Personality Change. New York, John Wiley & Sons, 1964, pp. 367-395.
4. ZUBIN, J., et al.: Experimental Abnormal Psychology. New York, Columbia University Bookstore (mimeographed), 1960, Chapter 12 A.

Part III: Perception under Special Conditions

8

SOME POSSIBLE BASIC DETERMINANTS OF DEPERSONALIZATION PHENOMENA

by NOLAN D. C. LEWIS, M.D.

THE PHENOMENON CURRENTLY CALLED "DEPERSONALIZATION" has been described under various terms as far back in time as recorded psychiatric observations have been made. In clinical work one meets with various degrees of comparatively mild disturbances of this nature on to complete loss of the sense of reality and identity. In the milder attacks or forms it consists of a subjective sense or feeling of estrangement or of unreality within the personality. The person feels strange and somehow different from his usual self. His feelings seem blunted and he may even say that his "emotions are dead"; that he cannot feel joy or sorrow, or experience love or hate. For example, a mother may assert that she has no feeling of love for her children. This lack of affective responsiveness seems to worry the patients most. It often extends to feelings of emotional indifference regarding former friendships, the church, and toward financial difficulties.

To the depersonalized person the world may appear strange, foreign and dreamlike. At times objects appear strangely altered. They may seem diminished or enlarged in size, or flat, or crooked and the tactile characteristics of objects may seem strangely changed. Sounds nearby may appear to originate at a distance. These patients complain of changes in their perceptibility, of alterations in their imagery, and some complain that they have lost power of imagination entirely.

In the ordinary setting, despite the strange and alarming situation there are no delusional components or bizarre interpretations and the subject understands that it is some psychological condition and usually fears that it will lead to "insanity." In somewhat more severe cases the subject has the impression that other people or objects are unreal, changed or are in the process of changing, or that they appear distorted in their physical characteristics and configurations (derealization). The subject may feel that current events or other experiences have happened before (*déjà vu*—"already seen").

In these non-psychotic patients, objective examinations by the psychiatrist usually fail to reveal any defect in the sensory apparatus, and the emotional capabilities are intact. Their facial expressions exhibit natural affective reactions, all of which indicates that they are capable of making and do make emotional responses. The psychological examination definitely establishes the fact that there is an inner conflict in the form of opposition to the experiencing of life. They do not give themselves wholly to their experiences. They try, but not quite successfully, to turn completely away from contact with the realities of life. In some cases it is possible for the therapist to discover what type of experiences, in particular, elicits this inner opposition.

The phenomenon, as such—that is, as a special emotional disorder—receives scanty attention descriptively in the textbooks of psychiatry although a number of its expressions are described in the symptomatology of neuroses and psychoses. In its mild form depersonalization is a relatively common experience. In more pathological states it is found among the expressions in various neuroses, depressive states, and, of course, among the early symptoms of schizophrenia. Its extreme expressions are found in mental states in which the patient is lost in fantasy, showing no interest in external experiences. Where it is an early expression of schizophrenia, it may gradually become the nucleus of a definite delusional formation. Here differential diagnosis is important since the inexperienced may diagnose a schizophrenia which is not present because of the vague unclear way some depressives and psychoneurotics describe these feelings. A change in the personality is felt and such remarks as "I am a stranger to myself" and "I feel lifeless—a mere automaton" may not indicate a deep splitting of the personality. Depersonalization phenomena are particularly prone to occur at the onset or termination of a neurosis or psychosis, and in some cases they dominate the entire picture as in severe schizophrenia.

Between depersonalization as a special entity and as a component or result of other more severe psychiatric disorders, a differentiation may be made according to some authors, on the degree of insight factor. Regardless of how fantastic the perceived changes may seem, they remain incredible to the uncomplicated depersonalized patient. I would suggest that the simpler episodes of depersonalization may be best understood, at present, as temporary partial regressions to earlier levels of the maturation of the personality, in the face of frustrating and intolerable life situations.

Some spectacular dissociative defenses appear in the form of hysterical fugues in periods lasting from a few minutes to several months or years with partial or total amnesias, all of which are precipitated by a serious adaptational problem. However, in schizophrenia the withdrawal and isolation is often colored by bizarre, fragmented symbolisms, compensating grandiosities and distortions in the various components of the body image as was so well described by Schilder[1] who also pointed out that the narcissistically invested organs are most commonly heavily involved in the depersonalization phenomena.

Cleveland and co-workers[2] experimented with 100 schizophrenics, 50 non-schizophrenics and 30 college students. They were compared as to their estimates of body size and parts and control objects, using various techniques. Schizophrenics were found to be less accurate in estimating the size of the body parts directly or from pictures to the extent to suggest, to the authors, the loss of boundary definiteness in the direction of ballooning of the body image. This did not occur with ordinary control objects.

There have been several reports[3-5] on experimental sensory isolation showing that this situation of deprivation can produce cognitive and perceptual distortions in the form of disorders of concentration and changes in the body image among other things. Some of these reactions resemble the transient conditions seen in post-operative cataract and other eye conditions when both eyes are bandaged[6,7] and in polio patients treated in a tank type of respirator. Common to all these and similar conditions is the disappearance of the symptoms when normal perceptual contact with the environment is re-established.

It is well known that in the depressive phase of the manic depressive psychosis, the patient may express the feeling that nothing exists. Although this may be said with emphasis, the patient is usually completely aware of the nature of his surroundings and behaves in keeping with his immediate environment. Often the patient complains of a loss of his identity and of his former interests in life, but retains his hold on the reality of his body and its environs. There is no impairment of memory as such but there are various degrees of loss of interest in what is taking place and therefore an attention defect.

Although the process of feeling dissolved, of losing one's identity, one's personality, the *l*, attains its most complete and lasting expression in schizophrenia where it may accompany fantasies of world destruction, somatic delusions and hallucinations or feelings of being passively controlled by outside forces, there are some benign non-schizophrenic cases, usually accompanied by feelings of dissolution, and practically always by fear. I refer to those instances where the whole body is projected to the outside without the impression that this projected body is distorted or different, but momentarily they are not sure which is the real one. The situation clears up rather promptly. Four such cases have come under my observation. One, a young woman, a secretary, was awakened by the telephone. When she reached the instrument, which necessitated crossing a room, she was shocked to find herself already there answering it. On another occasion the same girl went to her bathroom only to find she was already there combing her hair. One teacher found himself to be double on several occasions ("one behind the other"), talking to his students. A somewhat different position was taken by the projection of a young man, a college football player. On two occasions he found himself running "beside myself," both carrying the ball—a complicating situation which removed him from the team. All of these persons sought psychotherapy with the desired results.

The etiology of depersonalization remains a controversial issue but it is generally accepted that it constitutes a disturbance of the body image and since its symptomatology is protean, being bound in a wide variety of psychic states and functions, the explanation may well be sought in the dynamics of personalization, or in the integration of the personality, or in ego formation to speak psychoanalytically. Dissociation of the self or of the personality into some of its components occurs quite frequently in daily life. This probably represents a continuous process of disjunction and reintegration. Introspection splits the perceptive self into its components whether it is the scrutiny of one's own bodily processes or the observation of one's mental processes, thoughts and emotions. In the former, special attention is being paid to the sensations which originate in the body. This is an inwardly directed observation, which differs from the usual self-observation characteristic of all of us when we have a painful spot or when something has gone wrong physically, for here the observed organ becomes a separate object often largely removed from subjectivity. It is thus an object of observation.

Physically ill persons or those suffering a painful spot often feel the presence of another person who is aching, especially during the hypnogogic state preceding deep sleep. A distinction might be made that here we are dealing with hypochondriasis whereas depersonalization should apply only to disorders of self-observation of the thought processes. Freud[8] once defined the term "depersonalization" as properly "referring to the sense of the loss of oneself. The sense of loss of the environment is known as estrangement." However, in all of these matters introspection characterizes and dominates the situation. Therefore hypochondriasis and depersonalization are closely related clinically as Schilder always insisted.[9]

Approaching the problem psychoanalytically, it would seem that these patients withdraw libido from their own experiences and from their personalities and from the environment and that this is then fixated by some special events or experiences. The particular experiences may not be obvious, but the dissociation of the personality is obvious by the fact that the patient fills the double role, simultaneously, of experiencer and observer.

The phenomenon of depersonalization appears to be the beginning of withdrawal from the outside world, a process which if not interrupted can terminate in the world destructive state of mind. When an individual is in a condition of depersonalization, libido is drawn both from the environment and from some aspects of the ego. Some parts of the perceptive self and of the ego-ideal which relate to the person's contact with his environment must remain active. One must be permitted to assume that the ego-ideal as well as the perceptive self have remained in partial investment, both in the sense that the outside world appears only estranged and not destroyed, and that the intact parts of the personality scrutinize critically and attempt to evaluate the situation. As Schilder once formulated the mechanism, we "see in the phenomenon of depersonalization two diametrically opposed tendencies. The one strives to keep the individual in touch with reality and experience and to invest the environment with libido in spite of its estrangement. The other tendency endeavors to turn the individual from reality and experience, to withdraw its cathexes from the environment."

Depersonalization has also been interpreted to be a pathological defense dynamism developed with the object of protecting the person from threatening outer or inner trauma on the assumed basis that what is experienced at the time is unreal and therefore not to be feared, or that not being entirely oneself one's observations are not quite true and accordingly are not dangerous.

It is certain that various other factors may play a role in the depersonalization picture. It has long been known that movements accompanying mental states exert an influence on the distortion of images due to shifts of attention. Jaensch demonstrated years ago that various qualities of optical impressions are influenced considerably by the state of attention which may, in turn, depend upon the integrity of the eye muscles. Shifts in attention have the capacity of distorting the appearance of the environment.

While, clinically, depersonalization may be interpreted, in degree, as a mild temporary partial regression, or may appear as a deep permanent regression as in schizophrenia, what is the relationship of these states to anatomophysiological structure and to biochemical processes? Certain brain diseases and other pathophysiological states can produce depersonalization either by direct cause or by releasing it. But through what channels? Personally, I have never been willing to accept the concept that an individual can have fixed patterns of abnormal behavior or ingrained personal experiences without concomitant or associated molecular changes or metabolic abnormalities in the central nervous system. The time is well in the past when it seemed justified that a concept or phenomenon which is understandable from the psychological point of view cannot be due to an "organic" or somatic process.

Since neurophysiology has not yet reached a degree of development which permits an accurate correlation with psychological experiences of this type, one must recognize that any attempt to interpret mental behavior in terms of our present knowledge of neurophysiology and neurochemistry must be based largely on speculation and that any attempt to jump across this gap or to cross on flimsy footing may dump one into a pool of error. However, as a stimulant, enthusiastic error is always preferable to complacent belief or even to static wisdom.

According to the biological evidence now available, in dealing with human behavior we have to return repeatedly to the old accepted concept that we are products of our anlages and multifarious surroundings, and it is well recognized, as the result of investigation, that certain characteristics may be transmitted in latent form through several generations only then to become overtly or objectively manifest in a certain individual descendant. Therefore, inherited characteristics somewhere in the structure-function may have some bearing on reaction patterns. According to the 2nd law of thermodynamics, the non-living physical world tends toward disorganization. This differs from the distinguishing character of the biological world which is the tendency to preserve, to build up, to integrate, and to continue in organization. The stuff of living organisms cannot be separated logically or even well physically from the stuff of the environment. Consciousness with its several components is peripheral and may well be operative at the juncture between that tendency which the organism has to preserve itself at its present level and the opposite tendency to regress. Depersonalization and other disorders of perception are involved in the operations of consciousness.

In the process of evolution, nature has endowed man essentially with three brains which, in spite of marked differences in structure, function together. The most ancient of these brains is basically reptilian, the second has arisen from the lower mammals and the third is the late mammalian development which has made man peculiarly what he is. During the past 20 years, studies have demonstrated that the lower mammalian derivative, the so-called "limbic system" which we share with all mammals, functions at a primitive level in emotional behavior. There are indications that it elaborates basic emotional and visceral feelings that guide behavior aimed at self-preservation and preservation of the species. It is sometimes referred to as the "visceral brain" with the term "visceral" being used in its 16th century connotation as a label for strong internal feelings. Nerve cells in the brain are grouped into functional patterns called "schemes," and possibly depersonalization and dissociation (e.g., schizophrenia) are involved in elements of broken integration in some of the junctions or connections between "old" and new structures, phylogenetically speaking.

A relationship between several abnormal psychological conditions of the order of which we are dealing today, and the control and sustaining of sensory input and attention is quite possible. The body image disturbances of the schizophrenic patient as well as depersonalizations in other settings may possibly have their origins in defective screening. In Luby's[10] hypotheses, such disturbed neural integrations, in schizophrenia, "might result either from the presence of an inhibitor substance or from a defect in energy."

The reticular formation in the brain has different parts and extensions—and thus probably different functions which, under certain circumstances, may become disturbed. According to Courville and co-workers[11] it has been "generally accepted in recent years that the reticular formation can exert some type of control over specific sensory input, even though the exact nature of this control and its precise sites of action are still matters of controversy. "Our working hypothesis was that if a synchronizing system did exist, in the reticular formation, its effect on the sensory input might be opposite to that of the activating system." Their researches indicated the presence of two antagonistic ascending systems in the reticular formation: one adrenergic, the other colinergic whose tonic activity "originates in the mesencephalic tegmentum in one case and in the caudal regions of the brain stem in the other."

The current trend in neuropsychopharmacological experimentation may eventually throw light on several of our present problems. The drug known commonly as LSD, an ergot derivative, has been proved, by widespread research, to produce a variety of symptoms including visual distortions, perceptual changes, depersonalizations, disturbances in self-identity and reality, and anxiety reactions. It is usually considered the most powerful psychomimetic compound yet discovered. Studies have also been made on other hallucinogens such as mescaline, extracted from a cactus native in our southwest; harmine, derived from a Turkish plant; psilocybin, a mushroom product and bufotenin, extracted from toad venom. In recent years a very large number of derivatives of these substances, as well as some new compounds, have been synthesized. These constitute important attempts to elucidate the functions of the brain by studying the effects on behavior, the mode and site of action and the metabolic characteristics.

The "model psychoses" produced suggest "the hypothesis of a disturbance in proprioceptive feedback mechanism."[10] They suggest a reduction in the cortical activity due to reduction in apparent flow. (See experiments by Hermandes-Peon et al.: Acta Neurol. Latino-Am., No. 1, 1957.) Continued clinical experimentation with LSD and other psychotomimetic compounds are indicated—while there may be room for argument concerning the similarity, or lack of same, of engendered symptoms to schizophrenia, it is in the area of depersonalization and derealization that similarity between the two experiences becomes most striking and acceptable, and depersonalization may be at the very core of schizophrenia as Paul Federn[12] emphasized over 10 years ago.

Whitehorn[13] makes a pertinent comment on maturity of the personality. "Human beings we may truly say never can become wholly mature and independent, in the sense that we might describe for some animals in their adult stage as mature and independent. Human beings achieve such a state as we usually call maturity only by developing a good working accommodation to the inescapable fact of their inevitable interdependence. . . . Each human being is born weak and helpless and survives only by the sufferance and sympathy of others, enduring a long period of helplessness and inadequacy—indeed an undying dependency." Similar to many other terms in use, "maturity" is difficult or practically impossible to define comprehensively, but it implies a flexibility of the capacity to get along in a living environment, to live on the level of human equation with a balanced inner sense of adequacy and importance without the necessity to underrate others in order to make oneself an equal. The difficulty, for one reason or another, to reach a maturity, with the failure to realize infantile satisfactions within the adult framework, results, according to many psychopathologists, in depersonalization phenomena which can be released by a variety of somatic and psychologic stresses.

In the foregoing account it has been pointed out that depersonalization can result from a number of experimental techniques, and by several varieties of brain lesions, as well as from emotional conflicts. The nature of, and the exact location of the physiological pathways and the relative weight or significance of these factors and how these differ in degrees of dysfunction remain for further research. The complicated human being can be studied only in parts or segments at present. It may be a long time before it will be possible holistically.

REFERENCES

1. SCHILDER, P.: Mind, Perception and Thought. New York, Columbia University Press, 1942.
2. CLEVELAND, S. E., et al.: Perception of body size in schizophrenia. Arch. Gen. Psychiat, 7: 277, 1962.
3. SHURLEY, J. T., Profound experimental sensory isolation. Am. J. Psychiat., 117: 539, 1960.
4. DAVIS, J. M.: Sensory deprivation. Arch. Gen. Psychiat. 5: 84, 1961.
5. ZISKIN, E., AND AUSBURY, T: Hallucinations in sensory deprivation: Method or madness. Science, 137: 992, 1962.
6. LEIDERMAN, H., et al.: A.M.A. Arch. Int. Med. 101: 389, 1958.
7. LEWIS, N. D. C.: Psychosomatic principles and patterns in disorders of the special senses: (Weir Mitchel Memorial Lecture). Psychoanalytic Rev. 35: 411, 1948.
8. FREUD, S.: Almanach für Psychoanalyse, 1937.
9. SCHILDER, P.: Introduction to Analytical Psychiatry. New York, Nervous and Mental Disease Publishing Co., Monograph #50, 1928.
10. LUBY, E. D., et al.: Model psychoses and schizophrenia. Am. J. Psychiat., 119:-61, 1962.
11. COURVILLE, J., et al.: Functional organization of the brain stem. Reticular formation and sensory input. Science, 138: 973, 1962.
12. FEDERN, P.: Ego Psychology and the Psychoses. New York, Basic Books, 1952.

13. WHITEHORN, J.: A Working Concept of Maturity of Personality. Am. J. Psychiat. *119:* 197, 1962.

Additional References Bearing on the Subject

ACHNER, B.: Depersonalization (*I & II*). J. Ment. Sci., *100:* 838 and 854, 1954.

ANDREW, R. J.: Evolution of intelligence. Science, 1937: 585, 1962.

ARIETI, S.: The microgeny of thought and perception. Arch. Gen. Psychiat., *6:* 454, 1962.

BLUESTONE, H., AND McGAHEE, C. L.: Reaction to extreme stress. Impending death by execution. Am. J. Psychiat., *119:* 393, 1962.

FEINBERG, I., AND GARMAN, E. M.: Studies of thought disorder in schizophrenia: Arch. Gen. Psychiat., *4:* 191, 1961.

FLINN, D. E.: Transient psychotic reactions during travel. Am. J. Psychiat., *119:* 173, 1962.

GALSTON, I.: On the etiology of depersonalization. J. Nerv. & Ment. Dis., *105:* 25, 1947.

LEVIN, M.: The levels of the nervous system and the capacity to function independently of each other. J. Nerv. & Ment. Dis., *132:* 75, 1961.

MASSERMAN, J. H.: The Practice of Dynamic Psychiatry. Philadelphia, Saunders, 1955.

ROTH, N.: Disorders of visual perception as detected in psychoanalysis. J. Hillside Hosp. *11:* 86, 1962.

9

SENSORY DEPRIVATION AND ITS EFFECT ON PERCEPTION

by THEODORE SCHAEFER, JR.* and NILES BERNICK†

T HE LITERATURE ON SENSORY DEPRIVATION is too broad for a detailed examination in the time available. Several exhaustive reviews have already been published.[12,25,44,45,50] We intend to discuss only the research in which an adult human is isolated in a special environment where the patterning or absolute level of external stimulation is reduced. Within this context, we shall consider only that class of perceptual effects which is commonly referred to as imagery or hallucinatory phenomena. It is generally accepted that humans subjected to prolonged periods of reduced or monotonous stimulation are likely to experience some degree of perceptual and cognitive disturbance, but this conclusion is based on research involving serious methodological and procedural problems which have not been fully recognized. Therefore, we shall further restrict the discussion to problems of method and procedure and to some underlying theoretical considerations in research on sensory deprivation.

Although it is possible to cite earlier work,[19] the research at McGill University reported in 1954 by Hebb's associates, Bexton, Heron, and Scott,[4] defined the basic procedure for the study of the effects of sensory deprivation on the adult human organism. In these studies, subjects were isolated for periods up to 3 days in a special, uniformly lighted, sound-treated chamber. Variations in visual, tactual, and kinesthetic stimulation were reduced by having the subjects lie quietly on a bed wearing translucent goggles, with hands and arms encased in gloves and cardboard cuffs. Variation in auditory stimulation was masked by a monotonous hum from fans, an air conditioner, and an amplifier driving earphones mounted in a foam rubber pillow. Gross behavioral, physiological, intellectual, and perceptual effects were

---

*Columbia University. Currently at Scientific Engineering Institute, Waltham, Mass.

†University of Chicago.

observed or tested before, during, and after the isolation. Bexton, Heron, and Scott reported that irritability, discomfort, heightened emotionality, and impairment of intellectual and cognitive performance occurred during and immediately after isolation, but they emphasized, under the heading *hallucinatory activity*, the unusual imagery, dream-like states, and abnormal thought processes which most of their subjects experienced.

These results had quite an impact. A symposium devoted to sensory deprivation was held in 1958, only 4 years after publication of the first study. In addition to providing a useful review of the work and thought which had accumulated by 1958, this symposium, finally published[44] in 1961, served to indicate the broad interest in sensory deprivation. Fifteen papers dealt with an array of topics ranging from cognition and perception, through physiological and motor, to psychiatric and clinical considerations. Although this may be taken as evidence for the interrelatedness of all aspects of the living organism, or for the peculiar importance of sensory deprivation, it might be of more value to consider why, in such a short time, sensory deprivation could capture the interest of people in so many varied fields.

Its special importance has been argued as a means of understanding such practical problems as maintaining vigilance while performing monotonous tasks like monitoring radar screens,[4,12,25] and flying planes or space vehicles,[3,7,20,25,29,40,43,50] or the possible use of sensory deprivation in brainwashing,[12,18,25,35] and research on psychopathology or therapy.[2,15,16,23,25,28,38,44,45] These features of the sensory deprivation procedure have been touted in newspapers and magazines,[1,5,33] where the emphasis, as in the original study, has been on the disruption of cognitive processes and hallucinations. Such coverage has instilled the widespread belief that isolation as well as reduced stimulation can produce perceptual and mental aberrations. In an interview[34] about his space flight, John Glenn humorously reported that when he described the small, bright particles he had observed floating outside his capsule at sunrise, the Mercury Project psychiatrist asked, "What did they say to you, John?" In the context of the news reports and much of the research literature, the psychiatrist's implication was clear, if not justified.

However, the popular appeal of sensory deprivation research cannot fully account for the fervid interest among many students of behavior. Two currently ascendant theoretical positions can be seen as predisposing factors for the enthusiastic and uncritical acceptance of the reported effects of sensory deprivation. One of these theoretical positions, the one which directly stimulated the original sensory deprivation experiment, is Hebb's[17] emphasis on the importance of environmental stimulation in the development and maintenance of normal behavior. The other orientation is that of activation as put forth, for example, by Malmo,[32] based on the neurophysiology of the reticular formation and associated areas in the brain stem. Both viewpoints emphasize the crucial role of sensory input in the maintenance of normal functioning. The reported disruptive effects of reduced stimulation provide a point of convergence for these two, broadly based movements in behavioral research and theory.

There are, however, other theoretical orientations which contradict the expectation that normal, adult humans would suffer much perceptual disturbance in the deprivation procedure. These theoretical predispositions emphasize internal factors in normal functioning, factors which operate continually to maintain a dynamic internal equilibrium in the face of wide differences in the state of the external environment. Such factors are described in Cannon's concept of homeostasis[8] and Lashley's notion of the determining tendency, or set, in brain functioning.[27] Both Cannon and Lashley conceived of internal, ongoing processes which are in continual, dynamic action, maintaining an overall equilibrium which keeps all life processes within certain necessary limits. In their view, behavioral and physiological responses to changes in the external environment are in the direction of maintaining the internal environment within normal limits. Cannon was interested, primarily, in what some call bodily processes, but Lashley's determining tendency was supposed to be a neurological process, possibly reverberating circuitry, through which higher mental processes, like thought and perception, could proceed along specific lines more or less independent of the immediate environment. Both these concepts, Cannon's homeostasis and Lashley's determining tendency, imply that the effects of any but the most extreme environmental events are severely limited, at least insofar as resulting in a pathological condition. Viewed from this perspective, any event in the environment would have to be very unusual, indeed, to drive the self-regulating, equilibrium-maintaining organism into a pathological, nonadaptive state such as hallucinations or marked cognitive impairment. In the course of evolution, dynamic internal processes have developed to buffer the organism against the easy production of pathology by environmental factors.

The extended periods of sensory deprivation used in the first experiments could be viewed as precisely the kind of extreme deviation from normal environmental stimulation which might be expected to overcome the organism's inherent mechanisms for maintaining stability. Or, perhaps, the reported hallucinatory phenomena could itself be considered a buffering mechanism which permitted the organism to adjust to extreme change in the environment without more serious pathology. However, these alternatives seemed unlikely when it became apparent in later studies that the deprivation procedure could be reduced to as little as one hour[9,21] or even less[24,35] with essentially the same effects as the longer periods. In fact, the original Bexton, Heron, and Scott study included some subjects who experienced the unusual imagery in 20 minutes.[18] Such short periods of reduced stimulation seem insufficient to upset the self-regulating mechanisms, unless one argues that the species, in the course of evolution, has not developed appropriate homeostatic mechanisms for conditions of reduced stimulation. But this seems unrealistic. Such conditions are not rare. Certainly, for many mammals, survival in nature requires the ability to spend long periods hiding or waiting in motionless silence, often in a burrow or quiet, isolated spot. Man, in fact, must have evolved, or inherited from his ancestors, the capacity for such inactivity while hiding or waiting in isolated, nonstimulating situations. Hallucinations or other severe disturbances of thought would be fatal in many naturally occurring circumstances. It seems likely that susceptible humans would have been eliminated by natural selection, and organisms would have evolved who could withstand reduced sensory input without adverse effects.

In the literature on sensory deprivation, much has been made of individuals who have reported mental and perceptual disturbances in more or less naturally occurring isolation or deprivation situations.[30,45,50] However, the cases cited might just as well serve to emphasize that such experiences are infrequent. The individuals who report them do so because they recognize that their experiences are unusual. It would be as easy to assemble examples of people who have spent long periods in isolation without bizarre or disturbing perceptual experiences. Schacter,[41] for example, interviewed prisoners after 3 to 5 days of solitary confinement. His evaluation was that such isolation was not productive of disturbance, temporary or otherwise.

Thoughts of homeostasis and internal capacities for withstanding environmental anomalies had been interfering with my acceptance of the reported effects of sensory deprivation when Vernon, Marton, and Peterson, in 1961, published[47] a review of their attempts to replicate the hallucinatory outcome of the McGill group. In a series of experiments, they varied factors in the deprivation situation such as the amount and type of minimal stimulation, and the duration or uninterruptedness of the confinement. They were unable to determine which, if any, of these factors had any special importance in the production of hallucinations. But of greater interest was their overall finding that imagery or hallucinations were rather rare, only 10 of 55 subjects in their experiments having reported any hallucinatory phenomena. A review of the work on sensory deprivation at that time revealed that hallucinations, mild or otherwise, were not the invariant result of the sensory deprivation procedure. A few studies[29,40] reported a failure to obtain hallucinations or imagery, and another[7] yielded results similar to those of Vernon. Moreover, there are many situations in which subjects are routinely isolated in dark, quiet rooms for psychophysical and other research without experiencing imagery or hallucinatory phenomena. Schacter[41] describes experiments in which he isolated subjects for 2 to 8 days without obtaining the results that have come to be expected from such treatment. Although Schacter's procedure was not identical to typical sensory deprivation procedures, the isolation was complete and stimulus variation was certainly below normal.

Several factors have been considered in attempts to explain the marked differences in the amount and extent of hallucinatory phenomena in sensory deprivation experiments. In his exhaustive and thoughtful review of the literature on sensory deprivation, Fiske[12] has discussed these factors and cited the relevant papers. Fiske emphasized the apparent association between reports of imagery and the restriction of the subjects' mobility, and he argued from theoretical considerations that the ever-present kinesthetic and associated tactual stimuli are important sources of arousal and activation in sensory deprivation situations. I shall not attempt a detailed review, but the following considerations have been mentioned in one or aonther paper. The extent to which the subject feels free to report;[9,10,30] how the reports are obtained (in retrospect or during the experiment);[9,10,26,30] the criteria for imagery and hallucinations,[26,49] the patterning or meaningfulness of stimulation,[11,39,48] social isolation,[10,13,26,40] freedom to move,[10,12,13] temporal duration of the experiment,[29,49] presence of monotonous stimulation,[11,13,15] absolute level of stimulation,[11,13,15] and the role of suggestion or instructions as to what to report.[9,21,22,36,37]

Our own review led to a conviction that suggestion, or the subject's expectations, were of prime importance. Ruff, Levy, and Thaler[29,40] and Cameron[7] did not give instructions about imagery and hallucinations and their results are notable for lack of perceptual disturbances, or imagery. Vernon's studies, on the other hand, were preceded by very deliberate and thorough instructions about the nature of sensory deprivation studies, with an emphasis on the stressful aspects of the deprivation situation. The instructions given in other studies are, typically, not reported in enough detail to permit an evaluation of how they might affect the results, so we undertook the following experiments[42] to study the role of expectations or suggestions in sensory deprivation procedures.

EXPERIMENT I

The first experiment was designed to test the effectiveness of suggestion, or expectation, in producing hallucinatory experiences *without* stimulus deprivation. Twenty-seven volunteers (13 males, 14 females) from an undergraduate experimental psychology course were assembled in the lounge of a recently vacated dormitory. The subjects were assigned, randomly, to individual rooms and the following instructions, aimed at producing a set to stay awake and attend to subjective phenomena without actually specifying the exact nature of such experiences, were read aloud.

"This is, in part, an attempt to test the validity of extrasensory perception, and in part it is a laboratory experience in introspection. Although I am skeptical of the theory of extrasensory perception, my bias is not shared by a great many people. We have with us today eight psychology graduate students who, in varying degrees, accept some of the ESP reports as constituting good evidence for the existence of some kind of communication which seems to be mediated in ways other than the usual sense modalities. I have consented to allow them to carry out an experiment which we feel will constitute a scientific test of ESP. The design calls for placing each subject in a separate room, away from disturbing and distracting influences, in a relaxed state. We have gone to the trouble of providing cots for this purpose.

"Outside, in the hallway, a male and female graduate student will station themselves to send perceptual images of one kind or another. Your task, as a subject, is to try to receive their message which will be in the form of sensory or perceptual imagery. We are using a man and a woman on each floor because sex differences in ESP abilities have been reported, and because distance has also been implicated. We are asking you to adopt a cooperative attitude, and to try to introspect the image or images which will be sent.

"It is felt that the best possibility for success is for you to relax, lie down, remain as still as possible, and allow yourself to introspect your sensations and imagery. The method of projecting, and the material used by the graduate students will be described later. For now you should know nothing other than the fact that a wide variety of images or sensations may be used. Try to remain aware of your introspections. We will ask you to describe them after approximately one hour. Don't worry about trying to remember in great detail or in sequence. You will be given a check-list to help you recall subjective experiences which you might have had. Are there any questions? If at any time you wish to terminate your part in the experiment, please come out into the hall and one of the experimenters will be there to help."

One male and one female graduate assistant had been assigned to each of the four floors on which the experiment rooms were located. After the instructions were read each pair of graduate students assembled those subjects who had been assigned to rooms on their floor and conducted them, in a group, to the proper floor. Thus, a male and female graduate student were present on each floor to monitor the experiment. In each room, shades on the windows were drawn, reducing the late afternoon sunlight but not actually darkening the room. Except for the subjects' cots, each room was bare of all furnishings. Subjects and monitors maintained silence throughout the experiment, but sounds were audible from occasional pedestrian and auto traffic outside the building, and from steam radiators, plumbing, and the elevator within the building. All subjects reported and identified these kinds of noises in written answers to a questionnaire at the end of the experiment.

Before entering their rooms the subjects were asked to use the lavatories (located on each floor) and were reassembled in the hallway to begin the experiment together. The 14 subjects who had been assigned to rooms on the second and fourth floors were reassembled in the hallways on these floors, and additional instructions were read. These instructions, aimed at eliciting more dramatic images or "hallucinations," were as follows:

"You may experience quite vivid, strange, and dramatic feelings, sensations, and perceptions. Some of these experiences may seem bizarre or unusual. Don't let this disturb you. Strange perceptual experiences are often reported in prolonged introspective situations. Please try to relax and allow your mind to be receptive to each subjective phenomenon to whatever degree seems reasonable. We will be interested in the range and extent, as well as the kinds of imagery and subjective experiences which may occur."

The 13 subjects on the first and third floors entered their rooms after using the lavatories but without these additional instructions. This procedural difference between odd and even numbered floors was introduced to produce different expectations in the hope that differences in the quality or quantity of subjective report phenomena might be obtained.

Forty-five minutes after the subjects had entered their rooms, a monitor entered and gave each subject a sheet of paper with the following statement dittoed at the top:

"Please describe any compelling, long-duration, or dramatic subjective sensations, perceptions, or feelings which you experienced. Indicate whether they were pleasant or unpleasant."

Five minutes later this sheet was exchanged for a 25-item, dittoed check-list of the kinds of subjective experiences reported by subjects in typical sensory deprivation experiments. This check list was based on one developed by Jackson.[21] In a statement heading the check-list, the subject was asked to indicate, by marking one through four, the intensity with which a given phenomena had been experienced. If the subject had not experienced the phenomenon, he left the item blank.

TABLE 1.—Subjects' Reports of Their Experiences (from written descriptions); Number of Check-list Items Chosen; and Mean Intensity Rating of Checked Items

| | Numbers of Subjects | Reported Imagery | | | Check List Mean Number Of Items | Mean Intensity Rating |
		None	Moderate	High		
Experiment I (No Stimulus Deprivation)	27	3	16	8	8.9	2.5
Experiment II (Stimulus Deprivation)						
"Psychophysics" Instructions	5	5	0	0	6.0	1.7
"Typical" Instructions	5	1	0	4	10.6	2.2
"Typical" plus "stress" Instructions	5	3	1	1	7.8	1.9

Results

The results are presented in table I. The top row of figures describe the outcome of this experiment. Twenty-four of the total number of 27 subjects reported at least some imagery or subjective sensations in their written descriptions of their experiences. Eight of these reported fairly elaborate subjective experiences, some of which are presented in Appendix A.

It seems necessary to present these verbatim typescripts of the subjects' written reports because it is impossible to assert, confidently, that any given description of thought processes or perceptual phenomenon is a true hallucination, or even an experience that is comparable to the imagery that is typically reported in sensory deprivation. These problems are present in any sensory deprivation experiment. Part of the difficulty is inherent in the nature of subjective private events. In addition, the issue of what constitutes a true hallucination is not clear. If hallucination is defined as a sensory experience with no basis in reality, I suppose that the reports of subjects in this experiment cannot be accepted as hallucinations because it is possible that objective visual and auditory stimuli could have initiated the imagery. If it is necessary to establish that a subject did not recognize the unreality of his perceptual experience, then it is again difficult to argue that these subjects hallucinated. Several subjects denied, when questioned individually after the experiment had ended, that they really thought the experiences were happening: It is not likely that a normal person will say yes when he knows the event could not have occurred. It is interesting to note, however, three subjects in this experiment who reported that they felt the cot moving. One of these subjects, a girl, stated that she got up and looked under the cot for strings which she suspected the monitors were manipulating from the hallway. A male subject said he looked under the cot for electric wires and some device that was vibrating the cot. The third subject said that he discovered he could control the movement by changing the position of his head and he concluded that his pulse beat was responsible for establishing some kind of harmonic with the canvas and frame of the cot. For the first two of these subjects, the subjective experience, whether or not it was based on reality in some way was certainly a compelling illusion, or misinterpretation of a perceptual experience, if not an hallucination. It is also clear that the subjective experiences described by subjects in this experiment are quite like those of typical sensory deprivation experiments. Actually, as should become apparent after the next experiment is described, the question of whether or not sensory deprivation, as such, produces any effects at all is more important than what to call the effects.

On the 25-item checklist the mean number of items reported as having been experienced was 8.9 per subject with a mean intensity rating, on the four-point scale, of 2.5 per checked item. There were no appreciable differences in the number of items checked, or in the intensity rating, between the groups of subjects given the added instructions and those given only the single set of instructions.

Five of the 14 subjects who had been given the extra instructions reported elaborate imagery in their written reports, and three of the 13 subjects who had not received the added instructions also reported elaborate imagery. However, two of the three subjects reporting no imagery were on the fourth floor, where the additional instructions were read. There were no detectable sex differences, nor were there any indications of ESP—unless a report of the taste of chocolate or the vision of a large cabbage can be construed as equivalent to *pie a la mode,* the image which some of the monitors, on their own, had decided to "send."

Although the additional instructions failed to produce clear differences between groups, it does seem obvious, from these results, that sensory deprivation—unless lying on a cot in a quiet room for 45 minutes can be construed as such—is not necessary for the production of hallucinatory subjective responses. The results indicate that suggestion alone is sufficient to elicit such subjective reports. Failure to find differences between the groups may be interpreted as an indication that instructions to the first group were as suggestive of an expectation of subjective sensory phenomena as the added instructions to group two.

Experiment II

The second experiment was designed to test whether or not, in a more typical sensory deprivation situation, suggestion or appropriate expectations are necessary, within the brief time-limit of the above experiment, for the production of hallucinatory experiences. In this experiment 15 male college students were each paid two dollars to serve as a subject for one hour. The subjects were divided into three groups which differed in the "sets" or expectations they were given by varying the instructions and the arrangement of experimental apparatus. All subjects, regardless of instructions, were placed on a cot, alone, in a totally dark, sound-treated room specially built for research in audition. Each of the five subjects in Group I was led, individually, into the sound-proof chamber through an adjoining observation room equipped with auditory and visual apparatus—an audiometer, a tape recorder, an intercom, and a slide projector, all arranged so as to appear to be part of the experiment. The subject was asked to lie down on the cot, and the intercom was designated as the means of communication between experimenter and subject. A one-inch cross, cut into a large, black pasteboard panel masking a window in the wall at the foot of the cot, was pointed out as the visual stimulus ,aperature, and the experimenter left the room, turning off the light and closing the soundproof, double door. The following tape-recorded instructions were then played over the intercom:

"This is an exploratory study of the relationship between auditory and visual stimulation. You are part of a control group for which auditory stimulation will be reduced by presenting the visual stimuli in this sound-proof room. Your performance, and that of the other subjects tested under these circumstances, will be compared with subjects tested while auditory stimulation is presented simultaneously with visual stimuli.

"Since the effect we are interested in is reported to occur only at low levels of stimulation, it will be necessary for you to spend about 30 minutes dark-adapting. You will have to do this in the sound-proof room because there is some possibility that auditory fatigue may be an important factor in the phenomena. We have provided a cot for your comfort during the period of adaptation, but we must ask that you don't fall asleep while adapting. The visual threshold is quite variable for some time after wakening due to fluctuating attention, and this will make it difficult to get reliable results in the time remaining within the hour." In order to insure, to some extent, that the subject remained awake, he was asked, after 30 minutes, to watch for a light in the stimulus aperature. In reality, no stimulus was presented, each subject reported no stimulus, and he was then told that it would be necessary to dark-adapt a little longer. Fifteen minutes later, the experimenter entered the stimulus deprivation chamber, turned on the light, and asked the subject to fill out the dittoed forms described in Experiment I.

Before subjects in the remaining two groups were brought into the sound-proof room, the apparatus and equipment, except for the tape recorder and intercom, were removed from the observation room. Each of these ten subjects was introduced to the cot, intercom, and dark room, using the procedure described for Group I, except that the stimulus panel was not pointed out, and the stimulus aperature had been masked. After the experimenter had left the chamber, the five subjects in Group 2 heard the following tape-recorded instructions on the intercom:

"This is an experiment on the effects of reduced sensory input on normal sensory processes. You are to stay in this sound-proof, light-tight room for about one hour. Then you will be asked to describe any sensory or perceptual experiences you may have had, and to complete a short questionnaire concerning your experiences. You may experience quite vivid, strange, and dramatic feelings, sensations, and perceptions. Some of these experiences may seem bizarre or unusual. Don't let this disturb you. Such subjective phenomena are often reported under the conditions of this experiment. Please try to relax and allow your mind to be receptive to such subjective phenomena to whatever degree seems reasonable. We will be interested in the range and extent as well as the kinds of imagery and subjective experiences which may occur. You will be able to communicate with me at any time during the experiment by depressing the lever on the intercom apparatus next to you."

The five subjects in Group 3 heard the same instructions with the following added paragraph, quoted from one of Vernon's [46, p. 91] sensory deprivation studies:

"This is not a study in endurance. This is not an attempt to break you down. We are simply trying to find out what happens to humans under these conditions. If at any time the confinement becomes too difficult, you are free to terminate the experiment and we insist that you do so rather than trying to be heroic. The ante-chamber to the confinement cell will always be occupied by an experimenter."

The instructions common to Groups 2 and 3 were indented to produce the set and expectations usually suggested by instructions to subjects in typical sensory deprivation studies. Group 3 was given the additional paragraph in an attempt to test a hypothesis that the low incidence of imagery or hallucinations which Vernon has found might be due to this paragraph in his instructions. Such instructions might influence the subject's expectations so that he suppresses or represses subjective phenomena in an attempt to not appear weak or victimized, or because he is afraid to give free reign to possibly disturbing subjective experiences.

Results

The results of Experiment II are presented in table 1 (p. 210). None of the five subjects in Group I, given instructions for a psychophysical study, described anything in their written reports more noteworthy or hallucinatory than initial, fleeting lights, colors, after-images, or a slight ringing in the ears, all of which faded after the first few minutes.

When questioned verbally about the nature of the experiences and how they had passed the time, these subjects reported that they had felt relaxed and had thought about everyday activities, course assignments, the experiment, etc. Upon direct questioning, these subjects denied having experienced any imagery or unusual subjective experiences. On the average, only six of the sensory experiences listed in the check-list were indicated by these subjects, and the mean rating of intensity was only 1.7 per item. These values are lower than the comparable figures of 8.9 items rated, and 2.5 per checked item for subjects in the first experiment.

In contrast, subjects in the second group, informed of typical expectations in a sensory deprivation study, described the same kind of subjective phenomena in their essays as the non-deprived subjects in the dormitory rooms of Experiment I. Examples of these descriptions are presented in Appendix B. The average number of check-list items experienced by Group 2 subjects was 10.6, with a mean intensity rating of 2.2 per checked item. These values include one subject in Group 2 who reported no effects. It is interesting to note that this subject, upon questioning, stated that the dark-room experience was not out of the ordinary for him because his hobby is spelunking and he is accustomed to spending long periods in dark, quiet caves without experiencing such subjective states. It seems likely that, for this subject, the instructions did not restructure his expectations based on his past experiences.

Only two of the five subjects in Group 3, whose instructions included the paragraph quoted from Vernon, described any imagery. The others reported none and, when questioned, they firmly denied having any strange or delusional sensations. Group 3 subjects, including those reporting no imagery, checked an average of 7.8 items on the list of subjective phenomena and gave a mean intensity rating of 1.9 per checked item. The two subjects in Group 3 who did report imagery or subjective phenomena had extreme scores of 18 and 11 items checked, and mean ratings of 2.0 and 2.2 on the 4-point scale of the intensity of experience of the items checked. Thus the added paragraph from Vernon appears to produce either no imagery or an extreme amount, a result that might be predicted if one considers that either a subject's defenses may be aroused, or his perception more severely affected. Perhaps the University of Chicago students in this experiment differ somewhat from Vernon's Princeton subjects, accounting for the higher proportion of subjective reports than Vernon obtained.

Results of both experiments, considered together, indicate that suggestion or expectation is a very important factor in sensory deprivation experiments. Perhaps it is as important as reduced stimulation in producing the subjective experiences of sensory deprivation. This conclusion, although based on a brief deprivation period, has implications regarding the factor of suggestion in the design of future studies of the effects of reduced sensory input. It has, perhaps, an even more important bearing on the popular belief, discussed in the mass media, that sensory deprivation has an awesome power as a means of brainwashing, torturing, or breaking down political and war prisoners. The results of this study indicate that suggestion or expectation, rather than isolation or sensory deprivation, may be serious considerations in such situations.

In late 1961, when we were planning the first experiment, suggestion had been mentioned in only a few published reports.[9,24] While we were discussing the design of our experiments with our colleagues at the University of Chicago, we learned of the unpublished dissertations of Jackson[21] and Cambareri,[6] both emphasizing the probable role of suggestion or suggestibility in imagery. Jackson, on the basis of the effectiveness of a one hour deprivation period (12 of his 14 subjects reported peculiar sensations), reasoned that the effects were primarily due to prior knowledge of the anticipated results, and the creation of an attitude that hallucinations are appropriate in the deprivation situation. Camborari demonstrated that suggestible and non-suggestible subjects, as determined by pre-testing, reported different amounts of imagery in a tank-type, sensory-isolation procedure similar to that used by Lilly.[31] More recently, Pollard, Uhr, and Jackson[36] have reported that subjects informed that imagery and bizarre sensations had occurred in previous experiments, experienced more imagery in 3 hours of deprivation than subjects who were given no prior information and deprived for 8 hours. In another study[37] in which subjects were isolated on two occasions a week apart, these investigators found fewer reports of imagery and subjective phenomena during the second session, and a lower report of imagery during the second half of each 6-hour session. They interpret both findings as evidence for the importance of expectations in the production of hallucinatory phenomena.

In a recent review of sensory deprivation research, Jackson and Pollard[22] summarized the evidence for the importance of factors such as the subject's expectations and motivation, and the requirement, in several studies, that subjective experiences continually be described. They suggest that current views of sensory deprivation research which emphasize reduced stimulation are not justified. One current view, they point out, is identified with psychoanalytic concepts in which personality disorganization is thought to result from the emergence of primary process material when the ego is no longer assailed by environmental input. Another interpretation of sensory deprivation is in terms of neurophysiological changes resulting from reduced input into the reticular formation. In this view cortical arousal is diminished and abnormal brain functioning results. Both of these theoretical orientations are compatible with the idea that the effects of reduced stimulation are similar to certain kinds of behavior pathology, such as schizophrenia. But if the perceptual effects of sensory deprivation are related, primarily, to factors like attention or set, it is difficult to conceive its relevance to pathology. Ziskind and Augsburg,[51] for example, offer a less sensational explanation of the perceptual effects of sensory deprivation, and their title "Hallucinations in Sensory Deprivation—Method or Madness?" indicates the growing concern about methodology and procedure in this research. They suggest that the "hallucinations" of sensory deprivation are fragments of normal imagery which usually go unnoticed because our attention is not directed toward the elaboration and description of such fleeting experiences. As such, sensory deprivation phenomena are similar to dreams, or reveries while dozing, and cannot readily be likened to pathological states, or disturbances.

It should be emphasized, perhaps, that the sensory deprivation procedure may be a fruitful technique for research in behavior, as illustrated by its use in studies of task performance, cognition, and aspects of perception other than imagery or hallucinations. It also seems likely that long-term sensory deprivation may have serious consequences, as indicated in the recent findings by Zubek[52] of changes occurring in EEG alpha during 14 days of isolation, changes which persisted for at least one week after deprivation. In fact, the basic proposition that sensory deprivation has a disruptive effect on behavior, perception, and cognition is still tenable, but future research must take account of the methodological or procedural problems having to do with suggestion, the subject's expectations, and his attempts to cooperate by reporting that which he has been asked. Currently, widely accepted opinions that sensory deprivation research has relevance to military and political problems seem unjustified if one considers all the evidence available, including those studies which indicate that subject's or experimenter's expectations have influenced the findings and interpretations, to date. It seems likely that humans isolated in monotonous stimulus conditions, will not risk perceptual or cognitive disturbances unless they expect to experience such effects.

To end on a more positive note, it should be recognized that the experiments described and cited in this paper indicate that perceptual processes are very sensitive to factors like attention, set, expectations, or suggestion. The procedures used in sensory deprivation research may provide a unique method for studying these factors and their role in perception and behavior.

Appendix A

The following descriptions were written by subjects in Experiment I. These subjects were not placed in a reduced stimulus situation, but were told to attend to their imagery, etc.

1. "Most of the sensations I experienced were with colors. There was a long series of images of colors and substances with the colors, such as peppermint sticks revolving with bright pink. Blues of sky and ocean color also of waves and rhythms, undulating blues that lead to an image of a train running through a burning landscape. None of this was unpleasant.

"There were many more such patterns but none so compelling or persistent as the combination of colors and rhythms."

2. "At first I felt 'heavy,' paralyzed, as if I were dead and aware of it. A heaviness upon me. This feeling lasted quite a while. After the feeling and really simultaneously with it I experienced a visual sequence which at most could be described as rainbow-like only shaped like a helix into which I proceeded to see myself fall.

"Other visual feelings were a violent rapids and a moonlit ocean.

"I felt during the later part after the rainbow a fear which quickly passed along with the pounding of my heart."

3. "Very often I could see before me the various stages of an atom bomb blast. At first I 'saw' a fire ball and then the cloud spreading out. Suddenly I 'saw' a tractor. I closed my eyes, and I still imagined that I could see a tractor. Then horses pulling a wagon. It seemed rather strange to me that I

imagined such things—I rarely think that sort of thing. Then I 'saw' a few kids playing on a sleigh—going down a steep bank—the atom bomb then came back—what a shame the world has to end that way. I saw a face come out of the cloud—but it disappeared, and I saw the sun. This I thought was rather curious."

4. "A finger being wrapped up in a chain.

"One image reappeared several times—flowers in a bunch. They seemed to vary in color. I would say they were rather morbid—flowers as of a funeral.

"Another image that appeared several times was that of a hand or foot or claw—in each case it was large, rough, and warty. I felt nothing unpleasant here but the scene was unpleasant.

"A half face appeared once or twice, as if illuminated from one side."

5. "I had a very pleasant and also compelling image of a very blue lake, softly rippled, with a white raft in the middle. It was a complete perception: blue sky (dark) with white stars, green grass leading down to it, and a red boat tied to the raft.

"I also had a series of short images—red ball, green star (came back several times), brown parallel lines. (I can't remember the others.) These were neutral in feeling.

APPENDIX B

The following reports were written by subjects given typical sensory deprivation instructions and placed in a soundproof darkroom for 45 minutes.

1. "I heard a ringing in my ears after about a minute. This ringing varied in intensity. I thought of long passages of music and the ringing decreased during these times. When I stopped thinking of the music the ringing returned to its original intensity. The ringing then became louder and lower in a very regular pattern, always the loudest times were equally loud and the softer sounds were also equal.

"The ringing sounded like the chirping of spring peepers, for awhile.

"I then saw some light gray shapes against dark gray (the room seemed dark gray, rather than black after the first few minutes). The light shapes were irregular long curved objects which moved across like waves. While I saw these shapes, which was only for a short time, the ringing in my ears stopped for brief moments.

"After the experiment my hands felt odd, and not as sensitive as usual.

"I completely lost my time sense. The experiment seemed to be over in about half an hour.

"For a brief moment I thought I heard one of my friends say a short phrase.

"All sensations were pleasant. I didn't like the shapes at first, but was a little sorry when they left."

2. "I felt or rather feared suffocation. This occurred during the latter part of my confinement. I started breathing deeply. I saw strange shapes and noticed a steady hum in my ears. The weird shapes and hum occurred frequently though."

3. "The first thing that happened to me was I fell asleep for a few minutes. When I awoke I saw fluorescent lines that made me feel "creepy" and I started to feel panicky. This quickly passed, however, and I saw myself back in grammar school just as I was ten years ago and I remembered little things like the color of my geography book or my third grade reading book. Then for some reason I saw a giant cigar floating around with a long gray ash and it came towards me and dissolved just before it got to me. Nothing happened for a while and then the quietness hit me and I didn't like it at all. I found myself back in my high school orchestra-band playing marches which is what I enjoyed most in high school. Then I relaxed and saw those long fluorescent lines that looked like a constant hazy discharge of electricity. It was very relaxing."

REFERENCES

1. As minds grow misty. Newsweek, *54:* 60, 1959.
2. AZIMA, H., VISPO, R., AND AZIMA, F. J.: Observations on anaclitic therapy during sensory deprivation. *In* Solomon, P., *et al.* (Eds.) : Sensory Deprivation. Cambridge, Harvard University Press, 1961, pp. 141-160.
3. BENNETT, A. M. H.: Sensory deprivation in aviation. *In* Solomon, P., *et al.* (Eds.) : Sensory Deprivation, Cambridge, Harvard University Press, 1961, pp. 161-173.
4. BEXTON, W. H., HERON, W., AND SCOTT, T. H.: Effects of decreased variation in the sensory environment. Canad. J. Psychol. *8:* 70-76, 1954.
5. Brief isolation causes neurotic behavior. Science Digest, *48:* 29, 1960.
6. CAMBARERI, J. D.: The effects of sensory isolation on suggestible and non-suggestible psychology graduate students. Unpublished doctor's dissertation, University of Utah, 1958.
7. CAMERON, D. E., LEVY, L., BAN, T., AND RUBENSTEIN, L.: Sensory deprivation effects upon the functioning human in space systems. *In* Flaherty, B. E. (Ed.) : Psychophysiological Aspects of Space Flights. New York, Columbia University Press, 1961, pp. 225-237.
8. CANNON, W. B.: The Wisdom of the Body. New York, N. W. Norton, 1932.
9. COHEN, B. D., ROSENBAUM, G., DOBIE, S. I., AND GOTTLIEB, J. S.: Sensory isolation: Hallucinogenic effects of a brief procedure. J. Nerv. Ment. Dis., *129:* 486-491, 1959.
10. COHEN, S. I., SILVERMAN, A. J., BRESSLER, B., AND SHANAVONIAN, B.: Problems in isolation studies. *In* Solomon, P., *et al.* (Eds.) : Sensory Deprivation. Cambridge, Harvard University Press, 1961, pp. 114-129.
11. DAVIS, J., McCOURT, W. F., AND SOLOMON, P.: Effect of visual stimulation on hallucinations and other mental experiences during sensory deprivation. Am. J. Psychiat., *116:* 889-892, 1960.
12. FISKE, D. W.: Effects of monotonous and restricted stimulation. *In* Fiske, D. W., and Maddi, S. R.. (Eds.) : Functions of Varied Experience. Homewood, Ill., Dorsey Press, 1961, pp. 106-144.
13. FREEDMAN, S. J., GREENEBAUM, H. V., GREENBLATT, M.: Perceptual and cognitive changes in sensory deprivation. *In* Solomon, P., *et al.* (Eds.) : Sensory Deprivation. Cambridge, Harvard University Press, 1961, pp. 58-71.

14. GOLDBERGER, L.: Homogeneous visual stimulation (Gansfeld) and imagery. Percept. mot. Skills, 12: 91-93, 1961.
15. ——, AND HOLT, R. R.: Experimental interference with reality contact Individual differences. In Solomon, P., et al. (Eds.): Sensory Deprivation. Cambridge, Harvard University Press, 1961, pp. 130-142.
16. HARRIS, A.: Sensory deprivation and schizophrenia. J. Ment. Sc., 105: 235-237.
17. HEBB, D. O.: The Organization of Behavior. New York, Wiley, 1949.
18. HERON, W.: Cognitive and physiological effects of perceptual isolation. In Solomon, P., et al. (Eds.): Sensory Deprivation. Cambridge, Harvard University Press, 1961, pp. 6-33.
19. HOCHBERG, J., TRIEBEL, W., AND SEAMON, G.: Color adaptation under conditions of homogeneous visual stimulation (Ganzfeld). J. Exp. Psychol., 41: 153-159, 1951.
20. HOLT, R. R., AND GOLDBERGER, L.: Assessment of individual resistance to sensory alteration. In Flaherty, B. E., (Ed.): Psychophysiological Aspects of Space Flights. New York: Columbia University Press, 1961, pp. 248-262.
21. JACKSON, C. W., JR.: An exploratory study of the role of suggestion in research on sensory deprivation. Unpublished doctor's dissertation, University of Michigan, 1960.
22. ——, AND POLLARD, J. C.: Sensory deprivation and suggestion: A theoretical approach. Behavioral Sc., 7: 332-342, 1962.
23. ——, ——, AND KANSKY, E. W.: The application of findings from experimental sensory deprivation to cases of clinical sensory deprivation. Am. J. Med. Sc., 243: 558-563, 1962.
24. KANDEL, E. J., MEYERS, T. I., AND MURPHY, D. B.: Influence of prior verbalization and instructions on visual sensation reported under conditions of reduced sensory input. Am. Psychologist. 13: 334, 1958 (abstract).
25. KUBZANSKY, P. E.: The effects of reduced environmental stimulation on human behavior: A review. In Biderman, A. D., and Zimmer, H. (Eds.): The Manipulation of Human Behavior. New York, Wiley, 1961, pp. 51-95.
26. ——, AND LEIDERMAN, P. H.: Sensory deprivation: A review. In Solomon, P., et al (Eds.): Sensory Deprivation. Cambridge, Harvard University Press, 1961, pp. 221-238.
27. LASHLEY, K. S.: The problem of serial order in behavior. In Jeffress, L. A. (Ed.): Cerebral Mechanisms in Behavior: The Hixon Symposium. New York, Wiley, 1951, pp. 112-136.
28. LEIDERMAN, P. H., MENDELSON, J., WEXLER, D., AND SOLOMON, P.: Sensory deprivation, clinical aspects. Arch. Int. Med., 101: 389-396, 1958.
29. LEVY, E. Z., RUFF, G. E., AND THALER, V. H.: Studies in human isolation. J.A.M.A., 169: 236-239, 1959.
30. LILLY, J. C.: Mental effects of reduction of ordinary levels of physical stimuli on intact, healthy persons. Psychiat. Res. Rep., 5: 1-9, 1956.
31. ——, AND SHIRLEY, J. T.: Experiments in solitude, in maximum achievable physical isolation with water suspension of intact healthy persons. In Flaherty, B. E. (Ed.): Physiological Aspects of Space Flights. New York, Columbia University Press, 1961, pp. 238-247.
32. MALMO, R. B.: Activation: A neuropsychological dimension. Psychol. Rev., 66: 367-386, 1959.

33. Man alone in the dark. Newsweek, *53:* 106, 1959.

34. MANDEL, P.: First off it was quite a day. Life, Mar. 2, 36 A, 1962.

35. MYERS, T. I., MURPHY, D. B., AND SMITH, S.: Progress report on studies of sensory deprivation. Research Memorandum, U. S. Army Leadership Human Research Unit, Presidio of Monterey, Calif., March, 1961.

36. POLLARD, J. C., UHR, L., AND JACKSON, C. W., JR.: A comparison of relatively neutral versus relatively suggestive instructions on sensory deprivation behavior. Paper read at Midwestern Psychol. Assoc., Chicago, May, 1962.

37. ——, ——, AND ——: The effects of repetition of sensory deprivation on men and women. Paper read at Michigan Academy of Sciences, Arts, and Letters, Detroit, March, 1962.

38. ROSENSWEIG, H.: Sensory deprivation and schizophrenia: Some clinical and theoretical similarities. Am. J. Psychiat., *116:* 326-329, 1959.

39. RUFF, G. C., AND LEVY, E. Z.: Psychiatric research in space medicine. Am. J. Psychiat. *115:* 793-797, 1959.

40. ——, ——, AND THALER, V. H.: Factors influencing reactions to reduced sensory input. *In* Solomon, P., *et al* (Eds.): Sensory Deprivation. Cambridge, Harvard University Press, 1961, pp. 72-90.

41. SCHACHTER, S.: The Psychology of Affiliation. Stanford, Calif., Stanford University Press, 1959.

42. SCHAEFER, T., AND BERNICK, N.: The role of suggestion in "hallucinations" attributed to reduced sensory stimulation. Paper read at Midwestern Psychol. Assoc., Chicago, May, 1962.

43. SOLOMON, P.: Motivations and emotional reactions in early space flights. *In* Flaherty, B. E. (Ed.): Psychophysiological Aspects of Space Flights. New York, Columbia University Press, 1961, pp. 272-277.

44. ——, KUBZANSKY, P. E., LEIDERMAN, P. H., MENDELSON, J. H., TRUMBULL, R., AND WEXLER, D. (Eds.): Sensory Deprivation: A symposium held at Harvard Medical School. Cambridge, Harvard University Press, 1961.

45. ——, LEIDERMAN, H., MENDELSON, J., AND WEXLER, D.: Sensory deprivation: A review. Am. J. Psychiat., *114:* 357-363, 1957.

46. VERNON, J.: Physical and social isolation, G.A.P. Rep., *3:* 89-102, 1956.

47. ——, MARTON, T., AND PETERSON, E.: Sensory deprivation and hallucinations Science, *133:* 1808-1812, 1961.

48. VERNON, J. A., MCGILL, T. E., AND SCHIFFMAN, H.: Visual hallucinations during perceptual isolation. Canad. J. Psychol. *12:* 31, 1958.

49. WEXLER, D., MENDELSON, J., LEIDERMAN, H., AND SOLOMON, P.: Sensory deprivation. Arch. Neurol. & Psychiat. *79:* 225-233, 1958.

50. WHEATON, J. L.: Fact and fancy in sensory deprivation studies. Aeromedical Reviews 5—59. (Air Univ. School of Aviat. Med., USAF, Brooks AFB, Texas, Aug. 1959).

51. ZISKIND, E., AND AUGSBURG, T.: Hallucinations in sensory deprivation: Method or madness? Science, *137:* 992, 1962.

52. ZUBEK, J. P., WELCH, G., AND SAUNDERS, M. G.: Electroencephalographic changes during and after 14 days of perceptual deprivation. Science, *139:* 490-492, 1963.

10

PERCEPTUAL DEFENSE

by CHARLES W. ERIKSEN*

THE CONCEPTS OF PERCEPTUAL VIGILANCE AND DEFENSE were introduced in a series of three articles by Bruner and Postman[6] and Postman, Bruner and McGinnies.[45]† These terms were used as descriptive and semi-explanatory concepts for differences in the recognition of threatening or emotional stimuli as opposed to neutral stimuli. In the first of these articles, Bruner and Postman invoked the concept of vigilance as an explanation for their finding that stimuli associated with experimentally produced anxiety had lower recognition thresholds than neutral stimuli. They suggested the principle of perceptual vigilance whereby stimuli important to the organism were enhanced in perception and recognized sooner. The concept of perceptual defense appeared in the subsequent two articles where the tachistoscopic durations necessary for recognition of emotional words or words representing low values as assessed by the Allport-Vernon Study of Values were found to have higher recognition thresholds than neutral words or words from high value areas.

In the second of these studies, Bruner and Postman administered a word association test to their subjects and then subsequently studied the tachistoscopic durations necessary for the recognition of words with long, medium and short association times. They found that for some subjects words with long association times, indicating emotional disturbance, required much longer durations for recognition than words with medium or short association times. They termed this heightened recognition threshold perceptual defense and likened it to the process of repression whereby anxiety-provoking stimuli were defended against in perception or prevented from attaining conscious awareness in order to minimize anxiety. They also found, however,

---

*University of Illinois.

†A third principle, that of value resonance, was also advanced by these experimenters, but little further was made of it either by themselves or in the research of others.

that in certain subjects long association time words had lower thresholds for recognition. They invoked their principle of perceptual vigilance to account for this lowering of thresholds for affect-laden words pointing out that in some subjects there was a range of emotionality beyond which defense did not operate, but was replaced by sensitization.

In the Bruner, Postman and McGinnies study, the duration thresholds for recognition of words representing the value areas in the Allport-Vernon were compared with individual subjects' scores on this test. It was found that there was a correspondence between a subject's score on the respective value areas and on his recognition for words denoting these values. Subjects who had a high score on the theoretical value, for example, had lower duration thresholds for words from this value area and had higher thresholds for words from value areas on which they scored quite low. The concepts of vigilance and defense were again invoked to describe or explain these results with vigilance being assumed for low thresholds for the high value areas and perceptual defense for the higher thresholds for low value areas.

One might question at this point why two separate concepts were needed to describe the results. Could not a concept of differing degrees of vigilance be sufficient? For example, with respect to words from different value areas one might say that for high value areas a person has a high degree of perceptual vigilance that becomes correspondingly less as his interest in an area decreases. If the only evidence was the difference in recognition scores there would be some justification for the parsimony of a single concept.

However, Bruner and colleagues felt the concept of defense was necessary to account for two factors in the data. First, there was the finding that for some emotion-laden words, thresholds were lowered whereas for other words and subjects they were elevated. Secondly, the subjects' prerecognition guesses in response to words with high thresholds suggested a defensive flavor to the authors. They likened it to the concept of repression where there seemed to be an active inhibitory process operating rather than just a matter of differential sensitization.

This implication of an active inhibition of recognition in perception and its analogy to the clinical concept of repression became much clearer in the study by McGinnies.[39] Here the perceptual duration thresholds for recognition of a group of neutral words and a group of taboo words such as whore, bitch, belly, Kotex, etc. was studied. In addition to obtaining the recognition thresholds, McGinnies concurrently measured the subject's GSR during the prerecognition and the recognition trials. Not only did he find that the taboo words tended to require higher durations for recognition but also subjects gave greater GSRs on the prerecognition trials to the taboo words than they did on the prerecognition trials for the neutral words. The higher recognition thresholds for the taboo words were considered a manifestation of perceptual defense and the greater GSR accompanying the prerecognition guesses to the taboo stimuli was considered to be not only an indication of the active nature of the inhibition occurring in perception but also suggested an unconscious detection or manifestation of anxiety elicited by these emotional words.

There were, however, much more prosaic interpretations available for McGinnies' results as Howes and Solomon[32] were quick to point out. They had two main criticisms. One concerned the question of intentional response suppression on the part of the subject. This is a rather telling criticism if we view the experiment from the point of view of the subject. Consider the typical undergraduate brought into the experimental situation by a professor. The subject is exposed to fragmentary perceptions through the tachistoscopic exposure. Let us assume that the word house is projected and the subject sees what looks like a medium length word with an h at the beginning and maybe an s toward the end. He tries to think of some word which will fit these partial cues and comes up with house. The next word exposed is whore. He may pick up a fragmentary perception of something resembling a w and maybe an h and he guesses "whom." On the next occurrence of this stimulus word he actually says to himself, "My God, that looked like whore, but it couldn't be. The professor wouldn't show a word like that." And so he waits for a longer duration before hazarding a guess or overtly he says "whom" again. Of course one would expect a very sizable GSR to accompany this rather startling subjective experience. On the subsequent exposure he may be even more certain the word is whore but he is not going to risk saying whore and being incorrect. After all what would the experimenter think of somebody who would say a word like this when it really wasn't that word that was being shown?

This possibility of deliberate response suppression is sufficient to account not only for the longer durations required for recognition of the taboo words but also for the greater GSRs accompanying the prerecognition response to these words.

The second criticism that Howes and Solomon leveled at McGinnies' experiment concerned the fact that the taboo and neutral words used differed markedly in familiarity or frequency of past occurrences in the subject's experience. Howes and Solomon showed that the frequency with which the taboo word occurred in the Thorndike-Lorge word counts[55] was appreciably lower than that for the neutral words. They advanced the hypothesis that differential recognition thresholds for words were a function of the frequency with which these words had been experienced in the past.

This criticism, it is to be noted, was not only of McGinnies' experiment but also of the previous work done on visual duration thresholds for words. The phenomena of perceptual vigilance and of defense, it would seem, could both be explained as a function of the differential frequency with which the stimuli had been experienced in the subject's past history. Stimuli of high frequency of prior occurrence would have low visual duration thresholds while infrequent or rare stimuli would be expected to have high thresholds. Solomon and Howes then went on in further studies[33,51] to demonstrate that duration threshold for recognition of words could be predicted by the Thorndike-Lorge tables of word frequency. The assumption was made in using these tables that they provided an adequate approximation to the frequency with which the subjects had been exposed to various written words during their past history.

In essence the frequency theory of Solomon and Howes considers perception as a response and therefore susceptible to learning as are other responses. The assumption is made that the more frequently a response is practiced the greater its habit-strength or lower its evocation threshold. Thus, because we have perceived the word house much more frequently than we have perceived the word beatific, we will, in a tachistoscopic situation, perceive the word house at a shorter level of exposure or in the presence of much more impoverished cues than would be required for the perception of beatific. This then is the mechanism by which differential recognition thresholds are assumed to occur.

As we shall see later, this interpretation of perception as a response following a single law of learning, namely that of frequency, is at the very best a gross oversimplification of perceptual behavior and of the evidence in the field of perception. We might here, however, take note of two points with respect to the role of frequency in perceptual recognition. First, the role of frequency as assessed by the Thorndike-Lorge word count tables in determining perceptual recognition of words has been greatly overemphasized, and second, the Thorndike-Lorge word counts have some serious inadequacies as estimates of the frequency with which college students have had past experiences with different words.

With respect to the first point, we might begin by looking at the original papers of Howes and Solomon[32,33] in which the evidence for a relation between recognition threshold and Thorndike-Lorge frequency was presented. These authors reported correlations of the order of —.7 between the logarithm to the base 10 of frequency in the Thorndike-Lorge magazine and general semantic counts and the duration of tachistoscopic exposure necessary for word recognition. Fortunately, the authors not only report the correlation coefficients but also present the scatter diagrams. Careful examination of the latter reveals that practically all of the relationship is due to a difference between words having 0 or very low frequencies in the Thorndike-Lorge counts and words having high frequencies. If one considers words in the frequency range of 10 to 3,000 occurrences per million in the Thorndike-Lorge count and examines only this part of the scatter diagram, it is seen that there is virtually no relationship between Thorndike-Lorge frequency and recognition threshold.

The use of the Thorndike-Lorge word counts as a measure or indication of word familiarity and as a means of controlling or matching words on familiarity for experiments on word recognition is in itself an extremely questionable procedure. The Thorndike-Lorge counts are based upon the frequency of occurrence of words in children's books or popular adult magazines and are designed for the use of teachers as a guide to what words it is important to teach a child at different age levels. Perhaps the Lorge magazine count is more appropriate but again it is considerably out of date and it is really questionable as to how representative it is for a population of college freshmen and sophomores upon whom most of the perceptual recognition experiments are carried out.

The Thorndike-Lorge tables are particularly inappropriate as a control for frequency of dirty or taboo words. Unfortunately most of the experimenters who have attempted to study differential recognition thresholds for taboo and neutral words, have, in view of the Solomon and Howes criticisms, taken the precaution of matching the taboo and neutral words according to the Thorndike-Lorge frequencies of occurrence. If this procedure were merely ineffective one could overlook it as a form of superstitious behavior, but actually the use of this supposed control seriously biases the experiment in the direction of negative results. If the familiarity of taboo words is seriously underestimated by the Thorndike-Lorge tables, then matching a neutral word and a taboo word according to these frequencies almost insures that the taboo word has a much greater degree of familiarity to the subject than the corresponding neutral word. This in itself would almost preclude the obtaining of a positive perceptual defense finding in such studies.

That the Thorndike-Lorge tables do grossly underestimate the frequency or familiarity of dirty words is suggested in a pilot study carried out in our laboratory some time ago. A large sample of words covering the entire frequency range from the Thorndike-Lorge semantic count was selected and a multiple choice vocabulary test devised for them. Also a selection of so-called taboo or dirty words was obtained, many of which were so infrequent that they were not listed in the Thorndike-Lorge tables but others varying to frequencies as high as or higher than 30 in a million. These also were included for definition in the multiple choice vocabulary test. The assumption was made that familiarity or frequency of past experience with a word should correlate rather well with the number of people who could correctly define the meaning of the word. This was our finding for the case of neutral words. The correlation between Thorndike-Lorge frequencies and the number of correct definitions in a sample of over a hundred undergraduates was .57. However, when the correlation between the Thorndike-Lorge frequencies and the number of subjects correctly defining the meaning was examined for the taboo words, the correlation was found to be .03.*

By way of summary we may note that the empirical relationship between frequency of past occurrence and recognition threshold has been amply demonstrated although the magnitude of this relationship has undoubtedly been considerably overestimated. To attempt to explain all the relationships obtained between needs or motives and recognition thresholds for corresponding need-related stimuli as being primarily or solely due to differential frequencies of prior occurrence is essentially equivalent to saying that frequency of occurrence is the only principle of learning.

As was pointed out above, the frequency argument is based upon

---

*The lack of correlation for the dirty words is not solely due to the reduced frequency range. If the correlation of the neutral words in the frequency range of 0-30 is computed, the relationship actually increases to .67.

the assumption that perception is a response and that it is modified by learning via frequency of prior occurrences. This is of course to deny or leave no place for the differential history of positive and negative reinforcement associated with different percepts. If perception is to be considered as a learned response then we should expect it also to be modifiable by the other factors that determine other forms of learning. When we permit the occurrence of differential reinforcement to effect the learning of this perceptual response, then we have again opened the door to the possible phenomena of perceptual vigilance and perceptual defense. In other words, we are now in a position where we might attribute perceptual vigilance to the effects of positive reinforcement upon perceptual responses and perceptual defense as a result of anxiety-provoking or negative reinforcement. As will be seen, such a conception fits more closely with the data although its application will have to be somewhat modified.

Perceptual Defense and Psychological Defense Mechanisms

In introducing the concept of perceptual defense, Bruner, Postman and McGinnies implied a definite relationship to the more general area of personality dynamics and defensive mechanisms as clinically conceived. In borrowing from these concepts it is unfortunate these experimenters didn't draw more extensively upon the knowledge and ideas from personality and clinical theory, for if they had more systematically and thoroughly related their concept of perceptual defense to the clinical conception of defense, a large number of needless experiments and controversy could have been avoided.

Eriksen [11,12,14] was the first to systematically relate perceptual defense phenomena to clinical conceptions of defensive mechanisms. He pointed out that the clinical concept of repression is more sophisticated than to assume that all people or even a majority automatically repress any sexual or aggressive ideation, or that all anxiety-arousing stimuli and materials lead to repression. Instead, repression is a defensive mechanism used sometimes by some people to handle anxiety-arousing thoughts or feelings whose anxiety-provoking nature are a function of the individual's own unique past experiences. Thus one would not expect a great deal of commonality among people in terms of the kind of stimuli that should lead to repression. Furthermore, theories of personality dynamics also recognize that there are other types of defensive mechanisms. Repression is not the only way individuals defend against ego-threatening stimulation.

Intellectualization, reaction formation and projection are defensive mechanisms that one might expect to actually lead to a sensitization for a stimulus related to the conflict. In the instance of reaction formation the person manifesting this defense seems to be particularly alert to finding and stamping out the evil that he denies in himself. Similarly, in the case of projection those manifesting this defense are considered to be rather alert in detecting the presence of the defended-against impulse in others. Intellectualization frequently leads to a considerable preoccupation with the subject matter of the unacceptable impulse.

These differences in defensive mechanisms would be expected to have different perceptual concomitants. In a case of repression or denial one might expect a tendency for the subject to manifest avoidance or higher duration thresholds for stimuli related to the sources of conflict. On the other hand, a subject manifesting defenses of intellectualization, reaction formation or projection might be expected to show a lower duration threshold for anxiety-related stimuli.

It is clinically naive to assume that even among subjects who characteristically employ avoidance or repressive types of defenses that any source of anxiety will be defended against. Defensive mechanisms are learned techniques and it is to be expected that in the learning process the subject also learns the types of situations or stimuli against which they are apt to be effective or rewarding. They would be expected to be maximally effective against one's own subjective train of thought or memories and associations. They would be valueless against the perception of a charging tiger. Thus the choice of anxiety stimuli and the context in which they are presented must be so selected as to permit the defense to be effective and not conflict with the subject's need to behave in a reasonable manner. It must be remembered that defenses are subtle devices, not to be revealed or studied by sledge hammer methods.

In view of these considerations an experimental attempt to show that repression manifests itself at the perceptual level by higher thresholds for recognition of threat-related stimuli (perceptual defense) must meet certain requirements. First, independent operations must exist to show that the stimuli for which perceptual defense is expected are indeed anxiety-arousing for the individual subjects in the experiment. Second, it is necessary, again through independent criteria, to show that the subject has or uses avoidance-type defenses.

The Postman, Bruner and McGinnies[45] and McGinnies[39] experiments do not meet either of these criteria. In the first of these studies the application of the term perceptual defense to account for the higher recognition thresholds for words representing value areas of low interest to the subjects would seem to have little or no relation to the clinical conception of repression. Even if the subjects had been shown to respond to ego-threat with characteristic avoidance defenses, there seems little justification for assuming that a value area in which a subject has low interest is ego-threatening to this subject or anxiety-arousing. It seems more likely that the results of this experiment are due to differences in familiarity with the words of different value areas which in turn might be expected to correspond with the subject's interests as well as differences in availability of these value words as responses to the fragmentary cues the subject received during tachisto-scopic exposures.

In the McGinnies study there was again no attempt to take into account individual differences in use of defense mechanisms and also there was no independent means for assuring that the taboo stimuli employed were indeed anxiety-arousing for all or even a majority of the subjects used. There is little justification for assuming that words like belly and Kotex would generate enough anxiety in the average college subject to lead to repression or repressive-like defensive measures. The results from this study are most likely attributable as Howes and Solomon suggest, to the subject's deliberate response suppression arising from the possible embarrassment of incorrectly verbalizing a taboo word.

The Bruner and Postman study[6,7] was the only one of the experiments introducing the concept of perceptual defense that approached satisfying the first requirement. Here the perceptual stimuli were selected for individual subjects on the basis of association times to the words on a word association test. Since word association techniques have long been recognized in clinical usage as an effective technique for determining psychic sore spots or areas of conflict, there is some justification for assuming the perceptual stimuli in this experiment were indeed anxiety-arousing or emotion-producing for the individual subjects. However, no provision was made in this study for possible individual differences in the way the emotion or threat was handled by the subjects. The importance of thees individual differences in response to anxiety is revealed in the findings of these experimenters that for some subjects recognition thresholds were higher for words with long association times whereas for other subjects long association-time words showed a lower recognition threshold relative to words with medium association times.

The failure of these early studies to test adequately the concept of perceptual defense in relation to the concept of repression is somewhat understandable. The clinical concept of repression has never been too clear a concept nor has the general theory of psychological defenses. However, as we shall see below, the work on perceptual defense has done considerable to help sharpen the clinical concept of defensive mechanisms and yielded valuable material in terms of understanding their functioning. The importance of satisfying the two requirements in an experimental design on perceptual defense would now seem self-evident although there are still experimenters who report studies supposedly disproving the phenomena which do not meet either of these requirements. As Brown[4] has perceptively pointed out, failure to satisfy both of these requirements in a design renders an experiment incapable of testing the perceptual defense hypothesis.

Although as yet not generally recognized, one of the most important contributions from the need-in-perception research has been the development of an effective experimental technique for studying personality dynamics and psychological defenses. Our understanding of psychopathology and neurosis has progressed little beyond the rather crude formulations of Freud. A large factor in our lack of progress in this area has been the difficulty of devising experimental methods whereby defensive mechanisms could be studied and analyzed in the laboratory. Nearly all of the experimental efforts in this area have centered around the single mechanism of repression using various learning and memory techniques. The methods that are effective are for the most part quite cumbersome. Thus if the perceptual recognition task could be shown to be an effective and valid method of demonstrating defensive mechanisms under laboratory situations, we would be in a position to identify the presence of these defenses in laboratory subjects, explore how they operate and investigate their antecedent conditions.

Fortunately, there is an impressive array of experimental evidence that defensive mechanisms as clinically conceived do reveal their presence in perceptual recognition behavior. In a series of experiments, Eriksen and his associates have shown quite clearly the relationship between defense mechanisms as clinically conceived and perceptual recognition behavior. Not only have these experiments revealed that defenses can be studied through perceptual recognition but also some major steps have been taken in tracing out personality characteristics associated with different types of defensive reaction and the separation of different defensive effects on perceptual recognition.

In the first of these studies Eriksen[11] used psychiatric patients who were selected on the basis of having problems in specified need areas and in whom avoidance-type defensive mechanisms might be expected to be operating. The amount of emotional disturbance in the three need areas of aggression, homosexuality and dependence was assessed by a modified word association technique and disturbance scores on this test were then related to the subjects' perceptual recognition threshold for pictures depicting neutral and need-related scenes. Patients with high disturbance indicators on a need area were found to require longer exposure intervals for recognition of the corresponding need-related pictures than for neutral pictures.

In another study Eriksen[12] found that emotional stimuli did not necessarily lead to higher perceptual recognition thresholds. Subjects who were found to show extensive overt aggressive behavior and to freely express aggressive content in stories to TAT pictures were found to have lower recognition thresholds for pictures depicting aggressive content than for neutral pictures. This individual difference response to emotional stimuli was further substantiated in an experiment by Lazarus, Eriksen and Fonda.[36] Here psychiatric out-patients were employed as subjects and were classified on the basis of their therapeutic interviews and other clinical tests as either sensitizers or repressors, depending upon whether they responded characteristically to anxiety in terms of intellectualization or rumination about the threat, or whether they tended to avoid and deny thoughts and ideas related to the conflict sources. These investigators found that the patients classified as sensitizers tended to give freely aggressive and sexual endings to a sentence completion test whereas those characterized as repressors tended to block or to distort into innocuous forms sentence completion stems that would normally suggest either aggressive or sexual completions. Further, when performance on the sentence completion test was compared with the auditory perception of hostile and sexual sentences heard against a noise background, the sensitizers were superior in recognition of the emotional content relative to the repressors.

A more clear-cut demonstration of the relation between repression as conceived in memory and perceptual recognition behavior is found in an experiment[13] where performance on a somewhat traditional memory-type repression study was subsequently compared with behavior on a perceptual recognition task. A group of freshmen premedical students who might be assumed to be strongly motivated to perceive themselves as intelligent were threatened by manipulated failure on a pseudo-intelligence test. Their subsequent recall for items on which they had been successful relative to items upon which they had failed was determined and compared with a control group. On the basis of this comparison it was apparent that the experimental manipulation of failure had been successful. Subjects were then selected who showed either an extreme preponderance of recall of successful items or failed items. These two groups of subjects were then administered a word association test and on a subsequent session their recognition thresholds for long, medium and short association time words were determined. It was found that subjects who were predominantly success recallers on the memory study showed higher recognition thresholds for long association time words whereas subjects who predominantly recalled their failures showed no significant relationship between recognition thresholds and association time.

There have been numerous studies by other investigators which have also revealed the individual differences in perceptual recognition of anxiety-related material. Postman and Solomon[46] reported that some of their subjects showed a significantly lower threshold for anagram solutions on which they had failed whereas other subjects showed significantly higher recognition thresholds for the failed solutions. Similarly, Spence[52,53] found individual differences in terms of either facilitation or impairment of recognition of words when the emotionality or threat of the words had been experimentally manipulated, again by means of failure or success on an anagrams test supposedly measuring intelligence. (In all of these experiments it is to be noted that the question of stimulus frequency is well-controlled by the experimental manipulation of the emotionality of the stimulus.)

Evidence that these individual differences in perception of anxiety-relevant stimuli are reliable, has been presented by Stein[54] and by Singer.[49] Stein demonstrated that a subject's recognition behavior for one set of anxiety and neutral stimuli significantly and appreciably predicted his behavior on subsequent sets of stimuli. Subjects who were found to require longer exposures for the perception of aggressive stimuli on the first stimulus set were found by and large to show this same pattern on subsequent different sets of hostile and neutral stimuli.

Similarly subjects who showed facilitation for the aggressive material tended to continue to show this facilitation on subsequent tests.

Singer selected neutral and emotional words on the basis of associative reaction times. For half of the selected words, thresholds were measured in the first session and for the remainder in a session 2 weeks later. He reports a significant positive correlation between subjects' performance on the first half and the second half even when scores were adjusted for differences in perceptual acuity.

While these studies did not make use of an outside criterion of the subjects' preferred mechanism of defense nor look for personality correlates that might predict these individual differences, nonetheless the patterns of the findings certainly are commensurate with those of the sensitizers and repressors of Lazarus, Eriksen and Fonda and the completed, incompleted task recallers of Eriksen.

Confirmation of the relation of these individual differences in perceptual recognition to clinical conceptions of defense are found in studies of other investigators. Carpenter, Weiner, and Carpenter,[19] in a study similar to that of Lazarus, Eriksen, and Fonda, selected groups of repressors and sensitizers using the sentence completion test. Repressors had significantly higher thresholds for sexual words than did those subjects who showed the sensitization pattern on the sentence completion test. Similar results were obtained for the aggressive stimuli. Kleinman[35] used subjects with a hysterical hearing loss and compared auditory recognition thresholds for neutral and emotional stimuli. The hysteric patients showed higher recognition thresholds for the emotional stimuli whereas a control group composed of patients with partial organic deafness showed no difference between the two classes of stimuli.

Blum[3] and Nelson[40] made use of the Blackie pictures not only to detect areas of anxiety but also to determine the type of defensive mechanism employed by the subject in this conflict area. They were successful in relating perceptual recognition behavior to the clinically assessed areas of conflict and defenses.

Eriksen and his associates have been successful in relating the sensitizer-repressor variable to a hysteria-psychasthenia dimension as measured by the corresponding scales in the MMPI. In current clinical conceptions of neurosis, the mechanism of denial or repression is predominantly associated with the hysteric, whereas intellectualizing, rationalizing defenses are supposedly characteristic of the obsessive-compulsive or psychasthenic neurotic. In one study Eriksen[14] found a correlation between a composite of the hysteria-psychasthenia scales and recall of completed-incompleted tasks where the tasks had been administered under ego-threatening conditions. In this experiment those scoring high on the hysteria pole tended to predominantly favor successful tasks in their recall while those scoring on the psychasthenia end of the dimension favored incompleted or failed tasks over successful ones.

A further link in the chain of evidence connecting the repressor-sensitizer dimension with the hysteria-psychasthenia and clinical conceptions of defenses was provided in a study by Eriksen and Davids.[18] Here it was shown that scores on the hysteria-psychasthenia dimension were significantly and appreciably related to clinical assessments of extroversion and the use of repression.

Eriksen and Browne[17] then extended the linkage back to perceptual recognition behavior in an experiment in which they found that subjects high on the psychasthenia scale of the MMPI tended to have lower perceptual recognition thresholds for words representing experimentally failed tasks whereas the low psychasthenia subjects (hysterics) had higher recognition thresholds for these items.

The relation of the hysteria-psychasthenia scales to differential response to ego threat has been well substantiated by other investigators. Mathews and Wertheimer[38] found essentially the same relationships between the hysteria and psychasthenia scales and perceptual recognition of threatening words as did Eriksen and Browne. Carlson[8] found that subjects high on the hysteria pole tended to recall fewer disturbing words in a learning experiment and Truax[56] reports that the repressors forget more in response to implied failure on a learning task.

A number of other investigators have made deductions based upon the differences in defensive reaction of the repressors and sensitizers and extended these to other aspects of behavior. Altrocchi, Parsons and Dickoff[2] have shown that repressors and sensitizers differ in self-ideal discrepancy. They found that sensitizers have more hostile and submissive self-concepts than repressors and therefore a greater discrepancy between self and ideal self. Repressors, on the other hand, tended to have positive evaluations of the self. Gordon has found meaningful differences in the interpersonal predictions of repressors and sensitizers[28] and in the stability of the assumed similarity response set.[29] In this latter study Gordon found that repressors tend to assume similarity between self and partner more frequently than do sensitizers when predicting responses to a personal inventory. Altrocchi[1] has further extended these findings showing again the usefulness of the distinction between the repressor and the sensitizer.

In sum, these studies and others have succeeded in demonstrating first of all a consistency in defensive reaction within individuals that extends across learning, perceptual and interpersonal situations. It is to be noted, though, that the repressor-sensitizer is a dimension and not a dichotomy. The marked consistency in defensive reaction that pervades these various aspects of behavior would be expected to occur only in extreme groups such as typically have been used in the above experiments. One would anticipate that the majority of people would be in between on this continuum and would show greater diversity and perhaps less consistency in their responses to ego threat.

The relationship of the hysteria-psychasthenia or repressor-sensitizer dimension to Eysenck's introversion-extroversion has been noted by Eriksen[14] and Altrocchi.[1] The similarities of the sensitizers to Eysenck's[22] findings concerning neurotic introverts are quite apparent as are the relations of the experimentally determined characteristics of the repressors to Eysenck's neurotic extroverts. A further suggestion of the interrelationships of these dimensions is reported in an experiment by Brown[4] where perceptual recognition differences comparable to those between sensitizers and repressors were related to the neuroticism and extroversion scales of the Maudsley Personality Inventory. Also Inglis[43] has speculated in an interesting way upon these possible interrelations.

Explanations of the Perceptual Defense Phenomena

The evidence surveyed in the preceding section comprises a convincing testimonial as to the genuineness of the perceptual defense phenomena. It demonstrates that when experiments employ adequate precautions to insure that the perceptual stimuli are indeed anxiety-arousing for the individual subjects and take into account the individual differences in defenses, defensive mechanisms, as clinically conceived, do reveal themselves in the perceptual recognition of stimuli. But if we accept the genuineness of the perceptual defense phenomena, then we are faced with the need to explain the mechanism or means by which it operates.

Before examining some of the proposed explanations of perceptual defense we should note that because of the very large amount of evidence relating perceptual defense phenomena to clinical defenses, any explanation of perceptual defense should also be an explanation of defensive mechanisms in general. The evidence is impressive enough by now to indicate that perceptual defense is one manifestation of the more general ego defensive processes. Many of the explanations that have been advanced for perceptual defense have neglected this consideration.

The frequency explanation that we have discussed before attempts to explain the phenomena as arising from differing degrees of familiarity or frequency of past experience with the stimulus. Many of the defects of the frequency explanation have been noted, but we are now in a position to point out that the most serious weakness of this explanation lies in its failure to take into account the large number of studies which were summarized above. It is exceedingly difficult to see how a frequency explanation could be extended to cover the results of experiments such as those of Eriksen and Browne,[17] Postman and Solomon[46] and Spence[52,53] where the anxiety was experimentally attached to the stimuli. Here the stimuli were of approximately equal familiarity to the subject and of equal recency of past experience. Nevertheless, in these studies differences were found in the recognition of the stimuli depending upon whether or not they had been associated with success or failure.

It is further difficult to see how the frequency explanation could handle the consistent individual differences that have been found in perceptual defense behavior. Why, for example, would one expect repressors or subjects scoring high on the hysteria scale of the MMPI to have had low familiarity or low frequency of past experience with essentially the same stimuli for which the sensitizers or high psychasthenia subjects show a high degree of familiarity? Perhaps it's a manifestation of perceptual selectivity in that those who have advocated a frequency explanation for the phenomena have managed to successfully ignore the experimental evidence where care was taken to insure the emotional nature of the stimuli for the individual subjects and independent criteria were used to predict whether or not the subject would show defense or sensitization.

One of the more popular explanations for perceptual defense has assumed a subception-like process. Drawing from clinical ideas concerning the properties of the unconscious, the assumption has been made that the subject is capable of unconsciously perceiving or discriminating among stimuli that are of too low an intensity or too short a time duration to yield conscious discriminations. In other words, the unconscious mind detects the presence of the anxiety-laden stimulus and sets into operation defensive processes designed to prevent the conscious recognition of the stimulus. Such explanations are advocated by McGinnies[39] and most explicitly by Blum. The Lazarus and McCleary[37] subception experiment seemed to provide an experimental basis for such an assumption of unconscious autonomic discrimination.

A critical survey of the experimental evidence, however, does not support the existence of a sensitive enough unconscious discrimination to account for perceptual defense effects. There is insufficient space available in the present paper to review this evidence but Eriksen[16] has provided a summary of the experimental evidence for unconscious discrimination and concludes from this survey that at present there is no convincing evidence that the human organism can make discriminations by any response system that are more accurate than what can be elicited by verbal (conscious) report.

Bruner[5] and Postman[43,44] have both advanced a general theory of perception that may be termed hypothesis theory. Both authors are concerned with the general theory of perception rather than a specific explanation of perceptual defense phenomena. However, Postman has specifically attempted to explain perceptual defense (higher recognition thresholds for emotional stimuli) in terms of his more general theory. He considers perceptual defense to be attributable to the "dominance of strong alternative hypotheses" which interfere and delay the recognition of emotional stimuli. He also takes into account the individual differences corresponding to repressors and sensitizers that have been considered. While the "defenders" have strong dominant positive, i.e., non-emotional hypotheses, which require a large amount of appropriate information before they are rejected, the "nondefenders" are considered to have stronger negative, i.e., emotional hypotheses, than the defenders.

An excellent evaluation of hypothesis theory in relation to perceptual defense phenomena may be found in Brown,[4] but its major weaknesses are that it deals with the phenomena at too general a level and fails to take into account the relationship of perceptual defense to the more general problem of clinically observed defensive mechanisms. Much of the theory has a characteristic of post facto explanation and little work has been done by either Bruner or Postman to obtain independent estimates of the subject's availability of hypotheses in order to predict perceptual performance. It is also somewhat strained as a theory to account for the differences between sensitizers and repressors in perceptual defense.

An adequate explanation of how perceptual defense operates must have something to say about clinical defensive mechanisms in general. An explanation that relates both the perceptual and the clinical conceptions of repression and defense has been advanced by Eriksen and Browne[17] and Eriksen and Kuethe.[20] They have made use of Dollard and Miller's[10] behavior theory analysis of defensive mechanisms and extended it specifically to the perceptual recognition experiment and to word association test performance. The essence of the Eriksen and Browne explanation for perceptual defense lies in denying that the phenomena exist in perception. Rather it is a manifestation of response variables and response effects. To understand this argument fully it is necessary to digress a bit and examine the general concept of perception.

It is not a novel idea to point out that perception is different than the responses from which it is inferred. In perceptual experiments the results may be the reflection of the perceptual process as well as response variables that the subject used in indicating his perception. Psychophysicists have shown awareness of this distinction for many years in that they do not use truly random series of stimulus presentations in threshold investigations. A long sequence of positives or long sequence of negatives can occur with true random sequences but subjects have distorted conceptions of randomness. Having had three positives in a row the subject is more apt to say "no" or fail to report the signal on the fourth successive occurrence because he feels it could not have occurred as many successive times as this would imply. This would be an example of a response variable influencing characteristics imputed to perception.

While the theoretical distinction between perception and response has been recognized for some time, Eriksen and Wechsler[21] and Eriksen and Hake[19] revived interest in this distinction by showing operational ways in which response effects could be separated from so-called perceptual phenomena. A more systematic treatment of the distinction between perception and response has been offered by Garner, Hake and Eriksen.[23] For them perception is a concept or construct of what intervenes between stimulation and response, and the concept becomes clearer and more exact as we are increasingly successful in eliminating stimulus and response variables from the concept. They further point out how, through the use of converging operations, response variables can be ruled out or eliminated from the general concept of perception.

Eriksen and Browne have pointed out that the typical perceptual recognition experiment has more in common with a task of guessing than with a perceptual task. The question is, what does the subject perceive in a brief exposure of a word? If the subject is asked to describe exactly what he perceives, we do not receive responses in terms of whole words such as, "That looked like the word 'small', or I guess you showed the word 'house'." Instead the subject gives discriptions such as, "Well I had the impression of maybe a word, a short word, and it looked like it had a tall letter at the end," or "It is a word that begins with s and has an o somewhere in the middle of it." But in the typical recognition experiment the subject is not asked to describe exactly what he perceives but is either implicitly or explicitly asked to respond in terms of whole English words or of whole units depending upon the stimulus material employed. If the subject's perception is most adequately described under the conditions where he is given the freedom of the English language to describe what he perceives and asked to do this, then the usual recognition experiment is essentially asking the subject to guess what word might fit these vague perceptual cues he has perceived. In other words, the subject associates or tries to find a word that fits the fragmentary letters and impression of word length that corresponds to his actual perception.

If we now consider thoughts and associations as responses following the treatment of Dollard and Miller, we are in a position to account for perceptual defense effects in terms of nothing more mysterious than the empirically established effects of punishment on the probability of occurrence of responses. We may assume that different words have different habit strength as responses to different cues. If, for example, the word hook is anxiety-arousing or leads to self-devaluating thoughts in the subject due to previous experiences he has had, then hook would be expected to have less habit strength to the fragmentary perception described by the subject, as "the impression of a short word that looks like it has an o in it and ends in a k." Look or took might be expected to have greater habit strengths to this particular cue. Thus, at a brief duration of exposure, if this cue is obtained in perception, look or took would have a higher probability of being elicited as a response than would the anxiety-associated word hook. But as the exposures lengthen, the subject's cues or perception changes and he gains more knowledge about the actual stimulus. Eventually the duration is long enough so that the actual perception is hook in which case to this cue hook has the greatest habit strength and occurs as the recognition response. The operation of such a process over a number of words will yield statistically higher recognition thresholds for anxiety-evoking words relative to neutral words.

The subject does not necessarily have to subjectively feel he is searching for a word to fit the partial cues he actually perceives. The association of a response to these cues may be as immediate and automatic as the association white is to the stimulus word black. This associative connection in response to cues underlies not only the perceptual recognition experiment but also the word association test and may well account for the correspondence between perceptual recognition thresholds and association times.

That word-association connections are modifiable by punishment was established by Eriksen and Kuethe.[20] They were successful in changing a subject's preferred associative responses to stimulus words by electric shock punishment, and introspective reports of the subjects, verified by reaction time data, indicated that the new associations became automatic after a few trials.

It is to be noted that the above conception of repression is consistent with the clinical concept of the process. The original defining operation for detection of repression came from the psychoanalytic free association procedure. Here the analyst detects or suspects the operation of a repressive mechanism when the patient's associations show peculiar gaps, blockages, or deviate from what the analyst considers to be a reasonable type of associative chain. A person has considerable latitude in the type of associative connections or trains of thought he subjectively experiences. There is room for considerable idiosyncrasy without it becoming too conspicuous to one's fellows. By learning to change directions of association the person effectively can prevent the occurrence of covertly stimulated anxiety and it is only under the controlled condition of the clinician's couch that these peculiarities in associations become evident.

The foregoing account of perceptual defense removes the phenomenon from the field of perception and places it back with response variables and relates it, then, to behavior theory. It differs from the frequency theory of Howes and Solomon primarily in that the latter theorists do not explicitly distinguish between perception and the responses from which it is inferred. One could advocate an explanation of perceptual defense that applied the effects of reinforcement to perceptual learning rather than to response variables. The preference for locating the source of action in response rather than in terms of learned percepts is decided primarily on the basis of the lack of convincing evidence showing the effects of learning on perception per se. Goldiamond and Hawkins[24] in an ingenious experiment were able to show that the frequency effects of Solomon and Howes upon perceptual recognition could be obtained in the absence of any perceptual stimulus. Also Pierce[42] in an experiment that successfully eliminated the possibility of differential response bias, was unable to find any effect of frequency or familiarity upon perception. Similar results have been obtained by Goldstein.[25]

With but few exceptions the research literature on need and perceptual recognition lends itself to an interpretation in terms of the response theory advanced above. As pointed out by Garner, Hake and Eriksen,[23] most of the experiments in this area have not contained the necessary converging operations to attribute the obtained effects to the perceptual process. There have, however, been several studies that would appear to contain the necessary converging operations to localize the perceptual sensitization and defense effects in the perceptual process. Blum[3] compared the frequency with which the names of different Blackie pictures, assumed to be anxiety-provoking, were given as responses to tachistoscopic exposures where the anxiety pictures, unknown to the subject, were not exposed. The response frequencies obtained were then compared with the frequencies obtained to the condition where the anxiety pictures were actually presented. The first measure of response frequency provided a control for differential response strengths. Blum assumed that if unconscious perception occurred, then the exposures with the pictures present would lead to unconscious perception of the conflict which in turn would trip off more anxiety and activate defensive mechanisms leading to an even less frequent usage of the anxiety responses. Although he obtained positive results, investigators in other laboratories[47,50] have been unable to replicate this aspect of his experiment.

A similar method of correcting for differential response strengths for anxiety material has been employed by Mathews and Wertheimer[38] and by Goldstein.[25] In both of these studies there was a significant perceptual defense effect even after statistical correction has been made for response bias. However, Goldstein and associates in a further series of careful studies have pursued the problem of separating response variance from perceptual variance in recognition tasks. The results of these studies[25,26,27] have suggested that statistical correction for response bias effects are not adequate. While they have consistently been able to obtain the perceptual defense effect in their studies, they have nonetheless built up an impressive amount of evidence through careful experimentation that shows this effect to be attributable to response bias which in turn is probably due to conditioned avoidance response to the anxiety-provoking stimuli.

A Summing-Up

It would appear that fifteen years of experimentation on the effects of need upon perception has resulted in a conclusion that needs do not effect perceptual process but only response occurrence. Nevertheless, the tremendously important contributions that this research has made to psychology must not be overlooked. The research in this area played an important role in sharpening our concept of perception by leading to the experimental isolation of response variables from this concept. This distinction has not only been important in the need and perception area but has influenced traditional work on perceptual problems as well.

A most significant contribution has been made to the field of personality by furthering our knowledge of ego-defensive mechanisms and providing a means by which they may be detected and measured in the laboratory. It has provided us with the beginnings of a behavior theory account of repression and in so doing has made available more precise concepts and language for dealing with psychopathology. In giving rise to the concepts of sensitizers and repressors, it has indicated an important dimension of ego defensiveness. The important work of Altrocchi and associates, as well as that of Ullman and Lim[57] have indicated the fruitfulness of this dimension in understanding a wide variety of defensive behavior. The relationship of this dimension to Eysenck's introvert-extrovert dimension has already been noted and there are a number of indications[18,30,41] that this same dimension is related to the Taylor Manifest Anxiety Scale and to the leveler and sharpener dimension of Klein and his associates.[31] The nature of these interrelationships will require a large research effort to confirm and consolidate. An important attempt at integration in this area has been made by Inglis[34] but the data are yet too scattered and too many links in the chain are missing to achieve more than suggestive consolidations.

Perhaps the major contribution of the need and perception experimentation will come from its provision of a means of detecting and measuring ego defenses. Our concepts of psychodynamics and defensive processes are primitive and inadequate largely due to the lack of experimentation in this area. This in turn has resulted from the inadequacy and the lack of techniques for conveniently studying defenses in laboratory settings. While experimentalists in the clinical and personality area have been slow to seize upon this new methodology for studying defensive processes, the work of Shannon[48] and Ullman and Lim,[57] who have used the perceptual recognition technique in working out a new classification of defensive mechanisms, should do much to stimulate research employing this methodology.

REFERENCES

1. ALTROCCHI, J.: Interpersonal perceptions of repressors and sensitizers in component analysis of assumed dissimilarity scores. J. Abnorm. Soc. Psychol., 62: 528-534, 1961.
2. ——, PARSONS, O. A., AND DICKOFF, H.: Changes in self-ideal discrepancy in repressors and sensitizers. J. Abnorm. Soc. Psychol., 61: 67-72, 1960.
3. BLUM, G. S.: Perceptual defense revisited. J. Abnorm. Soc. Psychol., 51: 24-29, 1955.
4. BROWN, W. P.: Conceptions of perceptual defense. Brit. J. Psychol., Monogr. Suppl., 1961.
5. BRUNER, J. S.: Personality dynamics and the process of perceiving. In Blake, R. R., and Ramsey, G. V. (Eds.): Perception: An approach to Personality. New York, The Ronald Press Co., 1951.
6. ——, AND POSTMAN, L.: Emotional selectivity in perception and reaction. J. Person., 16: 69-77, 1947.
7. ——, AND ——: Tension and tension-release as organizing factors in perception. J. Person., 15: 300-308, 1947.
8. CARLSON, V. R.: Individual differences in recall of word association test words. J. Person., 23: 77-87, 1954.
9. CARPENTER, B., WIENER, M., AND CARPENTER, J.: Predictability of perceptual defense behavior. J. Abnorm. Soc. Psychol., 52: 380-383, 1956.
10. DOLLARD, J., AND MILLER, N. E.: Personality and Psychotherapy. New York, McGraw-Hill, 1950.
11. ERIKSEN, C. W.: Perceptual defense as a function of unacceptable needs. J. Abnorm. Soc. Psychol., 46: 557-564, 1951.
12. ——: Some implications for TAT interpretation arising from need and perception experiments. J. Person., 19: 283-288, 1951.
13. ——: Defense against ego-threat in memory and perception. J. Abnorm. Soc. Psychol., 47: 430-435, 1952.
14. ——: Psychological defenses and ego strength in the recall of completed and incompleted tasks. J. Abnorm. Soc. Psychol., 49: 45-50, 1956.
15. ——: The case for perceptual defense. Psychol. Rev., 61: 175-182, 1954.
16. ——: Discrimination and learning without awareness: A methodological survey and evaluation. Psychol. Rev., 67: 279-300, 1960.
17. ——, AND BROWNE, C. T.: An experimental and theoretical analysis of perceptual defense. J. Abnorm. Soc. Psychol., 52: 224-230, 1956.
18. ——, AND DAVIDS, A.: The meaning and clinical validity of the Taylor Manifest Anxiety Scale in the hysteria-psychasthenia scales from the MMPI. J. Abnorm. Soc. Psychol., 50: 135-137, 1955.
19. ——, AND HAKE, H. W.: Anchor effects in absolute judgments. J. Exp. Psychol., 53: 132-138, 1957.

20. ——, AND KUETHE, J. L.: Avoidance conditioning of verbal behavior without awareness: A paradigm of repression. J. Abnorm. Soc. Psychol., *53:* 203-209, 1956.

21. ——, AND WECHSLER, H.: Some effects of experimentally induced anxiety upon discrimination behavior. J. Abnorm. Soc. Psychol., *51:* 458-463, 1955.

22. EYSENCK, H. J.: Dimensions of Personality. London, Routledge and Kegan Paul, Ltd., 1947.

23. GARNER, W. R., HAKE, H. W., AND ERIKSEN, C. W.: Operationism and the concept of perception. Psychol. Rev., *63:* 149-159, 1956.

24. GOLDIAMOND, I., AND HAWKINS, W. F.: Vexierversuch: The log relationship between word frequency and recognition obtained in the absence of stimulus words. J. Exp. Psychol., *56:* 457-463, 1958.

25. GOLDSTEIN, M. J.: A test of response probability theory of perceptual defense. J. Exp. Psychol., *63:* 23-28, 1962.

26. ——, AND HIMMELFARB, S.: The effects of providing knowledge of results upon the perceptual defense effect. J. Abnorm. Soc. Psychol., *64:* 143-147, 1962.

27. ——, ——, AND FEDER, W.: A further study of the relationship between response bias and perceptual defense. J. Abnorm. Soc. Psychol., *64:* 56-62, 1962.

28. GORDON, J. R.: Interpersonal predictions of repressors and sensitizers. J. Person., *25:* 686-698, 1957.

29. ——: The stability of the assumed similarity response set in repressors and sensitizers. J. Person., *27:* 362-373, 1959.

30. GREENBAUM, M.: Manifest anxiety in the tachistoscopic recognition of facial photographs. Percept. mot. Skills, *6:* 245-248, 1956.

31. HOLZMAN, T. S., AND GARDNER, R. W.: Leveling and repression. J. Abnorm. Soc. Psychol., *59:* 151-155, 1959.

32. HOWES, D., AND SOLOMON, R. L.: A note on McGinnies' emotionality and perceptual defense. Psychol. Rev., *57:* 229-234, 1950.

33. ——, AND ——: Visual duration threshold as a function of word probability. J. Exp. Psychol., *41:* 401-410, 1951.

34. INGLIS, J.: Abnormalities of motivation and "ego functions." *In* Eysenck, H. J. (Ed.): Handbook of Abnormal Psychology. New York, Basic Books, 1961.

35. KLEINMAN, M. L.: Psychogenic deafness and perceptual defense. J. Abnorm. Soc. Psychol., *54:* 335-338, 1957.

36. LAZARUS, R. S., ERIKSEN, C. W., AND FONDA, C. P.: Personality dynamics in auditory perceptual recognition. J. Person., *19:* 471-482, 1951.

37. ——, AND MCCLEARY, R. A.: Autonomic discrimination without awareness: A study of subception. Psychol. Rev., *58:* 113-122, 1951.

38. MATHEWS, A., AND WERTHEIMER, M.: A 'pure' measure of perceptual defense uncontaminated by response suppression. J. Abnorm. Soc., Psychol. *57:* 373-376, 1958.

39. MCGINNIES, E.: Emotionality and perceptual defense. Psychol. Rev., *56:* 244-251, 1949.

40. NELSON, S. E.: Psychosexual conflicts and defenses in visual perception. J. Abnorm. Soc. Psychol., *51:* 427-433, 1955.

41. OSLER, S. F., AND LEWINSOHN, T. M.: The relation between manifest anxiety in perceptual defense. Am. Psychologist, 9: 446, 1954 (abstract).

42. PIERCE, J. R.: Some sources of artifact in studies of the tachistoscopic perception of words. J. Exp. Psychol., 66: 363-370, 1963.

43. POSTMAN, L.: Towards a general theory of cognition. In Rohrer, J. H., & Sherif, M. (Eds.): Social Psychology at the Crossroads. New York, Harper & Bros., 1951.

44. ——: On the problem of perceptual defense. Psychol. Rev., 60: 298-306, 1953.

45. ——, BRUNER, J. S., AND McGINNIES, E.: Personal values as selective factors in perception. J. Abnorm. Soc. Psychol., 43: 142-154, 1948.

46. ——, AND SOLOMON, R. L.: Perceptual sensitivity to completed and incompleted tasks. J. Person., 18: 347-357, 1950.

47. RASKIN, A.: A learning theory paradigm for perceptual-vigilance and perceptual-defense phenomena. Unpublished doctoral dissertation, Univ. of Illinois, 1954.

48. SHANNON, D. T.: Clinical patterns of defense as revealed in visual recognition thresholds. J. Abnorm. Soc. Psychol., 64: 370-377, 1962.

49. SINGER, B. R.: An experimental inquiry into the concept of perceptual defense. Brit. J. Psychol., 47: 298-311, 1956.

50. SMOCK, C. D.: Replication and comments: "An experimental reunion of psychoanalytic theory with perceptual vigilance and defense." J. Abnorm. Soc. Psychol., 53: 68-73, 1956.

51. SOLOMON, R. L., AND HOWES, D.: Word frequency, personal values, and visual duration thresholds. Psychol. Rev. 58: 256-270, 1951.

52. SPENCE, D. P.: A new look in vigilance and defense. J. Abnorm. Soc. Psychol., 54: 103-108, 1957.

53. ——: Success failure and recognition threshold. J. Person., 25: 712-720, 1957.

54. STEIN, K. B.: Perceptual defense and perceptual sensitization under neutral and involved conditions. J. Person., 21: 467-478, 1953.

55. THORNDIKE, E. L., AND LORGE, I.: The Teachers Word Book of 30,000 Words. New York, Columbia Univer. Press, 1944.

56. TRUAX, C. B.: Repression response to implied failure as a function of the hysteria psychathenia index. J. Abnorm. Soc. Psychol., 55: 183-193, 1957.

57. ULLMAN, L. P., AND LIM, D. T.: Case history material as a source of the identification of patterns of response to emotional stimuli in a study of humor. J. Consult. Psychol., 26: 221-225, 1962.

11

PERCEPTION DURING SLEEP

by WILLIAM C. DEMENT*

THE FINAL ANSWERS TO THE PROBLEMS OF PERCEPTION, particularly as they overlap the classical problem of the relation between brain and mind, undoubtedly lie at the top of the mountain. As Wilder Penfield has put it, "Those who hope to solve the problem of the neurophysiology of the mind are like men at the foot of the mountain. They stand in the clearings they have made on the foothills, looking up at the mountain they hope to scale. But the pinnacle is hidden in eternal clouds and many believe it can never be conquered."[33]

In a sense, every investigator who deals in some way with the nervous system and behavior is clearing land on the foothills and, in the long run, his contribution will have the same value whether he derives his inspiration from a lofty image of the summit or from the fertility of the soil beneath his feet. In any case, the mountain cannot be completely ignored. Its presence pervades our lives. Thus, whenever we look up from our specific tasks, we are confronted with the ubiquity of the phenomena we call perceptual. We are unable to talk about human behavior without talking about perception, and we must continue to do so even though we realize, as Teuber has stated, that as yet "there is no adequate definition of perception and no neurophysiological theory."[41]

In practice, perception is almost always defined by describing a number of characteristics that serve to differentiate perceptual phenomena from other kinds of activities. Taken together, these characteristics seem to apply to a set of variables that intervene between sensory stimulation and awareness or sensory stimulation and behavior.

One can distinguish two kinds of endeavor which deal with perceptual phenomena: a) that which attempts to account for the "facts" of perception, i.e., to explain how the intervening variables operate; b) that which is concerned more with the procedures of verifying the occurrence of perception.

---

*Department of Psychiatry, Stanford University.

According to Osgood,[30] there have traditionally been three points of view in attempting to account for the "facts" of perception (more or less independent of whether the "facts" are made available by subjective or objective observations) : physiological, gestalt, and behavioristic. There is little doubt that the first of the three has gained ascendency in recent years. Its aim is to account for all the phenomena of perception in terms of peripheral and central neurophysiological mechanisms. However, since neurophysiologists now make frequent use of behavioral techniques and have also begun to study and manipulate electrical fields within the central nervous system, it would be better to say that the other viewpoints have not been transcended, but rather, that they have been incorporated into a larger and more enriched neurophysiological attitude. At any rate, most investigators seem to believe, and there is a mounting record of accomplishment to sustain this faith, that when enough is known about the neurophysiology of the nervous system, we will be able to explain all perceptual phenomena. In this context, it does not matter whether the end result of the perceptual process is differential awareness, differential behavior, or both together.

When we come to the problem of verifying or defining the occurrence of perception, however, we find that the end result is crucial, and that there are still two widely divergent and equally valid viewpoints. One viewpoint is generally termed phenomenological and its data are derived solely from the content of awareness as communicated by language. The other viewpoint makes use of data obtained from behavioral observations and may thus be termed behavioristic. As philosophical systems, the two viewpoints are irreconcilable. In practice, however, nearly everyone who deals with the human organism quite happily adopts some compromise form of psychophysical parallelism, which essentially involves making temporal correlations between the two sets of data. There is some hesitancy to allow that perception has taken place unless such a correlation has been made. We do not seem to have very much confidence in subjective data unless they are bolstered by logically interconnecting behavioral observations, and somehow, we are not satisfied with the ultimate value of behavioral data in isolation.

Although the behavioristic viewpoint is scientifically more satisfactory and leads to fewer experimental difficulties, there are compelling reasons for adopting a dualistic approach. In the first place, both kinds of data are generally available in abundance. In the second place, the great complexity of the human organism cannot, at our present level of knowledge, be encompassed by the behavioristic approach. Thus, we find it convenient and helpful, at the very least, in ordering our thinking, to fill in the gaps with phenomenological linkages. Finally, we are studying ourselves, and when pushed to the wall, we find, like it or not, that we are not nearly so interested in nerve impulses as we are in how we feel.

At any rate, we get along very well with our psycho-physical parallelism and often actively seek to establish such a compromise. We stimulate a subject and ask him what he feels while at the same time recording his galvanic skin response and which key he presses. Some of our most treasured data come from the simultaneous observation of content of awareness and behavioral responses as a result of direct stimulation of the human cortex. Those who do not have access to both sets of data often seem a little wistful. "It must be great fun to put a question to the 'preparation' and have it answer." So commented Sir Charles Sherrington, the neurophysiologist, to Wilder Penfield, the neurosurgeon.[32]

What makes the topic "perception during sleep" of special interest in this context is precisely the fact that we cannot conveniently gather two parallel sets of data during the sleep state. In addition, a consideration of this topic will afford perhaps the best illustration of our tendency to demand that the occurrence of perception satisfy a dual criterion. Take, for example, the oft-cited case of the sleeping mother. The muted cries of her baby are added to the random noise of the city, and she immediately awakens; but she awakens with a question rather than certainty, and only after awakening does she identify the reason. What intervened between the stimulus and the awakening certainly has the behavioral qualifications of perception, but we prefer to speak of the process in terms of discrimination and habituation. On the other hand, from the phenomenological point of view, the dream certainly involves perception. However, after a number of earlier attempts to relate the dream to some objective variable had failed, the study of dreaming never quite achieved scientific respectability, despite its undeniable phenomenal reality. Thus, in contrast to the waking state where a multiplicity of real events (external stimuli, motor patterns, etc.) can be readily observed to interconnect with sensations and ideas, the sleeping state has seemed to offer for examination only the monotonous regularity of its own isolated vegetative functioning.

If this were still the case, I would certainly not be here today, talking about perception during sleep. Fortunately, recent closer scrutiny aided by modern techniques has shown that the sleeping organism is much more than a pulsating blob of protoplasm. There is a suggestion that the complexity of its functioning, particularly with reference to the central nervous system, may not be very much less than when it is awake. There is, in fact, a myriad of observable physiological events that may be paired with subjective data to define the occurrence of perception, if we expand our concept of behavior, and if we are willing to make the effort.

Physiological Variables

In the human subject, electroencephalographic (EEG) rhythms recorded during sleep vary through a continuum from the low voltage patterns of wakefulness to the high amplitude, slow waves that are presumed to be indicative of deep sleep. To facilitate a description of the recordings, this continuum is usually divided into a series of stages or levels. This system that we have used is as follows: *Stage 1*, a low voltage, irregularly mixed fast and slow pattern. *Stage 2*, characterized by the presence of 12-14/sec. sleep spindles with a low voltage background. *Stage 3*, an intermediate amount of high amplitude, slow activity with some spindling. *Stage 4*, a predominance of high amplitude, slow activity. When the EEG is recorded continuously throughout an entire night of sleep, a regular, cyclic alternation of stages is seen (fig. 1). Individual cycles are defined by the repetitive reappearance of lengthy periods of Stage 1 EEG. This "emergent" (to distinguish it from the brief period of Stage 1 at the sleep onset) Stage 1 thus alternates with periods in which Stages 2, 3, and 4 are present. Most of the Stage 4 patterns occur early in the night. Later, the changes consist mainly of an alternation between Stages 1 and 2.

A number of physiological variables have been observed together with the EEG in all-night recordings; for example, heart rate, respiratory rate, finger pulse volume, electromyogram (EMG), etc., and they all show some kind of unique behavior during the periods of "emergent" Stage 1. Perhaps the most prominent and exclusive feature of these periods is their association with bursts of rapid, conjugate eye movement; and for this reason, they have been designated rapid eye movement (REM) periods, while the interspersed intervals containing Stages 2, 3, and 4 have been referred to as non-rapid eye movement (NREM) periods. Thus, REM periods are associated with a constellation of physiological attributes that serve to set them apart from the remainder of sleep. We may go a step further, and state that physiological measurements during sleep have permitted us to distinguish two entirely different kinds of sleep, REM and NREM.[10,23] Variations *within* the two kinds of sleep are essentially quantitative and generally do not exhibit sufficient magnitude or persistence to warrant further subdivision.

In view of this formulation, the description of four EEG stages in human sleep recordings becomes somewhat redundant. While only one EEG stage is present during REM sleep, all four stages may be present

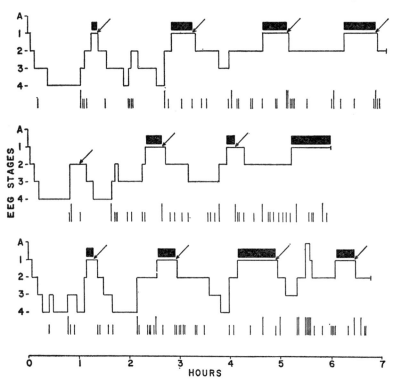

FIG. 1.—Continuous plotting of the EEG patterns for three representative nights. The thick bars immediately above the EEG lines indicate periods during which rapid eye movements were seen. The vertical lines below stand for body movements. The longer lines indicate large movements, changes in position of the whole body, and the shorter lines represent smaller movements. The arrows indicate both the end of one EEG cycle and the beginning of the next.

(Reprinted, by permission, from Dement, W. & Kleitman, N: Cyclic variations in EEG during sleep and their relation to eye movements, body motility, and dreaming. EEG Clin. Neurophysiol. *9:* 673-690, 1957).

in the interspersed intervals of NREM sleep without, however, showing any significant co-variance with other physiological measurements. Figure 2, which shows a plot of the data from an all-night recording of EEG and respiration, may be used as an example to clarify this point. A glance at this figure reveals that increases in both rate and variability of respiration during REM sleep stand out rather sharply against a rather stable respiratory background. In the first EEG cycle, there is a complete swing from Stage 1 at the sleep onset, through Stages 2 and 3 to Stage 4, and back to Stage 2. However, almost no change in respiration is associated with this wide fluctuation. The same is true for succeeding cycles, although this cannot be accorded equal significance because the EEG changes are less marked.

Looking at this figure, it would only be a very slight exaggeration to say that all EEG stages outside of REM periods are associated with a uniform rate and regularity of respiration. We have additional evidence suggesting that heart rate, muscle tone, body temperature,

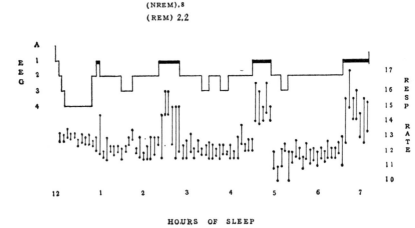

Fig. 2.—Variations in respiratory rate during an entire night of sleep. The top line is a continuous plotting of the EEG in terms of the four stages, and the dark bars indicate the eye movement periods. The number of respirations in each successive minute were counted and each vertical line represents the range of minute counts for each successive five minute period. It can be seen that during rapid eye movement periods, there is an overall increase in both range and rate.

(Reprinted, by permission, from Dement, W.: Eye movements during sleep. U.S.P.H.S. Symposium on the Oculomotor System. April 14-15, 1961, New York), and electrically elicited H-reflexes, similarly do not co-vary with the EEG. This is not to say that EEG shifts in NREM sleep are entirely without significance; merely that they are not associated with changes of a degree that would warrant further qualitative separation.

As is well known, the rapid eye movements of sleep were first described in human subjects by Aserinsky and Kleitman in 1953,[1] and their relation to the EEG sleep cycle was elucidated shortly thereafter. [11,12] Since then, analogous EEG variations during sleep, with REMs related to the appropriate phases, have been observed in a number of other species such as the cat,[8,23] monkey,[43] dog,[40] and rat.[28] In nearly all instances where identical variables have been measured, their behavior in defining the rhythmic alternation of two kinds of sleep has shown high cross-species consistency. In fact, the concept of two distinct kinds of sleep was first stated clearly by Jouvet from his experimental results with the cat,[23] and in addition, he described many features of the contrasting neuroanatomical mechanisms subserving each.

Because of their greater accessibility to experimental and operative manipulation, sleep research with animals has accumulated a large amount of information which is not available from human subjects. However, in view of the fact that analogous results have been obtained from the observation of physiological variables that *can* be measured in both humans and animals, it seems justifiable to make use of the data that can be obtained only from animal research in interpreting some of the results of human studies.

It is interesting that the dual nature of sleep was so long in being recognized. It might be suspected, since the physiological contrast is so striking, that REM sleep constitutes a very small fraction of the total sleep period, and was thus easily overlooked. However, this is far from the true state of affairs. In the human adult, for example, REM sleep accounts for 20 to 25 per cent of the total sleep time; in the adult cat, around 30 to 40 per cent; and in the newborn infant, about 50 to 80 per cent.[37]

CORRELATION WITH DREAMING

There can be little question that dreams qualify as hallucinations. Accordingly, if hallucinations are to be regarded as perceptual phenomena, and that seems to be the position taken by Professor West in his presentation, then it follows that dreams must also be accorded that status. But perceptions of what? Should endogenous stimulation be invoked, or should we assume that these experiences arise in the complete absence of any afferent activity? What really bothers most people about hallucinations and especially dreams, is the lack of certainty that they really occurred as claimed. It seems equally possible that descriptions of hallucinatory experience are artifacts of self-delusion and confabulation, that they may be spuriously elaborated in the attempt to communicate intelligibly some prior vague and disorganized sensations. An analogous situation might be seen in the hypothetical adventure of a little boy walking through a dark woods at night. A sudden noise, perhaps a falling branch, leads to a panic-stricken dash for home. His parents ask what happened, and the little boy tells a story of being chased by wolves or robbers. By the time he is through telling his tale, there is no question that he believes it really happened.

Many studies in recent years have shown that if subjects are abruptly awakened during REM sleep, they are very likely to report the occurrence of a dream and to be able to describe the complex imagery of its content.[1,6,13,14,17,24,25,38,46] Even so, the above objection could still be raised, namely, that some meaningless neuronal upheaval in REM sleep was misinterpreted upon awakening, or that REM sleep somehow predisposes to spurious recall. What is needed is the demonstration of a valid parallelism between the ongoing dream experience and the progression of physiological events in REM sleep. One step in this direction was the finding of a significant correlation between the length of the dream as measured by the number of words in the narrative, and the duration of REM sleep preceding arousal.[14] However, the most conclusive demonstration is that the spatio-temporal pattern of the rapid eye movement coincides with or parallels the dream events in a manner suggesting that the oculomotor apparatus is being stimulated to "view" and "scan" just as it would be by an analogous retinal input in the waking state.

Several studies have hinted at such a relationship[13-14] but its full extent was only recently demonstrated in a series of experiments by Roffwarg et al.[38] which I will describe in some detail because of their great importance to the topic of perception during sleep.

In this study, subjects were awakened immediately after or during the occurrence of a wide variety of spatio-temporal REM sequences by an experimenter who continuously monitored the write-out of the electro-oculogram (EOG). A second experimenter, who had no knowledge of the EOG, interrogated the subjects. From the details of their subjective dream experience, he derived a verbal description of the eye movement sequence that he felt must have occurred prior to the awakening. Several examples will clarify the procedure and the nature of the results:

Dream #1 (recorded and transcribed)

> "Right near the end of the dream I was walking up the back stairs of an old house. I was holding a cat in my arms."
> "Were you looking at the cat?"
> "No, I was being followed up the steps by the Spanish dancer, Escudero. I was annoyed at him and refused to look back at him or talk to him. I walked up, as a dancer would, holding my head high, and I glanced up at every step I took."
> "How many steps were there?"
> "Five or six."
> "Then what happened?"

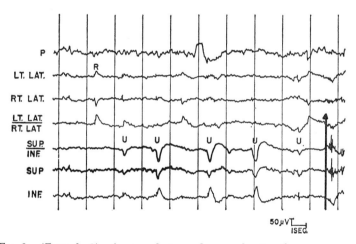

50 μV
1 SEC.

Fig. 3.—(Example 1): An a.c. electro-oculogram showing the eye movements during the last 20 seconds before the awakening (arrow) Electrode positions: P, parietal (EEG); Lt. Lat., left lateral canthus; Rt. Lat., right lateral canthus; Lt. Lat./rt. lat., same leads in bipolar arrangement; Sup/. supraorbital Inf., infraorbital; Sup./Inf., same leads in bipolar arrangement. REMs: R, right; U, up. Note the 5 distinct upward deflections recorded in the vertical leads corresponding to the interrogator's prediction of 5 upward movements. The EEG pattern throughout the record was low-voltage, fast and non-spindling (Stage 1 sleep).

(Reprinted, by permission, from Roffwarg, H., Dement, W., Muzio, J. and Fisher, C.: Dream imagery: relationship to rapid eye movements of sleep. Arch. Gen. Psychiat. 7: 235-258, 1962).

"I reached the head of the stairs and I walked straight over to a group of people about to begin a circle dance."

"Did you look around at the people?"

"I don't believe so. I looked straight ahead at the person across from me. Then I woke up."

"How long was it from the time you reached the top of the stairs to the end of the dream?"

"Just a few seconds."

Interrogator's Prediction

"There should be a series of five vertical upward movements as she holds her head high and walks up the steps. Then there should be a few seconds with only some very small horizontal movement just before the awakening."

The EOG associated with this dream is shown in figure 3. It can be seen that the interrogator's predictive verbal description almost exactly specifies the temporal sequence and direction of the eye movement potentials.

Dream #2

"Were you dreaming?"

"Yes, just as you were awakening me. I can't remember—oh, yes, I was on a subway train, riding down to—I can tell you exactly what I was looking at— I think I was using a pay phone on one wall of the train, you know, in those little compartments at the end. The train was moving between stations, and I was talking, and I remember saying something about soundproofing. But my eyes at that moment were moving very quickly I think."

"Were you facing the wall of the train?"

"Yes."

"What direction was the train moving in?"

"I believe it was going toward my right."

"Were you looking at the phone or away from the phone?"

"I was looking through the door window on the opposite wall at the wiggly lights in the tunnel whizzing by toward my left."

"How long before you awakened did this happen?"

"About 30 seconds, maybe a little more. I didn't look out that window continuously. I looked back at the phone on the wall."

"What happened just before you awakened?"

"I think I looked from the phone to the window and back to the phone quickly, then I woke up."

Interrogator's Prediction

"About a half a minute before the awakening, there should be a period of jerky, nystagmoid movements with a quick component to the left. Then, just before the buzzer, there should be a large horizontal movement to the left, followed by one to the right."

Again, the verbal description almost exactly describes the associated EOG (fig. 4). The dreamer is in a typical situation for producing optokinetic nystagmus and with the burst of nystagmoid movements in the record, we see one of the most remarkable examples of correspondence between dream content and rapid eye movements. This example also illustrates the value of the interrogator, since the subject himself had neither the experience nor the knowledge to infer the presence of optokinetic nystagmus.

Dream #3

(The dreamer is sitting among a group of people watching a violinist. Then someone sits down directly in front of her and blocks her view.)

"—there was a girl sitting to my right, but I don't think she's the one who blocked my view."

"From which direction did the girl walk before she sat down in front of you?"

"I don't know. It wasn't like real life, where you would watch a person walk over. She was just suddenly there in front of me."

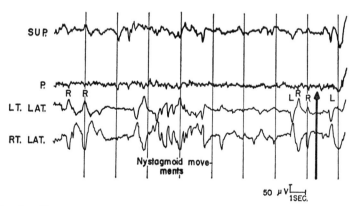

Fig. 4.—(Example 2): An a.c. electrooculogram of the last 17 seconds before an awakening (arrow). Electrode positions: Sup., supraorbital; P, parietal (EEG); Lt. Lat., left lateral canthus; Rt. Lat., right lateral canthus. REMs; R, right; L, left. This tracing is of special significance because of the presence of a period of rapid, saccadic eye movements with the quick, component to the left (nystagmoid movements). The subject had described watching tunnel lights go quickly by as he rode in a subway car. The P lead shows a Stage I sleep record.

(Reprinted, by permission, from Roffwarg, H., Dement, W., Muzio, J. and Fisher, C.: Dream imagery: relationship to rapid eye movements of sleep. Arch. Gen. Psychiat. 7: 235-258, 1962).

"Did you keep your eyes on the violinist until your view was blocked?"
"Yes."

Interrogator's Prediction

"Quiescence while listening to the music, then a quick right-left eye movement."

The associated EOG recording in figure 5 shows that the last eye movements were purely vertical, as a literal interpretation of the dreamer's report would have suggested. The interrogator introduced his own error by choosing to assume that the person blocking the dreamer's view must have come in from the side. However, the remainder of the prediction is correct. The main reason for presenting this example is to point out that the eyeballs are quiescent when the dreamer is staring at something, in this case, at the violinist. In other words, dreams do not stop in between bursts of eye movement. Rather, visual fixation (ocular quiescence) or scanning (REMs) take place in sequences appropriate to the dream activity within the REM period.

In the overall results, 77 of 121 dreams were recalled within 3+ clarity. In the hands of two independent judges, the correspondence

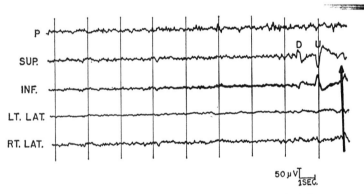

Fig. 5.—An a.c. electrooculogram showing the last 17 seconds before an awakening (arrow). Electrode Inf., infraorbital; Lt. Lat., left lateral canthus; Rt. Lat., right lateral canthus. ReMs: D, down; U, up.

Note the extended period of eye-movement quiescence preceding the burst of vertical deflections. This corresponds to the dream report of the subject watching an individual playing a violin on a stage. The deflections occurred at the point in the dream when the subject watched someone sit down just in front of her. The P lead shows a Stage 1 sleep record.

(Reprinted, by permission, from Roffwarg, H., Dement, W., Muzio, J. and Fisher, C.: Dream imagery: relationship to rapid eye movements of sleep. Arch. Gen. Psychiat. 7: 235-258, 1962).

between the predictions derived from the high clarity dreams, and their associated EOG's was rated as "good" (the prediction is an exact or nearly exact description of the directions, timing, and sequence of the actual movements recorded on the EOG) in 80.5 per cent of cases by one judge, and in 75.3 per cent of cases by the other. The percentage of "good" correspondences was somewhat lower in the remaining 44 dreams where clarity of recall was rated by the subjects as 2⁺ or 1⁺.

The conclusion that the oculomotor apparatus is actively responding to the dream imagery seems inescapable. The alternative explanation that the eyeballs are moving more or less at random as part of a purposeless increase in neuronal activity during the REM phase, and that dream images are elicited by the proprioceptive feedback, is unlikely. In the first place, the role of proprioception in the integration of eye movements and visual stimulation is not thought to be of crucial importance.[2] Secondly, REMs are not a necessary concomitant of "emergent" Stage 1 sleep and associated dream recall, as was demonstrated by observations made on congenitally blind subjects.[5,29] Finally, I am acquainted with a man who had both eyes enucleated and has subsequently experienced visual dreams.

The data of Roffwarg, et al. suggest, then, that the REMs represent a highly elaborate perceptual response, and of a much higher order, as we shall see, than can be elicited by any kind of external stimulation given during sleep. During REM sleep, dream images are, in effect, being substituted for retinal stimulation at some point in the stimulus-response process. Furthermore, at whatever point in the chain substitution occurs, that which is substituted must be virtually identical to the spatio-temporal pattern of neuronal discharge that would ordinarily be taking place as a result of the retinal stimulation consequent to "looking" at the analogous "real" objects.

Is the central nervous system capable of such a complicated substitution, particularly during sleep? Let us consider in the somewhat greater detail, the physiology of REM sleep and its relation to other states. Our purpose will be to see to what degree the neurophysiological background of the dreaming state warrants an affirmative position.

In the first place, the EEG during REM sleep suggests a fairly high level of arousal. In the cat, dog, and monkey, it cannot be differentiated by visual inspection from the patterns of alert wakefulness. In the human, a difference can be seen, but this may be due mainly to the presence of the so-called "saw-tooth" waves in the EEG of REM sleep, whose significance is unknown.[5,39]

The oculomotor apparatus is functioning at a rather high level. The REMs are binocularly synchronous, and their velocity appears to equal or approach that seen during fixational shifts in waking visual perception.[9,22]

In cats and dogs, hippocampal "theta" rhythms have been reported during REM sleep which the authors state are identical to activity elicited by the presentation of "meaningful" stimuli to the same animals in the waking state.[19,40]

Kanzow and his collaborators[26,27] have found that in cats, cortical blood flow is unchanged in passing from NREM sleep to wakefulness if there is no significant increase in behavioral activity. The highest values for blood flow are reached if the animals are distracted by an interesting object or event, e.g., approach of a human, opening of the cage, feeding, introducing a mouse into the cage. Throughout NREM sleep, the cortical blood flow remains at a low level, but with the development of REM sleep, it consistently rises to levels seen in the waking state during the periods of active attention described above.

Huttenlocher[21] studied unit discharge in the mesencephalic tegmentum during quiet arousal, strong arousal (by a puff of air), NREM sleep, and REM sleep. He found that spontaneous discharge rates were highest in the latter state.

Perhaps the most provocative observations are those of Evarts[15,16] He found high rates of spontaneous unit discharge in the visual cortex during REM sleep. NREM sleep and quiet wakefulness were associated with low rates of discharge in the same neurons. However, high discharge rates, not significantly different from those occurring during REM sleep, occurred in the waking state if the cats were presented with patterned visual stimulation. Unpatterned visual stimulation (diffuse light) had no effect.

Taken together, these studies of REM sleep paint a picture of a central nervous system, or at least its forebrain portion, that is highly aroused and engaged in the complex process of sensory-motor integration. Complex oculomotor behavior (REMs) is being elaborated. Arduini's observation (personal communication to the author) that pyramidal tract discharge is at a high level during REM sleep suggests that a motor output to the spinal cord is also being elaborated. If this is true, the lack of body movement and complete suppression of muscle tone[4,23] associated with REM sleep must be accounted for.

Dr. Robert Hodes and I have recently studied the H-reflex during sleep in adult human subjects. The posterior tibial nerve was stimulated every five seconds throughout the night while the EMG was continuously recorded from the calf muscles. During the onset of sleep and throughout NREM sleep, the reflex response was essentially unchanged. A complete suppression of the response occurred during REM sleep, but returned when the phase was terminated. We have interpreted this result as indicating that inhibitory influences are acting directly on the alpha motor neuron or that its excitability is greatly reduced by a concomitant reduction of activity in the gamma efferent system. Inhibition at this level forms the basis of the loss of muscle tone characteristic of REM sleep. It may also explain why gross body movements are not prominent at this time, even if a motor output appropriate to the dreamer's movements in the dream is being elaborated at higher levels. In line with this formulation, it might be suggested that this peripheral inhibitory mechanism is what makes the difference between a dreamer and a sleep walker.

A number of studies have shown that the complete picture of REM sleep occurs in complete independence of environmental stimuli.[9,10,12,14,23] The possibility that a crucial role is played by some trivial endogenous stimulus which has an exaggerated effect at higher levels cannot be ruled out. However, it seems just as likely that complex impulses are somehow elaborated from memory traces *within* the central nervous system and directed toward perpetual-motor areas. The psychomotor effects of temporal lobe stimulation in humans may be an analogous process.[34] As far as the forebrain is concerned, there is no difference between dream and reality. The phenomenological data have long emphasized that the salient feature of the dream experience is a heightened sense of reality. In olden days, this led philosophers to pose such questions as, "Am I a man dreaming I am a butterfly, or a butterfly dreaming I am a man?" From the point of view of the neurophysiological behavior of the forebrain, an exact parallel seems to be present. Thus, if we have adequately demonstrated a valid psychophysical parallelism, we may have no hesitation in saying that the REM phase is a period of perception during sleep. However, the perception is of endogenous material—material that must have many similarities with that which arises from patterned sensory stimulation in the waking state.

There is no evidence that accurate perception of environmental stimulation takes place during REM sleep. External stimuli occasionally modify the ongoing dream,[14] but they are almost always misinterpreted. Several experiments suggest that input from the environment is actively blocked out. For example, Huttenlocher demonstrated that the mesencephalic slow wave response to auditory clicks virtually disappeared during REM sleep.[20] Williams, Tepas and Morlock found that the average response to auditory stimuli recorded from the human scalp had the lowest amplitude during the REM phase.[45] Finally, several studies have demonstrated the relatively high arousal threshold of REM sleep in both man and animals.[3,12,23,44] Huttenlocher's suggestion that incoming sensory impulses are occluded because of the high degree of spontaneous neuronal discharge seems reasonable.[20]

A final thought is that the startling neurophysiological properties of the REM phase and their role as the background or basis of hallucinatory dream experiences must raise some interesting questions about the function of this peculiar kind of sleep and its role in the overall biological economy of the organism.

NREM SLEEP

In the little time that remains, we must turn our attention to the other kind of sleep. In the hands of several investigators,[17,25,35] awakenings during NREM sleep have produced reports of visual imagery. In many instances, these images were described as isolated and static. In some cases, however, it was claimed that the content of the recall could not be differentiated from the vivid dream experiences typically elicited from REM awakenings. Thus, from the phenomenological standpoint, dreaming (i.e., perception) can also occur during NREM sleep. If this is true, one is greatly puzzled by the lack of behavioral response to the imagery, and by the associated low level of physiological activity. If an experience is really occurring in NREM sleep that is identical with a dream experience, why are there no scanning eye movements, no heart rate accelerations, no increase in spontaneous neuronal discharges? In addition, this lack of change or fluctuation in physiological variables also means that there are no temporal landmarks to relate to the subjective reports. Accordingly, it cannot be established that NREM experience definitely occurs during sleep rather than being confabulated or elaborated at the moment of arousal.

There *is* one point in NREM sleep where it seems fairly safe to assume that imagery is actually experienced in the sleep state. This is at the onset of sleep. The rather complex imagery that is often recalled at this point is called "hypnagogic" imagery. From the subjective point of view, it is not usually accepted as "real" and is not as involved as the typical dream. Occasionally, however, hypnagogic imagery has all the subjective attributes of a dream experience.

Perhaps the most sensitive indicator of the onset of sleep is not the EEG, but rather the breakdown of visual fixation which is indicated by the appearance of *slow*, rhythmical, side-to-side swings of the eyeballs. This slow activity is an invariable concomitant of the onset of sleep and at least the first five or ten minutes of the NREM phase.[9]

Experiments were done in our laboratory in which subjects reclining in bed with their eyes closed were signaled when slow eye movement

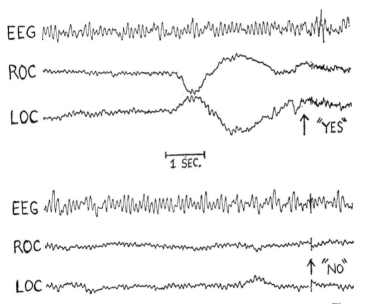

Fig. 6.—Relation of slow eye movements to hypnagogic imagery. Electrode placements: EEG, monopolar parieto-occipital electrode; ROC, right outer canthus monopolar electrode; LOC, left outer canthus monopolar electrode. With these derivations, a conjugate eye movement will give a potential change that is out-of-phase on the two eye pens. In the upper eye tracings, there is a rightward, leftward, rightward sequence of low swings after which the buzzer is sounded (arrow). Note that each directional component lasts about one second as compared to .05-.1 second for rapid movements. In the lower tracings, the buzzer (arrow) is sounded when there are no eye movements. Although there is no change in the continuous waking alpha rhythm in the EEG, the subjects reported hypnagogic imagery in instances illustrated in the upper tracings, and abstract thought in instances illustrated in the lower tracings. If the buzzer had not been sounded, the slow eye movements would have continued and in a few seconds, the EEG would have undoubtedly changed to Stage 1 sleep onset patterns.

was absent or at brief increments of time after its initial appearance. An attempt was made to select only instances when the EEG showed sustained alpha activity. Figure 6 shows an example of this procedure. If the subject was signaled during the presence of waking alpha and no slow eye movements, he invariably responded that he was awake and "thinking." If the signal followed the acceptance of the slow activity, he frequently reported a visual experience and diminished awareness of the environment. For example, in the instance of slow movement shown in figure 6, the subject said that he had to go to the bathroom and was wondering if he should call the experimenter, when "all of a sudden, I saw a man urinating." An important point is that within a narrow range, there was a definite tendency for greater subjective duration and complexity of hypnagogic imagery to be associated with longer periods of slow eye movement. Thus, if slow eye movement may be accepted as defining the onset of NREM sleep, it seems reasonable to conclude that the imagery actually occurred during sleep. It is obvious that slow side-to-side swings of the eyeballs are inappropriate to the visual experience. Our question, then, is why don't the images evoke the appropriate scanning movements, particularly in those instances where they are subjectively identical with REM imagery?

A striking example of a vivid hypnagogic experience failing to evoke a behavioral response in another system has been reported by Reiser:[36] "A 30 year old, healthy physician was serving as a volunteer subject for daily measurements of blood pressure, heart rate, and ballistocardiogram. One morning, he fell asleep on the ballistocardiogram table with all of the apparatus running and recording. After a few minutes, his left hand was observed to twitch and then to move. Immediately, he woke up and reported having experienced a nightmare. He had dreamed that he was parking his car at the top of his driveway, when the brakes failed so that his car was careening down to crash into the house. He was reaching for the emergency brake as he awoke, and he experienced all the subjective symptoms of severe anxiety, including palpitations. The records of blood pressure, heart rate, and ballistocardiogram showed *no change whatsoever.*"

Again, why didn't the experience and the associated anxiety evoke some change in the cardiovascular system? Such changes apparently occur during REM sleep. One can only say that the basis for the hypnagogic and dream images must be different. From the viewpoint of behavioral parallelism, (either in terms of REMs or other central and peripheral processes) hypnagogic imagery does not constitute perception. It may be that the hypnagogic and dream images arise from the same source, but that the contrasting nature of the two kinds of sleep permits radically different activity on the output side. However, this would mean that the image-input would be completely independent of such a vast difference in state, which seems unlikely. Obviously, the above considerations also apply to subjective experiences that are reported from awakenings in the middle of NREM periods.

On the purely behavioral side, a fairly high level of interaction with the environment can apparently be elicited during NREM sleep. The experiments of Oswald, Taylor and Triesman,[31] and Toman, Bush and Chachkes[42] demonstrate that complex stimuli can be discriminated. The results of Buendia, et al.[7] in the cat suggest that for certain tasks, discrimination is even better during NREM sleep than it is in the waking state. Finally, Granda and Hammack[18] have shown that complex operant behavior can be elicited during all EEG levels of NREM sleep. No indication was given in the above studies that any manifestation of awareness accompanied the discriminatory or operant behavior.

Summary and Conclusions

In its most general sense, the adjective, "perceptual," may be applied to nearly all processes that are presumed to operate upon input from sensory receptors. Certain classes of perceptual phenomena may be selected to emphasize the importance of central transformations, namely, those instances in which the final experience varies despite the constancy of underlying sensory events, and those in which the final experience is constant despite variations in underlying sensory events. As has been pointed out, it is most commonly assumed that we eventually will be able to explain these mediating transformations in terms of neurophysiological mechanisms.

In the case of the human, the end result of perceptual activity has been traditionally defined as a "state of awareness." However, philosophers and scientists have long recognized that there is no way of translating the presumed neurophysiological processes described in physical terms into the contents of awareness which are described in psychological terms. Consequently, there has been a shift to a reliance upon behavioral response as the end result so that when enough is known, the total process can be specified in a single mode of discourse. However, from the standpoint of both convenience and comprehensiveness, as well as their compelling nature, the subjective data are extremely difficult to ignore. Thus, we have come to adopt a psycho-physical parallelism with regard to perception which postulates an inextricable temporal relation between subjective experience and nervous function, although one cannot be explained in the terms of the other. We merely assume that a specific "content" of awareness is somehow dependent upon a specific neural event and will not occur in the absence of the latter. It may also be assumed that awareness arises from neural events that are more toward the terminal phases of perceptual elaboration, and further, that the neural events need not necessarily be initiated by peripheral stimuli as in the case of hallucinations.

It may safely be said that most of our attempts to make experimental inroads into the vast uncharted areas of perception are more concerned with the preliminary phases of the process than the final translation into either subjective awareness or behavioral response. We are even less concerned, at present, with the problem of which end result, behavioral or awareness, should be the legitimate index of the occurrence of perception. In human subjects, both sets of data are available in abundance, and it might even be asked whether a process is to be termed "perceptual" if it cannot be demonstrated that it has resulted in both awareness and behavior. The insistence upon a dual criterion of perception is certainly implied by our attitude in viewing certain extreme examples. Thus, we find the notion of perception without awareness as exemplified by the studies of sub-liminal stimulation a little difficult to handle. On the other hand, it is difficult even to conceive of awareness without behavior or potential behavior, particularly if characteristic neural events or verbal reports constitute behavior.

The reason for making this somewhat artificial distinction between the perceptual process and its end result is to highlight the unique problems that have confronted us in the consideration of the topic of perception during sleep. In this case, we are not so much concerned with how perceptual processes operate, as with whether or not they actually occur. We have found that many of the recent studies of sleep have dealt with the problem of relating the subjective and behavioral indices of perception, and implicit in these efforts seemed to be the principle that one was not valid without the confirmation of the other. This is, in part, due also to the fact that in sleep we cannot readily specify the input side of the paradigm. The point is not to suggest that there ought to be a dual criterion of normal perception in the human, but rather to emphasize that contrary to what is ordinarily encountered in the waking state, several combinations of end results are commonly seen in sleep and this situation may, in turn, have interesting implications for our consideration of normal perceptual processes and their background states.

We have seen that during REM sleep, there appears to be a rather remarkable correspondence between behavior, as indicated by eye movement patterns, and awareness, as indicated by the recall of dream content. Would we seriously consider the dream as a perceptual event if such a behavioral correlate had not been demonstrated? At any rate, in the case of REM sleep, both criteria of the occurrence of perception appear to be met, and in addition, the less specific behavior of the nervous system suggests that perceptual processes are going on. This allows us to further assume that some kind of "sensory input" is occurring and to speculate about its nature. It might be suggested that the essential difference between the waking state and REM sleep lies in the nature of the perceptual input, and in how much of the usual preliminary elaborations of peripheral sensory input are absent in the latter state.

During NREM sleep, the problem of defining the occurrence of perceptual activity is brought to the fore. If we accept the subjective data, we must conclude that we may have the experience of seeing, hearing, or thinking in this state. However, in contrast to REM sleep, there seems to be no physical counterpart either in overt behavior or in the kind of non-specific neurophysiological background that we are accustomed to associate with perceptual activity in the waking state. It may be that the essential neural events are present in both REM and NREM sleep, but that in the former, they are completely overshadowed by more dramatic but not necessarily crucial changes. If not, we must postulate that an exception to psycho-physical parallelism occurs in NREM sleep, or that the subjective reports reflect some other process not strictly perceptual which acquires an experiential attribute as an artifact of the attempt to describe it.

If subjective reports from NREM sleep are thought of as an awareness without parallel behavior, the examples of complex discrimination would appear to be just the opposite, behavior without awareness, although one may postulate a memory defect rather than the lack of subjective apprehension of the stimuli. At any rate, lacking a subjective counterpart, is such discriminatory behavior to be called perceptual?

And what is necessary beyond the neural processes involved in the discrimination to elicit some manifestation of subjective awareness? In summary, three combinations of behavior and awareness seem to be possible in the sleeping state. It might be suggested that only in the case of REM sleep can we confidently state that perceptual activity actually occurs. To the extent that this is a matter of definition, we do not wish to quibble. We only wish to point out such a definition is more of a problem in sleep than in wakefulness, and to suggest that further work in this area may help to shed some light on the neurophysiological basis of perceptual processes and their final translation into behavior and awareness.

REFERENCES

1. ASERINSKY, E., AND KLEITMAN, N.: Regularly occurring periods of eye motility, and concomitant phenomena during sleep. Science, 1953, *118:* 273-274.
2. BACH-Y-RITA, P.: Extraocular proprioception. Acta Neurol. Latinoamer. *5:* 17-39, 1959.
3. BENOIT, O. & BLOCH, V.: Seuil d'excitabilité réticulaire et sommeil profond chez le chat. J. Physiol (Paris), *52:* 17-18, 1960.
4. BERGER, R.: Tonus of extrinsic laryngeal muscles during sleep and dreaming. Science *134:* 840, 1961.
5. ——, OLLEY, P., AND OSWALD, I.: The EEG, eye-movements and dreams of the blind. Quart. J. Exp. Psychol. *14:* 183-186, 1962.
6. ——, AND OSWALD, I.: Eye movements during active and passive dreams. Science *137:* 601, 1962.
7. BUENDIA, N., SIERRA, G., GOODE, M., AND SEGUNDO, J.: Conditioned and discriminatory responses in wakeful and in sleeping cats. Unpublished manuscript.
8. DEMENT, W.: The occurrence of low voltage, fast, electroencephalogram patterns during behavioral sleep in the cat. EEG Clin. Neurophysiol. *10:* 291-296, 1958.
9. ——: Eye movements during sleep. *In* M. Bender (Ed.): The Oculomotor System. New York, Paul B. Hoeber, Inc., 1964.
10. ——: An essay on dreams: the role of physiology in understanding their nature. *In* T. Newcomb (Ed.): New Directions in Psychology, Vol. II. New York, Holt, Rinehart, & Winston, 1965.
11. ——, AND KLEITMAN, N.: Incidence of eye motility during sleep in relation to varying EEG patterns. Fed. Proc. *14:* 216, 1955.
12. ——, AND KLEITMAN, N.: Cyclic variations of EEG during sleep and their relation to eye movements, body motility and dreaming. EEG Clin. Neurophysiol. *9:* 673-690, 1957.
13. ——, AND KLEITMAN, N.: The relation of eye movements during sleep to dream activity: an objective method for the study of dreaming. J. Exp. Psychol. *53:* 339-346, 1957.

14. ——, AND WOLPERT, E.: The relation of eye movements, body motility, and external stimuli to dream content. J. Exp. Psychol. *55:* 543-553, 1958.

15. EVARTS, E.: Activity of neurons in visual cortex of cat during sleep with low voltage fast EEG activity. J. Neurophysiol. *25:* 812-816, 1962.

16. ——: Patterns of neuronal discharge in visual cortex during visual inspection, waking and sleep. XXII Int. Cong. Physiol. Sciences, Leiden, Sept. 10-17, 1962.

17. FOULKES, W.: Dream reports from different stages of sleep. J. Abn. Soc. Psychol. *65:* 14-25, 1962.

18. GRANDA, A., AND HAMMACK, J.: Operant behavior during sleep. Science *133:* 1485-1486, 1961.

19. GRASTYAN, E.: The hippocampus and higher nervous activity. *In* M. Brazier (Ed.) : The Central Nervous System and Behavior. Trans. Sec. Conf. J. Macy, Jr., Found., New York, pp. 119-205.

20. HUTTENLOCHER, P.: Effects of state or arousal on click responses in the mesencephalic reticular formation. EEG Clin. Neurophysiol. *12:* 819-828, 1960.

21. HUTTENLOCHER, P.: Evoked and spontaneous activity in single units of medial brain stem during natural sleep and waking. J. Neurophysiol. *24:* 451-468, 1961.

22. JEANNEROD, M., AND MOURET, J.: Etude des mouvements oculaires observés chez l'Homme au cours de la veille et du sommeil. C.R. Soc. Biol. *156:* 1407-1410, 1962.

23. JOUVET, M.: Recherches sur les structures nerveuses et les Mécanismes responsables des différentes phases du sommeil physiologique. Arch. ital. Biol. *100:* 125-206, 1962.

24. KAHN, E., DEMENT, W., FISHER, C., AND BARMACK, J.: Incidence of color in immediately recalled dreams. Science *137:* 1054-1055, 1962.

25. KAMIYA, J.: Behavioral, subjective and physiological aspects of drowsiness and sleep. *In* D. W. Fiske and S. R. Maddi (Eds.) : Functions of Varied Experience. Homewood, Illinois, Dorsey Press, 1961.

26. KANZOW, E.: Electrical activity and blood flow of the cerebral cortex of unanesthetized, unrestrained cats correlated to behavior. Excerpta Medica— Int. Cong. Series #37, 1961, 97-98, 5th Int. Cong. EEG & Clin. Neurophysiol. Rome, Sept. 7-13, 1961.

27. KANZOW, E., KRAUSE, D. AND KÜHNEL, H.: Die Vasomotorik der Hirnrinde in den Phasen desynchronisierter EEG-Aktivität im Naturlichen Schlaf der Katze. Pflügers Archiv. *274:* 593-607, 1962.

28. MICHEL, F., KLEIN, M., JOUVET, D., AND VALATX, J.: Etude polygraphique du sommeil chez le rat. C.R. Soc. Biol. *155:* 2389-2392, 1961.

29. OFFENKRANTZ, W., AND WOLPERT, E.: The detection of dreaming in a congenitally blind subject. J. Nerv. Ment. Dis. *136:* 88-90, 1963.

30. OSGOOD, C.: Method and Theory in Experimental Psychology. New York, Oxford University Press, 1953.

31. OSWALD, I., TAYLOR, A., AND TRIESMAN, M.: Discriminative responses to stimulation during human sleep. Brain *83:* 440-453, 1960.

32. PENFIELD, W.: Studies of the cerebral cortex of man. A review and an in-

terpretation. *In* J. Delafresnaye (Ed.): Brain Mechanisms and Consciousness. Springfield, Illinois, Charles C Thomas, 1954.

33. PENFIELD, W.: Neurophysiological basis of the ligher functions of the nervous system—introduction. *In* J. Field, H. Magoun and V. Hall (Eds.): Handbook of Physiology 1, Sect. 1, Vol. III: 1441-1445, 1960. Washington, D. C., American Physiological Society, 1960, pp. 1441-1445.

34. PENFIELD, W., AND RASMUSSEN, T.: The Cerebral Cortex of Man. New York, MacMillan Company, 1952.

35. RECHTSCHAFFEN, A., VERDONE, P., AND WHEATON, J.: Reports of mental activity during sleep. Canad. Psychiat. Assoc. J. *8:* 409-414, 1963.

36. REISER, M. F.: Reflections on interpretation of psychophysiologic experiments. Psychosomatic Med. *23:* 430-439, 1961.

37. ROFFWARG, H., DEMENT, W., AND FISHER, C.: Observations on the sleep-dream pattern in neonates, infants, children and adults. Child Psychiat. Mong. *2:* 60-72, New York, Pergamon Press, 1964.

38. ROFFWARG, H., DEMENT, W., MUZIO, J., AND FISHER, C.: Dream imagery. Relationship to rapid eye movements of sleep. Arch. Gen. Psychiat. *7:* 235-258, 1962.

39. SCHWARTZ, B.: EEG et mouvements oculaires dans le sommeil de nuit. EEG Clin. Neurophysiol. *14:* 126-128, 1962.

40. SHIMAZONO, Y., HORIE, T., YANAGISAWA, Y., HORI, N., CHIKAZAWA, S., AND SHOZUKA, K.: The correlation of the rhythmic waves of the hippocampus with the behaviors of dogs. Neurol. Medico-chir. *2:* 82-88, 1960.

41. TEUBER, H.: Perception. *In* J. Field, H. Magoun and V. Hall (Eds.): Handbook of Physiology, Sect. 1, Vol. III. Washington, D.C., American Physiological Society, 1960, pp. 1595-1668.

42. TOMAN, J., BUSH, M., AND CHACHKES, J.: Conditional Features of Sound-evoked EEG Responses during Sleep. Fed. Proc. *17:* 648, 1958.

43. WEITZMANN, E.: A note on the EEG and eye movements during behavioral sleep in monkeys. EEG Clin. Neurophysiol. *12:* 790-794, 1961.

44. WILLIAMS, H. HAMMACK, J., DALY, R., AND DEMENT, W.: Auditory Arousal and the EEG stages of sleep. EEG Clin. Neurophysiol. *16:* 269-279, 1964.

45. WILLIAMS, H., TEPAS, D., AND MORLOCK, H.: Evoked responses to clicks and electroencephalographic stages of sleep in man. Science *138:* 685-686, 1962.

46. WOLPERT, E., AND TROSMAN, H.: Studies in psychophysiology of dreams. I. The evocation of sequential dream episodes. Arch. Neurol. Psychiat. *79:* 603-606, 1958.

12

EFFECTS OF EARLY EXPERIENCE ON BEHAVIOR: EXPERIMENTAL AND CONCEPTUAL CONSIDERATIONS

by RONALD MELZACK*

T HERE IS CONVINCING PHYSIOLOGICAL EVIDENCE that stimulation of the sensory systems evokes patterns of nerve impulses that undergo continuous filtering and selection during their transmission through successive synaptic levels. An analysis of responses in frog optic-nerve fibers by Lettvin et al. (1959) and Maturana et al. (1960) has shown that these fibers carry information that has already been abstracted from the mosaic representation of the outside world which exists in the rods and cones. Only information on moving objects is transmitted by most of the optic fibers, so that specific shape and movement patterns must be selected right at the retinal level for transmission to the optic tectum. In higher animals such as the cat, sequential selection of information from the total visual input appears to go on during transmission through successive synapses at the cortex (Hubel and Weisel, 1959; 1962). Evidence such as this, together with data that demonstrate central control over sensory input (see Livingston, 1959; Melzack and Wall, 1962), makes it reasonable to assume that perceptions are subserved by processes of abstraction and selection of particular neural patterns from the total sensory input throughout the course of afferent transmission.

Müller's classic theory of specific nerve energies, and its implication of straight-through transmission from receptors to specific brain centers, has led to the implicit assumption that all the known psychological properties of sensation must be synthesized by the "higher

*Psychology Section and Research Laboratory of Electronics, Massachusetts Institute of Technology. Now at the Department of Psychology, McGill University, Montreal, Canada.

(This research was supported in part by the U.S. Army Signal Corps, the Air Force Office of Scientific research, and the Office of Naval Research and in part by the National Institutes of Health Grant MH-04235-03).

nervous activity" of the cortex. Yet it is now becoming apparent that the selection and filtering of information that occur at synaptic regions along the afferent pathways are under the dynamic control of the higher nervous activity about which we know so little (Hagbarth and Kerr, 1954; Magni et al., 1959). It now appears that central nervous system processes subserving memories, attention, emotional states, and so forth can block, facilitate or otherwise modify sensory input patterns by means of systems of fibers that run from the brain to synaptic regions in the afferent pathways (see Livingston, 1959; Melzack, 1961). The cortex, then, in this conceptualization, is not an end station but another relay, with specialized functions in the continuous processing of information.

It is reasonable to suppose that inhibitory processes play an especially important role in filtering out irrelevant information during afferent transmission, and Milner (1957) has already pointed out the necessity for inhibitory mechanisms in higher central nervous system processes to prevent a sensory stimulus from triggering an avalanche of activity that could overwhelm the organism. Physiological studies of centrifugal control systems show, moreover, that stimulation of cortical and subcortical brain areas leads to inhibition as well as facilitation of afferent volleys (see Livingston, 1959). Furthermore, there is evidence (Meulders, 1962; Guzman-Flores et al., 1962) to suggest that the cortex exerts a tonic inhibitory influence over portions of the sensory input pattern, so that information selection may involve release from inhibition as well as excitation per se. Part of the complexity of the interactions is revealed by the demonstration by Guzman-Flores et al. (1962) that the reticular formation exerts a direct facilitating effect on transmission through the dorsal column nuclei while it inhibits transmission in these nuclei by means of relays through the cortex.

While it is essential to understand the physiological mechanisms of pattern selection, it is equally important to ascertain by psychological experiment the extent to which selection and filtering processes are determined by innate and acquired contributions, and the consequences of an organism's failure to learn the significances of stimuli during early development. Thus the selection of particular sensory patterns is primarily determined by innate processes in many lower organisms (Tinbergen, 1951). However, experiments described below on restriction of sensory experience in higher organisms such as the dog indicate that selection and filtering at the early stages of synaptic transmission must also be under the control of brain processes that correspond to prior experience with the environment. The reason for assuming that these central nervous system processes, based on early learning, must play an active role in information selection will be discussed in the light of work on the effects of early sensory restriction carried out at D. O. Hebb's laboratory beginning in 1950, as well as recent behavioral and electrophysiological studies currently under way.

BEHAVIOR OF SCOTTIES RAISED IN A RESTRICTED SENSORY ENVIRONMENT

Severe restriction of the early sensory experience of dogs produces striking abnormalities in their behavior at maturity. The characteristic behavior of Scottish terriers raised in restriction cages, which drastically reduce (but do not eliminate) patterned sensory inputs can be summarized as follows:

1) *Extremely high level of behavioral arousal or excitement:* The most pervasive feature of the behavior of restricted dogs is the extremely high level of behavioral excitement. During the first few days after release from the restriction cages, the dogs "froze," or crept along the walls of the laboratory room. With increased contact with the environment, however, they became increasingly active. The excitement was most evident when the dogs were first permitted to enter a new environment. They showed gross bodily activity as they dashed from one object to another, sniffed actively at each, and excitement increased as they encountered each new object. Innocuous but fear-producing objects (Melzack, 1952; Mahut, 1958), as well as human beings playing different social roles (Melzack and Thompson, 1956), produced diffuse emotional excitement consisting of rapid circling movements or vigorous dashing to-and-fro with a characteristic bodily posture. Almost anything new in their environment, such as a new kind of food pan or dog biscuit, could bring about this excited activity. The peak of emotional arousal or excitement was manifested in the form of "whirling fits" (Thompson et al., 1956). These fits were frequently driven by sudden excessive stimulation. But they were also observed to occur spontaneously and were even observed in some dogs before they were removed from their home cages. These whirling fits were sometimes of such violence that the dogs cracked their tails or broke the skin on their heads against the walls of their cages.

2) *Failure to attend selectively to environmental stimuli.* The restricted dogs rarely showed sustained attention to stimuli in the environment. They appeared to be "driven" by novel stimuli as they dashed

from one object to another, inspected each momentarily, and returned often to the same object as though it were totally new. Their random exploration was in sharp contrast with the normal dog's methodical, sustained investigation of social (Melzack and Thompson, 1956) or physical (Thompson and Heron, 1954b) objects. The restricted dogs also failed to habituate to novel stimuli as rapidly as the control dogs. Both groups initially showed a high level of activity in the course of investigating a new dog or a new room, but the level of activity of the normal dogs dropped rapidly, while that of the restricted dogs dropped more slowly or even increased with increasing presentations of the new animal or room.

3) *Abnormal response to noxious stimulation.* Another remarkable feature of the behavior of the restricted Scotties was their frequent lack of response to noxious stimuli that produced avoidance behavior and other indices of pain perception in their normally reared littermates (Melzack and Scott, 1957). It was clear from the behavior of the restricted dogs that they did not fail to perceive all noxious stimuli; that is, they were not insensitive to pain. Rather, they often failed to perceive low- or medium-level noxious stimulation that was normally perceived and responded to by the control dogs. Of the ten Scottish terriers raised in restriction that were tested with a flaming match, three dogs poked their noses into the flame, four did not sniff at the flame but offered no resistance when touched with it many times, while three squealed and tried to avoid the flame. Similarly, of eight restricted dogs tested with pinprick, four showed only localized twitches and no other indication of pain perception, while four dogs pulled their bodies aside and yipped, but remained in the presence of the experimenter who continued to prick them. Moreover, the restricted dogs were also observed to bang their heads on low-lying water pipes, one dog having done this more than thirty times in a single hour. This behavior was observed when the dogs were exploring a room with their usual excited activity. Thus the behavior of the restricted dogs suggested that they sometimes perceived pain and sometimes not; some responded to pinprick and not to burn, while some responded to both but not when they hit the water pipe. High levels of noxious stimulation, however, such as intense electric shock, invariably produced a violent response in all the dogs.

4) *Difficulty in delayed response and other cognitive tests.* When the restricted and control dogs were tested in a delayed response apparatus, a striking difference emerged between the two groups

(Thompson and Heron, 1954a). The median maximum delay that permitted the control dogs to perform to criterion was 240 seconds. Among the restricted dogs, however, only one performed to criterion after a delay of 25 seconds and none of the others could perform the task after any delay at all. The restricted dogs also had difficulty in other cognitive tasks that were presented to them (Thompson and Heron, 1954a). They made a significantly higher number of errors on the Hebb-Williams maze than the normally reared dogs. The Umweg problem also presented difficulties to the restricted dogs, who tended to spend more time than the control dogs trying to push through the barrier rather than circumventing it.

5) *Social submissiveness.* The restricted dogs, despite their heavy weight and powerful build (see Hebb, 1955b), were submissive to the normally reared dogs (Melzack and Thompson, 1956). Restricted dogs not only allowed a control dog to take a bone away from them, but even refused to touch a bone if a control dog were in the same room and some distance from them.

6) *Excessive licking behavior.* Licking behavior was the characteristic response of the restricted dogs to attempts by the experimenter to pat them on the head or back. They withdrew from any contact and instead vigorously licked his outstretched hand. This licking behavior continued for prolonged periods of time and frustrated any attempts by the experimenter to actually make contact with the animal (Melzack and Thompson, 1956).

MECHANISMS UNDERLYING THE EFFECTS OF RESTRICTION

There are a number of possible explanations for the abnormal behavior exhibited by the restricted dogs and each will be examined to see how well it fits the evidence.

1) It is possible that the sensory restriction led to a degeneration of peripheral fibers or central afferent neurons. Animals reared in darkness, for example, exhibit definite structural abnormalities of the macula and even in the chemical composition of optic fibers (Riesen, 1958). Cats raised with the lids of one eye sewn together, thereby preventing pattern perception, later exhibit a degeneration of the corresponding geniculate cells and an abnormally small number of cortical cells that are capable of responding selectively to stimulation of the previously covered eye (Hubel and Wiesel, personal communication). Yet it is highly unlikely that neural degeneration or other neuropathology could have developed in the restricted dogs, since they

were not deprived of stimulation. Although the range of stimulation was drastically reduced, the dogs nevertheless received considerable patterned visual and auditory stimulation, smells and a variety of somesthetic inputs ranging from itch (they scratched) to noxious stimulation (such as banging violently against the cage walls).

2) The second interpretation is that the reduction of patterned sensory stimulation was sufficient to produce a deficit in perceptual processes. Thus, cats deprived of pattern vision during early development (by means of special goggles or lenses covering the eyes) fail to discriminate between simple visual patterns at maturity (see Riesen, 1961a). These effects are generally attributed to a deficit in pattern perception. This interpretation, however, does not satisfactorily account for the behavioral syndrome of the restricted dogs. First, they were able to perform organized, goal-directed responses in their home cages, but failed to do so after they were transferred from their cages to the "normal" laboratory environment (Melzack, 1954), so that the behavior of the adult restricted dogs appears to reflect a disruption of behavior rather than a simple perceptual lack or deficit. Second, although the restricted dogs frequently failed to perceive noxious stimuli, their positive responses to these stimuli at high intensity must be accounted for, as well as their failure to respond to lower intensities. The behavior of the restricted dogs, then, cannot be attributed in any simple way to a deficit in perceptual processes.

Indeed, this interpretation for even the deprivation experiment (Riesen, 1961a) is open to question (Melzack, 1962). Pattern-deprived animals are also restricted to small cages or rooms and show excessive arousal, hyperexcitability and seizure activity (Riesen 1961b) that resemble behavior observed in the restricted dogs. Moreover, Riesen (1961a) has reported that visually deprived animals have much less difficulty in discriminating patterns if the differences to be discriminated are replicated throughout the stimulus figures. It seems reasonable, then, that at least part of their difficulty in discrimination may be attributed to inability to select relevant patterns from the total sensory input rather than to a deficit in pattern perception. This possibility points to an alternative explanation for the behavior of the restricted dogs.

3) The third interpretation conceives of a two-part process in which (a) there is inadequate filtering of inputs on the basis of memories (phase sequences) of the significances of stimuli normally acquired in early experience, so that (b) the total input bombarding the central

nervous system produces an excessive central nervous system arousal which, as Hebb (1955a) has suggested, could be responsible for the correspondingly low cue properties necessary for discrimination and adaptive response.

This conceptual model is based in part on knowledge of the somesthetic sensory system (see Melzack and Wall, 1962). It is known that sensory stimulation of the skin evokes nerve impulse patterns travelling centrally along fibers having different conduction velocities. Thus, some properties of the stimulus, such as the lightest deformation of the skin when the stimulus configuration is applied, generate impulses in the fastest conducting fibers that traverse the dorsal columns and thence (after possible selection and filtering by activities of the motor system; see Magni et al., 1959; Towe and Jabbur, 1961; Guzman-Flores et al., 1962) are transmitted by the "classical" lemniscal fibers to thalamic and cortical areas. It is assumed that these signals, carrying precise information about the stimulus, do not evoke "sensation," but mark an important further step in the process involved in information selection and, ultimately, detection and categorization of the patterns to allow perception and response.

It seems reasonable to believe that these inputs arriving at the cortex via the fastest conducting fibers activate "phase sequences" corresponding to earlier experience which are then able to exert dynamic control over patterns ascending along more slowly conducting fibers that carry information on a number of stimulus properties (Wall, 1960; Wall and Cronly-Dillon, 1960; Hunt and McIntyre, 1960a,b). In this way past experience would be able to influence the selection of particular patterns to subserve perception and response while other patterns (or portions of them) are inhibited or otherwise filtered out (see Melzack and Wall, 1962). Thus the "phase sequence," developed on the basis of prior experience, is a crucial part of this model. It is conceived to be actively engaged in information selection in the early stages of sensory transmission rather than passively evoked to subserve perception per se. Experience with the environment, however, is not gained only during early development, though this may be the period when learning occurs most easily and provides the foundation for all later learning (Hebb, 1949). Learning also occurs during the entire life process, even in the adult restricted dogs. Thus the particular meanings and associations of stimuli, which can be acquired throughout the organism's life, will act in the process of information selection and abstraction.

In the absence of prior experience, then, all stimuli in a totally new environment would be equally meaningful (or meaningless); no associations could provide a basis for selective attention to one stimulus rather than another. As a result, there would be inadequate filtering at the early stages of information transmission, so that all inputs, "irrelevant" as well as "relevant," would reach the brain where they could bombard the neural systems that produce sensory and affective arousal. Hebb (1955a; 1949) has described some of the behavioral abnormalities that can be expected in the organism undergoing excessive central nervous system arousal: disorganized behavior patterns ranging from "freezing" responses to irrelevant and aimless activity, failure to discriminate and respond adaptively to relevant cues in the environment, and disruption of higher central nervous system processes such as utilization of relevant memory stores, attention, perception, and so forth. These kinds of behavior are characteristic of the behavior of restricted dogs released in a totally new environment.

The model, then, describes a "vicious circle" in which failure to filter out irrelevant information (on the basis of prior experience) leads to excessive arousal which, in turn, interferes with mechanisms (perhaps innately determined) that would normally act in the selection of cues for adaptive response.

Experiments with Beagles Raised in Restriction Cages

The model just described leads to a number of predictions at both behavioral and physiological levels. It predicts that the exceptionally high level of arousal induced in the restricted dogs by unfamiliar environmental inputs should produce a general impairment in the selection of cues, so that the restricted dogs should have difficulty in discriminating among environmental stimuli in all sensory modalities. Moreover, the hypothesized failure of the nervous system in restricted dogs to select relevant neural sensory patterns and to filter out irrelevant patterns on the basis of past experiences should also apply to the output side; that is, there should be a similar failure in selection of nerve impulse patterns that excite muscular activity, so that nerve patterns producing irrelevant responses should not be filtered out as rapidly as they are in the normally reared dog. Thus, natural response tendencies or particular acquired responses should continue long after they have become irrelevant and impede the organism in its adaptive responses to the environment.

The physiological predictions are obvious: the EEG of the restricted dogs should show a high degree of arousal to all novel stimuli (such as an unfamiliar cage or dog) indicated by a disproportionately large amount of high-frequency components. Concurrently, the high arousal should be accompanied by a reduction or modification of afferent signals during the transmission process (see Buser and Borenstein, 1959; Hirsch et al., 1961; Meulders, 1962). Moreover, since attentional processes play an important role in determining the amplitudes of evoked responses (see Livingston, 1959), the characteristic fluctuations in attention indicated by the behavior of the restricted dogs should be reflected by continuous changes in the amplitude and waveform of the evoked responses.

BEHAVIORAL STUDIES

Beagles are being used as subjects in a restriction experiment currently under way, since a recent stereotaxic atlas (Lim et al., 1960) for the beagle permits accurate placement of recording and stimulating electrodes in their brains. Each dog in the experimental group was placed, at three weeks of age, in a specially constructed cage (see fig. 1) that permitted feeding and care but prevented the dog from making contact with the outside environment. Each cage was well lit, so that the dogs were able to see visual patterns provided by the cage construction (lines, angles, circles, and rectangles) and their own bodies. In addition, auditory and olfactory stimuli from the laboratory were able to penetrate their cages. But the variety of patterned stimuli, compared with that in a normal environment, was drastically reduced. Starting at ten months of age or later, the restricted dogs were released from their cages for varying periods of time each day so that they could participate in the experiments described below. The dogs comprising the control group were raised normally on a farm until they were ten months old. They were then brought to the laboratory, where they lived two in a cage and were frequently permitted to run in a large outdoor enclosure.

Three kinds of experiments were carried out with the dogs: (1) observations of activity levels, since they provided an index of arousal that is fundamental to the model described above; (2) studies of discrimination in a number of modalities, since it is predicted that the high level of arousal should interfere with cue detection in all sensory systems; and (3) tests of their ability to "inhibit" irrelevant responses, since the model predicts difficulty in selection of relevant neural patterns on the output side comparable to failure in selection of inputs.

1) *Excessive Behavioral Arousal*

The extremely high level of behavioral activity manifested by the restricted beagles is one of the characteristic features of their behavior. Figure 2 shows a comparison of activity levels recorded in the two groups of dogs. Each dog was placed in a large testing chamber that

Fig. 1.—Restriction cages. The front doors slide open to permit the dogs to eat and drink from the food compartments which are attached to the cages.

contained two lucite panels that they had learned to press for a food reward, an overhead light, and other pieces of apparatus. The number of movements was counted by means of a photoelectric apparatus that registered a movement whenever the animal crossed from one side of the testing chamber to the other. During five-minute periods chosen randomly on each of three days, the restricted dogs showed approximately 125 crossing movements per five-minute period compared with 30 for the control dogs. Some of the restricted dogs exhibited brief "whirling fits" at moments of peak excitement, in which they turned in narrow circles at great speed. This "whirling" behavior, however, is rare in the beagles compared with the Scotties.

2) *General Impairment in Sensory Discrimination*

   a) *Difficulty in performing simple visual discriminations.* Significant

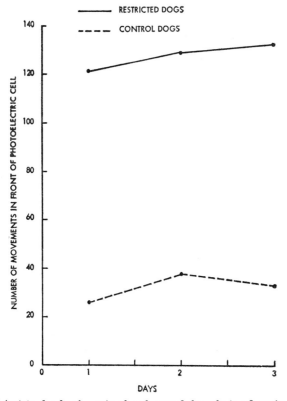

Fig. 2.—Activity levels of restricted and control dogs during five-minute periods on three successive days.

differences between restriction-reared beagles and their control litter-mates were observed (Melzack, 1962) when they had to discriminate between a white card (positive stimulus) and a black card (negative stimulus) which were located on the doors of a visual discrimination box. The response patterns of the two restricted dogs that were tested in this experiment were almost identical (fig. 3). Each showed rapid initial learning of the problem, presumably a transfer from an earlier brightness discrimination (learned during preliminary train-ing), which was followed by a rise in errors before they finally achieved criterion performance. The increase in errors was accom-panied by vicarious trial-and-error behavior at the choice point, in which the dogs appeared suddenly to become aware of the cues pro-vided by the cards on the doors. The control dogs, on the other hand, showed a smooth decrease in errors after the second day. The difference in error scores between the two groups is significant at better than the .05 level (t = 3.08).

The differences between the two groups were even more marked in reversal training, which was carried out six weeks later. The procedure was reversed so that the black card now signaled food and the white card was on the locked door (fig. 4). The control dogs showed a

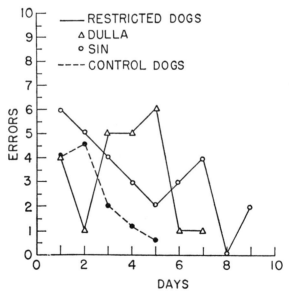

Fig. 3.—Errors made by restricted and control dogs during white (+) vs black (—) discrimination training.

gradual decrease in errors, while both restricted dogs made significantly higher error scores (t = 4.1; p = .02) for a prolonged period. The plateaus in the curve reflect a position habit that was developed by both dogs during the training. One ran only to the right-hand side and the other only to the left on nine or ten trials each day. Both dogs also showed a high level of excited behavior during the entire training period. Only after one of the dogs was permitted to correct its errors (on the twenty-second day) was it able to learn the reversal problem. Dogs raised in a restricted environment, then, encounter more difficulty than normally reared littermates in learning a simple visual discrimination and in utilizing it in a new situation (the reversal problem).

b) *Failure to respond normally to auditory stimuli.* A series of tests was carried out to study the effects of auditory stimuli on the be-

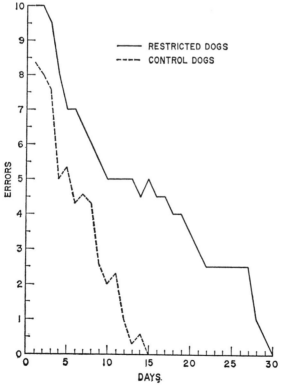

FIG. 4.—Errors made by restricted and control dogs during black (+) vs white (−) reversal training.

havior of the two groups of dogs. The subjects of the experiments were two restricted dogs (Dulla and Sin) and three normally reared litter-mates. The five dogs were each placed daily in a large cage that had two windows, and their behavior was "shaped" so that a press on either window triggered an apparatus that dropped a food reward (a piece of frankfurter) into the cage. Both groups of dogs learned the response relatively quickly, and there was no difference between the two groups in the number of rewards necessary to "shape" satisfactory pressing behavior.

The dogs were then given 12 ten-minute periods (one period per day) to achieve a stable response output.

Two tests with auditory stimulation were carried out. (i) On three successive days the dogs were given a ten-minute period in the test box each day, in which they received a food reward each time they pressed the window. No sounds were presented the first day, but on the second and third days a 15-second tape recording of lion roars was presented every two minutes (fig. 5a). (ii) On four successive days the dogs pressed the window to obtain a food reward. On the fourth day a 15-second tape recording of a cock crowing was presented every two minutes (fig. 5). Since one of the restricted dogs (Sin) sometimes regurgitated her food after five minutes of pressing, the two groups are compared for their response output for the first five-minute periods.

Figure 5 shows the effects of the auditory stimuli on the window-pressing responses of the two groups. The lion roars and cock crows produced a severe disruption of pressing behavior in the control dogs but had virtually no effect on the behavior of the restricted dogs. The control dogs exhibited a startle response at the beginning of the presen-tation of the auditory stimuli, assumed a crouching posture typical of fear behavior in the dog (Melzack, 1952; Mahut, 1958) and moved away from the window into a corner where they generally remained for the duration of the test period. Records of activity levels parallel almost exactly those of window-pressing responses. The restricted dogs showed marked excitement when the stimuli were first presented—one had a brief whirling fit—but both resumed pressing and moved freely around the apparatus. One of the dogs showed orienting responses to the lion roars on the first day, but rarely gave any sign of having "heard" the lion roars or cock crows during the subsequent presenta-tions. The other restricted dog investigated the apparatus during each auditory presentation but resumed her normal activity immediately

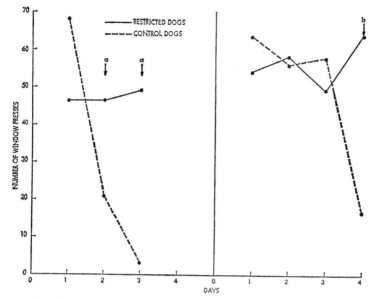

Fig. 5.—Effects of presentation of auditory stimuli (indicated by arrows) on window-pressing behavior. (a) Lion roars. (b) Cock crows.

after. While the auditory stimuli dominated the behavior of the normally reared dogs, they failed to elicit responses that would indicate that they had any emotional significance to the restricted dogs. These results, obtained with auditory stimuli, are similar to observations of the effects of innocuous but fear-producing visual stimuli in restricted and normally reared Scotties (Melzack, 1954).

c) *Failure to discriminate sexually relevant cues.* During the tests in which the dogs were pressing for food reward, one of the female dogs in the colony (not used as a subject in the current tests) came into heat. The behavior of the two male control dogs was strikingly different from that of the restricted male. When each control male dog was allowed access to the female, his behavior was goal-directed and the goal was unmistakable. Each began courting behavior, followed by mounting and intromission. When these dogs were in the testing apparatus, each whined, jumped excitedly about, ignored the food in the apparatus, and spent the ten-minute test period trying to leap out of the cage.

The male restricted dog, however, ignored the presence of the female and continually avoided her approaches. Although the presence of the female appeared to evoke a generalized excitement, it failed to produce any goal-directed behavior. Moreover, the behavior of this dog (Dulla)

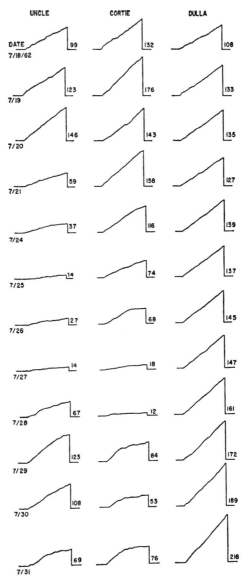

FIG. 6.—Effects of sexually relevant stimuli on window-pressing rates by one restricted (Dulla) and two control (Uncle, Cortie) male dogs.

in the testing apparatus was totally unlike that of the control dogs: his rate of pressing for food increased day by day, in sharp contrast to the lack of interest in food exhibited by the control dogs.

Figure 6 shows the cumulative window presses made during the 12-day period when each dog was placed in the cage for ten minutes a day. The increased pressing rate of Dulla and the sharp drop in pressing by the control dogs (Uncle and Cortie) at times of maximal interest in the female are clearly seen. The graphs also reflect the fact that Uncle's interest in the female was aroused before Cortie's. It is evident, then, that olfactory and related stimuli that elicited goal-directed behavior in the control dogs served only to increase the general state of activity of the restricted dog.

d) *Abnormal responses to noxious sitmulation.* Of the two restricted dogs, one crashed violently into the wall of a large wooden test box (after running 25 feet from his cage) every day for more than a month without ever giving any indication of pain. This dog, during the visual discrimination test described above, also struck a door in the apparatus with great force at least five times a day for more than four months and frequently hit the top of the apparatus with his head without ever wincing or squealing. Both dogs accidentally cut their rear paws, tearing the muscle until bone was exposed, without showing any signs of pain. Response to burn and pinprick has not yet been systematically investigated.

3) *Failure to "Inhibit" Irrelevant Response Patterns*

(a) Observations made during the experiments on visual discrimination and reversal learning suggested that the restricted dogs had difficulty in inhibiting or "holding back" incorrect responses. They usually developed a *position habit* (running at least 9 out of 10 trials to the same side of the apparatus) that dominated their behavior and that seemed to interfere with attempts to run toward the correct stimulus. The mean percentage of training days on which the dogs exhibited a position habit was 64 per cent for the restricted dogs and 16 per cent for the control dogs.

(b) An experiment was undertaken to test the hypothesis that restricted dogs have difficulty in inhibiting irrelevant responses. After the restricted and control dogs had achieved a stable window-pressing output for food reward (in which there was no difference in the mean number of presses made by the two groups), they were given daily 20-minute extinction periods for six days in which their presses were no longer rewarded. They were usually fed 4 to 6 hours after each extinction session so that feeding would not be temporally associated with activity in the box. Figure 7 shows the extinction rates for the two groups of dogs. It is clear that the restricted dogs showed a higher rate of pressing during extinction. Although they easily learned to press the window, they had difficulty in "inhibiting" the response when it became inappropriate.

(c) *Stereotyped response patterns.* The window-pressing responses of the two restricted dogs developed a remarkable stereotypy. Dulla turned a complete circle before each press on the window and again before eating the reward. This response pattern disappeared slowly over a five-day period. Sin developed an entirely different behavior pattern. As soon as the first food reward landed in the cage, she licked the slice of meat, rolled it around the cage, rubbed her head against it, and finally left it in a corner. She pressed again and repeated the same pattern until she collected a small pile of rewards (one to two dozen); she then ate them voraciously, sometimes regurgitating them and re-eating them. She pressed normally for the remainder of the test period. Behavior patterns like those of Sin and Dulla were never observed in the control dogs in the window-pressing apparatus.

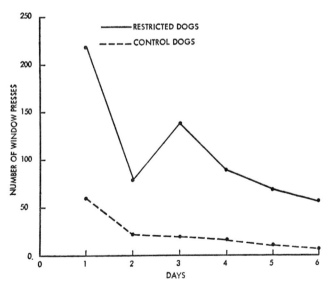

Fig. 7.—Number of window presses made by restricted and control dogs during six extinction periods.

Stereotyped behavior patterns were observed in one of the control dogs, however, during the visual discrimination tests. During training on a simple discrimination between an horizontal and vertical line, one of the "normal" control dogs (Uncle) underwent a remarkable change in personality and, in terms of both general behavior and error scores, became indistinguishable from the restricted dogs. He showed an increasingly high level of behavioral excitement and struggled violently when he was picked up. At the same time he developed a strong position habit, as well as stereotyped behavior patterns, such as turning two complete circles before responding to the stimuli. In the course of this dramatic behavioral change, his error scores shifted into the range of the restricted dogs (see fig. 8).

In summary, these experiments carried out with restricted dogs show

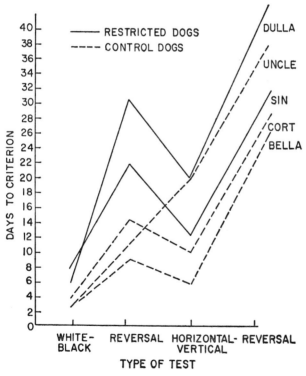

Fig. 8.—Number of days required by restricted and control dogs to solve four visual discrimination problems. One of the control dogs (Uncle) underwent a "breakdown" during horizontal-vertical discrimination training (see text).

that (1) they become extremely active after they are removed from the restriction cage and are placed into a new environment, (2) they exhibit abnormal perceptual behavior to visual, auditory, olfactory, and noxious stimuli, and (3) they have difficulty in "inhibiting" irrelevant responses such as position habits, responses that no longer bring food rewards, and stereotyped behavior patterns.

PHYSIOLOGICAL STUDIES

Physiological studies on the effects of early restriction are currently being carried out in collaboration with Stephen K. Burns, a graduate student in the Communications Biophysics Laboratory at M.I.T. Although the results so far must be considered preliminary, some consistent trends are emerging from the data. (1) When the restricted dogs are first permitted to look at a novel environment through their open cage doors, their electroencephalograms (EEG's) show a dramatic shift from low to very high frequencies, and shift back to low frequencies only when the door is closed. The control dogs' EEG's may show momentary shifts to higher frequencies, but they generally revert to lower frequencies long before the novel stimulus is removed. (2) The restricted dogs' EEG's after they have been released from restriction, show a significantly greater proportion of high frequencies (normally associated with high levels of central nervous system arousal) than the control dogs'. Moreover, the high arousal level, which appears most consistently at the frontal cortex, cannot be attributed solely to proprioceptive inputs from bodily activity, since it occurs when the restricted dogs are at rest. (3) The responses evoked by light flashes or clicks in the reticular formation of the restricted dogs show striking fluctuations in amplitude when a novel stimulus (another cage) is presented, so that the averaged evoked response is considerably reduced in amplitude. At the same time, responses at the cortex are often (although not always) modified during the stimulus presentation period. Thus during the period of high level of arousal produced by an unfamiliar environment, responses evoked by specific stimuli arrive at the brain in modified form. The evoked responses of the control dogs show similar modifications during their brief periods of EEG arousal, but they quickly return to normal as the slower EEG rhythms return. These preliminary results, then, tend to support the conceptual model discussed above.

IMPLICATIONS OF THE CONCEPTUAL APPROACH

The behavioral and physiological data obtained with the restricted beagles lend support to the conceptual approach based on current knowledge of information selection in the central nervous system. The impressive body of data on central control over afferent input reviewed by Livingston (1959) makes it reasonable to assume that the neural correlates of experience of the environment (phase sequences) act in the beginning stages of information selection to prevent massive sensory inputs from overwhelming the organism. The restricted dogs, in the absence of such prior experience, had difficulty in attending and responding selectively to relevant information and in replacing irrelevant, aimless responses with more adaptive behavior.

This conceptual approach has no difficulty in dealing with the obvious genetic contributions to behavior. It is clear from the experiments of Lettvin et al. (1959) and Hubel and Wiesel (1959; 1962) that there are innately determined mechanisms of information selection in the frog, cat, and monkey. At the same time, it is reasonable to believe that conditions at synapses that determine the selection and abstraction of particular patterns can be influenced by central nervous system activities such as memories of prior experience. Thus innate and acquired contributions would act together to determine the properties of the nerve impulse patterns that subserve perception and response.

GENETIC CONTRIBUTIONS

The genetic contributions to behavior are clearly revealed in studies of early restriction of experience. It is difficult to imagine a more homogeneous environment than a restriction cage in which each dog is surrounded by an identical set of four walls, ceiling, floor, light fixture, and air vent. Yet there are striking differences from litter to litter and even among dogs of the same litter. One beagle may be so active that he has occasional fits, while a littermate appears normal until a stimulus calls out excessive excitement that differentiates him from the control dogs. Similarly, a restriction experiment carried out by R. L. Solomon and his colleagues (personal communication) showed that all but one of the dogs of one litter failed to avoid shock, all dogs of a second litter learned normally, while in a third litter, half learned and half did not. Dogs in all three litters, however, licked boiling-hot radiator pipes to get at food smeared on them. With environment held so constant, this variability of behavior can only be attributed to genetic contributions.

There are also obvious breed differences between Scotties and beagles raised in restriction, such as the high frequency of whirling fits in Scotties and their infrequency in beagles, and the characteristic "teasing" stance of the Scottie during emotional excitement (Melzack, 1954) and its absence in the beagle. These differences are consistent with observations that each breed tends to show characteristic responses to fear-producing objects (Mahut, 1958) and that rearing methods have different effects in different breeds (Freedman, 1958).

Finally, there are striking species differences which suggest the possibility that physiological mechanisms subserving information selection may be radically different in different species. Thus the frog's eye selects patterns produced by small moving objects (Lettvin et al., 1959) while cat and monkey visual cortical cells select specific, complex geometrical patterns (Hubel and Wiesel, 1959; 1962). At the behavioral level, interspecies differences among mammals are just as striking. Dogs (Thompson et al., 1956) and cats (Riesen, 1961b) raised in restricted environments show excessive excitement, while the restricted monkeys described by Harlow and Harlow (1962) and the hospitalized human children described by Spitz (1945), all raised in astonishingly similar environments, show marked apathy and are almost polar opposites from the cats and dogs on an excitement dimension. The results are such as to suggest that the neural mechanisms in one group permit a continuous cephalad transmission of almost all information, both relevant and irrelevant, while in the other an excessive inhibition keeps out most of the sensory inputs.

Comparison of Effects of Restriction and Brain Lesions

A further implication of the conceptual model is that brain lesions that tend to (1) disrupt central control over selection of sensory information, (2) increase the level of central nervous system arousal produced by stimulation or (3) prevent selective utilization of prior experience should produce patterns of behavior that are similar to those of restricted dogs. One or more of these mechanisms has been implicated in the effects of lesions of the lateral brainstem and the frontal lobes, and, indeed, the behavioral syndromes produced by these lesions resemble in many respects the behavior of restricted dogs.

Lesions of the Lateral Brainstem

Sprague, Chambers, and Stellar (1961) have found that lateral brainstem lesions in cats produce (1) general sensory deficits in all modalities, with particularly striking effects in the visual system which they describe as "a failure in the capacity to utilize sensory information in making adaptive responses to the environment, in attending to relevant stimuli, and in localizing stimuli in space or on the body surface . . . the cat seemed to fail to appreciate the significance of a mouse or an aggressive dog or cat . . . and thus responded inappropriately to these stimuli"; (2) hyperexploratory behavior characterized by incessant stereotyped wandering, sniffing, and visual searching; (3) exaggerated oral activities; and (4) abnormal emotional responses, in which they show little or no defensive and aggressive reaction to noxious and aversive situations and no solicitation of affection or petting.

Sprague et al. (1961) have already noted the striking resemblance between the behavioral patterns of cats with lateral brainstem lesions and those observed in restricted dogs, and, indeed, the conceptual model described above lends itself well as an explanation of the cats' behavior. The model proposes that the lateral pathways evoke processes in the brain (including those subserving memories of prior experience) that act on sensory inputs ascending along more slowly conducting fibers to bring about selection of relevant cues. In addition, there is evidence (Adey et al., 1957; Desmedt, 1957; Kuypers et al., 1960) that a large portion of the fibers involved in central control over afferent inputs descend in the lateral brainstem. The lesions of the lateral pathways described by Sprague et al. (1961) must have eliminated fibers involved in both of these processes so that the reduction of central control over sensory inputs would produce a failure in selection of meaningful information, together with increased arousal and its concomitant effects. This kind of interpretation is consistent with the general sensory abnormalities observed in the cats, as well as the ceaseless hyperexploratory activity and the increased licking ("as though some inhibitory influence had been removed"; Sprague et al., 1961, p. 171).

Lesions of the Frontal Lobes

The manifold effects of frontal-lobe lesions have been reviewed by Russell (1948), Rosvold (1959) and more recently by Gross and Weiskrantz (1963). The primary behavioral effects (some of which are specifically characteristic of lesions of the lateral, medial or orbital surfaces of the lobes) appear to be the following: (1) a striking hyperreactivity to novel stimuli or to changes in stimulus intensity so that a stimulus that normally increases motor activity in a non-operated animal produces significantly higher levels of activity in the frontal operated animals (Isaac and DeVito, 1958; Gross and Weiskrantz, 1963); (2) impairment on visual learning-set and discrimination-reversal problems, which has been attributed to mechanisms such as failure to utilize immediate memory stores (Gross and Weiskrantz, 1963) but not to any simple sensory deficits; (3) impairment on delayed response tasks, which has been attributed to mechanisms such as failure to perceive the distinctiveness of relevant cues in the test situation (Pribram and Mishkin, 1956) but not to simple memory loss; (4) a profound disinhibition in conditioning procedures (Brutkowski et al., 1956); and (5) changes in emotional behavior (in the human) characterized by brief, intense emotional outbursts to simple emotion-provoking stimuli (resembling the emotional responses of the developing child; Russell, 1948) and, at the same time, decreased emotional disturbance by thoughts of death or by intractable clinical pain (Freeman and Watts, 1948).

The frontal cortex, then, appears to have two major spheres of activity: (1) it plays a role in the over-all responsiveness of the organism to changes in magnitude of environmental inputs, as well as in the more selective aspects of attention and sensory discrimination, and (2) it is somehow involved in processes that determine the emotional or affective consequences of sensory stimulation. A possible interpretation of these activities derives from the suggestion by Russell (1948) and Bousfield and Orbison (1952) that the frontal lobes are involved in the development and control of emotional behavior. Emotion characteristically involves massive autonomic, proprioceptive, and other sensory inputs arriving at the brain (Lindsley, 1951). If we assume that the frontal cortex mediates associations between (1) magnitude changes in sensory inputs (since it receives a large afferent inflow from the thalamic reticular system; Starzl and Whitlock, 1952) and (2) emotion or affect (through its abundant afferent and efferent connections with the limbic system; see Pribram, 1959) then the role of the frontal cortex could be to control the *amount* of input permitted access to higher brain areas. Thus the inhibitory influence exerted by frontal cortex on the reticular activating system (Adey et al., 1957) would provide a feedback mechanism to decrease arousal levels and thereby allow other brain processes such as those involved in utilization of prior experience and evaluation of the situation to achieve control over emotional responses generally accompanied by high arousal states.

Many of the effects of frontal-lobe lesions, then, as Isaac and DeVito (1958) and Rosvold (1959) have suggested, may be due to the removal of inhibitory or other regulating effects exerted by the frontal cortex on the reticular activating system (Adey et al., 1957). The heightened central nervous system arousal that would be produced could result in the disruption of neural processes involved in memory formation (see Mahut, 1962), as well as in the failure to select relevant cues in discrimination and delayed response problems.

This interpretation alone still does not account for the complex behavior pattern observed in animals with frontal cortical lesions. The frontal cortex could play a decisive role in sensory processes, however, if we assume that the associations of affect with particular properties of sensory inputs are retained permanently in the brain. Phase sequences developed by prior associations could contribute (together with other brain areas) to the selection of sensory information. The fact that stimulation of the lateral frontal cortex in the monkey can inhibit or facilitate sensory transmission in the brainstem (Adey et al., 1957) is consistent with such a possibility. Moreover, frontal cortical connections with the caudate nucleus (see Rosvold, 1959) would permit frontal activity to exert inhibitory and facilitatory influences on afferent patterns before they arrive at cortical sensory areas (Fox and O'Brien, 1962). The disruption of this contribution to selection and differentiation of sensory inputs on the basis of their acquired affective significance, together with the heightened central nervous system arousal, would both tend to produce behavior resembling that of the restricted dogs.

Lesions of the lateral brainstem or of the frontal lobes, then, produce effects that are consistent with a conceptual model in which central nervous system processes such as memory and attention contribute to the selection and filtering of sensory information. Clearly, each of these areas (and sub-areas within them) has particular specialized functions; but in a model such as this, "function" does not reside in any one area. Rather, each specialized portion of the brain contributes to information selection and to similar processes on the output side. If the model is valid, it suggests that physiological experiments would demonstrate EEG and evoked response effects similar to those observed in restricted dogs.

Nature of the Effects of Sensory Restriction

The dogs raised in restriction, within the framework of the conceptual model proposed here, do not have behavioral deficits but are on a continuum with normal animals on the various dimensions that define psychological processes. They are on the low end of the dimensions that define the extent and nature of prior experience and at the high end of the dimensions of behavioral and central nervous system arousal. Normally reared animals, however, show behavior that at times is qualitatively similar to that observed in the restricted dogs. Scotties raised in homes, for example, show diffuse emotional excitement like that exhibited by restricted dogs when they are confronted with a social stimulus (a "timid man") for which they have no ready response (Melzack and Thompson, 1956). They develop adaptive responses, however, more rapidly than the restricted dogs (see Melzack, 1954). Similarly, the physiological responses to new stimuli are initially similar in both restricted and control groups, but the restricted dog continues to be highly aroused for prolonged periods of time while the normally reared dog habituates rapidly.

It is significant, then, that when the control beagles that had been raised on a farm were placed in laboratory cages, they exhibited an extremely high level of behavioral excitement that subsided weeks or months later. One dog (Uncle) subsequently suffered a breakdown during a simple discrimination test in which he again showed a high level of excitement and became almost indistinguishable from the restricted dogs. A radical change in environment, whether it be from a restriction cage or from a farm, confronts the organism with stimuli that have little or no meaning, and prior experience is relatively useless in determining the relevance or irrelevance of social and physical stimuli. Under such conditions experience fails to make its normal contribution to the detection of relevant cues and the performance of adaptive behavior. The early environment, however, appears to set the stage for later learning, for the irrelevant, aimless activity tends to disappear in normally reared dogs long before it begins to decrease in dogs raised in restriction cages.

These observations, taken together, suggest that the restricted dogs are on a continuum, behaviorally, with the normally reared organism. The conceptual model developed above is consistent with this suggestion, since their abnormalities are attributed to inadequate selection and abstraction of relevant inputs, with the symptomatic excessive arousal which can then itself contribute to further behavioral anomalies. The excessive arousal, in this conception, is a symptom of failure in filtering and only secondarily a cause of the response patterns that characterize the behavior of dogs released from restriction cages into a totally novel environment. The primary selection process has been conceptualized by Head (1920, pp. 745 f) as follows:

> Between the impact of a physical stimulus on the peripheral end-organs of the nervous system, and the simplest changes it evokes in consciousness, lie the various phases of physiological activity. The diverse effects produced on the living organism . . . must be sorted and regrouped; some are facilitated, others are repressed. . . . This process is repeated throughout the central nervous system until the final products of integration . . . excite those conditions which underlie the more discriminative or more affective aspects of sensation. . . . Afferent physiological processes are most complex at their origin; they become continuously more specific and simpler as they are subjected to the modifying influence of the central nervous system.

REFERENCES

1. ADEY, W. R., MERRILLEES, N. C. R., AND SUNDERLAND, S.: The entorhinal area: behavioral, evoked potential, and histological studies of its interrelationships wtih brain stem regions. Brain 79: 414-439, 1956.

2. ——, SEGUNDO, J. P., AND LIVINGSTON, R. B.: The cortifugal influences on intrinsic conduction in cat and monkey. J. Neurophysiol. 20: 1-16, 1957.

3. BOUSFIELD, W. A., AND ORBISON, W. D.: Ontogenesis of emotional behavior. Psychol. Rev. 59: 1-7, 1952.

4. BRUTKOWSKI, S., KONORSKI, J., LAWICKA, W., STEPIEN, I., AND STEPIEN, L.: The effect of the removal of the frontal poles of the cerebral cortex on motor conditioned reflexes. Acta Biol. Exptl. (Lodz) 17: 167-188, 1956.

5. BUSER, P., AND BORENSTEIN, P.: Reponses somesthesiques, visuelles et auditives, recueillies au niveau du cortex associatif suprasylvien chez le chat curarise non anesthesie. EEG Clin. Neurophysiol. 11: 285-304, 1959.

6. DESMEDT, J. E., AND MECHELSE, K.: Sur un phenomene d'inhibition centrifuge dans la voie acoustique centrale chez le chat. Comptes rendus Soc. Biol. 12: 2209-2212, 1957.

7. FOX, S. S., AND O'BRIEN, J. H.: Inhibition and afferent information by the candate nucleus. Science 137: 423-424, 1962.

8. FREEDMAN, D. G.: Constitutional and environmental interactions in rearing of four breeds of dogs. Science 127: 585-586.

9. FREEMAN, W., AND WATTS, J. W.: Pain mechanisms and the frontal lobes: a study of prefrontal lobotomy for intractable pain. Ann. Intern. Med. 28: 747-754, 1948.

10. GROSS, C. G., AND WEISKRANTZ, L.: Some changes in behavior produced by lateral frontal lesions in the macaque. In K. Akert and J. M. Warren (Eds.): Frontal Cortex and Behavior. In press, 1963.

11. GUZMAN-FLORES, C., BUENDIA, N., ANDERSON, C., AND LINDSLEY, D. B.: Cortical and reticular influences upon evoked responses in the dorsal column nuclei. Exper. Neurol. 5: 37-46, 1962.

12. HAGBARTH, K.E., AND KERR, D. I. B.: Central influences on spinal afferent conduction. J. Neurophysiol. 17: 295-307, 1954.

13. HARLOW, H. F., AND HARLOW, M. K.: The effect of rearing conditions on behavior. Bull. Menninger Clinic 26: 213-224, 1962.

14. HEAD, H.: Studies in Neurology. London, Frowde, Hodder and Stoughton, 1920.
15. HEBB, D. O.: The Organization of Behavior. New York, John Wiley and Sons, Inc., 1949.
16. ——: Drives and the C.N.S. (Conceptual nervous system). Psychol. Rev. *62:* 243-254, 1955a.
17. ——: The mammal and his environment. Am. J. Psychiat. 1955b, *111:* 826-831.
18. HIRSCH, J. F., ANDERSON, R. E., CALVET, J., AND SCHERRER, J.: Short and long latency cortical responses to somesthetic stimulation in the cat. Exper. Neurol. *4:* 562-583, 1961.
19. HUBEL, H., AND WIESEL, T. N.: Receptive fields of single neurones in the cat's striate cortex. J. Physiol. *148:* 574-591, 1959.
20. HUBEL, H., AND WIESEL, T. N.: Receptive fields, binocular interaction and functional architecture in the cat's visual cortex. J. Physiol. *:160* 106-154, 1962.
21. HUNT, C. C., AND McINTYRE, A. K.: Properties of cutaneous touch receptors in cat. J. Physiol. *153:* 88-98, 1960a.
22. ——, AND McINTYRE, A. K.: An analysis of fiber diameter and receptor characteristics of myelinated cutaneous afferent fibers in cat. J. Physiol. *153:* 99-112, 1960b.
23. ISAAC, W., AND DeVITO, J. L.: Effect of sensory stimulation on the activity of normal and pre-frontal lobectomized monkeys. J. Comp. Physiol. Psychol. *51:* 172-174, 1958.
24. KUYPERS, H. G. J. M., FLEMING, W. R., AND FARNHOLT, J. W.: Descending projections to spinal motor and sensory cell groups in the monkey: cortex versus subcortex. Science *132:* 38-40, 1960.
25. LETTVIN, J. Y., MATURANA, H. R., McCULLOCH, W. S., AND PITTS, W. H.: What the frog's eye tells the frog's brain. Proc. IRE *47:* 1940-1951, 1959.
26. LIM, R. K. S., LIU, C-N., AND MOFFITT, R. L.: A Stereotaxic Atlas of the Dog's Brain. Springfield, C. C Thomas, 1960.
27. LINDSLEY, D. B.: Emotion. *In* Stevens, S. S. (Ed.): Handbook of Experimental Psychology. New York, John Wiley and Sons, Inc., 1951.
28. LIVINGSTON, R. B.: Central control of receptors and sensory transmission systems. *In* Handbook of Physiology. Washington, American Physiological Society, *1:* 741-760, 1959.
29. MAGNI, F., MELZACK, R., MORUZZI, G., AND SMITH, C. J.: Direct pyramidal influences on the dorsal-column nuclei. Arch. Ital. Biol., *97:* 357-377, 1959.
30. MAHUT, H.: Breed differences in the dog's emotional behaviour. Canad. J. Psychol. *12:* 35-44, 1958.
31. MAHUT, H.: Effects of subcortical electrical stimulation on learning in the rat. J. Comp. Physiol. Psychol. *55:* 472-477, 1962.
32. MATURANA, H. R., LETTVIN, J. Y., McCULLOCH, W. S., AND PITTS, W. H.: Anatomy and physiology of vision in the frog (*rana pipiens*). J. Gen. Physiol. *43:* 129-175, 1960.
33. MELZACK, R.: Irrational fears in the dog. Canad. J. Psychol. *6:* 141-147, 1952.
34. ——: The genesis of emotional behavior: an experimental study of the dog. J. Comp. Physiol. Psychol. *47:* 166-168, 1954.
35. ——: The perception of pain. Sci. Amer. *204:* 41-49, 1961.

36. ——: Effects of early perceptual restriction on simple visual discrimination. Science *137:* 978-979, 1962.

37. ——, AND SCOTT, T. H.: The effects of early experience on the response to pain. J. Comp. Physiol. Psychol. *50:* 155-161, 1957.

38. ——, AND THOMPSON, W. R.: Effects of early experience on social behavior. Canad. J. Psychol. *10:* 82-90, 1956.

39. ——, AND WALL, P. D.: On the nature of cutaneous sensory mechanisms. Brain *85:* 331-356, 1962.

40. MEULDERS, M.: Etude comparative de la physiologie des voies sensorielles primaires et des voies associatives. Brussels, Editions Arscia S. A., 1962.

41. MILNER, P. M.: The cell assembly: Mark II. Psychol. Rev. *64:* 242-252, 1957.

42. PRIBRAM, K. H.: The intrinsic systems of the forebrain. *In* Handbook of Physiology. Washington, American Physiological Society, *3:* 1323-1344, 1960.

43. ——, AND MISHKIN, M.: Analysis of the effects of frontal lesions in monkey: III. object alternation. J. Comp. Physiol. Psychol. *49:* 41-45, 1956.

44. RIESEN, A. H.: Plasticity of behavior: psychological aspects. *In* H. F. Harlow and C. N. Woolsey (Eds.): Biological and Biochemical Bases of Behavior. Madison, University of Wisconsin Press, 1958.

45. ——: Stimulation as a requirement for growth and function in behavioral development. *In* D. W. Fiske and S. R. Maddi (Eds.): Functions of Varied Experience. Homewood, The Dorsey Press, Inc., 1961a.

46. ——: Excessive arousal effects of stimulation after early sensory deprivation. *In* P. Solomon, P. E. Kubzansky, P. H. Liederman, J. H. Mendelson, R. Trumbull and D. Wexler (Eds.): Sensory Deprivation. Cambridge, Harvard University Press, 1961b.

47. ROSVOLD, H. E.: Physiological psychology. Annu. Rev. Psychol. *10:* 415-454, 1959.

48. RUSSELL, W. R.: Functions of the frontal lobes. Lancet *254:* 356-360, 1948.

49. SPITZ, R. A.: Hospitalism: an inquiry into the genesis of psychiatric conditions in early childhood. Psychoanal. Stud. Child *1:* 53-74, 1945.

50. SPRAGUE, J. M., CHAMBERS, W. W., AND STELLAR, E.: Attentive, affective, and adaptive behavior in the cat. Science *133:* 165-173, 1961.

51. STARZL, T. E., AND WHITLOCK, D. G.: Diffuse thalamic projection system in monkey. J. Neurophysiol. *15:* 449-468, 1952.

52. THOMPSON, W. R., AND HERON, W.: Effects of restriction early in life on problem-solving ability in dogs. Canad. J. Psychol. *8:* 17-31, 1954a.

53. ——, AND ——: Exploratory behavior in normal and restricted dogs. J. Comp. Physiol. Psychol. *47:* 77-82, 1954b.

54. ——, MELZACK, R., AND SCOTT, T. H.: "Whirling behavior" in dogs as related to early experience. Science *123:* 939, 1956.

55. TINBERGEN, N.: The Study of Instinct. New York, Oxford University Press, 1951.

56. TOWE, A. L., AND JABBUR, S. J.: Cortical inhibition of neurons in dorsal column nuclei of cat. J. Neurophysiol. *24:* 488-498, 1961.

57. WALL, P. D.: Cord cells responding to touch, damage, and temperature of skin. J. Neurophysiol. *23:* 197-210, 1960.

58. WALL, P. D., AND CRONLY-DILLON, J. R.: Pain, itch, and vibration. Arch. Neurol. *2:* 365-375, 1960.

Discussion

by HOWARD P. ROFFWARG, M.D.

D R. ZUBIN, LADIES AND GENTLEMEN, I feel it a great privilege to have been invited to discuss these four excellent papers. A great emphasis has been placed on perception at this meeting. It has excited a considerable number of thoughts within me about what really constitutes a percept and what is the actual relationship between a response and the percept that it ostensibly reflects. Perception is not yet really a single concept. Those who are interested in it frequently take a kind of poetic license in defining it. It seems to me that some of the confusions in our conceptionalizations are highlighted by the following story I cannot resist passing on even though it is most likely apocryphal. It is alleged that a somewhat eager and ingenuous young Harvard freshman was taking Dr. Skinner's introductory course in Psychology. He was forever being fascinated by such complicated and diverse behaviors as could be elicited from experimental animals in response to the brilliantly conceived programs of stimulation. One day while in the laboratory, he observed a pigeon being conditioned to press levers in response to color cards. Under each lever was printed the name of the particular color which the pigeon was learning to pair with that lever. As the freshman watched, the pigeon perceived the colors and proceeded to press the levers above the names of the colors in question. He somewhat hastily surmised that the bird had indeed read the printed words. Surfeited with the intellectual excitement of new discovery, he dashed out into the Harvard yard where he happened upon a rather urbane member of the senior class, a major in English literature. Our freshman ran up to him and sputtered, "Do you know what those behaviorists are doing in the psychology lab? They're teaching pigeons how to read!" The literature major glanced up somewhat bemusedly, then momentarily paused in serious reflection. Finally he looked at the newsbearer and asked, "Oh, ... and what do they say about what they have read?"

Humbly, then, I would like to direct my attention to the four papers presented this afternoon. I would first like to offer my appreciation to Dr. Schaefer for his excellent review of sensory deprivation phenomena, and for a clear exposition of his own experiments on suggestion as related to sensory deprivation hallucinations. It is becoming increasingly clear that we must question further the methods and conclusions that previous workers have employed to support the allegation that the sensory deprivation situation results in the production of hallucinations. There seems to be a growing body of evidence that many of these phenomena may be either a result of suggestion, or of a distorted interpretation of the eidetic imagery which many people experience on occasions that are not particularly restrictive.

Be that as it may, it is of interest that consideration is given to the possibility that the not yet fully understood sensory phenomena which subjects report during states of immobilization and deprivation may have a role to play in homeostatic balance. Does it not at least seem to be an accepted finding that if an individual is placed in a situation in which he is deprived of the great bulk of normal sensory stimulation, some form of endogenous sensory experience fills in for what has been subtracted from the normal environment. Some of the data from sleep physiology also bear on this point. It has been demonstrated in studies of age differences that there is an inverse relationship between the proportion of time spent awake each day and the amount of dreaming (Stage 1) sleep. In other words, it appears that the less time an individual is awake each day the more sensory stimulation must come from within. Zubek and Welch's finding that alpha wave frequency is reduced during long term sensory deprivation may constitute a bridge in our understanding of these phenomena.[1] During drowsiness, when alpha begins to attentuate, hypnogogic imagery is experienced. Moreover, dreaming takes place when the EEG pattern is close to that of the waking state with the exception of the relative infrequency of alpha. And subjects who manifest a good deal of alpha during Stage 1 sleep seem to have poor recall of visual phenomena in their dreams. Accordingly, the hallucinations reported during sensory deprivation might be explained as follows: during sensory deprivation when alpha diminishes, the neurophysiological basis for imaging is created, without it being necessary or universal that subjects will hallucinate under these conditions.

The hypothesis that endogenously arising sensations may be part of a buffering mechanism has been considered but apparently abandoned by Dr. Schaefer. It is nevertheless intriguing in the light of Fisher and Dement's[2] finding in one case that incipient psychotic decompensation is accompanied by a significant augmentation of dreaming sleep, and Fisher's[3] demonstration that borderline patients run high baseline dream percents.

Turning to Dr. Eriksen, I have been thrown somewhat off base by the title of his paper, "Perceptual Defense," which is an extraordinarily careful review of the variations in the perceptual defense theories during the last 15 years. I approached this meeting prepared to discuss investigations of perceptual processes. But I have come away from Dr. Eriksen's review with the firm conviction that in general he is describing an area of interest which offers much of our understanding of psychological defense mechanisms but little to our knowledge of perception taken in the strict sense of a sensory or perceiving process.

Most attempts at defense of all types are motor operations. Dr. Eriksen's paper illuminates our view of psychological defensive operations, and I concur with him that the explanations of the so-called "perceptual defense" phenomena reside more with reaction and response than with perception *per se*. In this regard, however, I would like to offer a conclusion differing from Eriksen's concerning the Howes and Solomon frequency theory (i.e., they argue that time threshold of word recognition is related to the frequency with which the word has appeared in the prior experience of the subject). The Howes and Solomon argument, according to Dr. Eriksen, relies on an understanding of perception as a response. I suggest, on the other hand, that these authors were merely attempting to show that previous exposure to words, or familiarity with them, rather than "psychological vigilance" and "defense," are the determining causes of disparity in recognition thresholds. Certainly the Howes and Solomon explanation is not in its own terms an oversimplification, though it accords also with Perceptual Set theory in that if an individual is familiar with a word he is "readier" to identify it. It is Dr. Eriksen who offers an association and response (defense mechanism) explanation of the "perceptual defense" data. Although he is correct that allegations about frequency of exposure are insufficient in themselves to explain response variation which, as he indicates, are highly complex functions, it is *he* who is concerned with the response side. Howes and Solomon were at pains to explain variations in response times only on the basis of *sensory* considerations—that is, in terms of recognition factors. It is my feeling that their arguments are basically valid as far as they go. We may concur with Dr. Eriksen, however, in his belief that the mechanisms of defense become involved in facilitating or delaying recognition *responses* (but not recognition) and, thus, are an essential and legitimate area of information about human behavior.

It may be concluded that many of the earlier studies of "perceptual defense" based their conclusions about perceptual thresholds on data which really measured response. Hence, we are indebted to these investigations for allowing us a better appreciation of response variables. A case may be made, however, for understanding these delays in response as perhaps partially attributable to perceptual factors as well, but only insofar as *perceptual set* or *central directive state* is involved. Dr. Melzack has told us something of central control over the admission of stimuli based on phase sequences in animal development. These findings may provide a beginning idea of the neurophysiological basis for the *central directive states* which have been thought theoretically to affect perception proper.

The "perceptual defense" model had originally gone further than Directive State theory. The differences are subtle but crucial. I would interpret "perceptual defense" as meaning defense *through* perception. But few would now claim that defense mechanisms are defenses *through* perception taken in the strict sense. These phenomena, as Dr. Eriksen maintains, seem to be for the most part consequences of central association, interpretation and motor responsiveness. Contrariwise, the "perceptual defense" hypothesis, Allport points out, depends upon a concept of a "preperceiver" who perceives and transmits to the CNS, which then shuts off further recognition of the perception.[4] This is what Dr. Melzack appears to be describing as a phase sequence phenomenon. But a "preperceiver" is inconceivable without rapid perception, even though the percept is subliminal. It is patently *not* a defense against perception. Actually, it may constitute the operation of a *perceptual set*.

To sum up my feelings, I feel that the early "perceptual defense" theorizers attempted to engage in a perception feast with a response cake. Dr. Eriksen has done much to clarify the issues for us.

Dr. Dement's paper has offered some persuasive arguments that we include dreaming, or the hallucinatory phenomena which occur during Stage 1-REM sleep, under the rubric of perceptual activity. He has shown that in a number of parameters—with the notable exception of attenuation of muscular activity—the neurophysiology and behavior of a dreamer's state bear a high order of similarity to an individual's state when he is awake and active. The eyes look at what he "sees"; the brain works vigorously in ways we can measure; pulse and respirations race on or slow down as is appropriate to the situation. And Wolpert, in as yet an unconfirmed study, finds action potentials present in the muscles of the particular limb he is using in a dream.[5] The more we investigate the phenomenology of the dream experience, the more we find it to be frighteningly similar to the waking state. One by one the myths about the dream world are failing to be substantiated. For instance, Kahn has shown that we *do* dream in color.[6] Moreover, Dement and Wolpert have shown that the appreciation of time duration in dreams closely approximates that in the waking state, and the time it takes to accomplish a particular feat in a dream is not a matter of an instant but is probably closer to the duration of the same events in waking life.[7] It is as if our discrete perceptions of the real world or, if you prefer, of our experience, are stored within us and are switched on in all their detail during Stage 1 sleep.

One recalls the exhortations of Bishop Berkeley, Professor Lovejoy and their schools of philosophical Idealism and Dualism. They endeavored to convince us that we can not claim the existence of a real world outside us; rather, what we perceive as real may not be substantive, but may reside only within us. How they would have liked to demonstrate their theories with a mechanism that is indeed able to titillate every sensory modality and recreate entirely within us every aspect of what we feel to be exposure to external reality. Unfortunately, they did not have the means. But they mounted such a strenuous apology for their view (which may be stated, "there is *no* reality, and were there one, we would not be able to know it") that McGilvary felt constrained to admonish them for their seemingly impregnable alienation. He observed:

> "Nature is not something existing by grace of logic, logicians exist from time to time by grace of Nature, and when they do, they proceed to pay attention to certain features of nature, abstracting these features and freely manipulating them, thus producing 'logical constructions.' Then some of these logicians are rapt in wonder as to why some of their 'constructions' fit nature so nicely. Others, their eyes in fine frenzy rolling, rave that Nature is their handiwork."[8]

The parallel I wish to draw here is that the dream process, more effectively than the Idealist philosophers, has made nature its handiwork, seemingly in every detail. And the dreamer, his eyes in fine frenzy rolling believes it! It is quite difficult to find any way that the dreamer can know his experience is not real. It seems so real, and as in the awake state, he feels an involuntary and unevoked quality to his sensations. Dr. Dement has written elsewhere that he finds only one difference between the experience of the dreamer and that of an awake individual—the dreamer seems to have relinquished his incredulity for the often fantastic circumstances in which he finds himself.[9] But I must take issue with Dr. Dement even on that point. It is my impression that the dreamer *does* feel perplexity and dismay. He *is* struck by the oddness of events. But his dream situation is so real and compelling upon his emotions and attentions, that he gives short shrift to his doubts in order to devote full energies to the struggles or pleasures at hand.

It does not appear useful to me to claim that the awake person knows (in some as yet undefined way), but knows with certainty, that he is awake, while the dreamer does not. For we may speculate that if a dreamer being pursued through an unfamiliar jungle by ferocious tigers were questioned about the reality of the experience, he might retort, "Of course it's real, man, do you think I'd be running for my life if it weren't." The fact is that most of us can make a good guess as to when we are awake rather than dreaming. When we cannot, we entertain the possibility of a pathological state interfering with what we loosely conceptualize as "reality testing." But we *expect* "reality testing" to be compromised during a dream.

The only way we know that our perceptions are veridical is that, in Dewey's words, ". . . we do not . . . know *them* but we know all things we do know *with* or *by* them. They furnish the ultimate evidence of the existence and nature of objects which we infer."[10] Thus by turning what we think and hope to be a door knob, the door opens and we may walk into another place. We put a coin into what we infer is a vending machine and out comes a stick of gum. Hence, we act on the world and it acts back upon us or allows us to function further. This *proof via response* constitutes, in reality, our only way of knowing that our perceptions are veridical, or close to the actual state of things.

We may in a dream sit down to consume a juicy steak and feel it to be in every respect a similar experience to that in waking life. How then may we state a case for *any* distinction between the dream world and this one? I think the point is, as Dr. Dement has maintained, that on perceptual grounds, we cannot make the distinction, and the brain is responding as if actually perceiving. But fortunately for us, we wake up and may eat a real beefsteak. For even a rich and steady diet of such fare during dreaming would not long sustain us, and satiated as we might feel in the dream, we would, if not otherwise nourished, die of starvation. Dreams, then, may be understood as very true hallucinatory percepts which have measurable neurophysiological and behavioral correlates.

The case is not so good for the hallucinations of psychosis, sensory deprivation or hypnosis where neurophysiological correlates have not yet been demonstrated. "What is an hallucination," is an interesting question. If cortical evoked potentials are monitored in an individual in response to auditory clicks, a particular wave form may be measured. If the individual is then hypnotized and told he will hear clicks all the time, he replies that he does. Yet the cortical potentials are found only when an actual click is interposed. There is, hence, no neurophysiological correlate of the hypnotic hallucination. This is not the case with dreams. I agree, with Dr. Dement that there is a difference between these so-called hallucinations and dream hallucinations. The latter seem to be, in the present state of our knowledge, the only hallucinations which may be said to be true percepts.

Time has grown short so I will confine my remarks about Dr. Melzack's paper to only a couple of points. For those interested in perceptual theory, Dr. Melzack's paper offers fascinating data which seem to validate the theory of *central directive states* influencing what is admitted to perception. The role of phase sequences seems to be that of exerting dynamic control over more slowly travelling information, the latter usually constituting the main body of a percept.

Dr. Melzack's experiments are carefully executed and very revealing. But he draws a number of conclusions concerning disordered perception in his experimental animals that I do not believe are warranted on the basis of the data presented. The behavior of these animals is so complexly pathological that it may be aberrant in many ways quite unrelated to disorders in perception or discriminatory power. For instance, the deviant practice of sexual avoidance in his sensory isolated animals was discussed by Dr. Melzack as a failure of discrimination. But, as a matter of fact, it seems to me that the animals make an excellent discrimination of the situation. They perceived its sexual possibilities rapidly. They respond to the situation with alacrity as witnessed by their heightened window pressing. In other words, a defense of regression to a previous (food oriented) level of functioning is exhibited. Clearly there is no failure to perceive the opportunity presented. What the animals abundantly display is an extraordinarily negative reaction to the opposite sex. Is this a problem of perception?

Finally, Scott in his review of the literature on periods of critical development, showed that the peak period of socialization learning ends as a new period of increasing negativism towards strangers begins.[11] I wonder if any of Dr. Melzack's current investigations throw any light on critical developmental stages in the animals he studied.

REFERENCES

1. ZUBEK, J. AND WELCH, G.: Electroencephalographic changes after prolonged sensory and perceptual deprivation. Science 139: 1209-1210, 1963.
2. FISHER, C. AND DEMENT, W.: Dreaming and psychosis: Observations on the sleep-dream cycle during the course of an acute paranoid psychosis. Bull. Phila. Assoc. Psa. 11: 130-132, 1961.
3. ——: Work in progress, Personal Communication.
4. ALLPORT, F.: Theories of Perception and the Concept of Structure. New York, Wiley, 1955.
5. WOLPERT, E.: Studies in the psychophysiology of dreams: II An electromyographic study of dreaming. A.M.A. Arch. Gen. Psychiat. 2: 231, 1960.
6. KAHN, E., DEMENT, W., FISHER, C., AND BARMACK, J.: Incidence of color in immediately recalled dreams. Science 137: 1054-1055, 1962.
7. DEMENT, W. AND WOLPERT, E.: The relation of eye movements, body motility, and external stimuli to dream content. J. Exp. Psychol. 55: 543-553, 1958.
8. MCGILVARY, A. B.: Memory and perceptual perspectives. J. of Philosoph. 30: 1933.
9. DEMENT, W.: An essay on dreams: the role of physiology in understanding their nature. University of California Far Eastern Institute Symposium, "Le Reve et les societies humanes." June, 1962, Royaumont (in press).
10. DEWEY, J.: Essays in Experimental Logic. Chicago, U. of Chicago Press, 1916, Chapters 9 and 10.
11. SCOTT, J.: Critical periods in behavioral development. Science, 138: 949-958, 1962.

Discussion

by JACK A. VERNON

I AM PARTICULARLY PLEASED that Dr. Schaefer has seen fit to attempt to replicate some of our Princeton studies of Sensory Deprivation. That we have had so little success in eliciting hallucinatory experiences where others seem to succeed so easily has long puzzled me. It is clearly the case that many studies cannot be compared because we have employed such divergent procedures. But even those that appear very similar to ours nevertheless obtain different results. We have, in the past, tended to believe that we were using a definition of hallucinations which would eliminate mere imagination. That is, for an experience to be classed as an hallucination it had to meet the following criterion: it had to appear to be real, i.e., "fool" the subject, it had to be "out there," and its coming and going could not be under the control of the subject.

Dr. Schaefer has found that our instructions to the subject may have prevented or drastically reduced the incidence of reported imagery. And this comes as something of a surprise to me since we have attempted without success, the opposite approach. That is, we deliberately suggested the presence of sound in the SD chamber. We used sound because most SD subjects report hearing things the identity of whose source is unknown to us. Without going into detail, suffice it to say we failed to elicit auditory hallucinations by our suggestions.

It would be a very important contribution to a confused literature if Dr. Schaefer is correct, for his results place great emphasis upon the procedure employed. There is, however, one point of caution even here. Dr. Schaefer has utilized confinements of only one hour which may not be enough. Even those investigators who do report the occurrence of hallucinations usually employ longer confinement times. In fact, Zubeck seems to feel that more than two days is necessary to get any real magnitude of such reports.

There is one further point I would like to make which is really in the nature of a suggestion for additional work. Whether or not SD is capable of producing hallucinations seems as yet unsettled to me. But if it is capable of such productions, then it would serve to potentiate the hallucinogen drugs. To my knowledge such an investigation has not been conducted.

Perceptual Defense

The work, of which there has been a great deal, in perceptual defense has in my opinion suffered from several unattended points. Dr. Eriksen has clearly pointed out the majority of the faults obtaining in earlier work. There still remain a few points or questions which I should like to raise.

The work of Peterson provides the basis for the first point of inquiry. He measured the reaction time to briefly exposed words. The subject's task was to classify each word as to animal, mineral, or vegetable by manipulating the appropriate switch. The words which were presented contained some taboo words mostly of a scatological nature. Peterson found that the reaction time to the taboo word was significantly slower than to the other stimuli but, and this is the main point, *only* for the first such occurrence. When the second and third, etc. taboo words came along reaction time was nearly normal. This suggests that perhaps set, or expectation, or novelty, are important dimensions to be considered in such work.

In the perceptual defense work much attention has been given to anxiety or anxiety-arousing stimuli. But there has been little attention to validating the anxiety potential of the stimuli. Thus in many cases the arguments have become circular. That which reflects perceptual defense is anxiety producing and vice versa. It is to be admitted, however, that the concept of anxiety is not one which is easily validated. The usual physiological indicators seldom provide sufficient reliability to be useful so that perhaps a new approach is indicated. One possible approach might be the preevaluation of whatever stimuli are to be employed by the semantic differential.

Perception during Sleep

The work of Aserinsky and Kleitman in 1953 suddenly brought the subject of dreams into a refreshingly new focus. Since that time, work has progressed to the point of making a convincing argument that animals other than man are capable of dreaming. The new technique of detecting *when* a subject was dreaming by observing eye movements made it possible to clear up one major point of confusion about dreams. It never seemed reasonable that some people should dream while others did not. The eye movement work revealed that if one does not awaken shortly after the dream, say within about ten minutes, the dream is not recalled. Does this suggest that there is something unsure about memory for dreamed events? Why should they not persist in memory for longer than about ten minutes?

In the recent past, there has been a fairly consistent failure to produce and/or influence dreams by external stimuli. Or for that matter, by internal stimuli, such as those generated by lack of water or food. Since one is still left with no answer as to what *causes* dreams, it is difficult to abandon the idea of external influences. After all if we become cold during sleep, we do some fairly intelligent things without awaking. Why then should not external stimuli influence dreams? The work of Dement and Hodes may have provided at least a possible solution to this problem. They found that the H-reflex will occur throughout sleep except for that period of REM sleep. The complete suppression of the reflex during the dream phase may mean, they suggest, the inhibition of the alpha motorneuron bypassing the gamma efferent system. Or in more general terms, could it mean that the introductory phases of the dream sequence serve to shut out or inhibit all peripheral afferent systems?

It may seem far fetched, but I cannot refrain from questioning whether the above may account for the generally negative findings for sleep learning studies (that is, negative findings in the case of really adequate studies). Could it be that the material presented during sleep was blocked and/or interrupted by dreams so as to prevent or retard learning?

Effects of Deprivation in Early Development

Dr. Melzack's finding that early deprivation does something to reduce pain sensitivity strikes me as an unexpected finding. In the Princeton Studies of Sensory Deprivation we came to question whether or not pain sensitivity would be influenced by the confinement experience. We raised a question of this sort as a result of trying to decipher the nature of pain. As Livingston and so many after him have pointed out, the perceptual side of pain is an extremely complex one. The experience of pain in man cannot be thought of as the simple presence of pain stimuli. Thus in a very simple-minded fashion we reasoned that Sensory Deprivation would reduce the amount of neural noise normally present in man and render him more sensitive to pain. We were not here thinking of distraction effects or absence or distraction but rather a more internal neural state of less activity produced by prolonged confinement. Our findings on the pain sensitivity of the SD subjects bore out our expectations. After 48 hours of SD the experimental subjects were significantly more sensitive to pain, i.e., their pain thresholds had dropped. The control subjects who were tested in the SD chamber (thus an absence of distraction) showed no change in pain threshold.

Of course the conditions employed by Melzack are entirely different from ours and thus probably account for the divergence in results. Since we cannot confine man in SD chambers from early childhood, it is my hope that Professor Melzack will use SD-like confinement on normal adult animals and then check their sensitivity to pain.

The early sensory restriction has led to so many more-or-less inferior performances of the experimental animals that it is little wonder that Melzack postulates possible neural degeneration. However, before one can accept such a notion it would be essential to demonstrate that the impaired or lost function was truly permanent.

Another puzzling finding is the occurrence of "whirling fits." That these fits occur at the height of excitement may be related to Melzack's notion of neural degeneration. It may be that normal inhibitor centers have not developed and that an irradiation process occurs.

It is very clear that Professor Melzack's work will eventually lead not only to a better understanding of sensory and neural mechanisms but possibly to the importance of early experience for learning. If learning can be hampered (and the permanency of the hampering must be determined) by early restrictions, what are the chances of reversing the effect by deliberately introducing special early training under the added conditions of restriction?

13

ADVENTURES WITH REPETITION: THE SEARCH FOR ITS POSSIBILITIES*

by D. EWEN CAMERON, M.D.†

SEVEN YEARS AGO WE STARTED OFF on a series of adventures in pursuit of repetition, a thing as everyday, as strange as a raindrop. Some things are so common, so inlaid into the fabric of our days, that they can pass us by in a thousand forms and yet never catch our thought. Only the most determined and somewhat dryly rewarding efforts bring us to wonder, for instance, at that extraordinary thing which is gravity. We use it each moment of each passing hour. Every house is in part an anti-gravity structure, as is every chair, and throughout the day, we make use of anti-gravity in our postures.

The same is true of friction. How little we know of it—how much we use it. The car moves forward on the road. The girl does not slip off the edge of the bed. And friction is the reason for each of these things and countless more besides. But certainly it is only quite rarely that we think of this strange universal force that has touched our every action since first we counted time.

So it is with repetition. We don't think much about it because we are far more concerned with the uniqueness of events—with the beginnings of things and sometimes with their endings—and rarely is our attention held by their continuous repetition. It is true, of course, that we make use of it in rote learning and we also know something of its consequences in conditioning. Every now and again, however, some little change, often minute, clicks into action and shifts the way in which things ordinarily run. Then for a fleeting moment we are free to stir and look through the rent in the curtain of the world of things as we currently believe them to be and see into another quite different world of things as they might be—if we choose to see them differently.

---

*Presidential Address
†Director, Allan Memorial Institute, Montreal; now Director, Psychiatry and Aging Research Laboratories, Albany Veterans Administration Hospital; Research Professor, Dept. of Psychiatry, Albany Medical College, Albany, N.Y.

There are many such worlds. Some are completely different from ours—radically, complexly different, interlocking in their differences so completely as to form consistent wholes, built as each believes, on the most obvious self-evident truths that no one in his senses would think of questioning. There stands the vanishing world of the Navahjo, of the Yoruba, the Easter Islander—in a word, of every culture in the world.

Turning to a smaller section of our world of things as they are, we have come to feel that some of our concepts of ourselves would have to be changed if we reconsider them in terms of the part played in human behaviour by repetition.

Very often, as you know, some of these twists and changes in the way we think about things come out of the blue, but other times you can see them linked up with some specific event in our days. I take the last century or so as being "our days." These twists very often follow upon the development of some new form of instrumentation. We have had to thrust into our hands a most extraordinary range of instruments. Every sensory organ that we have now has added to it a quite magnificent array of prosthetic agents. We can see into and hear from regions which are absolutely closed to our unaided powers. We can perceive temperatures, radiations, vibrations, utterly beyond the range of our natural sensory equipment.

At the intellectual level, the giant computers manipulate in a moment a number and range of symbols far beyond the capacity of 1000 men.

The instrument that started us off on our adventures is quite simple. It was known as far back as the time of Edison: that is a means of preserving and reproducing sound. However, in the last several decades, this has become vastly improved until we have the extremely simple, accurate and clear, tape recorder. Now these tape recorders almost spell out the word repetition.

Many of us quite early were impressed with the wealth of material which could be rescued from immediate oblivion through the tape recorder—the shifts in cadence, the tiny blocks, the changes in speed and emphasis; the world of non-verbal auditory communication could be recorded, and indeed there has been some indication that there may be a whole universe of non-verbal communication carried on below the perceptual level.

In 1953 I was working as I had for some years with a tape recorder during a period of psychotherapy. The patient was a blonde and sultry girl from Bermuda whom I roundly suspected of incestuous, but carefully covered up, feelings for her father. He would wait up for her, she would come home late. She would undress noisily. He would come in. He would pour out angry accusations. She would become furious. He would hit her. She would grapple with him. Both would fall to the floor and engage in what was outwardly a furious—but I believed mutually enjoyed—scuffle from which both emerged exhausted. The father on the surface was the stern parent, the girl the outraged adolescent. I made many fruitless attempts to get her frankly to agree that all was not as it seemed.

Eventually one hot and sticky summer afternoon she said a few words which seemed to tell what I was seeking. The recorder was on and so with great satisfaction I played it back to her and said, "There!" To which she replied, "There nothing!" I was exasperated and thought to myself, "You will hear" and so I played back these few sentences ten, twenty, thirty times, turning the switch of the machine rapidly back and forth. As I watched her, she grew more and more disturbed, angrier and angrier, and eventually she jumped off the couch: "You're a damn fool." She ran out of the Institute and down the avenue and was retrieved with some difficulty.

I was immensely struck by this and wondered for days why many repetitions of this statement should have an effect that the initial utterance did not. Now ordinarily such things don't shape themselves up as puzzles at all. We just take for granted that nobody wants to go on listening to the same thing. But why not? Heaven knows our breathing is repetitious enough and our walk is simply a fall from one foot onto the next endlessly repeated.

There seemed no answer to the question, so I repeated this procedure with all the other patients I had in psychotherapy and got much the same thing—discomfort, aversion, embarrassment and resentment. And indeed I even noticed in myself a reluctance to do this—I felt that I was being unkind, insensitive, imperceptive—that in a word one simply didn't do this sort of thing to people. For these reasons, namely, the patient's feelings and my own, I felt increasingly sure that there must be something of importance lying hidden. Eventually—as so often happens when one goes on repeating and repeating an experiment—an additional thing occurred which threw a flood of light on the whole matter.

This observation was a statement by one patient that he could not get the sentences, which we had played back, out of his mind for the whole week that intervened until his next therapeutic hour. He said, "I kept thinking about it. It came back to my mind on the most unexpected and undesired occasions". I then looked over the other cases and saw what had hitherto been missed, namely, that both things which he pointed to had occurred in them also, though in quite varying degree. First they had tended to keep on thinking about the sentences that had been played back to them so often. At times they had noticed a change in the way they had thought about the topic, and nearly always they had found that new recollections had come into awareness. Indeed, for some people it was almost as though the topic we had lit up by repetition had started to blaze out like a fire blizzard, drawing in with greater and greater rapidity more and more recollections of a related nature.

In our early experiments, we used the term 'dynamic implant' to denote the repetition material we used. Actually at this time we were implanting nothing. We were simply lighting up a topic already encoded by the patient's memorial processes.

These observations only served to sharpen up the enigma. Repetition, was so clearly beneficial to the individual and yet it was something to which he showed a most definite aversion. And indeed we knew it to be much more than a simple aversion, for in the meantime we had shifted from excerpts taken from the patient's communication in psychotherapy to the exploration of what would happen if we attempted to establish behavioural patterns by repetition of signals of our own devising. The connection between this and our early observations was simple enough. Seeing that the patient did change and for the better following repetition of his own statements, would he not change more decisively and in a more controllable way if we set up the statements ourselves? By this time we were calling them 'verbal signals' and, for convenience of discussion, we were calling the procedure 'psychic driving'.

Driving it was, since clearly if this thing worked after thirty repetitions, it was only common sense to see what would happen if the repetition was increased tenfold, a hundredfold or even more. And eventually our patients were listening to verbal signals we had set up ourselves on the basis of our knowledge of the patient, and listening from 6 in the morning until 9 at night day after day and week after week.

We very soon found, however, that it did not work out quite as we had planned it, and the patient's aversion was now reinforced by his capacity to protect himself against the impact of repetition. Amazing though it may sound, my colleagues and I—Dr. Levy, Dr. Ban and Mr. Rubenstein—found it was possible for the individual to be exposed to the repetition of verbal signals, such as I have described, a quarter to one-half million times and yet be unable to repeat these few short sentences at the end of this extraordinary large number of repetitions. In other words, the individual has a means of blocking the effects of repetition.

When we explored the literature on repetition, we found to our interest that at the physiological level too, the organism protects itself against the effects of prolonged repetition. The neurophysiologists have discovered a number of mechanisms which operate to produce what they call 'response decrement'. In other words, mechanisms which result in a response to a stimulus becoming progressively less with repetition—thus protecting the organism against damage that might result from too frequent repetitions.

These observations then led us to another long period of conjecturing, reading up on other men's experiences and their thoughts about them. Eventually we came to the working hypothesis that repetition is an exceedingly powerful force. Everywhere you look at living things you will find that repetition is used and at the same time the living creature protects itself against excessive exposure to repetition. In the human subject, this is particularly necessary because no creature is as rapidly and as extensively adaptive as is the human being. Hence, while it is of immense value to use repetition—and we do use it in rote learning, conditioning, habit formation, in the structuring of work schedules and in many other ways—at the same time we must protect ourselves against repetition lest it force us into adaptation which we do not wish. Every human being has a greater or lesser urge to go on being himself—to preserve his identity—and this is no less true of the neurotic than of the normal person—so he must protect himself against disturbing reorganizations in his thinking and his feelings.

We now found ourselves squarely facing the next chapter in our pursuit of repetition. How could we block the mechanisms which the human being sets up to protect himself against adaptation and thus ensure that our driving statements would enter and become established as new patterns of behaviour?

At this point, as so often happens in a long research, we took a wrong turning and continued to walk without a glint of success for a long, long time. I won't recount to you all the things we tried to do to stop the working of these mechanisms of defense against repetition. Let me simply say that we vastly increased the number of repetitions to which the individual was exposed, that we continued driving while the individual was asleep, while he was in chemical sleep, while he was awake but under hallucinogens, while he was under the influence of disinhibiting agents. We tried driving under hypnosis, immediately after electroshock, we tried innumerable combinations of voices, of timing and many other conditions, but we were never able to stop the mechanisms.

Other lines of our research were however showing successes. We were now able to produce desired changes in almost every patient that we tried, but these changes always took, we felt, far too long and many of them were far too unstable. But we had begun to notice that where our patients, after driving, took their new-found behaviour patterns back to homes in which there was plenty of support, enthusiasm for the new change and a good deal of understanding, these patterns became long lasting and finally established. But where, on the other hand, the home was a disturbed and destructive one, the patterns quite soon disappeared. From these observations, we developed the idea of primary and secondary reinforcement leading to consolidation.

Primary reinforcement was carried out in the institute by the nurses and the doctors giving praise and expressing enthusiasm for the newly appearing behavioural patterns. Secondary reinforcement was the name which we gave to long-term followup of these patients—having them come back and listen once or twice a week to their driving in the Out-Patient Department, and also consisted in the instruction of the relatives regarding the desirability of giving acceptance to the patient's new way of doing things.

We went further than this and began to recognize something which we had already seen from studies in other related fields. In this field which I am discussing with you tonight, you will readily see that what we are trying to do is to set up in the memory systems of the individual new behavioural patterns. In another area, we have found it expedient to try to destroy pathological behavioural patterns held in the memory storage systems. This we do by depatterning. And once we had extended our depatterning to chronic neurotic patients, we began to recognize the very important part played by the neurotogenic home in maintaining neurotic behavioural patterns. And this idea we carried over into the area of psychic driving. To give expression to the idea we set up a plan whereby our patients were placed in other homes for 6 weeks to 3 months after discharge. It might be that these other homes also had neurotogenic factors, but they were not the factors to set into operation the particular neurotic tendencies of our patients and, hence, consolidation of the new behavioural patterns could take place.

At the outset of my talk tonight, I indicated that these studies on the effects of repetition had provided us with new ideas. Some of these ideas, as you can see, we translated into procedures, but others have been translated into new theoretic concepts. One of these is that recovery is not always a matter of the resolving of a conflict. Indeed with passing time, we have begun to wonder if this is actually a very realistic concept and how well grounded it is in experimental data. Certainly from our experience we can say that much of recovery is really due to acquisition of dominance within the patient of what are considered to be normal behavioural patterns.

We have postulated the idea that every personality trait which is dominant has also a contra-trait which is sub-dominant. Where the individual is prudent and cautious and conservative, we may be reasonably sure that this trend has been set up by the suppression of urges to be impulsive, to be rash and to be reckless and that these impulses still remain although sub-dominant.

And the same thing we have thought is true of the individual who has dominant characteristics of aggressiveness, sadistic behaviour and a disregard for others. Submerged beneath, we think there are contra-traits composed of urges for closer relationships with others, for belongingness rather than independence and for the exchange of affection and tenderness.

In part, we are inclined to think that driving serves to activate these contra-traits—but however only in part—since as you will hear later, we have succeeded in developing traits to which it seems most unlikely that there are contra-traits.

May I now return to our long wandering in the wilderness in search of a means directly to overcome the mechanisms which the individual sets up to block the effects of repetition. It was only within the last year that we turned away from this pursuit and began to seek a totally different solution and this was by developing means of involving the patient in listening to the statement. In this way we got him to do the work of setting aside his own blocking agents rather than our trying to force them.

Quite early in our experiments we had carried out a series of studies on the nature of talking and on the nature of listening. It had become quite clear to us that complete attention was far from what we wanted. Because complete attention simply means complete absorption with reception. What we wanted from our patients—and I think what many speakers want from their audiences—was attention. When a man attends and thinks, he naturally doesn't hear as much as the man who merely listens, as part of the time he is engrossed in his own thinking of some aspect of the problem that his attention to the speaker has started up. The fact that his attention under these circumstances was necessarily incomplete did not trouble us however, as with the vast number of repetitions, the patient was bound to attend to every aspect of the statement if not the first time round, at least the one thousand and first time round. And his thinking and feeling—in a word, his involvement—is fundamentally what brings about reorganization.

If you look through the psychological literature, you will find that the phenomenon which we call 'involvement' has not been dealt with by anyone, but this is what we have found to be the most desired response and it is the kind of response that has gotten us past the operation of the blocking mechanisms.

How were we to know that we were actually getting this involvement? This proved easy enough. Instead of running repetition continuously from 6 in the morning until 9 at night, we now decided to give recognition to the fact that the response we wanted from the patient called for far more active work than required by passive attention or, as it more commonly turned out to be, continuous blocking. So we cut down the driving periods to about 4 hours a day—2 hours in the morning, 2 hours in the evening. Moreover, we set the continuous tapes up in such a way that they were run for about 4 minutes and then there would be a period of silence of about 6 minutes and the cycle would repeat itself throughout the 2 hours. During the 6-minute period, we asked the patient to write down everything that he had thought about or was thinking about in consequence of the signals he had heard, and this written material was handed in so he could have a pretty good idea of how much involvement was going on.

A still more important question of course is how did we know that we were getting any change in the behaviour of the individual? Here, as you know, we are getting into one of those vastly important areas of the human sciences which has never been very satisfactorily organized. How do we measure change in behaviour and how can we relate it to specific causal events? Our verbal signals portrayed certain changes of a desirable nature which we hoped the patient would incorporate—that he would become more assertive; that he would become more confident; that he would become free of his anxiety; that he would mature and take responsibilities; that he would show more drive and enterprise. It is of course not too difficult to demonstrate that this was achieved. We have had growing success over the years in just this direction, and relatives and patients and employers and social workers and nurses and the ward staff themselves have agreed that just such changes appeared in our patients. In order that there would be as little doubt about it as possible we would take movies before and after, we would run psychological batteries before and after, some of them being self-rating, others involving ratings by a psychologist.

However, an awkward thought kept recurring to us, namely, that these changes are to some extent although not completely the changes which might appear in almost anyone on recovery from a neurosis. We felt that we must find some more objective measure of the effects in repetition in changing behaviour. We chose to add a tracer to our driving signals. This would be something that had nothing to do with getting better or showing improvement in performance. It was at the same time clear that this tracer—if it were to show itself—would have to contain some urge to action, and hence we called such signals 'imperative tracers.' The tracer if incorporated shows itself in action within the first week after exposure to repetition.

Our first imperative tracer which we used 3 or 4 years ago consisted in a statement, "You like to be close to other people. You like to reach out and touch them." And, sure enough, it happened not in all, but in a number. In some patients it disappeared within a few days. In others, however, it persisted for an embarrassingly long period of time and apparently was sustained by secondary gain. Eventually we came to feel that we should find an imperative tracer having fewer social consequences. Our present imperative tracer—involving picking up pieces of paper—is very simple. It usually appears within the first week after exposure and disappears quite quickly after cessation of the driving, since it is rare that the patient finds any secondary gain to reinforce it.

Now we come to the last in a long series of adventures in our search for the effects of repetition. I mentioned to you a little while ago our deep interest in involvement. This, as you can gather resulted in a great deal of written material which we read. But before discussing this, may I divert for a moment to say that in the last 2 or 3 years we have been dividing our driving statements into what we call negative signals and positive signals, both kinds being specifically designed to evoke the appropriate psychotherapeutic mechanisms. The negative signals consisted essentially of all the criticisms that the patient had made of himself or heard made of himself. These we started with in each case and the patient at first accepted them as being only too true. But in the course of a few days, he would begin to express some doubts as to whether things were really quite as bad and finally he would show a growing resentment and rejection. When this point was reached in about 10 days, we would regard it as the point of maximum intensity, and we would shift to the positive driving statement, reflecting the aspirations of the patient—what he wanted to become.

Now to go back to the written material which the patients produce, we began to realize that actually the negative driving signals set in motion certain of the mechanisms of psychotherapy—problem identification, desensitization, the beginnings of the patient-therapist relationship and sometimes the development of explanation. The positive driving signals, on the other hand, showed a great deal of the principle of reorganization, much of the development of explanations and a maturing of the patient-therapist relationship.

And may I add that in order that this new procedure of involvement may be as productive as possible, we have begun to drive these statements while the patient is under the influence of sodium amytal and desoxyn. The amount of material which some patients bring out under these circumstances is really tremendous.

So now we have actually two main ways of using repetition. The first is to produce direct reorganization exemplified by the creation of the habit of picking up pieces of paper and the account of the extensive changes in personality brought about by the positive signals. The second is an indirect method of producing reorganization by bringing into play the mechanisms of psychotherapy.

In this long recital of our quest after the effects of repetition on behaviour, I have shown you a few of the exciting new things which can be discovered. I have also shown you some of the side roads which one might take leading into quite different fields, and I have shown you one or two which lead apparently into a sterile wilderness.

We are still far away from being able to set up the truly compelling patterns of behaviour which sometimes occur naturally as, for instance, in the sexual patterns of behaviour, nor can we set up patterns with anything like the durability that one finds in some habits or in imprinting in animals, but we have made a beginning.

I feel quite confident that the journey if continued with hopefulness and a touch of serendipity is one that will interest and stimulate and has much greatly to reward the determined traveller—and ultimately the patients for whom all such travels are undertaken.

APPENDIX

Officers:

Jerome D. Frank, M.D., Pres.
The Johns Hopkins University
Baltimore 5, Maryland

Franz Kallmann, M.D., Pres. Elect
722 West 168th Street
New York 32, New York

Seymour S. Kety, M.D., Vice-Pres.
National Institute of Mental Health
Bethesda 14, Maryland

Fritz A. Freyhan, M.D., Secretary
National Institute of Mental Health
c/o Saint Elizabeths Hospital
Washington 20, D.C.

Bernard C. Glueck, Jr., M.D., Treasurer
Box 2070
Hartford 2, Connecticut

D. Ewen Cameron, M.D., Councillor
1025 Pine Avenue, West
Montreal 2, Canada

Benjamin Malzberg, Ph.D., Councillor
240 State Street
Albany 1, New York

Committee on Program

Paul H. Hoch, M.D., Chairman
722 West 168th Street
New York 32, New York

Joseph Zubin, Ph.D.
722 West 168th Street
New York 32, New York

(L) = Life Member
(H) = Honorary Member

Committee on Membership

Benjamin Pasamanick, M.D., Chairman
Columbus Psychiatric Institute
Ohio State University
Columbus 10, Ohio

Members:

Theodora M. Abel, Ph.D.
Palisades
Rockland County, New York

David Abrahamsen, M.D.
1035 Fifth Avenue
New York 28, New York

Nathan Ackerman, M.D.
43 East 78th Street
New York 21, New York

Alexandra Adler, M.D.
30 Park Avenue
New York 16, New York

Leo Alexander, M.D.   (L)
433 Marlboro Street
Boston 15, Massachusetts

Edward B. Allen, M.D.   (L)
21 Greenbridge Avenue
White Plains, New York

George S. Amsden, M.D.   (L)
Acworth, New Hampshire

Leslie R. Angus, M.D.
1120 East Market Street
Danville, Pennsylvania

Silvano Arieti, M.D.
22 East 72nd Street
New York 21, New York

Irma Bache, M.D. (L)
1 East 368
Pentagon Building
Washington 25, D.C.

Walter W. Baker, M.D.
Asoc. Prof. of Psychopharmacology
Medical College of Philadelphia
1025 Walnut Street
Philadelphia 7, Pennsylvania

Lauretta Bender, M.D.
44 Malone Avenue
Long Beach, New York

Paul Bergman, M.D.
Clinical Center
Room 2N 238
National Institute of Mental Health
Bethesda 14, Maryland

Herbert Birch, Ph.D.
Department of Pediatrics
Albert Einstein College of Medicine
New York 61, New York

H. Waldo Bird, M.D.
1313 East Ann Street
Ann Arbor, Michigan

James Birren, Ph.D.
Section on Aging
National Institute of Mental Health
Bethesda 14, Maryland

Daniel Blain, M.D. (L)
1320 K Street
Sacramento 14, California

Henry Brill, M.D.
Pilgrim State Hospital
West Brentwood, New York

Eugene Brody, M.D.
University of Maryland
School of Medicine
Baltimore, Maryland

Albert Browne-Mayers, M.D.
55 East 86th Street
New York 28, New York

Hilde Bruch, M.D.
Baylor University Medical School
Houston, Texas

A. Louise Brush, M.D. (L)
55 East 86th Street
New York 28, New York

Dexter M. Bullard, Sr., M.D. (L)
M.H.A., 500 West Montgomery Avenue
Rockville, Maryland

Ernest W. Burgess, Ph.D.
University of Chicago
1225 East 60th Street
Chicago 37, Illinois

Dale C. Cameron, M.D.
Assistant Superintendent
Saint Elizabeths Hospital
Washington 20, D.C.

Carl D. Camp, M.D. (L)
304 South State Street
Ann Arbor, Michigan

Douglas G. Campbell, M.D.
490 Post Street
San Francisco 2, California

Eric T. Carlson, M.D.
60 Sutton Place, South
New York 22, New York

Edward J. Carroll, M.D. (L)
121 University Place
Pittsburgh 13, Pennsylvania

James P. Cattell, M.D.
880 Fifth Avenue
New York 21, New York

Brock G. Chisholm, M.D. (H)
Seawood, West Coast Road
R.R. 2, Victoria
British Columbia, Canada

Robert Clark, M.D.
Friends Hospital
Roosevelt Blvd. & Adams Avenue
Philadelphia 24, Pennsylvania

John A. Clausen, Ph.D.
1963 Yosemite Road
Berkeley 7, California

Hollis E. Clow, M.D. (L)
121 Westchester Avenue
White Plains, New York

Robert A. Cohen, M.D.
4514 Dorset Avenue
Chevy Chase 15, Maryland

Jonathan O. Cole, M.D.
7111 Edgevale Street
Chevy Chase 14, Maryland

Oskar Diethelm, M.D.
New York Hospital
525 East 68th Street
New York 21, New York

Roy M. Dorcus, Ph.D.
University of California
Los Angeles 24, California

John M. Dorsey, M.D. (L)
Wayne St. University
Detroit 2, Michigan

Leon Eisenberg, M.D.
2610 Whitney Avenue
Baltimore, Maryland

William W. Elgin, M.D.
Sheppard & Enoch Pratt Hospital
Towson 4, Maryland

Joel Elkes, M.D.
9902 Cedar Lane
Bethesda, Maryland

Milton H. Erickson, M.D. (L)
32 West Cypress Street
Phoenix, Arizona

Jack R. Ewalt, M.D.
72-76 Fenwood Road
Boston 15, Massachusetts

Raymond Feldman, M.D.
9900 Old Spring Road
Kensington, Maryland

Robert H. Felix, M.D.
Dean, School of Medicine
St. Louis University
St. Louis, Missouri

Max Fink, M.D.
Missouri Inst. of Psychiatry
5400 Arsenal Street
St. Louis 39, Missouri

Barbara Fish, M.D.
70 East 10th Street
New York 3, New York

Arthur N. Foxe, M.D.
9 East 67th Street
New York 21, New York

Richard L. Frank, M.D.
15 East 91st Street
New York 28, New York

Alfred M. Freedman, M.D.
161 West 86th Street
New York 24, New York

Arnold J. Friedhoff, M.D.
32-25 168th Street
Flushing 58, New York

John Frosch, M.D.
1 Gracie Terrace
New York 21, New York

Daniel H. Funkenstein, M.D.
74 Fenwood Road
Boston 14, Massachusetts

W. Horsley Gantt, M.D.
Johns Hopkins Hospital
Baltimore 5, Maryland

Bernard C. Glueck, Sr., M.D. (L)
University of North Carolina
Box 1020
Chapel Hill, North Carolina

Murray Glusman, M.D.
50 East 72nd Street
New York 21, New York

William Goldfarb, M.D.
530 West End Avenue
New York 24, New York

Jacques Gottlieb, M.D.
Lafayette Clinic
951 East Lafayette
Detroit 7, Michigan

Milton Greenblatt, M.D.
Superintendent
Boston State Hospital
591 Morton Street
Boston 24, Massachusetts

Roy R. Grinker, Sr., M.D.
Michael Reese Hospital
29th Street & Ellis Avenue
Chicago 16, Illinois

Ernest M. Gruenberg, M.D.
722 West 168th Street
New York 32, New York

A. Irving Hallowell, Ph.D.
Box 14, Bennet Hall
University of Pennsylvania
Philadelphia, Pennsylvania

Professor Ward C. Halstead
5537 University Avenue
Chicago 37, Illinois

David A. Hamburg, M.D.
Department of Psychiatry
Stanford Medical School
Stanford, California

Donald M. Hamilton, M.D.
121 Westchester Avenue
White Plains, New York

Irving B. Harrison, M.D.
142 Garth Road
Scarsdale, New York

Lynwood Heaver, M.D.
61 Irving Place
New York 3, New York

Morris Herman, M.D.
30 East 40th Street
New York 16, New York

Harold E. Himwich, M.D.
State Research Hospital
Galesburg, Illinois

Hudson Hoagland, Ph.D.
Deerfoot Road
Southboro, Massachusetts

Leslie B. Hohman, M.D. (L)
Duke Medical School
Durham, North Carolina

Bernard Holland, M.D.
Emory University
P.O. Box 459
Atlanta 22, Georgia

William A. Horwitz, M.D.
722 West 168th Street
New York 32, New York

Joseph Hughes, M.D.
111 North 49th Street
Philadelphia 39, Pennsylvania

Howard F. Hunt, Ph.D.
New York State Psychiatric Institute
722 West 168th Street
New York 32, New York

William A. Hunt, Ph.D. (L)
Northwestern University
Evanston, Illinois

Paul E. Huston, M.D.
500 Newton Road
Iowa City, Iowa

Lissy Jarvik, M.D., Ph.D.
722 West 168th Street
New York 32, New York

George A. Jervis, M.D., Ph.D.
Research Department
Letchworth Village
Thiells, Rockland County, New York

Lothar B. Kalinowsky, M.D.
115 East 82nd Street
New York 28, New York

Abram Kardiner, M.D. (L)
1100 Park Avenue
New York, New York

Solomon Katzenelbogen, M.D. (L)
9305 Parkhill Terrace
Bethesda 14, Maryland

William Raymond Keeler, M.D.
484 Avenue Road
Toronto 7, Ontario, Canada

Edward J. Kempf, M.D.
Wading River
Long Island, New York

Isabelle V. Kendig, Ph.D.
Sandy Spring, Maryland

Richard D. Kepner, M.D. (L)
P.O. Box 3119
Honolulu 2, Hawaii

Lawrence C. Kolb, Sr., M.D. (L)
6645 - 32nd Street, N.W.
Washington 15, D.C.

Vojtech Adalbert Kral, M.D.
4145 Blueridge Crescent
Montreal 25, Canada

Morton Kramer, Sc.D.
9612 Sutherland Road
Silver Spring, Maryland

Emma Layman, Ph.D.
104 West Second Street
Mt. Pleasant, Iowa

Zigmond M. Lebensohn, M.D.
1712 Rhode Island Avenue, N.W.
Washington 6, D.C.

Heinz E. Lehmann, M.D.
6603 LaSalle Boulevard
Montreal, Quebec, Canada

Alexander H. Leighton, M.D.
Payne Whitney Clinic
525 East 68th Street
New York, New York

Paul V. Lemkau, M.D.
615 N. Wolfe Street
Baltimore 5, Maryland

David M. Levy, M.D.
47 East 77th Street
New York 21, New York

Aubrey J. Lewis, M.D. (H)
The Maudsley Hospital
Denmark Hill, S.E. 5
London, England

Nolan D. C. Lewis, M.D. (L)
Rural Route 5
Frederick, Maryland

William T. Lhamon, M.D.
Cornell University
Medical College
525 East 68th Street
New York 21, New York

W. T. Liberson, M.D., Ph.D.
Chief, Physical Education
   and Rehabilitation Service
V.A. Hospital
P.O. Box 28
Hines, Illinois

Ogden R. Lindsley, Ph.D.
Behavior Research Laboratory
Harvard Medical School
Metropolitan State Hospital
Waltham 54, Massachusetts

Maurice Lorr, Ph.D.
1521 Erskine Street
Washington 12, D.C.

Reginald S. Lourie, M.D.
Children's Hospital
Washington 9, D.C.

John W. Lovett-Doust, M.D.
University of Toronto
2 Surrey Place
Toronto, Ontario, Canada

Hans Lowenbach, M.D.
Duke University Medical Center
Durham, North Carolina

Donald J. MacPherson, M.D. (L)
1101 Beacon Street
Brookline 46, Massachusetts

Sidney Malitz, M.D.
722 West 168th Street
New York 32, New York

Robert Malmo, Ph.D.
1025 Pine Avenue West
Montreal 2, Quebec, Canada

Edwin E. McNiel, M.D. (L)
3875 Wilshire Boulevard
Los Angeles 5, California

Paul Meehl, Ph.D.
Mayo Box 390
University Hospitals
Minneapolis 14, Minnesota

William C. Menninger, M.D. (L)
Menninger Foundation
Topeka, Kansas

James G. Miller, M.D.
Mental Health Research Institute
University of Michigan
Ann Arbor, Michigan

Neal E. Miller, Ph.D.
615 Wayland Road
Plymouth Meeting, Pennsylvania

John A. P. Millet, M.D.
25 East 92nd Street
New York 28, New York

Thomas Verner Moore, Ph.D., M.D.
(H)
Ven. P.D. Pablo Maria Moore
O. Cart
Cartuja de Miraflores
Apt. 43
Burgos, Spain

Robert S. Morrow, Ph.D.
16 Pietro Place
Dobbs Ferry, New York

Leon Moses, M.D.
19 East 74th Street
New York 21, New York

Hobart Mowrer, M.D.
445 Gregory Hall
University of Illinois
Urbana, Illinois

Harry M. Murdock, M.D. (L)
Sheppard & Enoch Pratt Hospital
Towson 4, Maryland

Henry A. Murray, Ph.D., M.D. (L)
48 Mount Auburn Street
Cambridge, Massachusetts

J. Martin Myers, Jr., M.D.
Institute of Pennsylvania Hospital
111 North 49th Street
Philadelphia 39, Pennsylvania

Leo P. O'Donnell, M.D.
36 Elm Street
Pawling, New York

Raymond L. Osborne, M.D. (L)
140 East 54th Street
New York 22, New York

Winfred Overholser, M.D. (L)
St. Elizabeths Hospital
Washington 20, D.C.

Joseph B. Parker, Jr., M.D.
University of Kentucky
Medical Center
Lexington, Kentucky

Grosvenor B. Pearson, M.D.
3101 W. DeBazan Avenue
St. Petersburg, Beach 6, Florida

Harris B. Peck, M.D.
11 East 68th Street
New York 21, New York

Harry H. Pennes, M.D.
611 West 239th Street
Bronx 63, New York

Zygmunt A. Piotrowski, Ph.D.
1025 Walnut Street
Philadelphia 7, Pennsylvania

Phillip Polatin, M.D.
5281 Independence Avenue
New York 71, New York

Hyman L. Rachlin, M.D. (L)
35 Park Avenue
New York 16, New York

Sandor Rado, M.D.
235 East 73rd Street
New York 21, New York

John Rainer, M.D.
9 Innisfree Place
Eastchester, New York

Fritz Redl, M.D.
20001 Warrington Drive
Detroit 21, Michigan

F. C. Redlich, M.D.
333 Cedar Street
New Haven 11, Connecticut

David McK. Rioch, M.D.
4607 Dorset Avenue
Chevy Chase 15, Maryland

Janet MacKenzie Rioch, M.D.
719 Monroe Street
Apt. 203
Rockville, Maryland

Margaret Rioch, M.D.
4607 Dorset Avenue
Chevy Chase 15, Maryland

Fred V. Rockwell, M.D.
Grasslands Hospital
Valhalla, New York

Howard P. Rome, M.D.
Mayo Clinic
Rochester, Minnesota

Mathew Ross, M.D.
Koniginne Gracht, 48 A
Den Haag
The Netherlands

Theodore Rothman, M.D.
415 North Camden Drive
Beverly Hills, California

William S. Sadler, M.D. (L)
533 Diversey Parkway
Chicago, Illinois

George S. Saslow, M.D.
University of Oregon
Medical School
Portland 1, Oregon

Isidore W. Scherer, Ph.D.
Veterans Administration Hospital
Northampton, Massachusetts

G. Wilson Shaffer, Ph.D.
Johns Hopkins University
Baltimore 18, Maryland

Charles Shagass, M.D.
The Psychopathic Hospital
State University of Iowa
500 Newton Road
Iowa City, Iowa

David Shakow, Ph.D. (L)
National Institute of Mental Health
Clinical Center
Bethesda 14, Maryland

Alexander Simon, M.D. (L)
Langley Porter Clinic
San Francisco, California

John L. Smalldon, M.D. (L)
104 Pleasant Street
Concord, New Hampshire

George W. Smeltz, M.D. (L)
Marlborough-Blenheim Hotel
Atlantic City, New Jersey

Lauren H. Smith, M.D. (L)
111 North 49th Street
Philadelphia, Pennsylvania

Harry C. Solomon, M.D. (L)
74 Fenwood Road
Boston, Massachusetts

Rene A. Spitz, M.D.
45 South Ash Street
Denver 22, Colorado

Edward J. Stainbrook, M.D.
509 Prospect Boulevard
Pasadena, California

Gregory Stragnell, M.D.
388 Homewood Road
Los Angeles 49, California

Joseph G. Sutton, M.D.
5 Roosevelt Street
Montclair, New Jersey

Hans C. Syz, M.D.
The Lifwynn Foundation
52 South Morningside Drive
Westport, Connecticut

William S. Taylor, Ph.D.   (L)
55 Dryads Green
Northampton, Massachusetts

Harry A. Teitelbaum, M.D.
1801 Eutaw Place
Baltimore 17, Maryland

William B. Terhune, M.D.   (L)
Silver Hill Foundation
Box 1114
New Canaan, Connecticut

Charles B. Thompson, M.D.
The Lifwynne Foundation
52 South Morngside Drive
Westport, Connecticut

Kenneth J. Tillotson, M.D.   (L)
1265 Beacon Street
Brookline, Massachusetts

Harvey J. Tompkins, M.D.
157 Chapel Road
Manhasset, L.I., New York

James S. Tyhurst, M.D.
Department of Psychiatry
University of British Columbia
Vancouver 9, British Columbia
Canada

Vladimir G. Urse, M.D.   (L)
Cook County Hospital
Polk and Wood Street
Chicago 12, Illinois

Roy McL. Van Wart, M.D.   (L)
10431 Bellagio Road
Los Angeles 24, California

Heinrich B. Waelsch, M.D.
722 West 168th Street
New York 32, New York

Raymond Waggoner, M.D.
University Hospital
1313 East Ann Street
Ann Arbor, Michigan

James Hardin Wall, M.D.
121 Westchester Avenue
White Plains, New York

George A. Waterman, M.D.   (L)
200 Beacon Street
Boston, Massachusetts

David Wechsler, Ph.D.
Bellevue Hospital
New York, New York

Edith Weigert, M.D.
12 Oxford Street
Chevy Chase 15, Maryland

Edwin A. Weinstein, M.D.
7101 Pyle Road
Bethesda 14, Maryland

Livingston Welch, Ph.D.
Hunter College
695 Park Avenue
New York 21, New York

Frederic Lyman Wells, Ph.D.   (L)
87 School Street
Belmont 78, Massachusetts

Louis Wender, M.D.   (L)
59 East 79th Street
New York 21, New York

Frederick L. Weniger, M.D.
3811 O'Hara Street
Pittsburgh 13, Pennsylvania

Louis J. West, M.D.
University of Oklahoma
Medical Center
800 N.E. 13th Street
Oklahoma City 4, Oklahoma

Robert W. White, Ph.D.
Harvard University
Cambridge, Massachusetts

John C. Whitehorn, M.D.
210 Northfield Place
Baltimore 10, Maryland

George B. Wilbur, M.D. (L)
Cove Road
South Dennis, Massachusetts

William Preston Wilson, M.D.
Duke University
Medical Center
Durham, North Carolina

Cecil L. Wittson, M.D.
9651 North 29th Street
Omaha 12, Nebraska

Lewis R. Wolberg, M.D.
55 East 86th Street
New York 28, New York

Joseph Wolpe, M.D.
University of Virginia
School of Medicine
Charlottesville, Virginia

S. Bernard Wortis, M.D. (L)
410 East 57th Street
New York 22, New York

Past and Present Officers of the
American Psychopathological Association

Presidents

1912	Adolf Meyer	1940	Douglas A. Thom
1913	James T. Putnam	1941	Roscoe W. Hall
1914	Alfred R. Allen	1942	Roscoe W. Hall
1915	Alfred R. Allen	1943	Frederick L. Wells
1916	Adolf Meyer	1944	Frederick L. Wells
1917	Adolf Meyer	1945	Bernard Glueck
1918	Smith Ely Jelliffe	1946	Robert P. Knight
1921	William A. White	1947	Frederick L. Wells
1922	John T. MacCurdy	1948	Donald J. MacPherson
1923	L. Pierce Clark	1949	Paul Hoch
1924	L. Pierce Clark	1950	William B. Terhune
1925	Albert M. Barrett	1951	Lauren H. Smith
1927	Sanger Brown II	1952	Joseph Zubin
1928	Ross McC. Chapman	1953	Clarence P. Oberndorf
1929	Ross McC. Chapman	1954	David McK. Rioch
1930	William Healy	1955	Merrill Moore
1931	William Healy	1956	Oskar Diethelm
1932	J. Ramsay Hunt	1957	Howard S. Liddell
1933	Edward J. Kempf	1958	Leslie B. Hohman
1934	Edward J. Kenpf	1959	Harry C. Solomon
1935	Nolan D. C. Lewis	1960	David Wechsler
1936	Nolan D. C. Lewis	1961	William Horsley Gantt
1937	Nolan D. C. Lewis	1962	Lauretta Bender
1938	Samuel W. Hamilton	1963	D. Ewen Cameron
1939	Abraham Myerson		

Vice Presidents

1924	William Healy	1933	Albert M. Barrett
	George H. Kirby		Trigant Burrow
1925	J. Ramsay Hunt	1934	Albert M. Barrett
	Sidney L. Schwab		Trigant Burrow
1927	Ross McC. Chapman	1935	J. Ramsay Hunt
	Edward J. Kempf		Smith Ely Jelliffe
1928	Edward J. Kempf	1936	J. Ramsay Hunt
	E. Stanley Abbott		Smith Ely Jelliffe
1929	Edward J. Kempf	1937	Samuel W. Hamilton
	E. Stanley Abbott		Ray G. Hoskins
1930	J. Ramsay Hunt	1938	Lydiard H. Horton
	Herman N. Adler		Hans Syz
1931	J. Ramsay Hunt	1939	Roscoe W. Hall
	Herman N. Adler		Douglass A. Thom

Vice Presidents

1940	George S. Sprague	1951	Harry M. Murdock
	Bernard Glueck		Lauretta Bender
1941	Frederick L. Wells	1952	William Horowitz
	Lowell S. Selling		S. Bernard Wortis
1943	Frederick L. Wells	1953	David McK. Rioch
	Lowell S. Selling		Merrill Moore
1944	Lowell S. Selling		Howard S. Liddell
	Flanders Dunbar		
1945	Thomas V. Moore	1955	Oskar Diethelm
	Robert P. Knight		Howard S. Liddell
1946	Paul H. Hoch	1956	Leslie B. Hohman
	Thos. A. C. Rennie	1957	David Wechsler
1947	William C. Menninger		
	Ruth Benedict	1958	David Wechsler
1948	Ruth Benedict	1959	Clara Thompson
	Lauren H. Smith	1960	Theodore M. Abel
1949	Arthur N. Foxe	1961	Donald M. Hamilton
	Norman Cameron	1962	Jerome D. Frank
1950	Harry M. Murdock		
	William S. Taylor	1963	Franz J. Kallmann

Secretaries

1921 H. W. Frink	1940-1948 Merrill Moore
1922-1926 Sanger Brown, II	1944-1951 Samuel W. Hamilton
1927-1929 Martin W. Peck	1952-1960 Donald M. Hamilton
1930-1939 L. Eugene Emerson	1961-1963 Fritz A. Freyhan

Treasurers

1924-1942 William C. Garvin	1952-1963 Bernard C. Glueck, Jr.
1943-1951 Joseph Zubin	

Honorary Members

Brock G. Chisholm, M.D.
Seawood, West Coast Road
R.R. 2, Victoria
British Columbia, Canada

Thomas Verner Moore, Ph.D., M.D.
Carthusian Foundation in America, Inc.
Sky Farm
Whitingham, Vermont

Aubrey J. Lewis, M.D.
The Maudsley Hospital
Denmark Hill, S.E. 5
London, England

INDEX